JAMIE WYETH

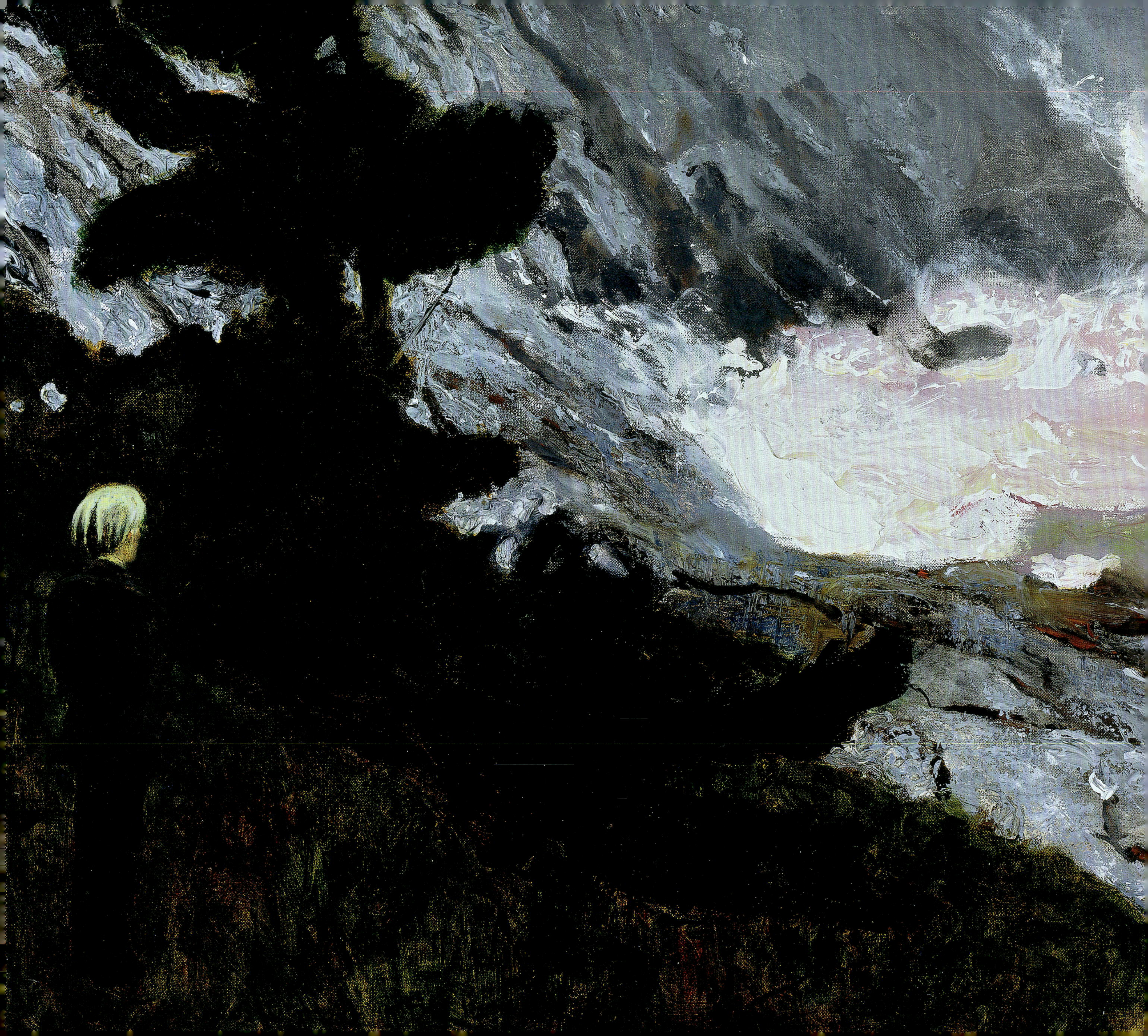

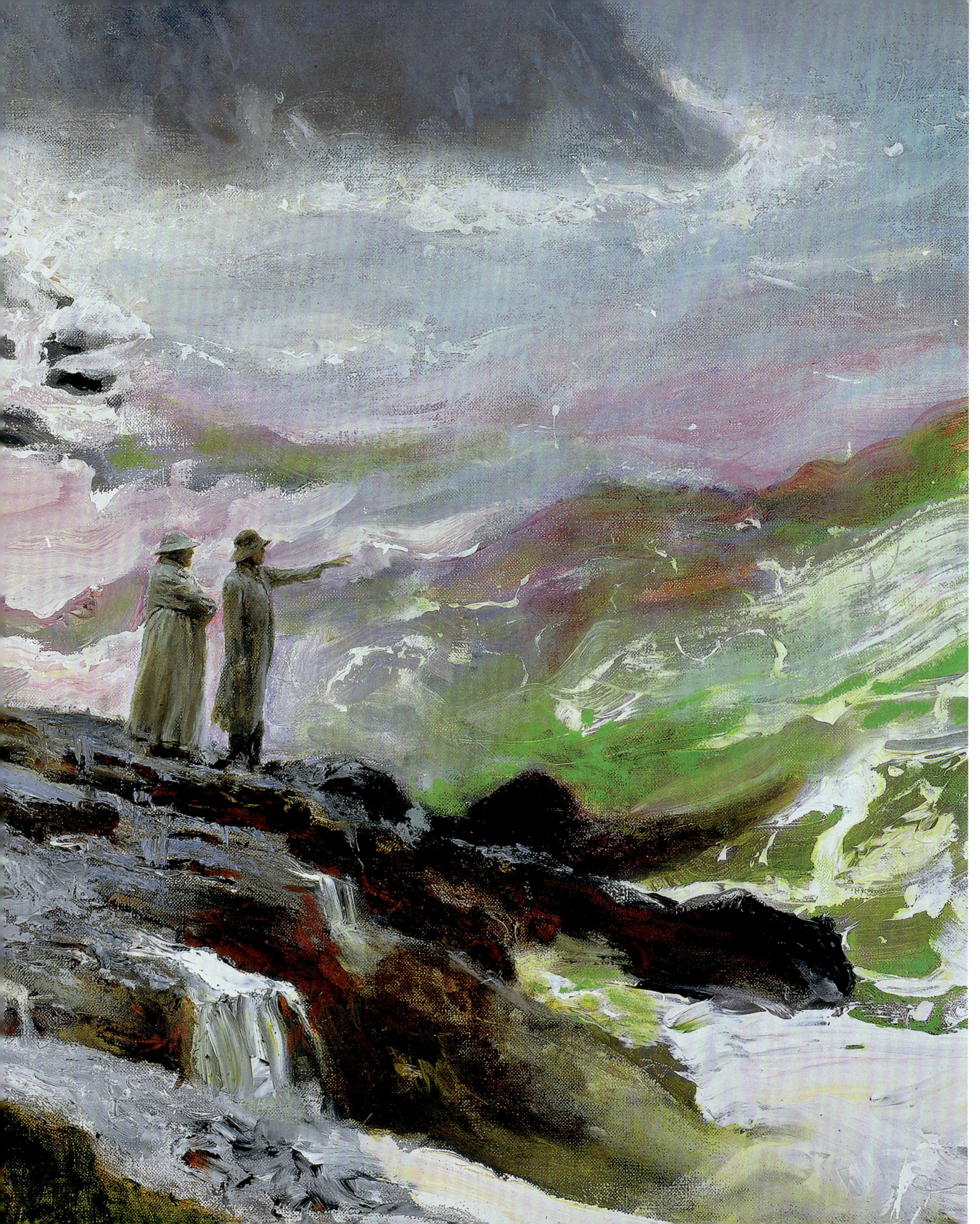

JAMIE WYETH

Elliot Bostwick Davis

With an essay by David Houston

MFA Publications
Museum of Fine Arts, Boston

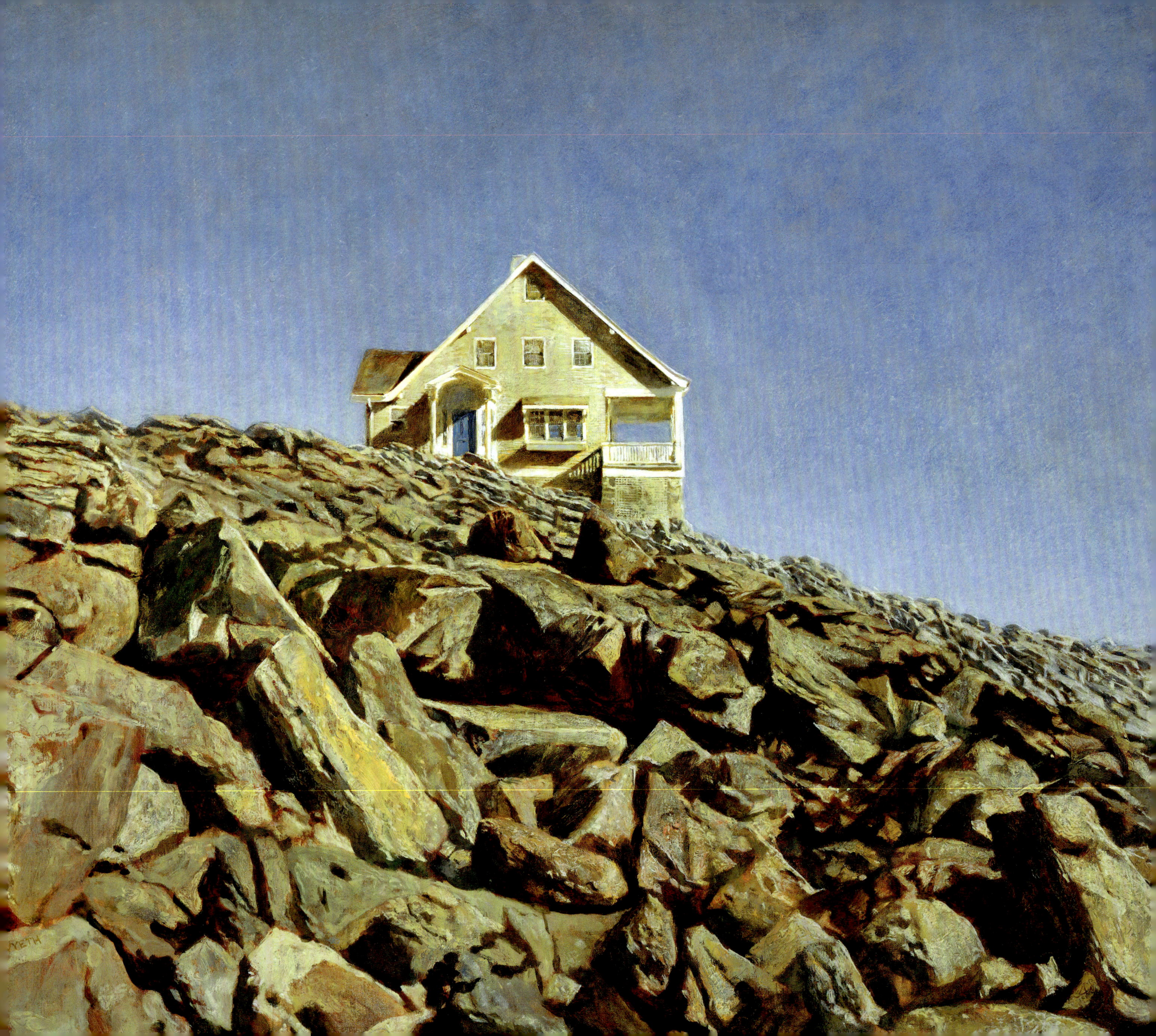

Contents

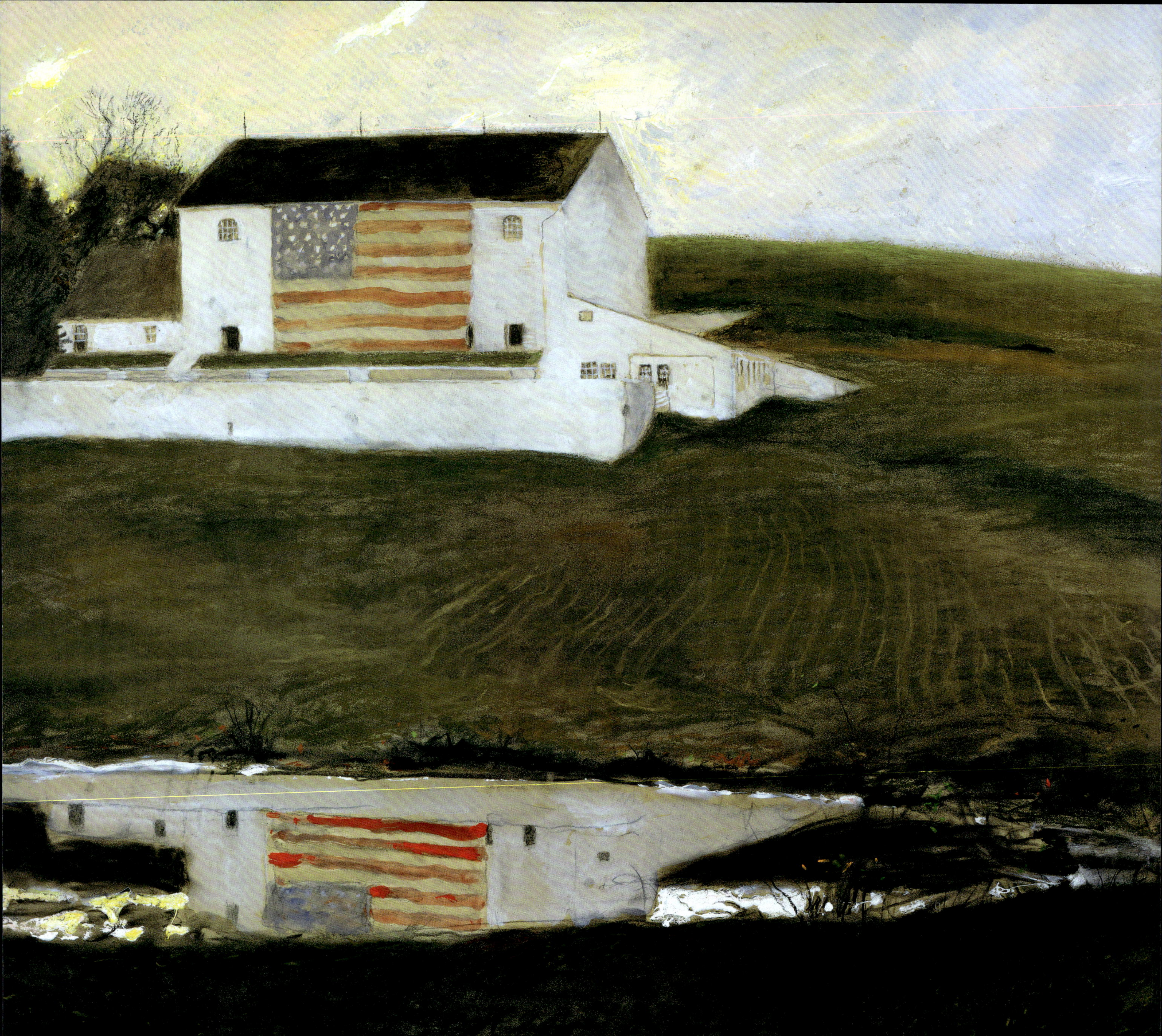

Director's Foreword

The **Museum of Fine Arts** is very pleased to welcome Jamie Wyeth back to the Boston area, where his family's roots go back to the seventeenth century. His grandfather, the great illustrator Newell Convers (N. C.) Wyeth, studied art in Boston as a young man, and his murals of sailing ships grace the foyer of the First National Bank of Boston building (now Bank of America). His father, the distinguished American realist Andrew Wyeth, is represented at the MFA by a select group of paintings, watercolors, and drawings.

Jamie Wyeth presents the first retrospective for this highly imaginative American artist since 1980. In the intervening years, Jamie Wyeth's work has often been exhibited together with the work of his grandfather and father. This publication and the exhibition it accompanies offer an opportunity to consider Jamie Wyeth on his own terms, tracing the arc of the artist's development from his earliest drawings through to his most recent compositions. We are pleased to be able to include lesser-known early works, such as the unforgettable portrait of Dr. Helen Taussig, as well as depictions of many other people, places, animals, and objects that have sparked the artist's imagination for over six decades.

We are profoundly grateful to the funders who have made this exhibition and its accompanying publication possible. We are especially indebted to our longtime partners at Bank of America for their sponsorship of the exhibition and their generous loan of Wyeth's watercolor painted in the aftermath of 9/11, *Patriot's Barn*. The continuing support provided by Bank of America for the MFA's exhibitions, programs, and Huntington Avenue Plaza is a beacon of leadership and a model of sustaining public-private partnerships in the arts.

I must also thank the funders who have provided additional support: for the publication, the Ann and William Elfers Publications Fund at the Museum of Fine Arts, Boston; for additional exhibition support, the Mr. and Mrs. Raymond J. Horowitz Foundation for the Arts and the Foundation's president, Warren Adelson, as well as Mr. and Mrs. Jeffrey E. Marshall and the Shelly and Michael Kassen Fund.

We are delighted that *Jamie Wyeth* will be shared with audiences at the Brandywine River Museum of Art, the San Antonio Museum of Art, and one of the youngest institutions dedicated to American art, Crystal Bridges Museum of American Art. For their part in making this possible, we are grateful to Thomas Padon, Director of the Brandywine River Museum of Art, and Virginia Logan, Director of the Brandywine River Conservancy, as well as former director James Duff; Katherine C. Luber, The Kelso Director, San Antonio Museum of Art; and Crystal Bridges' executive director, Rod Bigelow, as well as President Don Bacigalupi and Deputy Director Sandra K. Edwards.

Malcolm Rogers
Ann and Graham Gund Director
Museum of Fine Arts, Boston

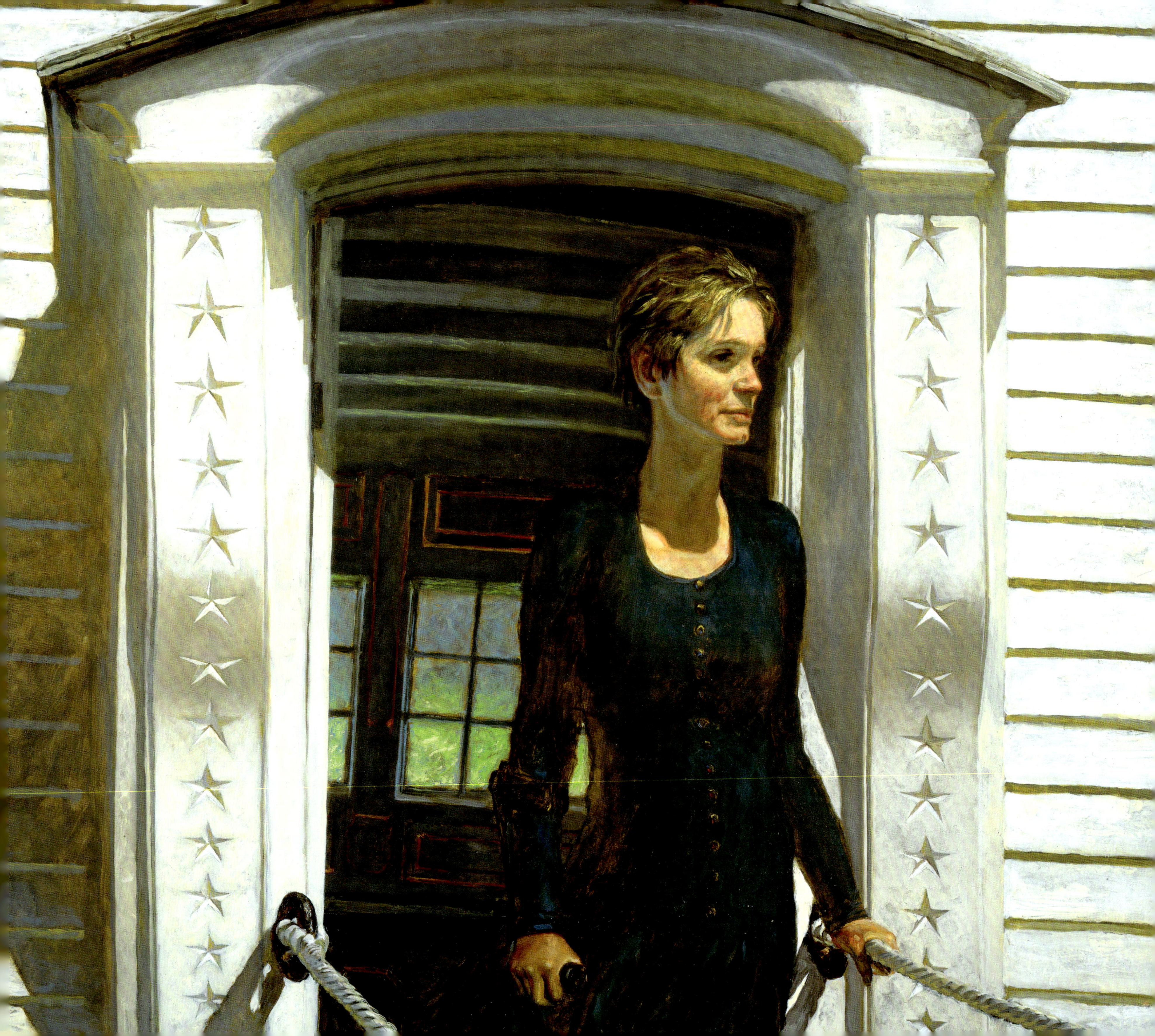

Preface

WYETH. Jamie Wyeth was born into a family whose name, depending on your point of view, is revered or reviled in the realm of twentieth-century and contemporary American art. Their work is unapologetically realistic, and yet their particular type of realism is hard to pin down. It has been related to social realism, surrealism, and magic realism, and condemned for not keeping step with Abstract Expressionism, color field painting, minimalism, and various forms of postmodernism. Wyeths and their art have appeared on the covers of many magazines from *American Artist* to *Time*. They have painted presidential portraits and official White House Christmas cards, created unforgettable illustrations to classic tales available at local libraries, and even holiday stamps that could be had at any post office window for a few cents. There may not be another artist working in our nation today whose family name and work are everywhere around us in plain sight, and yet whose own artistic vision remains so little known.

This catalogue, which accompanies the first comprehensive retrospective of Jamie Wyeth's work, traces the larger arc of the artist's development from his earliest drawings as a child to his current compositions, examining them in the context of American art both past and present. Previous presentations of his work have focused primarily on specific themes, selected according to the various animals, people, and places he portrays.[1] Over time, these exhibitions have obscured a sense of the artist's personal evolution, with the exception of an early retrospective mounted at the Pennsylvania Academy of the Fine Arts in 1980, when he was thirty-four years old.[2] Jamie Wyeth's compositions have more often appeared in multiple-generation exhibitions of works by a varying cast of characters from the Wyeth family, although they have always featured his grandfather, Newell Convers Wyeth, and his father, Andrew Wyeth.[3] In these contexts, Jamie Wyeth's own aesthetic perspective has been diluted in favor of the Wyeth family brand of realism, and the unifying curatorial vision has favored family similarities rather than highlighting the individual artists' distinct contributions and personalities. Add to this history the strained relationship between the Wyeths' name and contemporary art, and we find that only rarely has Jamie Wyeth's work been considered more broadly in the context of his generation. David Houston's essay in this volume is an attempt to begin addressing this oversight.

One exhibition, proposed by the artist, that examined his relationship to contemporary art and was brilliantly executed by a team of capable scholars is the 2006 *Factory Work: Warhol, Wyeth, Basquiat*.[4] Another recent exhibition, *Farm Work* (2011), displayed signs of cracking past curatorial codes by looking broadly at Wyeth's art over several decades and has contributed significantly to bringing his career into sharper focus. This time around, we have risked opening the trapdoors of various silos that have contained Jamie Wyeth's work in the past and letting his artistic production pour forth. From that massive pile of images, we examine only a small selection of Wyeth's compositions—just over one hundred, in a range of media—against a spectrum of artistic traditions. In so doing, we seek to shed light

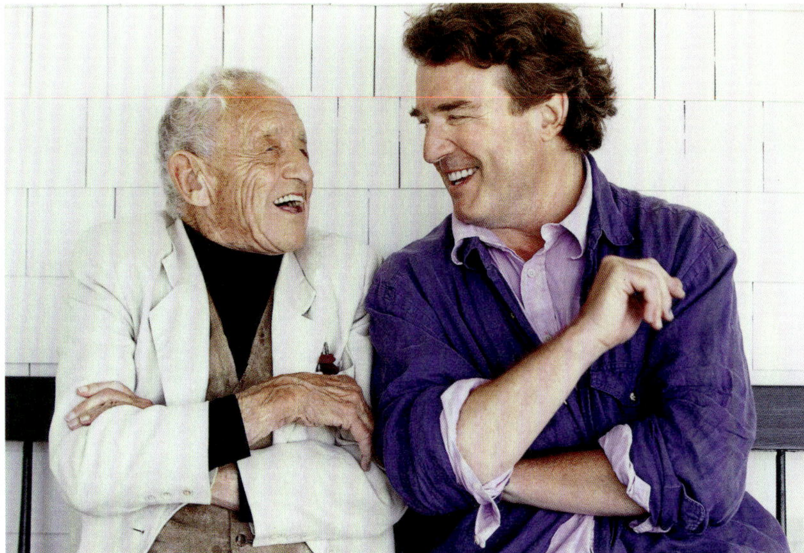

Fig. 1. Peter Ralston (born in 1950)
Of a Feather, 2008
Archival pigment print
43.2 x 55.9 cm (17 x 22 in.)

on how Wyeth's artistic imagination creates this hybrid form of realism that is so elusive.

The dualities of polar opposites that thread through Jamie Wyeth's artistic career electrify his best works. Within his own family, there are the relationships to the two male figures of his father and grandfather. And, on the female side, his wife, Phyllis Mills Wyeth, and the role of his mother, the family matriarch, author, archivist, and collaborator for Wyeth's first illustrated book, *The Stray* (1979); and his aunt, Carolyn Wyeth, his first formal teacher.[5] There are the two Andys, Wyeth and Warhol. There are artists that Wyeth acknowledges as inspirations, such as John Singleton Copley, Thomas Eakins, Sandro Botticelli, and Rockwell Kent; and those he has not: Winslow Homer, Edward Hopper, John Singer Sargent, and Mary Cassatt.

Then there are the two worlds the artist inhabits in the Brandywine River Valley and Maine. Wyeth travels frequently—primarily by airplane—between his home at Point Lookout Farm in Wilmington, Delaware, and the islands of Maine, where he maintains studios on Southern Island in Tenants Harbor and on Monhegan Island. The two landscapes in which the Wyeth family has lived and worked have reinforced the tension between these polar opposites and inspired their creativity for generations.[6] The American artist Marsden Hartley, who was born in Lewiston, Maine, and returned to the state frequently during his later career as he became more invested in the concept of "nativeness," found that the process of shifting locales heightened his artistic sensibility and deepened his sense of identity.[7] Wyeth's frequent travels between Brandywine and Maine—and, within Maine, between the distinct realms of the two islands he works on—also have enhanced his aesthetic experience of each place.

Each of these destinations contains many smaller worlds, like a set of Russian nesting dolls; it is possible to have opened only a few while working on an exhibition project of several years' duration. To place these two worlds within the broader context of American art, the contrast between Brandywine and Maine may be best explained perhaps in terms of the great New England transcendentalist, Henry David Thoreau, who wrote eloquently about his experience of nature and the self as circumscribed within his farm and cabin at Walden Pond, as well as during his explorations of the wilderness near Mount Katahdin in *The Maine Woods*. The writings of Thoreau, a significant figure for N. C. and Andrew Wyeth and the broader Wyeth family, offer us various paths for examining these two distinct natural worlds as represented and expressed by Jamie Wyeth.

Beyond a consideration of how various competing dualities enhance the creative process, in evaluating the trajectory of any artist's development, it is important to bear in mind that artistic imagination is porous and dynamic, and subject to infinite variables, not least the changing seasons of the year and changes of emotional mood. A switch of medium, from drawing, to watercolor, to oil, to sculpture and assemblage, can jolt an artist's aesthetic sensibility, just as location or subject matter can, and thus it is important to consider how these distinctions play into the work over time, as an artist visits and revisits particular interests, themes, and modes of representation.

Jamie Wyeth's career spans a period of unprecedented change from the emergence of Pop Art in the 1960s, the figurative revival of the New Realism, and the unfolding pluralism of the 1980s and 1990s, to the current expansion of a global contemporary art world. Not easily associated with any specific school or movement, Wyeth consciously avoids following newly minted trends, although he is well aware of what is being shown in the museums and galleries, especially those of New York City (where he also maintains a residence). His media and his subjects—whether mentors, muses, landscapes, family pets, wild animals, or the vast array of objects that he collects—are richly diverse. During the more than six decades that Wyeth has been honing his artistic vision, we find the past has continually informed the present. His personal quest to discover the purpose fundamental to art is expressed by his Monhegan muse, Rockwell Kent: "To be entitled to the honor that society bestows upon it, it must unquestionably have a social value; that is, as a potential means of communication it must be addressed, and in comprehensible terms, to the understanding of mankind."[8] Wyeth's own form of realism and his distinctive artistic perspective capture the wonder, beauty, and strangeness of his many worlds, in a lifelong quest to approach the universal truths of nature.

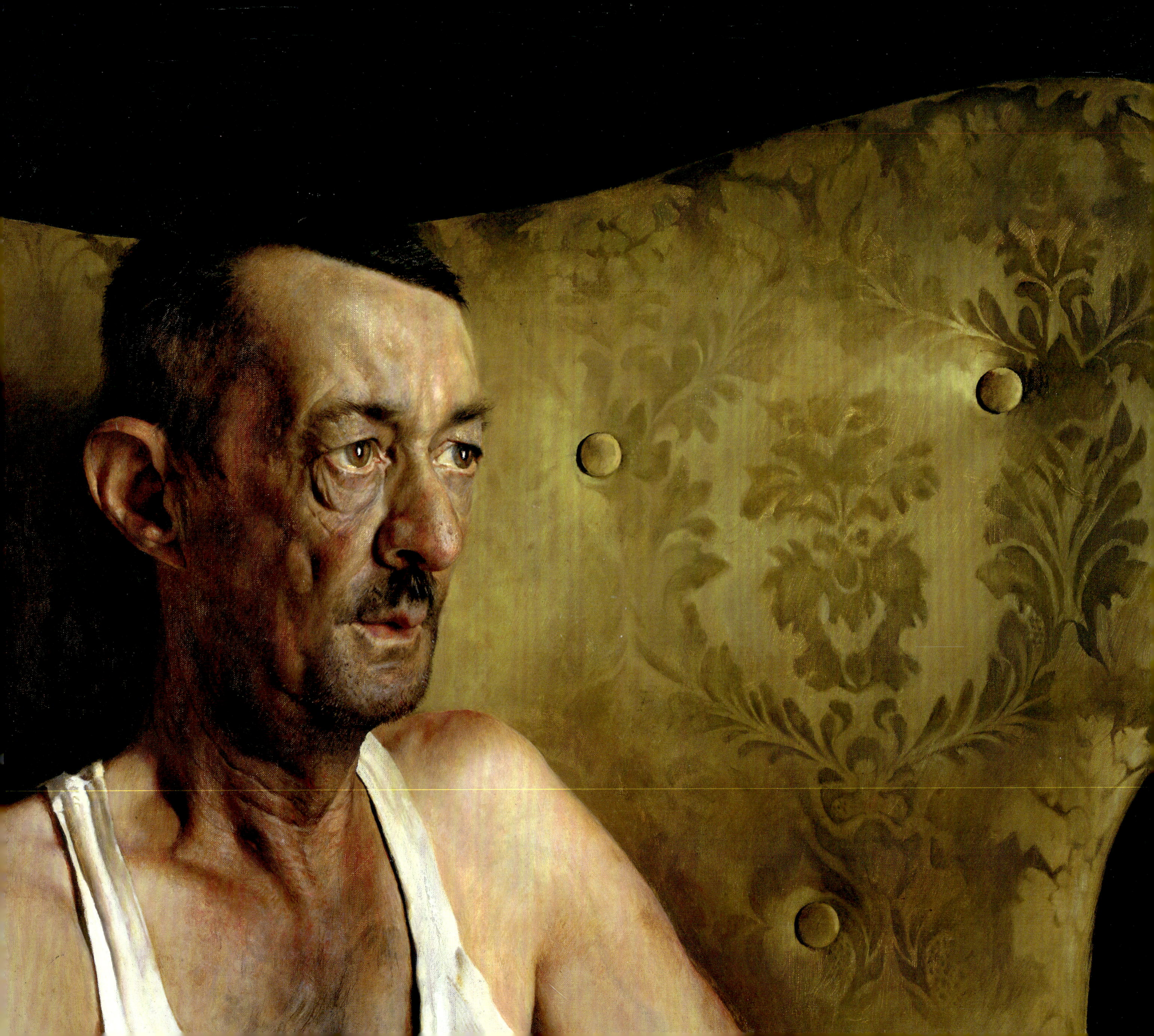

Jamie Wyeth and Recent American Realism

DAVID HOUSTON

From the elegantly discontinuous proto-modern paintings of Edouard Manet to the revival of the last three decades, realist painting has been in a constant state of flux. Representational painting was assigned an uneasy status during the long march of modernism, and it has continually redefined itself in ways that both reinvigorate long-standing traditions and explore new directions in the radical aesthetic pluralism that defines our visual world. Jamie Wyeth occupies a unique position within the revival of realism; he is an artist working in an unbroken line of realist painters that extends back to the nineteenth century, but he also continues to evolve a distinctive strain of traditional American realist painting today. As a member of the Wyeth clan, he remains a well-known but elusive artist, one whose skill continues to dazzle and whose diversity of subjects and styles can also mystify. Like his father's before him, his work enjoys popular recognition, and it has influenced several generations of realist painters. Unlike many artists of his generation, he is not identified with a specific contemporary trend or stylistic movement. For some, his work is too traditional for the New Realism and too individualistic to fall into mainstream contemporary trends. As the last in a line of artists that spans a century of narrative painting, Wyeth matured early and developed in splendid isolation from the growing influence of popular American culture. To this day, he has chosen to remain aloof from the visibility, mechanisms, and celebrity culture of the art world and continually revisits the places and subjects of his chosen orbits of the Brandywine River Valley and the coast of Maine.

Jamie Wyeth's place in American art is often situated within the "Brandywine tradition" of painting—a line of American realism that stretches from the Civil War to the present. The Brandywine School encompasses the work of Howard Pyle, Jamie's grandfather N. C. Wyeth, his celebrated father, Andrew, and Jamie Wyeth himself; these artists have a shared sense of values and a shared geography, but no common formulaic style. Although he has traveled the world, Jamie Wyeth chooses to paint the landscape, the people, and the animals in his immediate worlds of Brandywine and Maine. The Brandywine heritage is characterized by strong narrative quality and a closely observed realism, grounded in a strong sense of place, and animated by an unwavering faith in the transformational power of the artist's imagination. Jamie Wyeth's place of importance within the Brandywine tradition sets him apart from many of the concerns of the contemporary art world, and it is an impediment for understanding Jamie Wyeth's work in the larger context of recent American art. The rural regions Jamie chooses to paint are almost premodern in their austere beauty, and the otherness of this timeless topography appears exotic and has fueled many romantic myths that have grown up around the Wyeth clan. This popular mythmaking and Jamie's interest in discussing and exhibiting his work in the context of family often preempt deeper analytical discussions of both his personal evolution and the inner voicing of Jamie's work outside the Brandywine association. The critical reception that continues to cast a long shadow over Andrew Wyeth's place in the history of American art also limits

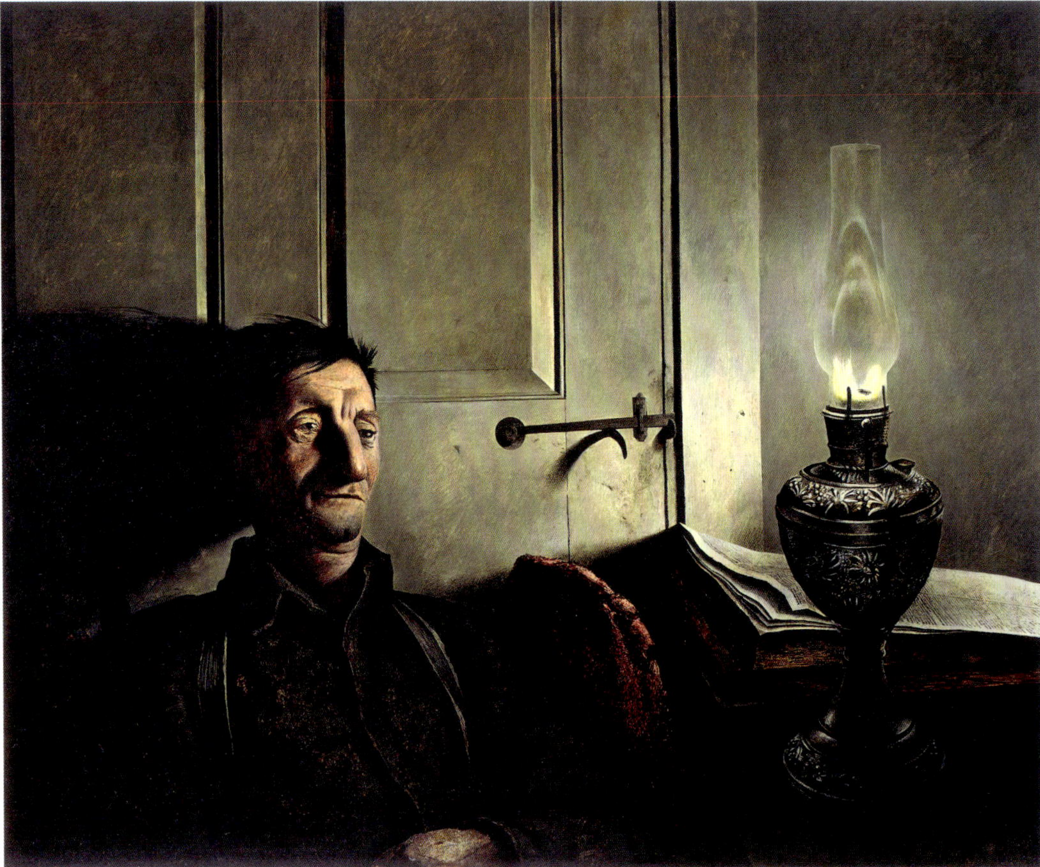

Fig. 2. Andrew Wyeth
(1917–2009)
Oil Lamp, 1945
Tempera on panel
86.4 x 106.7 cm (34 x 42 in.)

an expanded critical discussion of Jamie's own vision and accomplishments beyond these obvious and well-documented historical associations. This, along with the dearth of artists' statements and in-depth interviews, often leaves critics and scholars at a loss for information beyond the purely visual, a situation the Wyeths seem to tolerate, if not encourage.

Jamie Wyeth was nurtured in a world whose rhythms, points of reference, and distance from American popular culture were radically different from those of most artists of his generation. This singular formation, based on private tutelage in a sequestered, enchanted realm, was also shared by Jamie's father, Andrew, who characterized his own youth as a circumscribed existence, more like staying "in Sherwood Forest with Maid Marion and the rebels."[1] In many ways young Jamie Wyeth did not choose his own path—through his family tradition, an ancestral tie to place, his natural talent, and a unique education, it chose him.

Jamie Wyeth's masterful early portraits were painted when most of his contemporaries were still filling out their art school applications. As a young artist with an abundance of natural talent and a storied family of accomplished individualism, Jamie set about making his own personal variations on traditional themes. His choice of conventional subject matter and perceptual approach was out of sync with both the dominance of Abstract Expressionism and the open-ended, playful experimentation that was transforming the new American art of the 1960s. Compared to Andrew's, Jamie's approach to portraiture is more detailed, contemporary in mood, and more tightly focused compositionally, and it expands outwardly to the world in a completely different way. When comparing Jamie's *Portrait of Shorty* (1963) with Andrew Wyeth's similar 1945 painting, *Oil Lamp*, we immediately see different compositional approaches and a different narrative concern in these works (cat. 9; fig. 2). Andrew's earlier painting is an environmental portrait and is as much a portrait (as the title suggests) of the oil lamp and the room as of the man. *Portrait of Shorty*, on the other hand, parallels the development of a new hyperrealistic approach to figure painting emerging in the work of Wyeth's contemporaries Philip Pearlstein and William Beckman, although with a softer edge. Even more contemporary in mood but traditional in approach is *Draft Age* (1965), the first of Jamie's forays into current political issues—in this case, the escalation of the Vietnam War (cat. 11).

Wyeth's *Portrait of John F. Kennedy* is an example of the mature work of a formidable young talent evolving along a different trajectory from his peers (1967; cat. 19). Lincoln Kirstein characterized the connection between artist and subject as the confluence of two American mandarins: "James was the hereditary professional painter, Jack Kennedy the hereditary political virtuoso."[2] Jamie's portrait of John F. Kennedy, though ultimately rejected as an official commission, is one of the few paintings of the era that captures the psychological drama and thoughtful introspection of Kennedy's handling of many of the critical events of his presidency. Composed to approximate the proportions of the golden mean, this painting uses traditional paint and canvas to capture a key figure of a culture in radical transition. A direct comparison with Robert Rauschenberg's equally iconic image of John F. Kennedy, *Retroactive I*, marks the transition from the representational realism of traditional portraiture to the new sensibility formed by the growing prominence of mass media and the mythmaking power of advertising and public relations (fig. 3). Rauschenberg's mixed-media approach exploits a commercial

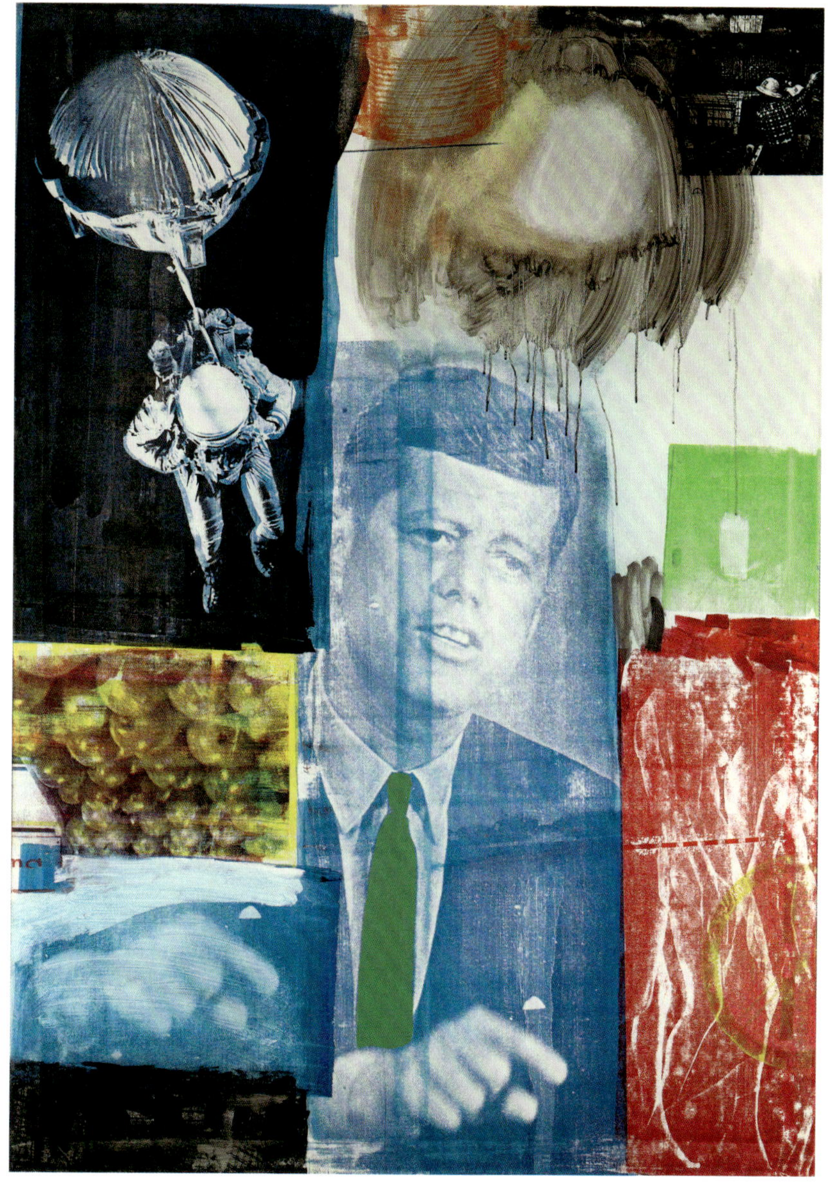

Fig. 3. Robert Rauschenberg
(1925–2008)
Retroactive I, 1963
Oil and silkscreen ink on canvas
213.4 x 152.4 cm (84 x 60 in.)

process (silkscreen printing) and refashions an image appropriated from a presidential press conference photo in a highly syncopated collaged image that includes a playful reference to the space race through another appropriated photograph of a parachuting astronaut in the top left of the composition. The sparkling detail and subtle psychological insight of Wyeth's portrait make it a late example of a centuries-old approach to portraiture descended from the humanism of the Renaissance. Rauschenberg's complex, multilayered composition decenters the primacy of the subject and replaces the artist's investigation of the subjectivity of the sitter's inner life with a manufactured media image floating in a nonhierarchical collage sensibility.

Portrait of Lincoln Kirstein (1965) is an unconventional composition and a work of psychological complexity among Jamie's early portraits (cat. 12). Its sophistication and confident execution exemplify the steady expansion of Jamie Wyeth's world beyond the confines of his father's aesthetics and the world of Chadds Ford. The painting is both an intimate portrait of a close family friend and an iconic image of a major American cultural figure. Along with the Kennedy portrait, it signifies the remarkably swift maturation of a young artist.

The growth of galleries, public institutions, and collectors in the late 1950s and the 1960s saw the creation of new styles and new aesthetic sensibilities, as well as the beginnings of today's globalized art world. Jasper Johns and Robert Rauschenberg were both examples of a younger generation of artists that did not share the same geography, influences, and sensibilities of the generation formed by the Great Depression and Second World War. Created, as Rauschenberg cleverly put it, in the "gap between art and life," the new art looked beyond the limiting aesthetics of Abstract Expressionism to embrace common materials and the everyday experiences that reflected the kaleidoscopic social, political, and technological changes reshaping American art and culture. The power of the newly minted media-driven consumer culture ruptured the purity of high art with the appearance of the Pop Art movement in New York City in 1962. Andy Warhol's serialized screen prints of Campbell's soup cans were first exhibited in that watershed year 1962, the same year that also saw him explore the growing influence of mass-media identity and fabricated glamour in the *Elvis* and *Marilyn* series. The renewed interest in figurative art was documented on the West Coast with an exhibition of the New Realism mounted by the Pasadena Museum, also in 1962, linking the emergence of Pop Art to a wide range of approaches to the new figurative art that were descended from modernism, but were also conscious of the growing influence of popular media and very much of the moment. The passion for experimentation continued in a parallel movement, and both Pop Art and the new media-based video art breached a barrier between the worlds of art and popular culture. The first exhibition of video as art was mounted by the pioneering Fluxus artist Nam June Paik at the Galerie Parnass in Wuppertal, Germany, and in New York, Dan Flavin pioneered the use of commercial fluorescent light tubes in his minimalist sculptures at the Judson Gallery.

From the later 1960s to the mid-1970s, Jamie Wyeth increasingly integrated himself into the world beyond Chadds Ford, documenting some of the significant events of this turbulent, transitional era. Among the works that resulted from his commission to record the Apollo space program, the haunting night painting *Moon Landing* (1969) is an important work in the artist's evolution (cat. 24). This carefully composed oil painting chooses to dramatize this historic event through the familiar landscape of the Monhegan coastline. The two bollards in the foreground become stand-ins for the viewer of the painting, a compositional device that Caspar David Friedrich uses in his 1819 painting *Two Men Contemplating the Moon* (Gemäldegalerie, Dresden).

One often overlooked work that offers keen insight into Jamie Wyeth's personal evolution and aesthetic choices at a critical moment in his career is a large, multipaneled mural he painted while serving in the Delaware Air National Guard from 1966 to 1971. The mural is surprising in scale and of unusual sophistication for a party backdrop (fig. 4). Based on the bibli-

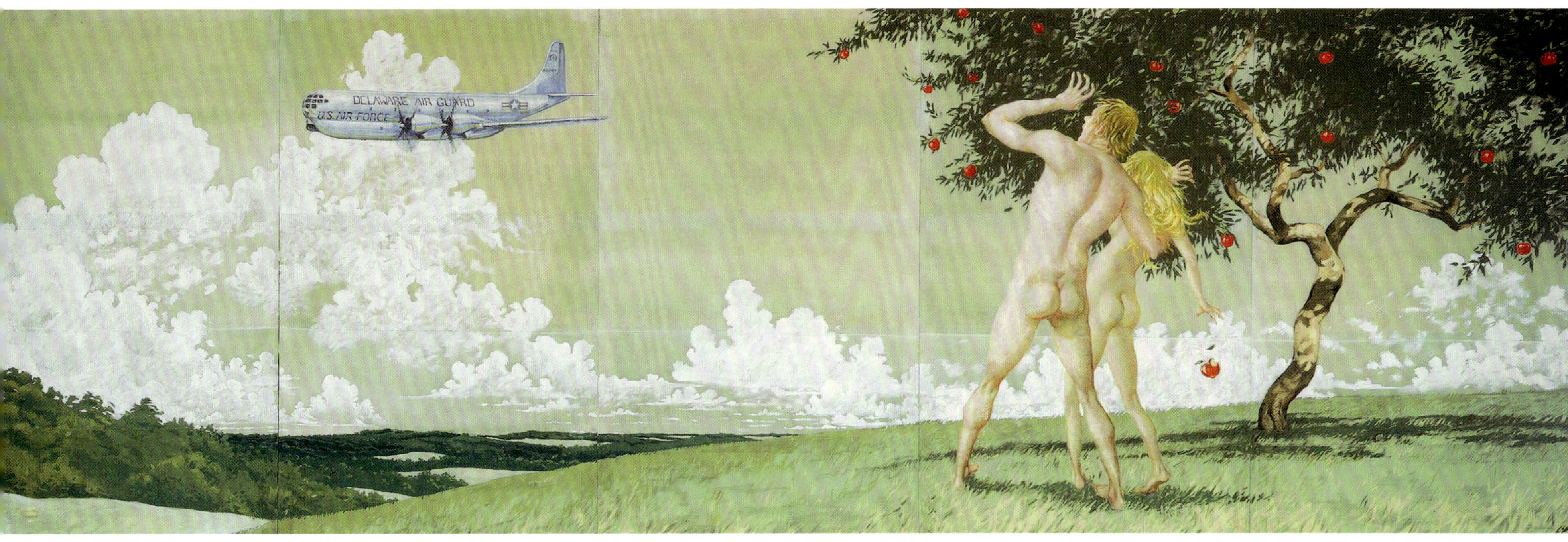

Fig. 4. *Adam and Eve and the C-97*, 1969
Oil on parachute nylon
2.29 x 7.03 m (7 ft. 6 in. x 23 ft. ¾ in.)

cal theme of Adam and Eve in the Garden of Eden, this mural is painted with mannerist drama, as a low-flying U.S. cargo plane takes Adam and Eve aback. As the foundational couple look to the sky, Eve drops the forbidden fruit she has plucked from the Tree of Knowledge. The work has an overwhelming narrative quality rendered in a light-green, post-Impressionist-inflected palette. The composition and overall mood reflect an awareness of both turn-of-the-century European painting and American New Deal public art.

Revisiting the mural from today's perspective, we can see that this painting simultaneously looks back to the grand age of American murals that flourished during the Great Depression and forward to the revival of grand narrative painting of the postmodern movement of the 1980s. Had he chosen to further pursue direct historical references and narrative monumentality in his work, this mural could have prefigured postmodern historicism and would have been a turning point in Jamie's career. He would have anticipated the recasting and remaking of history painting as seen later in the paintings of Mark Tansey and Jack Beal, and the return of monumental narrative painting with the advent of the Neo-Expressionist movement. The mural is large and compositionally well resolved, and it demonstrates Jamie's technical facility and strong narrative abilities. It is at once grand, playful, and unlike any other painting from the late 1960s.

One important source is undoubtedly the painting by N. C. Wyeth commissioned by the Wilmington Savings Fund Society Bank in Wilmington, Delaware, during the golden age of American mural painting, and completed in 1932. *Apotheosis of the Family*

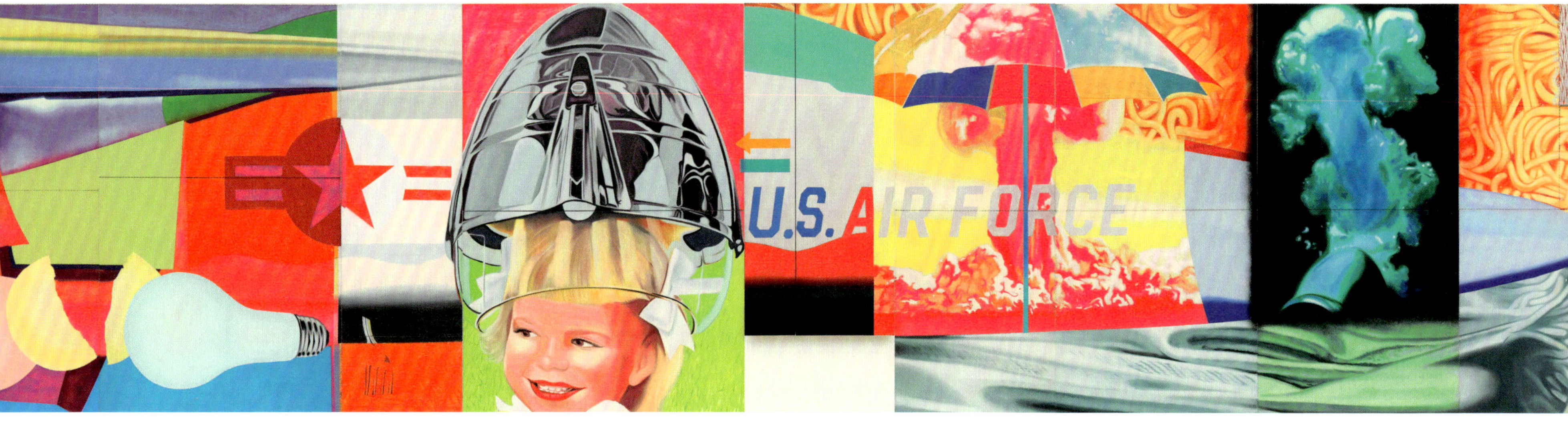

Fig. 5. James Rosenquist (born in 1933)
F-111 (detail), 1964–65
Oil on canvas with aluminum, overall: 3.05 x 26.21 m (10 x 86 ft.)

(Collection of the Historical Society of Delaware), N.C.'s nineteen-by-sixty-foot mural, is a series of vignettes of brightly painted figures in a large colorful landscape, including a fifteen-year-old Andrew Wyeth, who was the model for a nude figure holding a bow and arrow. At the time that Jamie Wyeth painted *Adam and Eve,* it would have looked decidedly out of date next to contemporary monumental works such as James Rosenquist's *F-111* (fig. 5). Composed of twenty-three panels that occupy all four walls of a room, Rosenquist's monumental work brings the aesthetics of billboards into the art gallery. Today it is Rosenquist's Pop Art mural that looks charmingly dated, while Wyeth's playfully historicist mural can be seen as distinctly contemporary, as it simultaneously looks back to history (including the artist's own family history) for inspiration and anticipates the monumental narrative painting of postmodernity.

Rather than applying the cool, objective blandness of Pop Art and the New Realism of the 1960s, Jamie's mural evokes the humanistic richness of late nineteenth-century European Symbolist painting through the prism of American New Deal art. It is a tantalizing work painted almost two decades in advance of the historical revivalism and playful irony that motivated a generation of painters at the center of the figurative revival. From the late 1950s to the mid-1980s realist pioneers such as Alfred Leslie, Alfred Russell, Lennart Anderson, Jack Beal, and Bruno Civitico looked beyond the confines of modernism to reinvigorate realist painting with both technique and content. Within this historical context, Jamie Wyeth may be understood as simultaneously a continuation of traditional American realism and a harbinger of the realist revival that redefined painting in the 1980s and 1990s.

The 1970s saw Jamie Wyeth working in New York in the epicenter of art, fashion, and high society. He was introduced to Andy Warhol by the photographer and socialite Peter Beard, and Warhol and Wyeth painted each other's portraits in 1976, an arrangement facilitated by Wyeth's friendship with Lincoln Kirstein. Over the next four years Wyeth enjoyed two extended residencies at the Factory, participated in four exhibitions, and shared an exhibition catalogue with Andy Warhol. Jamie Wyeth's portraits of his Factory days are at once grander in spirit and more loosely rendered and casual in mood. His sketches of Warhol on brown cardboard are freely handled and capture a casual snapshot aesthetic typical of the Factory, but unique in Wyeth's work. The telling Stanley Tretick photograph of Warhol and Wyeth standing with their reciprocal portraits exemplifies the difference between both the men and their work (fig. 6). Jamie's natural good looks are given the typical unemotional glamorization that Warhol bestowed on socialites and celebrities, while Jamie's less-than-flattering portrait of Andy Warhol stands in sharp contrast to his more formal, and highly empathetic, portraits of John F. Kennedy and Lincoln Kirstein of the previous decade.

What does Jamie Wyeth's foray into the New York art world mean in the larger context of his life and work? From the documentary works of the Apollo missions and the Watergate hearings to his celebrity portraits of Warhol, Arnold Schwarzenegger, and the Russian ballet star Rudolf Nureyev, Jamie Wyeth was moving beyond the confines of the Brandywine tradition and engaging with the world of contemporary celebrity and the unfolding of major historical events. This moment could have been a major turning point in Wyeth's career, one that moved him from the margins of his rural worlds to the center of the New York worlds of art and high society. Instead, this period from 1975 to 1980 was a mere flirtation; Wyeth did not permanently relocate to New York City and integrate himself into the rapidly changing trends of the New York art world. Following his own singular and circuitous path, he chose to remain deeply rooted in his rural worlds of Brandywine and Maine and stay true to his chosen path. In most respects, he continued to be the same artist he had been before his foray into the gloss of Manhattan and the demimonde of the Factory. Wyeth, in an act of self-definition, chose to pursue an independent path, one that remained aloof from the mechanisms of the mainstream art world, the influence of powerful dealers, and the lure of the art market. He once again consciously chose to be firmly grounded in the rural world and familiar subjects that continue to nourish his life and work.

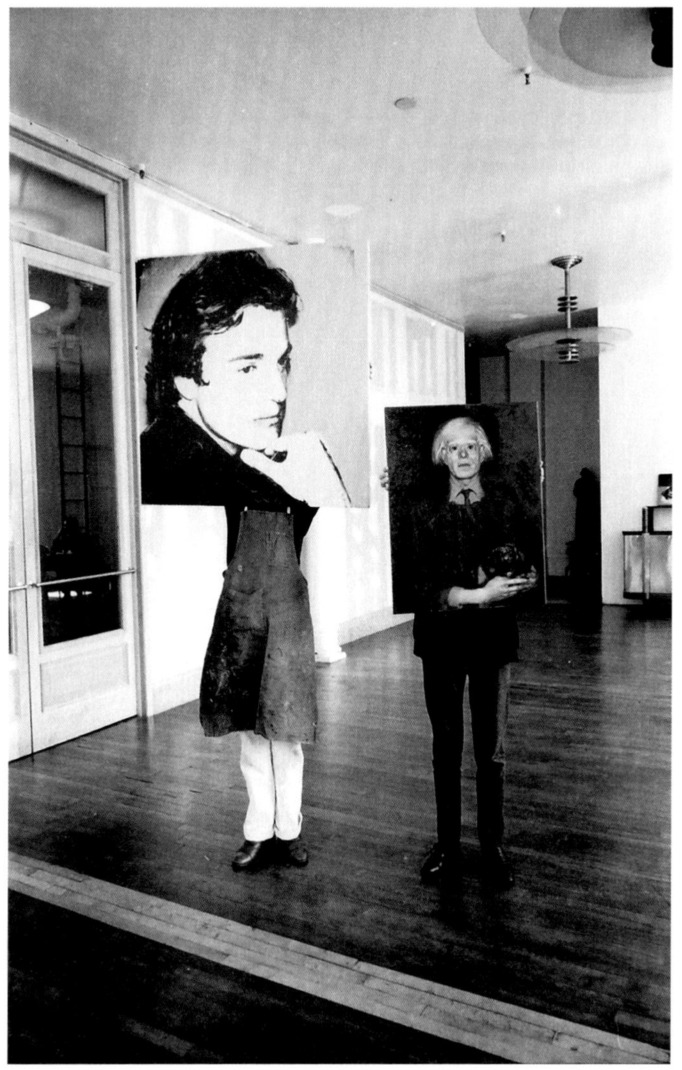

Fig. 6. Stanley Tretick (1921–1999)
Andy Warhol and Jamie Wyeth, 1976

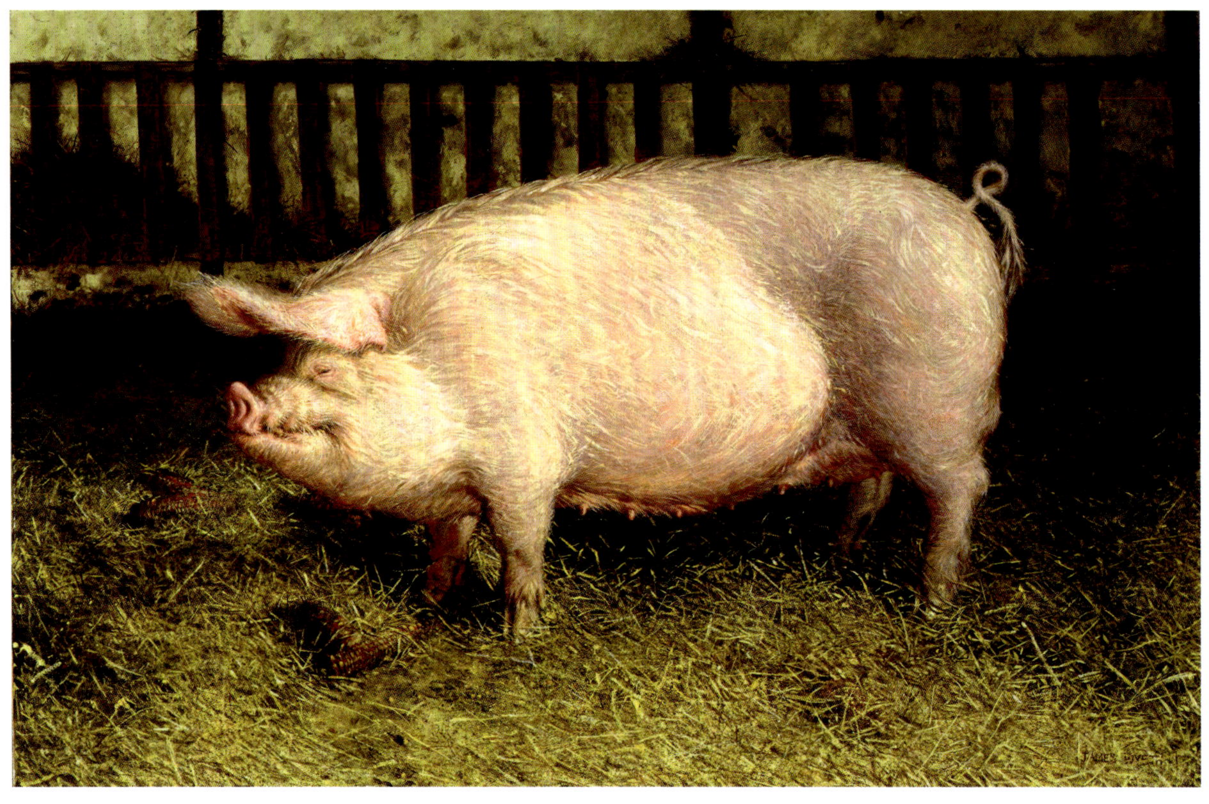

Fig. 7. *Portrait of Pig*, 1970
Oil on canvas
130.8 x 211.5 cm (51½ x 83¼ in.)

Fig. 8. Damien Hirst (born in 1965)
This Little Piggy Went to Market, This Little Piggy Stayed at Home, 1996
Glass, pig, painted steel, acrylic, stainless steel, plastic, formaldehyde solution, and painted steel with motorized base; two parts, each 120 x 210 x 60 cm
(47¼ x 82⅝ x 23⅝ in.)

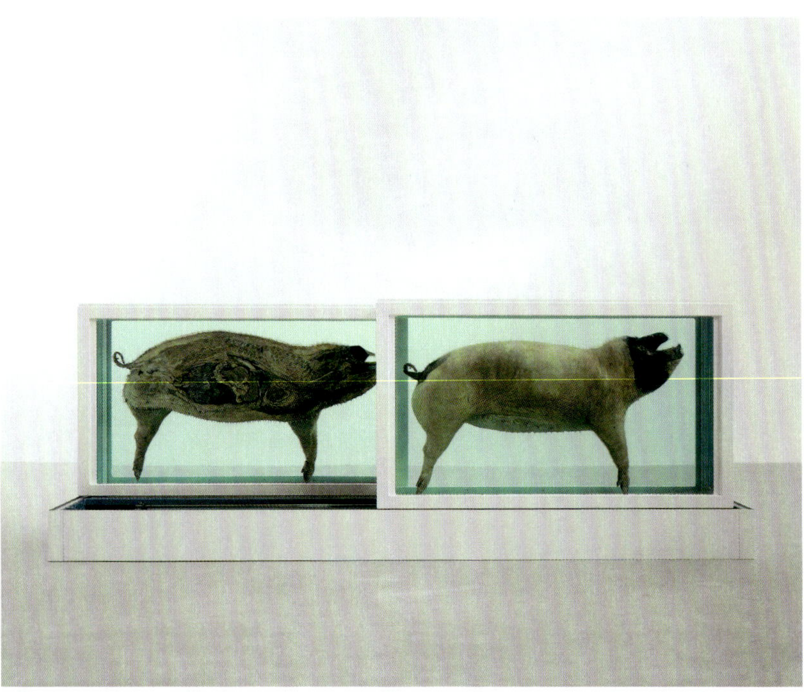

No other major American artist of our time has painted animals with the intimacy and depth of understanding that Jamie Wyeth has. As Lincoln Kirstein observed of Wyeth's youth, "His closest companions were beasts and birds of the Brandywine's riverbanks and fields, a domain whose aspects had barely changed since before the eighteenth century."[3] Jamie Wyeth had painted the animals of the Brandywine River Valley since his early years, and it is possible to parallel these animal paintings alongside all the phases of his evolution as an artist. One of his most significant paintings, *Portrait of Lady* (1968; cat. 81), was painted shortly after his portraits of John F. Kennedy and Lincoln Kirstein. An image of a ewe rendered with the same intense observation and tight detail as seen in those of his human subjects, *Portrait of Lady* is nevertheless a painting of a different order and offers an important insight into the underlying assumptions of Jamie Wyeth's artistic practice. Simultaneously real and hyperreal, detailed and oddly abstract, *Portrait of Lady* is an early example of Wyeth's animal paintings that reaches beyond appearances and suggests that the accrued detail of realism can also create a deeper resonance between the visible and invisible worlds. The viewer senses an immediate visible and emotional connection between the animal and the landscape that implies a pantheistic continuity of the natural order. Lady's dark face harmonizes with the darkness of the earth, and the intensity of her gaze merges with the yellow sky. The directness of her bold, challenging gaze links the viewer with the animal, and the animal with nature, establishing continuity in the natural order of things.

Jamie's bird paintings, descended from *The Rookery* (1977, private collection) and the monumental *Raven* (1980; cat. 85), introduce a complex, multilayered range of new expressive content to his work. Although explored as a unique body of work in the 2005 exhibition *Gulls, Ravens, and a Vulture*, these compositions have yet to be discussed fully within the context of Wyeth's career. Like his father, Andrew, Jamie uses bird's-eye perspectives and animal imagery in a deeply symbolic manner. Andrew's *Soaring* (1942–50) contains both elements, which offer an important precedent for Jamie's obsessive exploration in his gull paintings (see fig. 20, p. 132). By the 1980s the seagulls and ravens had become a major preoccupation in Jamie's work. Whereas the sheep, wolves, and cows boldly stare out of the paintings to directly engage the viewer, the gulls are captured and anthropomorphized in a diverse array of activities as if on a stage. In contrast to the gulls, the ravens are more of a type, portrayed as enigmatic and passive and often rendered in profile. They never achieve the kineticism or extroverted expression of the gulls, painted in a complex array of postures and attitudes. Each of Wyeth's animal subjects suggests a different intent and content and invites the viewer to interpret it as a character with strong human psychological associations, sometimes in a general way, but often in a way specific to the artist's own world.

In comparison to the importance accorded to animals as the main subject in Jamie Wyeth's recent work, the portrayal of animals in contemporary art seems slight, superficial, or exploitative. Among the most important examples of successful animal imagery in recent art are Susan Rothenberg's horses from the mid-1970s. Painted at a time when recognizable imagery, and even the act of painting itself, was called into question, Rothenberg's large expressionistic paintings of horse silhouettes set against a painterly ground opened new possibilities for a revival of expressionist painting. Much of her success was due to timing, but her empathetic understanding and archetypal portrayal of horses were not insignificant to the success and historical importance of this body of work. Similarly, Lucian Freud has always painted animals as an indirect subject appearing in his figure paintings or as "portraits," where they are the main focus of the painting. Many of his portraits feature his beloved whippet dogs standing alongside the sitter or in the sitter's lap. His most curious animal paintings, which have a unique place in his work and a kindred resonance with Jamie Wyeth's animals, are his horse paintings from late in his career. Freud lavishes the same perceptual intensity on the horses that he does on his human subjects. Perhaps the most famous, or infamous, use of animals in contemporary art is in the sculptures of Damien Hirst. Hirst's *This Little Piggy Went to Market, This Little Piggy Stayed at Home* and Jamie Wyeth's *Portrait of Pig* contrast an urban, conceptual understanding of an animal with a rural perspective that knows both the living creature and its habitat (figs. 7, 8).

Jamie Wyeth's figure paintings are diverse and complicated. His most straightforward figures are the youthful portraits from the 1960s and the Factory years paintings of Warhol, Schwarzenegger, and Nureyev. In *Lighthouse* (1993) and *The Wanderer* (1992, both in private collections), Wyeth utilizes the silhouette as a symbolic presence of the viewer, a device that first appeared in *Moon Landing* (1969; cat. 24). Wyeth's most fully developed and evocative figure paintings are the series of portraits of the adolescent islander Orca Bates, which resonate with the contemporary concerns of identity, sexuality, and psychological introspection (cats. 67, 68). Based on the device of the open narrative prominent in the art of the 1980s and early 1990s, these are among Jamie Wyeth's most contemporary works. An obvious comparison is Eric Fischl's many paintings of adolescent boys from the 1980s. Fischl's adolescents are knowing, eroticized youths caught up in a contemporary urban world of events largely defined by the adults around them. Whereas Orca Bates is symbolic of an inward journey of soul-searching self-identity, Fischl's young men are often characters in a contemporary morality play that tells us more about the adults of their world than the young men themselves.

It is impossible to understand Jamie Wyeth's accomplishment as an artist without discussing the shifting frames of the critical context in which the work is produced, exhibited, and interpreted. One of the unexplored stories in Jamie Wyeth's evolution as an artist is the role of his father's lifelong struggle for critical acceptance in the art world. As a realist in an age dominated by abstraction, Andrew Wyeth was cast as the arch-villain of reactionary conservatism in midcentury American art. The critical discussion of Andrew Wyeth's painting was for years also applicable to Jamie's work as well.

The belief that realist painting was rendered obsolete by the verisimilitude of photography and the advent of abstract art is an argument that is central to the narrative of modernism. One of the most influential books that argues this point, and one that still has resonance today, is Wassily Kandinsky's *Concerning the Spiritual in Art* (1911). This text, part aesthetic manifesto and part historical argument, is unified by a hefty dose of theosophical mysticism couched in the Bergsonian terms of human evolution. At the heart of Kandinsky's complex ideas was the simple belief that humankind was evolving toward a higher spiritual plane and that art was a powerful tool that would lead the human spirit to this elevated level of understanding. Kandinsky argued that abstract painting was a new spiritual language that was leading humanity away from the evils of materialism and in the direction of the realization of our spiritual destiny. Kandinsky's ideas have found continuing life in important schools such as the Bauhaus, Black Mountain College, Illinois Institute of Technology, and the Yale School of Art, after he migrated to America with the wave of immigrants fleeing the chaos of the Second World War. One of Kandinsky's important American champions was the painter and curator Hilla Rebay, a founder of the Guggenheim Museum (originally called the Museum of Non-Objective Painting), and many of his observations from *Concerning the Spiritual in Art* reverberated in the mid-twentieth century through the influential teaching and writing of Hans Hofmann. This idea—the deeply held belief that nonobjective art represents the historical imperative through the irrepressible progressive spirit of modernity—became common among the majority of forward-thinking members of the art world.

The most outspoken and authoritative proponent of American abstract painting was the critic Clement Greenberg, who shared Kandinsky's belief that nonobjective painting was the most significant development in the art of the modern era. By 1942 Greenberg had declared that realist painting was dead, replaced by work that corresponded to his own ideas about the flatness of the picture plane that made the medium a means in itself. Those who persisted in illusionistic, perceptual-based art were thought to be out of touch with the new imperatives of culture and seen as reactionary romantics. As the painter Frank Stella stated in 1966, "It's just that you can't go back. It's not a question of destroying anything. If something's used up, something's done, something's over, what's the point of getting involved with it?"[4] These emanations of Greenberg's exclusionary progressive thinking dominated the art world, and especially the academic world, well into the 1980s. Within this climate of either-or, then and now, the art press saw Andrew Wyeth's painting, and perceptual realism in general, as obsolete, nostalgic, and completely out of date. Wyeth's continued and overwhelming popular appeal was also seen as supporting evidence that his work was less serious than that of his abstract contemporaries.

As Jamie Wyeth watched Andrew Wyeth living the life of a celebrated but nonetheless embattled realist artist, and possibly because of it, his career moved with its own self-determined inner logic apart from the mainstream art world. His early hyperrealistic portraits were contemporary with the development of Pop Art and New Realist painting, but his critical reception was often in the same negative context or aggressive indifference within the realist-abstraction opposition that dominated the art criticism of the 1960s. Jamie Wyeth's inner-directed path followed an independent evolution, one often at odds with his contemporaries and continually circling back to revisit favorite topography and themes. As an artist of the eternal pursuing a circular evolution in a linear-thinking world, Wyeth continually revamped familiar places and subjects while the many mainstream American art movements from Abstract Expressionism, through Pop Art, minimalism, the New Realism, and postmodern pluralism came and went.

The German art historian Udo Kultermann's *The New Painting* (1969), a wide-ranging survey of contemporary art from abstraction to the New Realism, purposefully ignores the classic American realist tradition exemplified by Andrew and Jamie Wyeth. The omission of the Wyeths from this pantheon of contemporary painters is an example of the powerful influence of the modernist narrative and the belief in the linear tradition of the New Realism. The new, heavily mediated realism is characterized by the author as "a groping attempt to deal with the new conception of realism."[5] He argues that the New Realism is a movement that cannot be ignored, and one that is fundamentally different from the traditional perceptual approach of the old realism. "There exists," he writes, "another kind of realist, more traditional and direct, such as Andrew Wyeth, who seems to be equally realistic. That kind of artist has played no role in formulating the new realism we are discussing here."[6] Kultermann still situates the new developments in realist painting firmly within the critical framework of the linear unfolding of modernism. In *New Realism* (1972), Kultermann clearly sees this new movement as an extension of the same ideas associated with minimalism and postpainterly abstraction rather than a new historical trajectory. The cool objectivity and unexpressive surfaces of the New Realism, to his mind, are a clean break with the past and diametrically opposed to traditional realism. The flat planes of color and cropped perspectives of the New Realism demote the importance of narrative content, which is presented as a mere romantic idealism of the past, and replace it with objectivity and a detached point of view that mediates the world through the camera lens and the prism of popular culture.

In the 1970s and 1980s museum curators mounted exhibitions that attempted to define contemporary realist painting, although they struggled with the lack of stylistic unity in the work as well as the contradictory nature of the critical debates around it.[7] What is clear is that in the landscape of contemporary realisms, diversity, in all its contradictory nature, is the norm, and that although there may be schools and movements, there are as many exceptions to their rules as praiseworthy examples. In the past three decades contemporary realism has continued to flourish, and its stylistic diversity continues to expand exponentially.

In rethinking the critical context for Jamie Wyeth's career, it would be a mistake to cast his work as an example of postmodern painting. His highly individual approach to realism lacks the self-conscious irony, historical revivalism, and media awareness associated with the diverse range of postmodern realist styles. In the words of the theorist Ihab Hassan, postmodern art shares a common interest in "fragments, hybridity, relativism, play, parody, pastiche, an ironic, anti-ideological stance, an ethos bordering on kitsch and camp."[8] Though similar in their shared realist approach, glaring differences of content, mood, and intent are apparent in the most basic comparison between Jamie Wyeth's recent work and those of postmodern neoclassicists such as Bruno Civitico, Edward Schmidt, and Lennart Anderson or high postmodern stylists such as Vitaly Komar and Alex Melamid or the clever neohistoricism of Mark Tansey. For an institutional world that is intent on categorizing art through periodization, stylistic labels, and contemporary trends, Wyeth's directness of experience, variety of subjects, and nomadic stylistic diversity present a challenge for contemporary critics and viewers alike. Although many of his subjects—people, animals, landscape, and architecture—are constants in his work, his approach to them is purposefully inconsistent rather than the result of a logical linear development. He often revisits subjects, looping back and painting the same themes in a different style or different context. What is consistent in the diversity of his long career is a point of view where the visible and invisible worlds intermingle through the force of imagination.

Contemporary realism, for lack of a better descriptive phrase, has its Old Masters, the important bridge figures in the 1950s and 1960s (Fairfield Porter, Alfred Russell, and John Koch); hyperrealists (Philip Pearlstein, Audrey Flack, and Chuck Close); detached practitioners of the Pop-inflected New Realism of the 1960s (Alex Katz, Will Barnet, Janet Fish, and William Bailey); and classicists (Lennart Anderson, Edward Schmidt and Bruno Civitico). It has the explorers of neobaroque drama, such as Alfred Leslie and Jack Beal, and expressionists, including the later Gabriel Laderman and Alice Neel. Among the younger generation, Steven Assael, Vincent Desiderio, Jeanne Duval, and Bo Bartlett, himself an artist associated with Andrew Wyeth and the Brandywine tradition, all reinforce both the vitality and the variousness of contemporary American realism. There are also the very recent practitioners of a playful, conceptual approach to realism, such as John Currin, George Condo, Neo Rauch, and Luc Tuymens. Within this context, Jamie Wyeth is a pluralist among the predictability of art-world stylists. Rather than mapping one consistent path, he continues to explore a range of realist strategies, which are sometimes related to consistently revisited subjects and sometimes not. Where Barnett Newman maintained the primacy of object matter, Jamie Wyeth has maintained the primacy of subject matter. In an era that values irony, conceptual strategies, and surface qualities over content, Wyeth's neotraditional work reinforces the narrative qualities of realist painting while also suggesting that a subject matter can reach beyond the obvious and the visible.

If we look beyond the obvious and well-known subjects and individual styles of the artists of the Brandywine School, theirs is a deeply shared set of values and beliefs that are foundational ideas behind their work. One of the many reasons that the critics respond negatively to the work of the Wyeths is that these shared values stand outside the changing critical and theoretical context of contemporary art. First of all, the geographical rootedness grounds both the subject matter and the content of the work to a place and time that rejects modernist abstraction, the collage sensibility of midcentury American art, and the virtual disengagement of postmodernity. This unbroken line of realism also bypasses the need for revivalism, ironic posturing, or conceptual mediation, because this link between the artist and subject is a real-time observation and traditional representation of that experience. The Brandywine tradition has deep conceptual roots in the American tradition of transcendentalism, which believes in the continuity between the material world and the invisible realm of spirit. In his first published essay, "Nature," Emerson writes, "Every fact is the symbol of some spiritual fact."[9] The origins of this mystical alliance between the visible and the invisible originated with the founder of the school, Howard Pyle, who was also a well-known follower of the visionary thinker Emanuel Swedenborg. Pyle was so taken with Swedenborg's writings that he mandated that they be read aloud to his students as they worked. Pyle was also tangentially connected to European Symbolism through the painter Giovanni Segantini. Pyle was impressed by his work, which he saw during his European travels. The 1897 Segantini monograph by William Ritter has been passed down through the artists of the school like a holy text.[10]

The simple Symbolist belief in the importance of nature as a storehouse of images that connects humanity to the larger spiritual world became a basic, unarticulated tenet of the artists of the Brandywine tradition. Much to the confusion of his admirers, Andrew Wyeth has been quoted as having said, "I am no more [a realist] than the man in the moon."[11] His work may, in fact, be read as a continuation of the Symbolist practice of the visible world of fact being an evocation of ideas, states of mind, and a way of addressing the mysteries of life. Jamie Wyeth is the inheritor of this unbroken tradition where the real and the intangible intermingle in the work of art, and his work is at once of our time and premodern and antirealistic in its point of view and intent. As Emerson suggests, "For every object has its roots in central nature, and may be so exhibited to us as to represent the world."[12] For the artists working in this grand tradition, a picture is not a mere image, but ultimately a representation of a world.

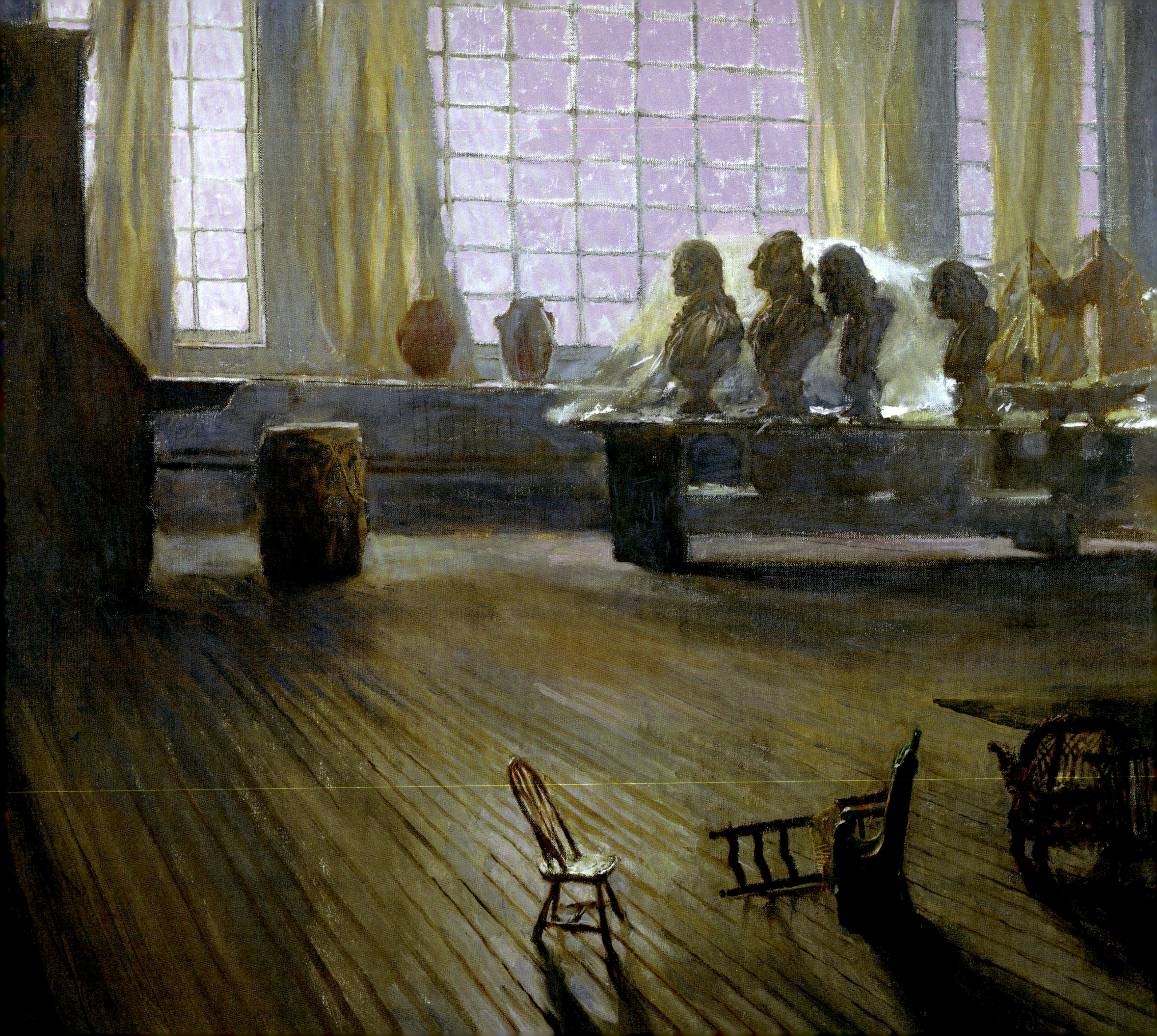

Early Life and Work

The world of working artists so surrounded Jamie Wyeth from the very moment he was born on July 6, 1946, in Chadds Ford, Pennsylvania, that he later quipped, "Everyone in my family paints, except, perhaps, the dogs."[1] The second son of Elizabeth (Betsy) James Wyeth and Andrew Wyeth, Jamie belonged to the third generation of the Wyeth family to live and work in the Brandywine River Valley between Pennsylvania and Delaware. His father was the youngest child of Newell Convers (N. C.) Wyeth, the first member of the Wyeth family to put down roots in Chadds Ford, who made his way to the area fresh from his studies in Boston, hoping to become a student of the celebrated illustrator Howard Pyle (1853–1911).[2] The rich, rolling landscape that had witnessed so many events of the American Revolution appealed to N. C. Wyeth's New England heritage and outlook, and though he retained close ties to his family in Needham, Massachusetts, he eventually settled permanently in Chadds Ford in 1908, studied with Pyle, and proceeded to dedicate himself to his art and, in time, his family.[3]

Jamie Wyeth's grandfather died the year before he was born, and yet the ethos and traditions established by the family patriarch—especially at Halloween and Christmas—carried on into Jamie's youth and beyond. The Wyeth family, especially N. C. Wyeth, derived great pride and strength from his New England roots, which extended back to an English mason, Nicholas Wyeth, who first purchased land in Cambridge, Massachusetts, in 1645. In 1881 Andrew Newell Wyeth married Hattie Zirngiebel, the daughter of a Swiss-born horticulturalist, Denys Zirngiebel; they established themselves at 284 South Street in Needham, where Newell Convers Wyeth was born the following year. Deeply moved by the American transcendentalists Ralph Waldo Emerson and, especially, Henry David Thoreau—whose Walden Pond in Concord was not far from his own birthplace and family homestead in Massachusetts—N. C. Wyeth was inspired to illustrate Thoreau's journals in *Men of Concord*, published in 1936. Andrew Wyeth was born on Thoreau's birthday, July 12, a happenstance that his father found remarkably fortunate, particularly given his profound sense of the spiritual qualities inherent in the natural world that he hoped to convey in his art. Beyond Chadds Ford, N. C. Wyeth began seeking summer respite in Maine in 1910, with his friend and fellow art student, Sidney M. Chase. He traveled to the St. George peninsula on the coast in 1918 and two years later established a home in the town of Port Clyde, which he named Eight Bells in honor of Winslow Homer.[4] He thus initiated a long tradition of Wyeth family members living on Maine's midcoast and nearby islands that continues today.

Creative pursuits seemed to come naturally to the Wyeths, as their family culture and dedicated work ethic supported a variety of artistic interests and aptitudes. Of Newell Convers and Carolyn Wyeth's five children, three were practicing artists (Henriette, Carolyn, and Andrew); one was a musician (Ann); and one was an inventor and engineer with several patents to his name (Nathaniel). The extended family of Newell and Carolyn included sons-in-law who were also artists: Peter Hurd, who initially came to study with N. C. Wyeth and later became Henriette's husband; and John McCoy, Ann's husband. The range of artistic talent expressed by the Wyeth family has often inspired comparison with the Philadelphia artists Charles Willson Peale and his brother, James Peale, along with their many progeny and spouses; however, key differences between these two clans are often overlooked. Charles Willson Peale apparently directed forms of artistic expression by assigning different genres of painting to his various children, setting his son Raphaelle on the path of still life painting, for example. The most distinguished painters of the second generation of Peales, Sarah Miriam Peale and Anna Claypoole Peale, daughters of James, were known for still lifes and miniatures, and of the third generation, Mary Jane Peale is perhaps best known for teaching her own father, Rubens, and for specializing in flower paintings.[5] The approach of the Wyeths seems to have varied by gender, but not in the ways that one would expect. Carolyn Wyeth was closely supervised by her father in making sketch after sketch of plaster casts and still life setups, whereas N.C. treated Andrew, the youngest, with benign neglect as a means of preserving his own vision, an approach that Andrew claims to have, in turn, extended to Jamie Wyeth.[6]

When Jamie Wyeth came along in 1946, Andrew Wyeth was working hard to make a name for himself, while also grieving the loss of his own father the year before.[7] Reflecting on what he considered an important turning point in his art, Andrew Wyeth observed of his father's death: "We had a wonderful friendship. Of course, he'd been my only teacher, and he was a wonderful, remarkable person. When he died, I was just a clever watercolorist—lots of swish and swash. . . . Now I was really on the spot and had this terrific urge to prove that what he had started in me was not in vain—to really do something serious and not play around with it, doing caricatures of nature. I had a vast gloomy feeling. Fortunately, I had always had this great emotion toward the landscape and so, with his death, . . . the landscape took on a meaning—the quality of him."[8] Soon thereafter, Andrew managed to sell his *Christina's World* (1948), a now iconic painting in the constellation of twentieth-century American art, to the Museum of Modern Art, setting him on the path to becoming one of the most famous and recognizable American artists of the second half of the twentieth century, if not the most celebrated by contemporary art critics.[9]

Artistic talent was taken seriously in Jamie Wyeth's home from his earliest years, as is amply demonstrated by the extensive cache of over a thousand childhood drawings that his mother saved and often annotated with his descriptions and dates. Such early drawings often provide tantalizing windows into the personality of the artist, as their subjects frequently point the way to themes that will occupy later stages of an artist's career.[10] The earliest drawings shown here reflect the youthful exuberance of the artist's vivid imagination, which was sparked and stoked by stories and images from his grandfather's repertoire created during the golden age of book illustration. We find cowboys fighting, knights coming to the rescue of damsels in distress, musketeers battling, and a special member of that band, d'Artagnan, triumphantly brandishing his sword while tossing his head back to unleash what we could imagine was a blood curdling laugh (cats. 1–3). In the charming winter scene *Boys Sledding*, Wyeth creates a sophisticated balance between the negative space of the winter landscape and two pairs of boys, one duo poised at the summit and one at the base of the hill. Our eye follows the arc of a boldly curving hillside before coming to a full stop where the large snowball and boy bending over are drawn at the bottom of the sheet. The placement of the two small boys at the top relative to the wide expanse below creates a sense of tension, intimating their fear at being on the edge of a precipice, from which the sled is about to launch at breakneck speed. Throughout his career the artist has continued to derive inspiration from the aesthetic energy created by juxtaposing simultaneous views of close and distant perspectives within the same image and has demonstrated a particular fondness for the creative possibilities presented by winter landscapes.

In *Ardent Lover*, the intense longing of the knight for his lady locked far away in a tower stretches out before us in the shape of an armored snake creeping stealthily up the vertical wall of a fortress. The twelve-year-old artist had already met his future wife, Phyllis Mills, and may have been anticipating his romantic quest to capture her heart.[11]

One of the most revelatory early drawings shows us Jamie Wyeth confronting his father's art (cat. 7).[12] The sheet appears to have been used initially by Andrew to render a profile portrait of Jamie in watercolor that was left unfinished, or at least cast aside in the studio. The three-year-old Jamie seems to have found this profile of him by his father as good a place as any to leave his own mark, and he proceeded to create his own pencil drawing of a fishing boat at the bottom of the sheet, all the while respecting the likeness made by his father. The act of drawing on Andrew Wyeth's watercolor of his own image boldly states Jamie Wyeth's identity, expressed by his lines as distinct from those of his father. In his composition Jamie responds to some of his father's shapes by placing a small hook at the top of the mast to balance a small triangular form (perhaps delineating the edge of a table) near his own image. Even at this early age, Jamie Wyeth reveals his developing interest in exploring the various realms he represents, showing us what is happening above, at, and below the waterline. A seagull soars above the scene at the left, while a man pilots a vessel with the distinctly blunt stern of a traditional Maine lobster boat over the water. Then, plunging his pencil beneath the surface of the water to depict a line perhaps for an anchor, Wyeth draws an enormous fish swimming directly beneath the boat.

Jamie Wyeth's path as an artist followed that of the traditional apprentice dating back to the Italian Renaissance when he succeeded in convincing his parents that he should leave school permanently to devote more time to the studio and his chosen profession. In 1957, when home schooling was not the norm, the stance was bold for a boy who had just finished sixth grade and was only eleven years old. And yet some of the most famous painters of the early Renaissance began this early, including the young Giotto, a poor shepherd boy out in the fields drawing his flock on flat stones, until he was spotted by the famous Florentine painter Cimabue and taken on as an apprentice.[13] Andrew Wyeth had acquired most of his formal schooling through private tutors, supposedly owing to poor health as a child, and did not consider a college education necessary for an artist.[14] Newell Convers Wyeth was highly skeptical of the benefit of the local public school that his children attended, noting frequently in his letters that the essential aspects of their education could be derived at home.[15] It appears that Betsy James Wyeth was opposed to the idea of their son's leaving school to study at home, although she eventually came around despite her misgivings, and, together, Jamie Wyeth and his parents developed a program for his education that would satisfy the Pennsylvania Board of Education and his determination to pursue his passion outside the realm of formal schooling.[16]

Rather than having Jamie become an apprentice to his father, who was in the midst of building his own career, Andrew Wyeth arranged for him to study with his aunt Carolyn Wyeth, who used N. C. Wyeth's studio as her own.[17] After quitting school, Jamie had his own idea of what he would do to become an artist. He had "been reading the retelling of the Arthurian legend in *The Once and Future King* by T. H. White, and had visions of giving himself whatever education he might need by observing animals in the woods, as Arthur had under Merlin's tutelage." Jamie Wyeth's parents were having none of that fantasy world as a substitute for his education, and certainly his idea of school was not going to pass muster with the educators of the local school board. In the mornings a tutor came, and Wyeth had to take regular examinations to demonstrate that he was keeping up with his grade level in academics.[18] Jamie would go to his aunt Carolyn's in the afternoons, "where for the first year he was assigned to drawing spheres and cubes." Although bored by those disciplinary exercises, he later understood their value; as he observed: "I just had to do it. I just wanted to get my tools as sharp as possible."[19] It was there that he was drawn to oil paint, as his father was working primarily in tempera and dry-brush watercolor by then. As he recalled, "I suppose my real interest started in oil because I loved the way [Carolyn] squeezed it out—it looked so edible."[20]

Jamie Wyeth sketched his aunt Carolyn (cat. 6), a free if somewhat eccentric spirit, retrieving her mail from the local postman in the nude behind a large blanket, and incorporated her distinctive style of surrealist landscape into his own compositions (see, for in-

Fig. 9. John Singleton Copley (1738–1815)
A Boy with a Flying Squirrel (Henry Pelham), 1765
Oil on canvas, 77.2 x 63.8 cm (30⅜ x 25⅛ in.)

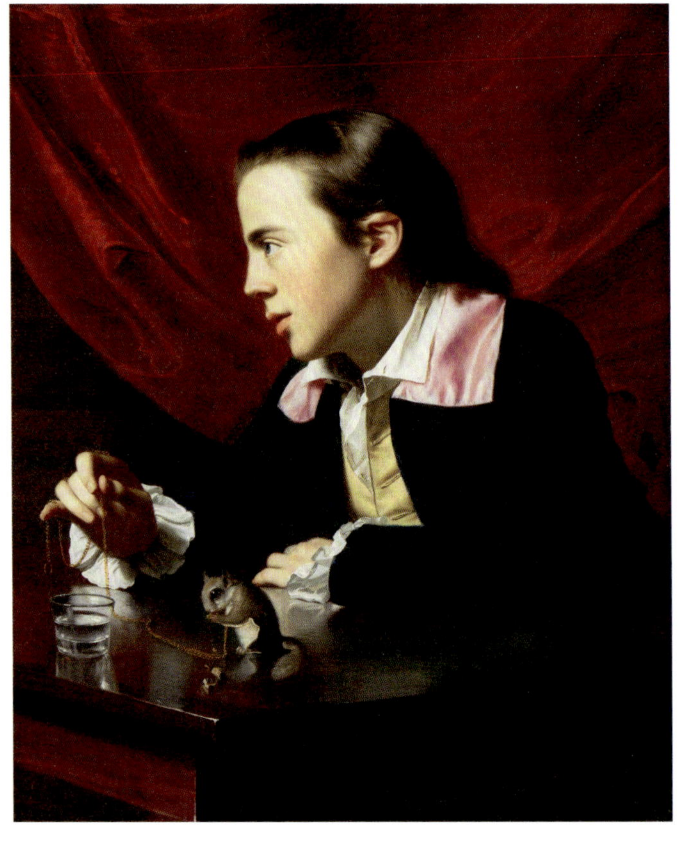

stance, the background of *Catching Snowflakes*, cat. 47), although no finished portraits of this important teacher are known.[21] A vivid glimpse of Carolyn's command of N. C. Wyeth's studio appears in Andrew Wyeth's biography, as she marched up and down in her black gaucho hat and her father's long brown coat. Jamie recalled, "She sort of *became* my grandfather. . . . It was the strongest visual exposure you could have, other than being with him physically. Maybe it was even stronger than if he had been there. His personality that I found later in his letters—such a Mama's boy—I don't know if I would've been that enamored of him."[22]

The importance of that studio space, especially the props that it contained as an inspiration for N. C. Wyeth's work, appeared later on in Jamie Wyeth's memory of the interior depicted in *The Children's Illustrator* (cat. 8).[23] Painted nearly fifty years after the artist had begun his formal studies there, the studio appears vacant at the heart of the composition. The busts of famous men that often looked down from their lofty perches near the cornice of the room in photographs of N.C. working there now line a makeshift table near the window, partially obscured by sheeting to protect them from the ravages of dust and time. The foreground is littered with an array of children's chairs that serve as counterpoints to the busts, suggesting childhood seats from which the great leaders of the future would emerge. One is toppled on its side, another is pulled up to a table, and two are positioned facing each other as though their former occupants were deep in conversation, perhaps recounting tales of their favorite heroes depicted in N.C. Wyeth's illustrations. The gleaming floorboards draw our eye toward the Palladian window that

N. C. Wyeth had installed to capture the northern light. Just as Andrew Wyeth expressed a sense of wanting to prove that what his father had started in him was not in vain, Jamie Wyeth evokes a melancholy nostalgia for the lessons that he learned as a child with his aunt Carolyn. And yet, the props scattered around the room ultimately give way to the dynamic presence of the sky's lavender haze, one of the most expressive colors from N. C. Wyeth's palette, which breathed such strongly felt emotions into his most memorable compositions, illuminating the past and shining optimistically toward a future vision waiting to be imagined and realized on canvas.

Following those early years studying with his aunt Carolyn in his grandfather's studio, Jamie Wyeth would demonstrate a remarkable ability to conjure up the personalities of his subjects. *Portrait of Shorty*, painted in 1963, when the artist was seventeen years old, represents the most highly accomplished portrait produced soon after he set out on his own. As his father and grandfather had recruited models from the local community, so Jamie Wyeth persuaded Shorty to pose for him.[24] *Portrait of Shorty* is startlingly simple in the quiet but jarring collision of two worlds. Shorty wears an undergarment without sleeves that is still known today by the slang term "wife beater"; the straps are grimy and the edges curled and tatty from wear. He sprouts a small mustache, a grizzly five o'clock shadow on his chin, and deeply creased cheeks, all entirely consistent with his attire. We might expect to see an empty beer can within arm's reach of the model, but in this portrait the figure's head is placed carefully within the arching wing of a richly upholstered chair. The fabric and complex curve of the seat offer a luxurious backdrop for Shorty's careworn stubble that suggest a makeshift throne. The elaborate, eighteenth-century foliate pattern of the silk brocade injects into the portrait a brilliant acid green rendered in remarkable verisimilitude that recalls one of the signature colors and the technique used by fifteenth-century Netherlandish Masters such as Jan Van Eyck. Asked how he came to pose Shorty in that particular upholstered chair, Wyeth quickly replied that it was just the chair that was around in his studio at the time.[25] It may well be that simple. And yet the artist chose to represent Shorty wearing his undershirt, with its frayed edges exposed, unshaven, and with heavy lids hooding his eyes as he stares into the distance with a casual, daydreaming look—ensconced within the lap of luxury. Regardless of why he made his choice, the resulting effect is one of bold contrasts that energize the image, making Shorty appear even more startlingly realistic. Wyeth's decision to set his humble subject against the backdrop of elaborate brocade ultimately transforms his model into a memorable and living image of visual worship, magnifying the manner in which Shorty's life story reveals itself both in the creases of his face and in his guts.

Wyeth's *Portrait of Shorty* reflects the culmination of his early years as an apprentice within his own family circle, richly augmented by the host of images available to him in the great museums of nearby Philadelphia and his family's wide-ranging interest in literature, art, music, and film. It can be compared with a "coming-of-age" portrait by an American artist whom Wyeth himself noted as a considerable influence on his development, John Singleton Copley.[26] In *A Boy with a Flying Squirrel*, Copley's portrait of his fourteen-year-old half brother, Henry Pelham, the artist enhances the youthful quality of Pelham's features by placing him in front of a heavy swag of soft velvet drapery (fig. 9). His rosy, youthful skin and silky brown hair appear every bit as smooth to the touch as the delicate fur on his pet squirrel, proudly posed on the gleaming mahogany tabletop. The composition is a visual lexicon and a feast of textures and surfaces. This overachieving, self-taught artist of colonial Boston intended to put his best efforts forward in rendering the objects and surfaces that form Pelham's portrait as a way of announcing his technical capabilities to the broader world, especially to the leaders of London's Royal Academy, where he hoped to earn a place for himself to study further.[27] Jamie Wyeth's *Portrait of Shorty* may well have served a comparable function, announcing to his parents and his teacher, Aunt Carolyn, that he had mastered the full repertoire of artistic tools and was now capable of going head-to-head with Copley, Van Eyck, or, for that matter, any other American painter, including the adult members of his own family.

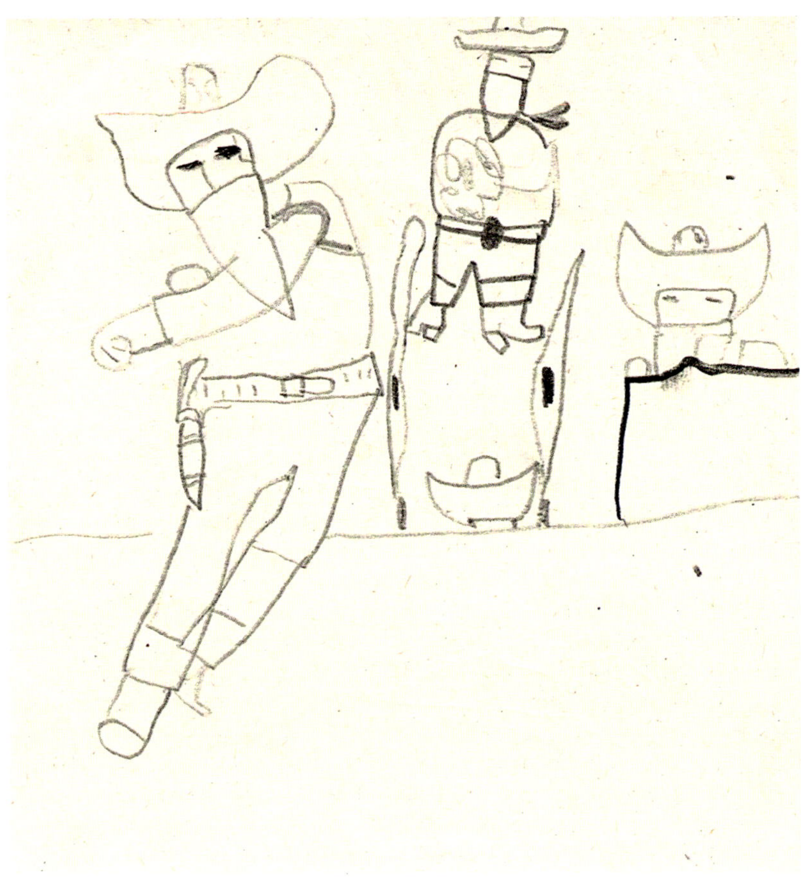

1. *Cowboys Fighting*, 1952. Graphite on paper, 9.5 x 9.5 cm (3¾ x 3¾ in.)

2. *Musketeers*, 1951. Graphite on paper, 27.9 x 21.6 cm (11 x 8½ in.)

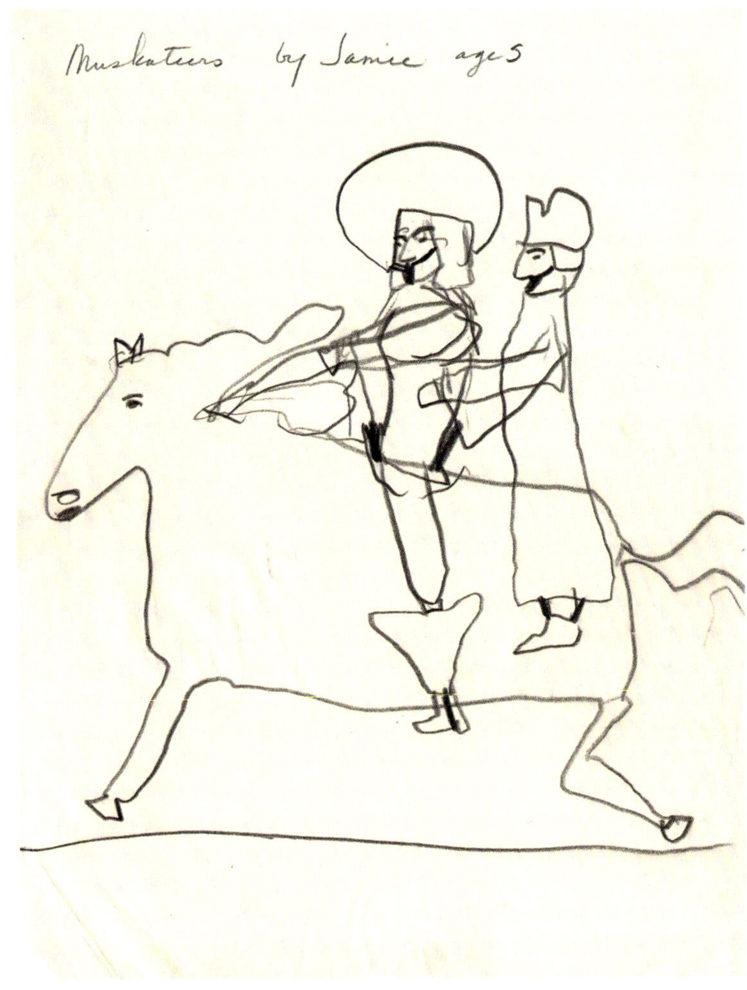

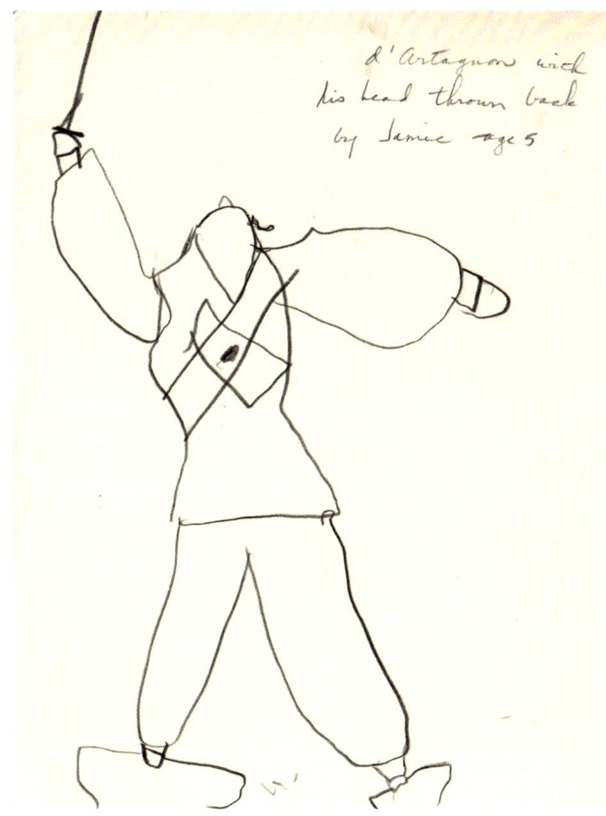

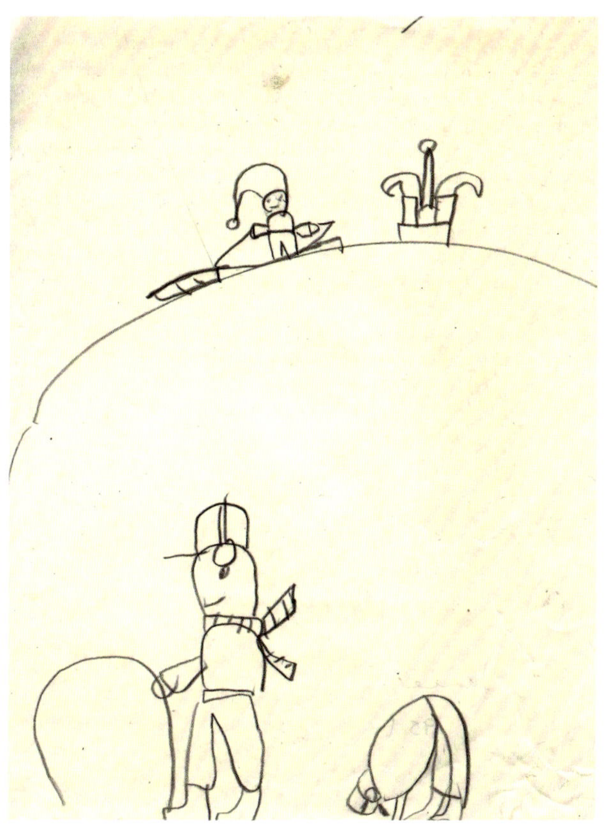

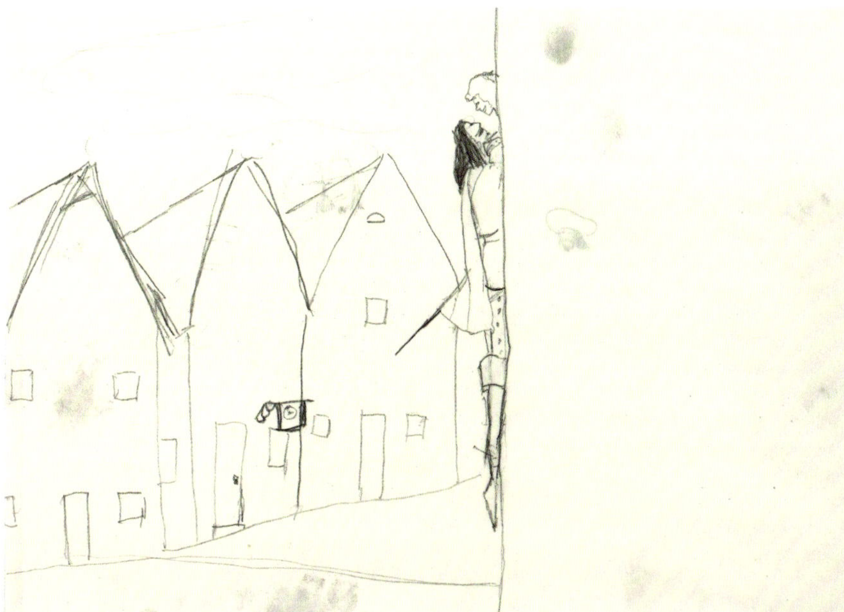

3. *D'Artagnan*, 1951. Graphite on paper, 27.9 x 21.6 cm (11 x 8½ in.)

4. *Boys Sledding*, 1951. Graphite on paper, 27.9 x 21.6 cm (11 x 8½ in.)

5. *Ardent Lover*, 1958. Graphite on paper, 21.3 x 27.6 cm (8⅜ x 10⅞ in.)

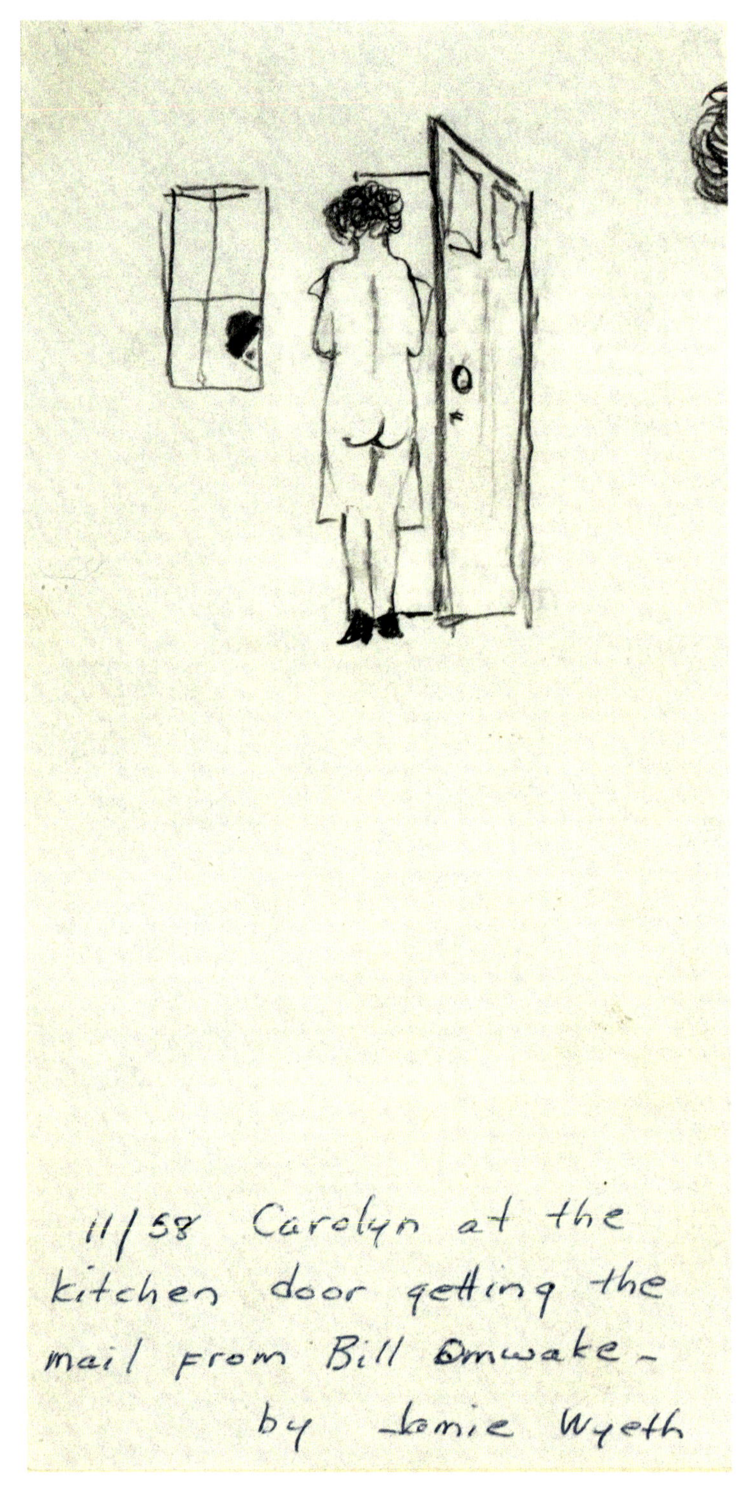

6. *Aunt Carolyn*, 1958. Graphite and ink on paper, 15.9 x 8.3 cm (6¼ x 3¼ in.)

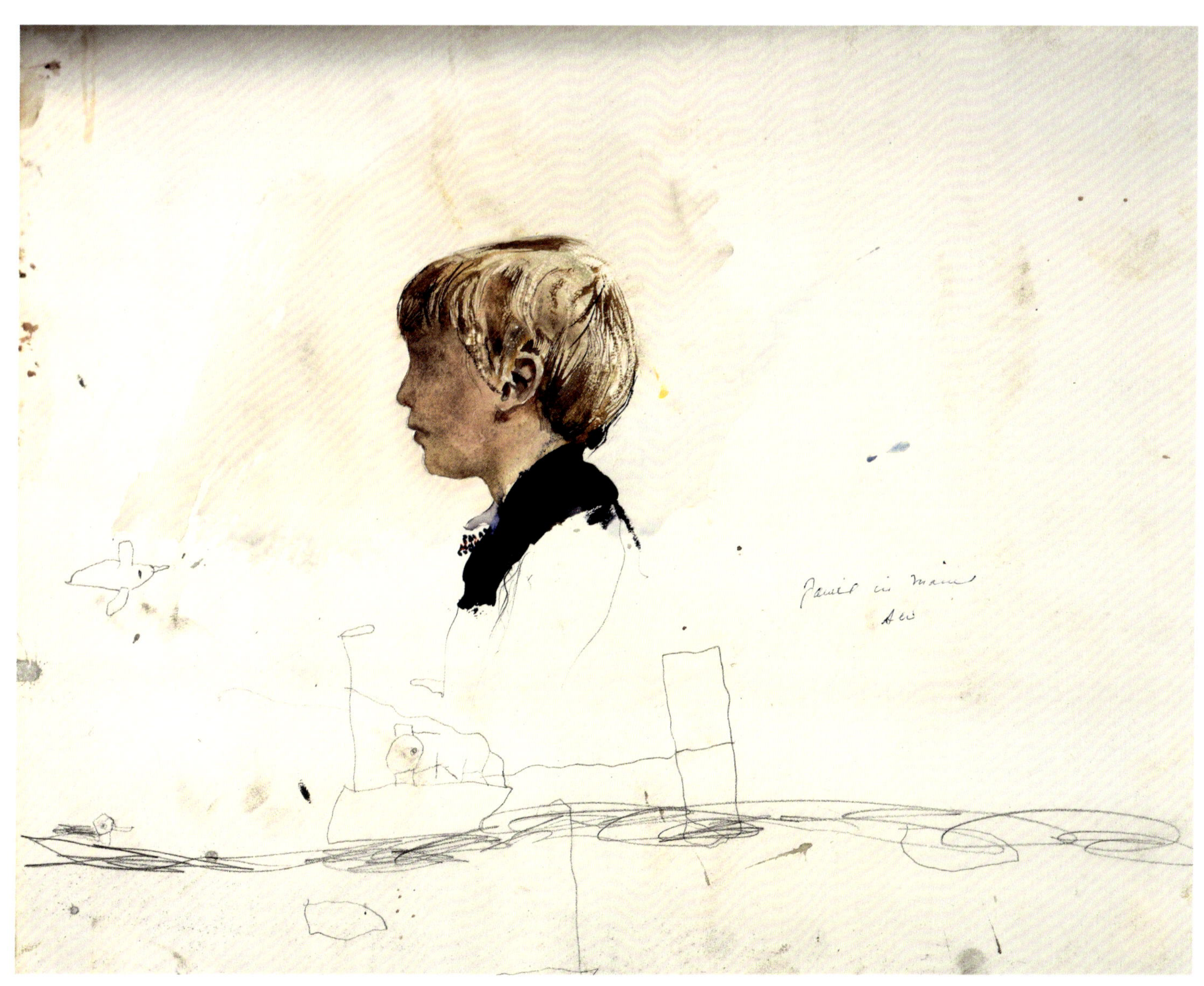

7. Andrew Wyeth and Jamie Wyeth, *Jamie in Blue Sweater,* 1949. Watercolor on paper; graphite on paper, 40.6 x 50.8 cm (16 x 20 in.)

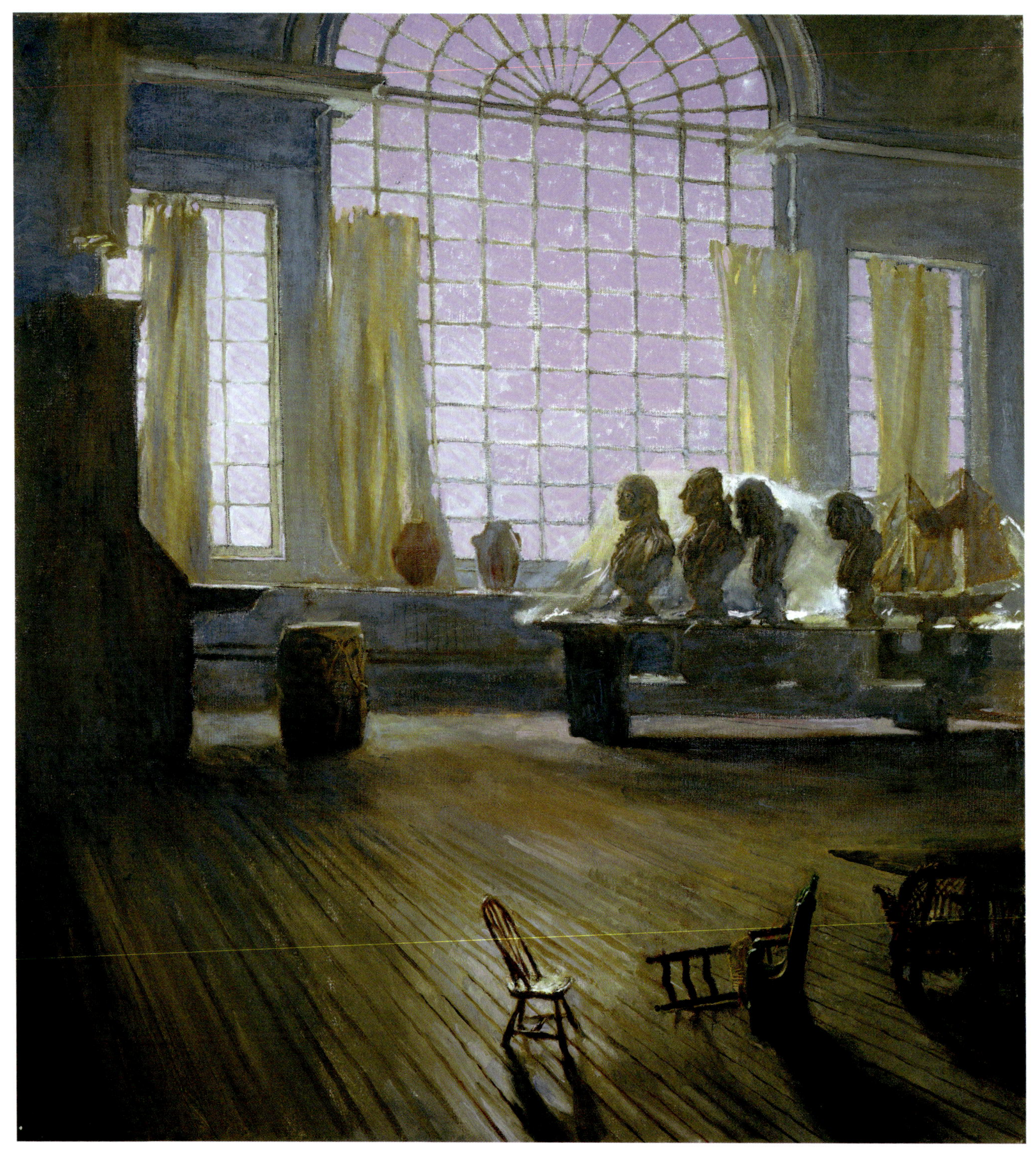

8. *The Children's Illustrator*, 2005. Oil on canvas, 71.1 x 66 cm (28 x 26 in.)

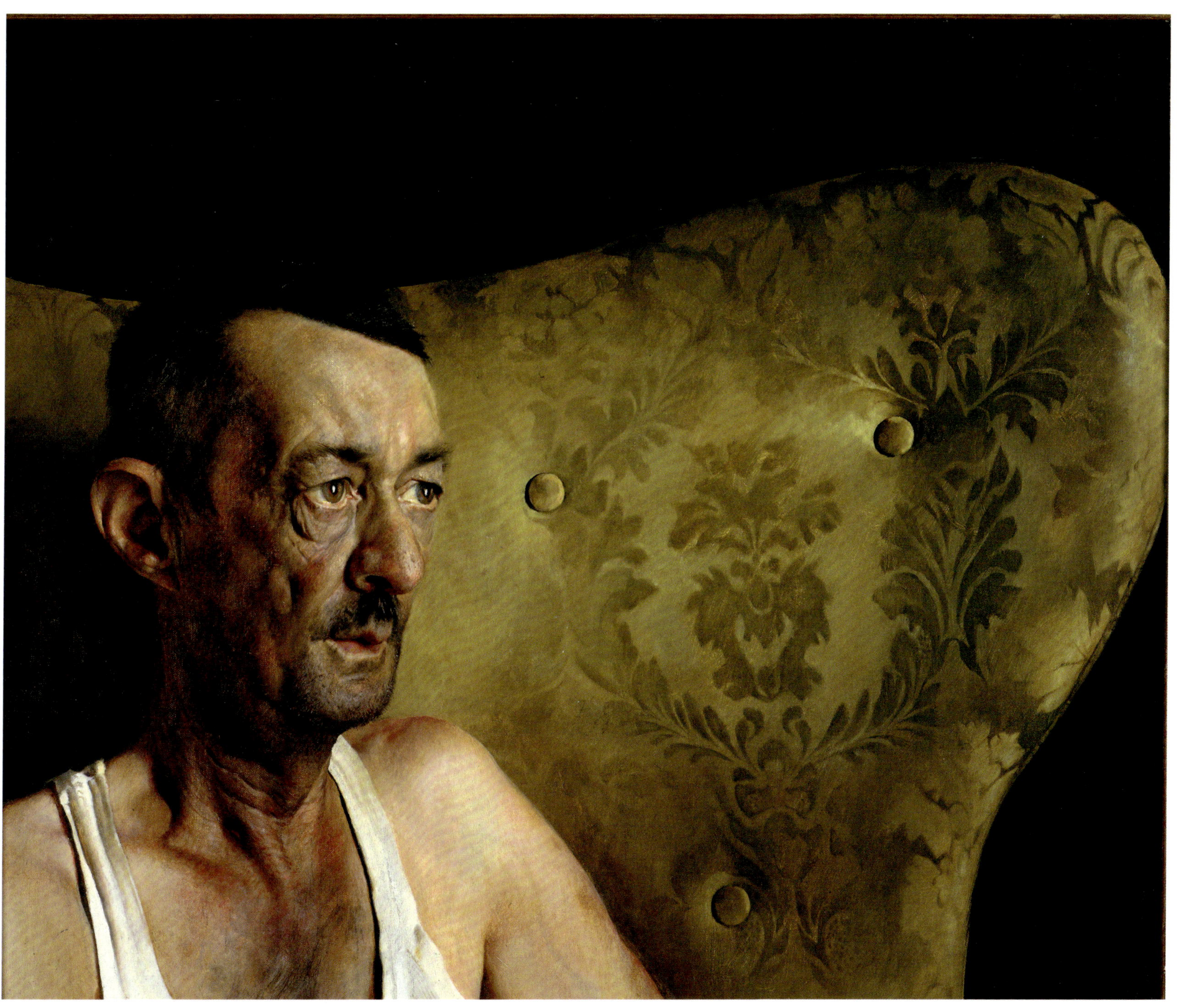

9. *Portrait of Shorty*, 1963. Oil on canvas, 45.7 x 55.9 cm (18 x 22 in.)

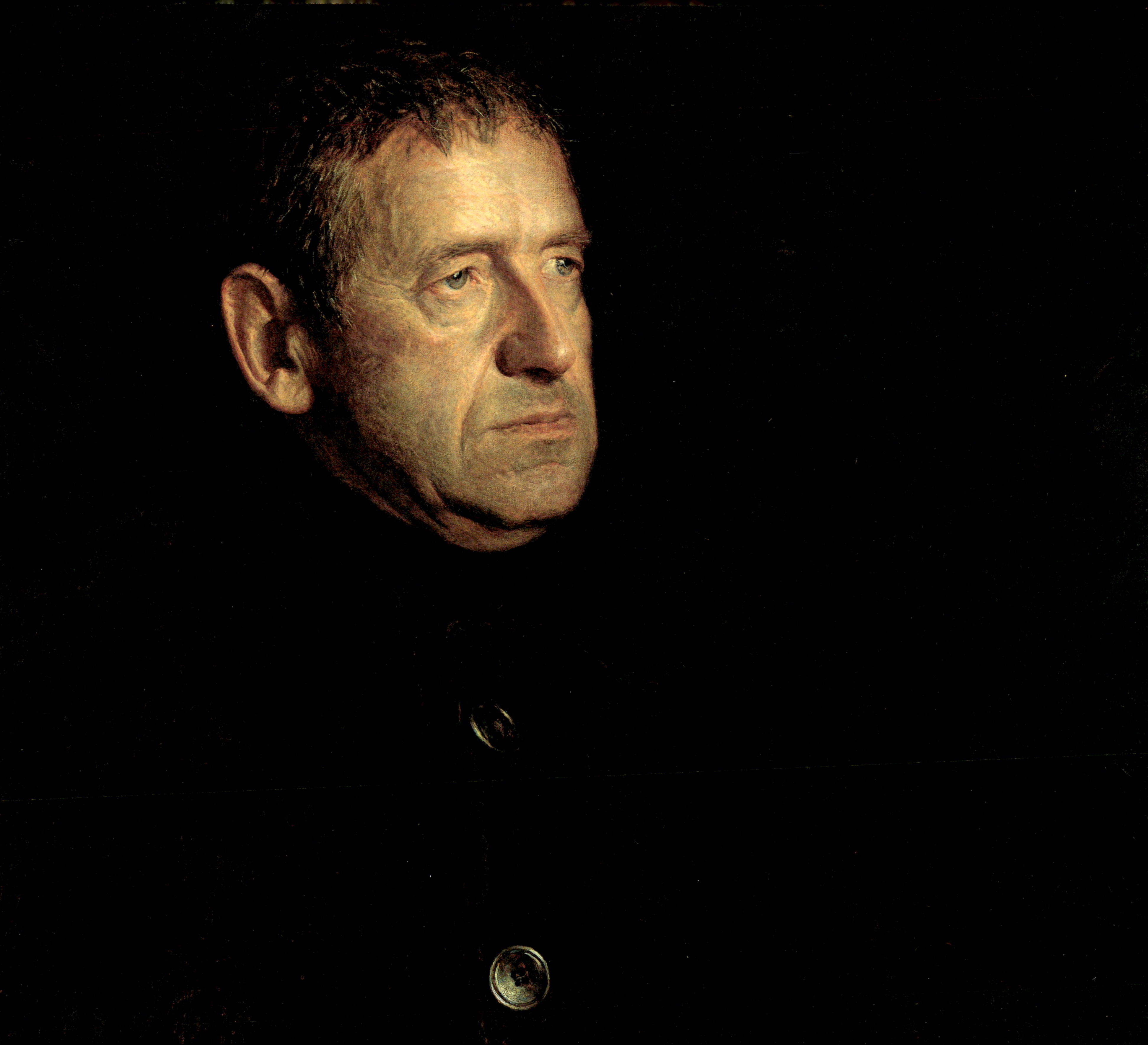

Formation

With ***Portrait of Shorty* behind him,** Jamie Wyeth began the process of emerging from the family's cocoon in Chadds Ford and midcoast Maine.[1] The demonstration of such virtuosity at a young age was not without pitfalls, as Andrew Wyeth noted that he did not want his precocious son to be a Shirley Temple, an allusion to the challenging transition to adulthood that befell the cherubic childhood star of the Depression era.[2] The younger Wyeth's subsequent development involved careful study of anatomy and some early forays into an immersive form of portraiture, which he frequently rendered as half-lengths against dark, monochromatic backgrounds.

The presentation of his first formal commission, *Portrait of Helen Taussig*, elicited tears and gasps of horror when his subject's face, with its piercing blue eyes staring intently at the viewer from behind cat's-eye glasses, was formally unveiled before Taussig's adoring colleagues and friends at Johns Hopkins Hospital.[3] Denied admission to Harvard Medical School because she was a woman, Taussig received her M.D. from Johns Hopkins and went on to become a pioneering pediatric cardiologist there; she was the second female member of the tenured faculty and is still considered one of the institution's most distinguished doctors.[4] Two hundred guests had assembled to honor Helen Taussig's retirement and her celebrated career, one of whom recalled the crowd's reaction: "It wasn't what we had expected, nor the way we saw her."[5] Dr. Engle, the head of the committee who had commissioned Wyeth, did not mince words when he observed of the portrait, "It looked like a mean old witch."[6]

Jamie Wyeth later recalled his youthful experience of painting Dr. Taussig: "I found her fascinating the more I got to know her." Drawn to her intense gaze, he observed that she would "just stare right at me intently with those blue eyes. It was so amazing. [I] don't think she had a care in the least of how she looked, to the point that I was fascinated by the fact she would powder her nose almost pure white. Even in the portrait you can see it. I loved the idea that everything was secondary to her work."[7] Working with a head-on format that is often used to represent omnipotent and regal figures, Wyeth captures Helen Taussig's intense intellectual focus by featuring her clear blue eyes as the windows of the soul. That her appearance was of little interest to her is evident by the way the neckline on her dress slips off her shoulder, in striking contrast to her unforgettable gaze.

After the Taussig debacle, the most emblematic of Wyeth's paintings from this early period is *Draft Age*. The sitter, James ("Jimmy") Lynch, was Wyeth's childhood friend and one of his partners in the various "crimes" of their adolescent adventures. Lynch spent an intense six hours a day, six days a week, over the course of three months, posing for *Draft Age*. Previously he had served as Wyeth's obliging model for various anatomical studies, observing that he didn't mind since he "had learned how to fall asleep while posing. [It] was great. I just lay down and went to sleep and Jamie paid me $1.50 an hour."[8]

An early drawing depicts Lynch sporting an aviator's scarf and goggles, but then they went to see Marlon Brando in *The Wild One* (1953). In honor of their hero, Lynch showed up to pose wearing the black leather jacket and sunglasses he has on in the painting; he recalled that Wyeth's initial reaction was "this will freak 'em out, this will really freak 'em out."[9] The result, in its youthful cockiness and bad-boy stance, is one of the most original of Wyeth's early portraits. Lynch, hidden behind the cool reflections of his dark glasses, wears his black leather jacket unzipped, revealing his bare chest, while the tongue of his belt dangles provocatively, daring us to expose him. The portrait stands as a sign of their times and a youthful symbol of the tumultuous generation facing the specter of Vietnam; Lynch received his draft notice the day the portrait was completed.[10]

Another important portrait from the same year reveals Jamie Wyeth's relationship with Lincoln Kirstein, who became a dominant influence in his life and his art for decades. Kirstein was a hulking polymath, described variously as godlike and senatorial by others and in his own words as a "suffering servant."[11] He was the son of Louis E. Kirstein, a self-made garment manufacturer who rose to become the chief executive of Filene's Department Store in Boston, and the former Rose Stein. Before graduating from Harvard in 1930, he managed to establish the Harvard Society of Contemporary Art, a forerunner of the Museum of Modern Art.[12] Armed with his inheritance from his father and his mother's sense of philanthropy, Kirstein was boldly determined to fulfill his remarkable vision for enhancing the arts in the United States.

Kirstein's travels in Europe during the late 1920s persuaded him to dedicate his energies to the world of ballet. The impresario later observed, "My whole life has been about trying to learn how things are done. What I love about the ballet is not that it looks pretty. It's the method in it. Ballet is about how to behave."[13] It was the role of discipline in artistic endeavors that would also have a lasting effect on Jamie Wyeth, especially when he was caught up in depicting the ballet star Rudolf Nureyev in the later 1970s.

During the late 1940s, Kirstein had been a champion of Andrew Wyeth's, promoting the purchase of *Christina's World* by the Museum of Modern Art in 1948 and encouraging him to finish *Soaring* (see fig. 20), at a time when the large Masonite panel painting, relegated to the family's basement, was used for the Wyeth boys' miniature train set. When Jamie was born in 1946, Kirstein was already married to Fidelma Cadmus, sister of the artist Paul Cadmus, though he maintained intimate relationships with a variety of men throughout their fifty years of marriage.[14] Andrew and Betsy Wyeth encouraged their son's close association with Kirstein, knowing how influential the impresario was in the New York art world of the 1960s.[15] When Jamie Wyeth arrived on the New York art scene in 1965, at the age of nineteen, Kirstein was clearly smitten by him, describing the young artist, whom he had known since infancy, as "golden-wheat-colored, fuzzy and clean like honey on the best bread."[16]

In many ways *Portrait of Lincoln Kirstein* signifies the outsize role that its subject would play in the artist's early formation and throughout his career. When Andrew Wyeth declined Kirstein's request to paint his portrait in favor of passing the torch to his son, it was a generous gesture that his father repeated on several occasions while Jamie Wyeth was working to establish himself.[17] Arriving on the doorstep of Kirstein's New York apartment just in time to see the great man dashing off to march in Selma, Alabama, Jamie took up residence in a spare room, and Kirstein, who rarely sat still, eventually dedicated some 165 hours to posing, considered to be a great testimony to his fondness for the young artist.[18]

Kirstein had collected numerous portraits by his contemporaries, and, although he hoped Jamie Wyeth would be able to achieve a combination of John Singer Sargent and Thomas Eakins for this one, in the end the painting has far more in common with Copley's portrayal of the similarly leonine orator Samuel Adams (about 1792, Museum of Fine Arts, Boston).[19] Kirstein was embarrassed by his hulking six-foot, three-inch, frame and his self-assessed lack of grace, and he attempted to mask his girth with an unvarying uniform of a double-breasted black suit, white shirt, and black tie, which often caused others to mistake him for a rabbi or clergyman.[20] Wyeth's portrait of the balletomane is highly contemplative, reflective of the active mind that Kirstein cultivated with the help of his extensive library, art collections, and wide-ranging interests. Wyeth depicts him from behind, a solution that evolved as the portrait was in progress, and a pose inspired by Kirstein's habit of watching performances from the wings backstage at the New York State Theater.[21] He appears here as the omnipresent and omnipotent impresario behind the scenes, watching something that is left to our imagination. His enormous back blocks our view, effectively offering up Wyeth's image of the giant's shoulders on which he would later stand to capture his own artistic vision well into the future.[22]

Through Kirstein, Wyeth had access to numerous performances throughout Lincoln Center and especially the performers in the world of the ballet. He became fascinated with the superstar Rudolf Nureyev and ultimately spent an intensive eighteen months portraying the dancer's every move (see cats. 37–42).[23] Kirstein did not extend his blessing to Wyeth's desire to portray Nureyev, as he considered him a "grandstander" rather than a "company dancer."[24] Despite Kirstein's assessment of Nureyev, these two giants of the ballet world enjoyed each other's company and respected one another. They are depicted in animated conversation at New York's fabled restaurant of café society in Wyeth's miniature tableau vivant *La Côte Basque* (cat. 13); also present is the author Truman Capote, who wrote about its habitués, including his dining companion, Joanne Carson.[25] Kirstein was keenly interested in artistic anatomy, and he connected Wyeth with Dr. Emanuel B. Kaplan, a prominent hand surgeon at Columbia Presbyterian Hospital, who made it possible for him to study anatomy in one of the New York City morgues (cats. 14–15).[26] In reflecting on his experiences in New York City during the mid-1960s, Wyeth credited his surroundings in Kirstein's apartment, where he had lived, and the opportunity to explore his vast collection, which included Paul Cadmus's series of paintings *The Seven Deadly Sins* (1945–49, Metropolitan Museum of Art), as the nascent idea for his own series of the *Sins* in 2007 (see cats. 92–98).[27] Above all, Kirstein, as Andrew Wyeth noted, took Jamie seriously, contributing an essay to the catalogue of the young artist's first exhibition at Knoedler's in 1966 and in 1987 to *An American Vision*.[28] Over time Kirstein's infatuation with Jamie Wyeth cooled, and he became quite unsparing in his criticism, although they remained friends until Kirstein's death in 1996. Jamie Wyeth himself noted that he was not an "easy man" and was "very tough and extremely hard on me."[29] Despite Kirstein's backhanded compliment that Jamie Wyeth was "beautiful, charming . . . hard as nails . . . as cynical as an experienced ambassador," he still considered him "the best young painter in the country" and, in the end, remained loyal to their friendship by honoring him as being "better than his father."[30]

If Kirstein pushed Wyeth out into the art world of New York City, Wyeth pushed himself into the larger world of Washington, D.C., and well out of his comfort zone by accepting the opportunity—or, as he described it, the prospect that scared "the hell out of me"—of painting a posthumous portrait of President John F. Kennedy.[31] Turning down the official commission, Wyeth agreed to paint a portrait if he could be given access to family members as a means of conceiving the image. The artist embarked on an intensely immersive process of watching all the available films, reviewing all the available photographs, reading about the president's life from a variety of perspectives, and eventually following Robert and Edward Kennedy around as a means of discerning family traits, gestures, mannerisms, and speech patterns that might offer insight into portraying John F. Kennedy. Scores of drawings reveal Jamie Wyeth studying every detail of the brothers' expressions, as is especially evident in *Senator Edward M. Kennedy's Eyes*. Within that sheet, we discover Wyeth zeroing in on what would become the final solution for the portrait: the president lost in thought, his clenched fist in front of his mouth, and his thumb rapping his front teeth. In the completed portrait the president's right eye wanders into the distance, while his left eye focuses on the middle ground. In the drawing *Senator Edward M. Kennedy's Eyes*, the irises are very nearly on axis, evident in the smaller studies around the corners and edges of the sheet in which we begin to see the artist exploring the drooping orientation of Kennedy's right eyelid. Wyeth locates the orientation of the eyes within Senator Kennedy's eye sockets and face, in each instance depicting them as tracking the same object, with the subtle distinction of the largest, most finished version at the center, in which the right eye begins to drift off course.

Portrait of John F. Kennedy was an important turning point for Wyeth, as it solidified in many ways a method that he had used throughout his early career. In a 1997 interview the artist offered one of the most concise statements about his process for representing a person on canvas:

> To me, a portrait is not so much the actual painting, but just spending time with the person traveling with him, watching him eat, watching him sleep. When I work on a portrait, it's really osmosis. I try to become the person I'm painting. A successful portrait isn't about the sitter's physical characteristics—his nose, eyeballs, and whatnot—but more the mood and the overall effect. I try not to impose anything of mine on him. I try to get to the point where if the sitter painted, he'd paint a portrait just the way I'm doing it. I'm never satisfied with one portrait. I think the studies probably are as important as the finished pieces. I do lots of drawings. It's sort of like having a love affair with the person.[32]

If, as Honoré Daumier is said to have observed, the camera is able to see everything and understand nothing, then the artist has the potential to understand everything—even those features and traits that others might not see or wish not to see. In many ways the Kennedy portrait succeeded too well in synthesizing what the photographs and films had not captured. What Wyeth understood and expressed visually about the president produced an image that others would have liked to forget. Although Mrs. Kennedy appreciated the remarkable likeness of her late husband, members of the president's family, especially Robert Kennedy, felt the portrait was an all-too-painful reminder of the way President Kennedy appeared during the harrowing events of the Cuban Missile Crisis. After Wyeth completed the painting, it hung briefly in the John F. Kennedy Library in Boston; in 1988 it was reproduced on a postage stamp in Ireland. It has also been displayed at the Washington, D.C., home of Vice President Joseph Biden.[33]

While Jamie Wyeth had been working on Lincoln Kirstein's and John F. Kennedy's portraits, his father was rapidly becoming one of the most recognizable contemporary artists in the United States.[34] The next segment of Jamie Wyeth's career could be seen as a gradual separation from his association with the work of the Wyeths, especially that of his father, as far as the outside world was concerned. Several important milestones bolstered his outward appearance of independence. He served in the Delaware Air National Guard from 1966 to 1971, and prepared to report to Vietnam in 1969 as a combat artist, in anticipation of his deployment painting watercolors such as *C-97 Landing in Vietnam* (1969, Delaware Air National Guard). The Tet Offensive, which began in January 1968, resulted in the cancellation of all noncombatant tours of duty, and, by the end of that year, on December 11, 1968, he married Phyllis Mills.[35]

Navigating personal and professional independence from a formative figure is challenging for anyone, and all the more so for one whose artistic mentor—his father—was enmeshed in the complex dynamic of family relationships. Artists since the Renaissance have often disregarded the generation of their fathers and direct teachers, reaching back to the preceding era in what is called the "grandfather's law."[36] By his own admission, Jamie Wyeth, a great admirer and collector of his grandfather's work, follows this pattern, having spent his formative years in his grandfather's studio and being taught by his grandfather's most intensely schooled pupil, his aunt Carolyn. In describing the contrasts between the two generations of artists, Jamie Wyeth recalled as a child walking into his father's studio, where he would find nothing but four bare walls and the dead crow he was drawing, while he could walk up the hill to his grandfather's studio, which was laden with a host of studio props such as cutlasses and muskets, along with classical busts and of course his grandfather's paintings (see cat. 8), all of which captured and cultivated his imagination.[37]

In painting his father in 1969, perhaps as a way of knowing the object of his affection well enough to let it go at that juncture,

Fig. 10. Thomas Eakins (1844–1916)
The Writing Master, 1882
Oil on canvas
76.2 x 87 cm (30 x 34¼ in.)

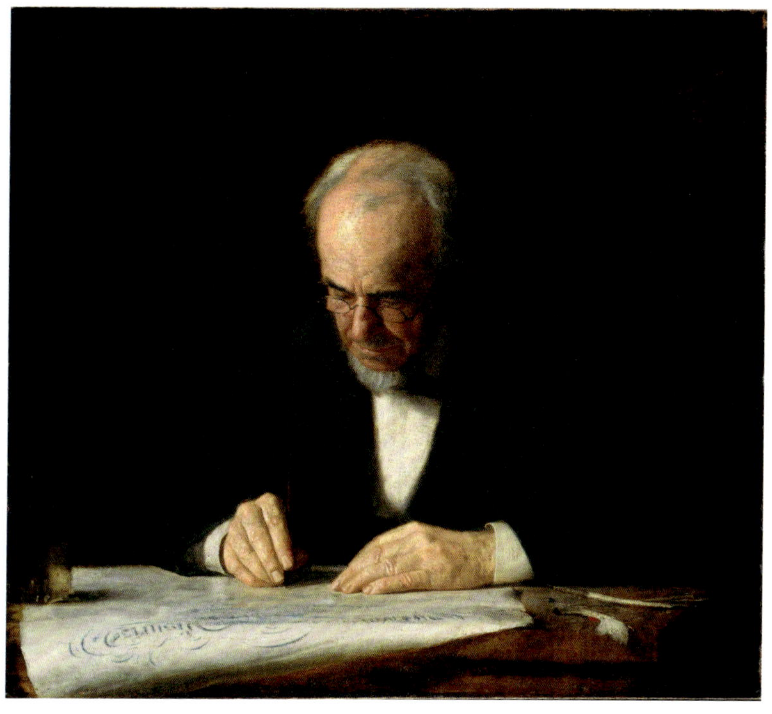

Jamie Wyeth offers a sober and respectful portrayal of the artist, who by then was well into middle age. Andrew Wyeth sits left of center, staring off into the right distance; his left eye tracking on one axis, while his right, more hooded by its lid, focuses on the middle distance. Jamie Wyeth does not spare the signs of his father's aging: folds of skin droop beneath his chin, and the hair at the top of his head is thinning and graying. Whereas in *Draft Age* Lynch vamps for us, pressing his body forward to all edges of the canvas, right up to his crotch, the subject of *Portrait of Andrew Wyeth* appears withdrawn from our space; a sense of reverence is bestowed on a courtly figure kept at a magisterial distance. Around his father's shoulders Jamie Wyeth tenderly draws the proverbial Wyeth mantle in the form of a black coat with a half-cape that resembles one of the Wyeth family costumes hanging around N. C. Wyeth's studio. Initially Jamie Wyeth conceived of painting his father wearing a German World War I helmet, as seen in one of the related drawings from the collection of the Morgan Library and Museum (*Portrait of Andrew Wyeth in a German Helmet*). In the finished composition, he has discarded the helmet in favor of leaving his father's bared head nearly touching the upper left edge of the composition.

Rather than showing his father in the act of painting or drawing, he stays close to his own past formula of posing his sitters against dark, monochromatic backgrounds, which recalls Thomas Eakins's portrait of his own father, *The Writing Master* (fig. 10). Unlike Eakins, who shows his father bowing reverently over a page of calligraphy that spills into our space, Jamie Wyeth leaves to our imagination Andrew Wyeth's manner of working. As he did in his early drawing on his father's portrait of himself, Jamie Wyeth paints his father, but he does not paint *over* his father, in the sense of replicating Andrew's painting in the composition. Perhaps as a tribute to their mutual respect for each other's work and pro-

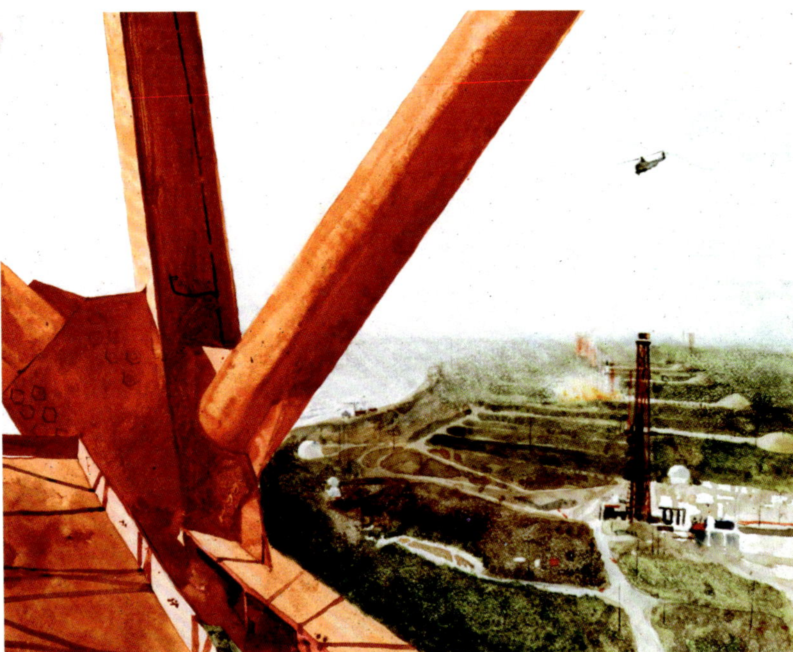

Fig. 11. *Support*, 1969
Watercolor on paper
53.3 x 61 cm (21 x 24 in.)

fession, Jamie Wyeth does not presume to represent Andrew's own painting within a portrait he is painting of his father. Andrew Wyeth believed that every artist is competitive and wants his work to be the best, even if that means besting your own child. In his biography he observes, "When you get fame—you see, I'm in competition with my son whether I want to be or not. Just the fact that I exist as a painter."[38] Jamie Wyeth's restraint in not including a painting or sketch by his own father within the composition effectively removes him from the arena of artistic competition, and, by so doing, allows him to assert his separation from his father and independence as an artist.

His *Self-Portrait* from about the same time presents a diffident view of the young artist. Wyeth thrusts his body backward into a neutral space and modestly covers himself in shadow. His glance is tentative, as though he has caught the eye of the viewer but is about to turn away. The bared flesh of his torso is rendered with soft modeling, and the figure's anatomy—despite the studies he subjected Jimmy Lynch to and those rendered in the New York City morgue—is not entirely convincing, especially relative to the distance between his shoulders and the relationship of his upper arm to his shoulder.

Andrew Wyeth was honest enough—some of the time—to admit that he competed with his son, and yet he did promote Jamie Wyeth for certain opportunities, just as N. C. Wyeth had helped his son garner experience by soliciting his participation in illustration projects, while also voicing his own envy of Andrew's talent.[39] In 1969, the same year he sat for his portrait, Andrew stepped aside in favor of promoting Jamie Wyeth's participation in the Eyewitness to Space program, a collaboration between the National Aeronautics and Space Administration (NASA) and the National Gallery of Art. Several well-known artists of the day also accepted the assignment, among them Norman Rockwell, Robert Rauschenberg, and Andy Warhol, along with several artists in Jamie Wyeth's extended family, including his uncles Peter

Hurd, John McCoy, and George ("Frolic") Weymouth, a cousin of Phyllis Mills Wyeth, who married Jamie Wyeth's first cousin Ann Brelsford McCoy.

Of all the notes, sketches, and paintings of the ongoing manned space flight operation made by the artists invited to participate, one of the most vivid accounts was written by Peter Hurd, who likened the herculean feat of landing men on the moon to building the great Gothic cathedrals. Hurd reflected on the Cape Kennedy (now Canaveral) experience: "Perhaps it was in witnessing a supreme gathering of forces, the sight of so many individuals engaged in a wide range of techniques, all addressed to achieving one objective: the successful completion of another orbital flight. The thought kept occurring to me that a similar mass effort built the great cathedrals; the same desire of man to attain his ultimate capacity. It seemed to me that the men of science today are the equivalents of those artists and artisans of great past periods of art; that while widely different in approach, they are linked in an urge to discover new horizons of the human spirit."[40] He also singled out the massive structure of the gantries that held the spacecraft in place as painted "an intense and subtly beautiful shade of red." That very feature captured Jamie Wyeth's imagination as well, and in *Support* he represents the gantry as the flying buttress for a cathedral like Notre Dame (fig. 11).

Jamie Wyeth's most dynamic images inspired by the Eyewitness to Space program reveal how he met the challenge of depicting the overwhelming nature of the race to the moon by falling back on to his ability to see the world as a series of basic forms, the first lessons of his formal training with Carolyn Wyeth. *Support* is in many ways the most architectural of the images. Several others, including *Gemini Launch Pad*, share his re-creation of the expansive landscape of the Eyewitness to Space experience and terrain—real and imagined—in terms of the basic elements of studio solids—cones, cylinders, blocks, and spheres.[41] In *Gemini Launch Pad* the artist zeroes in on a massive, pyramidal building that effectively shears off the distant silhouette of the red gantry against a cloudy Florida sky. To provide a sense of scale and a means of humanizing this strange, otherworldly edifice, he includes a red bicycle, which was part of the scene at Cape Kennedy as a practical means of traversing the vast distances between offices, a humorous touch in its reminder that the simple, two-wheeled cycle enabled humans to launch into flight at Kitty Hawk.

Wyeth's *Gemini Launch Pad* bears a striking resemblance to Edward Hopper's watercolors of simple New England buildings that he reduces to bold arrangements of geometric forms early on in his career during the late 1920s, including *House of the Fog Horn, No. 2* (1927, Museum of Fine Arts, Boston), effectively an exploration of how geometric, architectural forms relate to the Maine landscape and ultimately block out the light that surrounds them. Wyeth's aptitude for and attraction to rendering architectural forms plays out on many levels beyond his paintings through his realization of architectural projects on a variety of scales—one-sixth scale, half-scale, and full scale—at Southern Island, Maine. We see Wyeth the architect imagining Southern Island buildings at full scale in *Bell Tower*, *Lighthouse Iris*, and *A Murder of Crows*, as well as in a half-scale building replicating Daniel Webster's birthplace, carefully reconstructed on Southern Island near a small pond (see cats. 74, 75, and 76). More recent architectural assemblages of one-sixth scale created at his Southern Island studio include *La Côte Basque* and *Factory Dining Room* (cat. 13; see cat. 29). Whereas Hopper is particularly attentive to the shapes of shadows cast by varied structures and the distinction between the wall that faces the light and the part left dark when blocking light, in Wyeth's *Gemini Launch Pad* cast shadows are eliminated to such a degree that the scene becomes disorienting. We are not quite sure where we are, but for the diminutive bicycle that indicates we are in a place where humans propel themselves by wheels and gears, even, in time, all the way to the moon.

The sense of scale and wonder inspired by the Eyewitness to Space program had an immediate and also a more lasting effect on Wyeth's work, and here it is important to bear in mind the nature of an artist's creative process as imagination and memory continue to revisit and re-envision subjects over the course of the near and longer term. Reflecting the nearer term is Wyeth's response to the Cape Kennedy experiences as expressed by *Moon Landing*, a composition dating from the year of the historic moon landing of the Apollo XI crew, on July 20, 1969. And yet, the early experiences in the Eyewitness to Space program even years later continue to shine through many of Wyeth's nocturnal compositions, including *Meteor Shower*, *Mischief Night*, and *A Recurring Dream* (see cats. 86, 78, and 104), among others. The low vantage point and dark atmosphere of *Moon Landing* recasts the two large bollards planted in front of his studio on Monhegan as ancient monoliths from Stonehenge that come into focus as our eyes adjust to the darkness of a vast, spooky sky. In this unsettling scene shimmering moonlight reflects off the surface of the sea, spilling onto the canvas like mercury, viscous and deadly. Even in daylight, the setting of Wyeth's Monhegan studio, located at the southern tip of the island, has the feeling of being at the edge of the world. With the glistening cloak of moonlight, the rocky Monhegan ledge has an otherworldly, surreal appearance that evokes pagan architecture.

Wyeth's welding together of earthly, lunar, and surreal landscapes in this composition may have resulted from the real-time collision of the worlds of Monhegan and the moon landing. Summoned to witness the historic splashdown from Cape Kennedy, Wyeth traveled from Monhegan by fishing boat, small plane, and then Air Force jet, completing the journey within six hours.[42] The painting that resulted expresses that sense of awe at being able to reach the moon, previously known for millennia on earth as a ghostly, gleaming image in the evening sky.

Wyeth's decision in 1974 to engage with contemporary events by executing drawings of the Watergate hearings could be considered a decided return to earth and another historical drama, played out on the smaller stage of a courtroom, that also generated shock waves. Politically libertarian, Andrew Wyeth had been an admirer of President Richard Nixon, whereas Jamie's wife, Phyllis, had been an aide in the Kennedy White House.[43] Jamie Wyeth's early association with the Kennedy entourage during the process of creating the late president's portrait offered another avenue by which he could establish himself politically as his own person, separate from his parents. By becoming one of the court artists at the Watergate hearings, Wyeth solidified his reputation for independence, and he ultimately produced numerous drawings from which several were later published in *Harper's Magazine*. To render the drawings he spent day after day in the courtroom where the drama of the Watergate hearings unfolded before the nation on television, an experience as an eyewitness to history that was dramatically different from that as an Eyewitness to Space.

Many American artists built a foundation for their later work by early on applying themselves out of necessity to illustration, a field that is certainly well respected in the Wyeth family. Jamie Wyeth has illustrated three books to date—*The Stray* (1979), *Cabbages and Kings* (1997), and *Sammy in the Sky* (2011)—and, he observed, all three projects had positive effects on his subsequent work (see cats. 57, 58, and 87). During the Watergate trials, his privileged perspective as a court artist granted him a ringside seat to the political drama, while the rest of the nation saw only the segments broadcast on television. The process of presenting in drawings what he could also see in the news media would later play out in his own work, in the way that the majority of his portraits painted during the later 1970s are of celebrities who were actively, intensely, and continually engaged with how their images were being projected to the world at large in the popular press.

Wyeth was drawn to the personalities on display during the hearings, and he focused his attention on those playing the starring roles, although he was occasionally inspired by those with bit parts as well. One sketch depicts a federal marshal guarding the door to the courtroom, and another shows a view of the jurors intently listening to the testimony that seemed to drone on endlessly.[44] The artist seems to have found the judge presiding over the whole circus, John Sirica, to be especially compelling (cat. 25). Wyeth renders him as the careworn, wise orator, recalling Rembrandt's *Syndics of the Cloth Makers Guild* (1662, Rembrandthuis Museum).

The process of drawing the events on parade before him each day offered Wyeth ample opportunity to study character, pose, and emotional tone in rapid succession, and he approached the task hoping to be as truthful a recorder as possible.[45] The discipline of courtroom drawing had been adopted earlier by the nineteenth-century French Master Honoré Daumier, who seems to have relished the process of honing his draftsmanship by depicting French lawyers gesticulating with flair and passion. In his images, fists pound, mouths gape, and fingers point at the end of outstretched arms, all the while maintaining a sense of the decorum that was based on the mannerisms of classical oratory. In Wyeth's scenes of the Watergate hearings, the protagonists are tame by comparison, and ultimately they have more in common with Winslow Homer's keen observation of quotidian life in the Union Army camps during the Civil War, as portrayed in *Harper's Weekly.* Both Homer and Wyeth record minute details of the mise-en-scène as a way of expressing the manner in which even milestones in the nation's history unfold at the human level. Special Counsel Albert Jenner, in a garish windowpane suit and a bow tie, appears with hands in his pockets and his foot planted firmly on a folding chair, exuding what he may hope is a sufficient dose of old-boy, nonchalant swagger and confidence to carry his client, while the television journalist Roger Mudd looks on from the lower left (cat. 26). On another sheet, Special Prosecutor James F. Neal appears in profile as he leans in to the microphone with great urgency and in three-quarter view at the upper left corner, while the Honorable Judge Sirica ponders the proceedings from the far right edge of the sheet (cat. 27). Wyeth often placed multiple figures or single figures like Neal from various angles on one page of drawing paper both for practicality, as the testimony unfolded rapidly, and to convey a sense of what was going on. And yet the simplicity of the scenes he depicted, coupled with the dreary drone of the proceedings as televised, belied the magnitude of the events that would rock the nation's confidence in executive authority to the core. In the end, Wyeth's drawings of the Watergate dramas appear fragmented. Each page conveyed the banality of daily events in minute detail with a detachment Wyeth later described as his way of taking the "art" out of the "job"; the series of drawings ultimately build toward a powerful contribution to the historic record. Taken together, Wyeth's Watergate drawings offer an alternative perspective to the televised broadcasts that shattered public perceptions of American politics and presidential power and planted a strain of skepticism toward government leaders that thrives to this day.

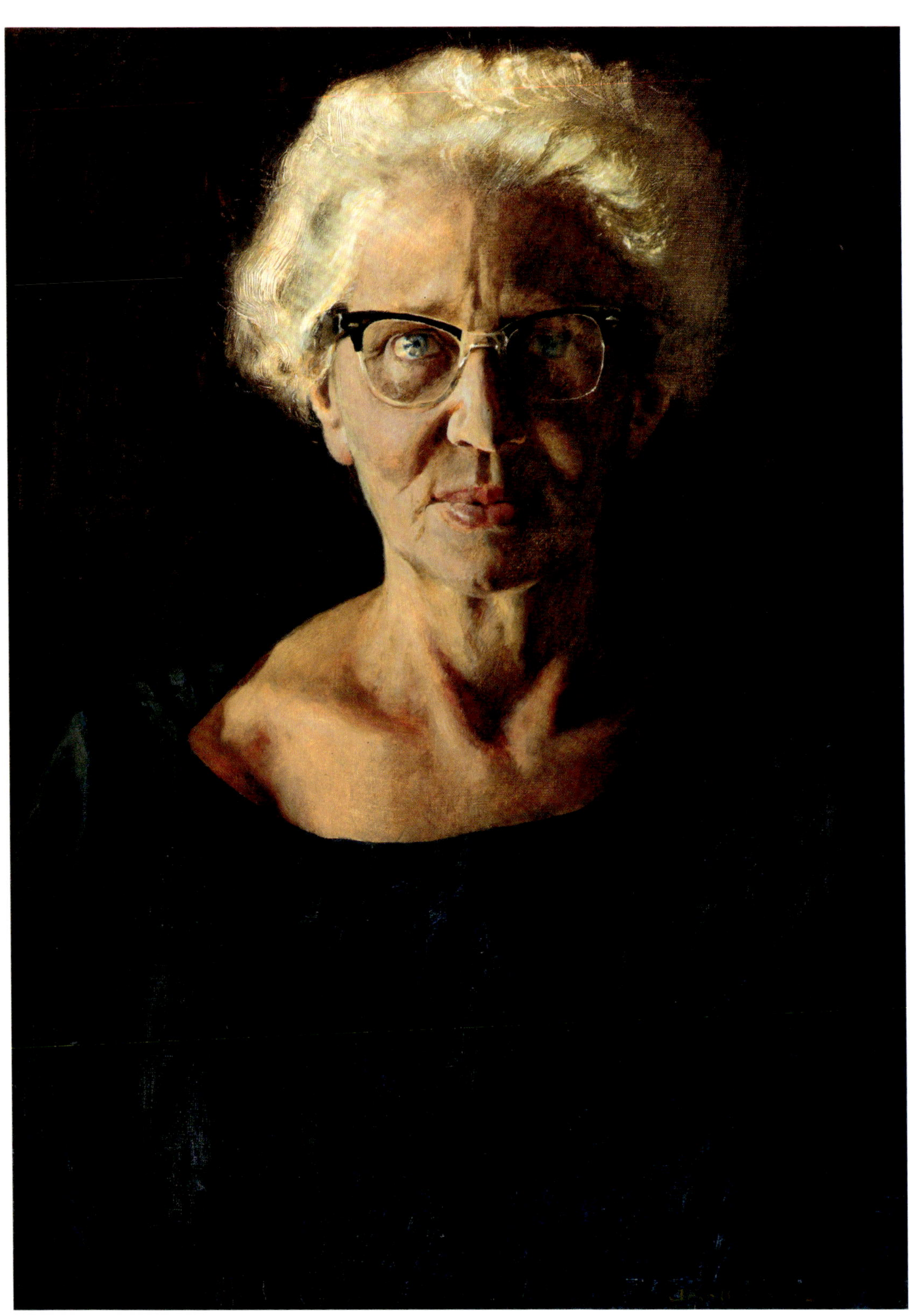

10. *Portrait of Helen Taussig*, 1963. Oil on canvas, 40 x 55.2 cm (15¾ x 21¾ in.)

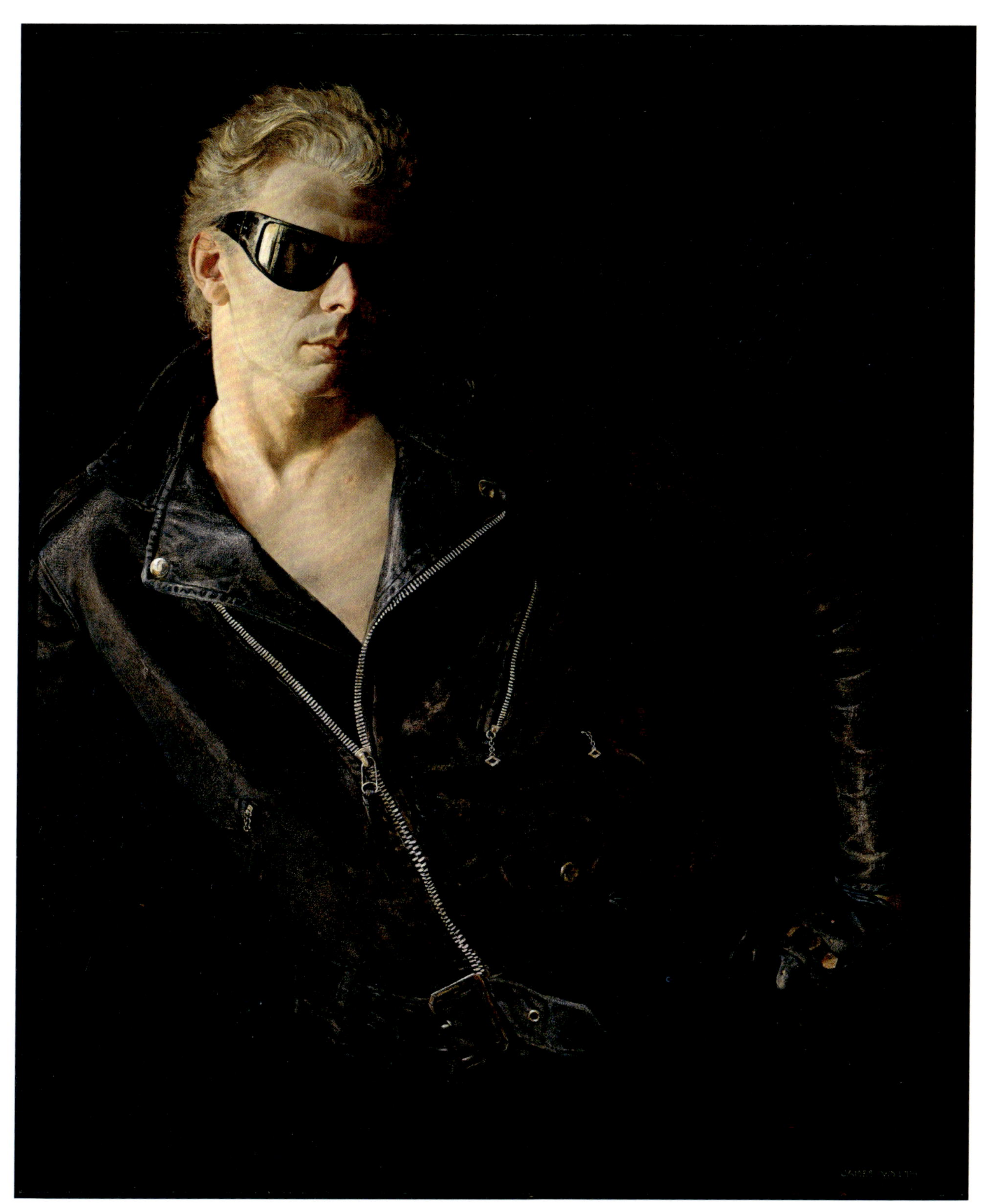

11. *Draft Age*, 1965. Oil on canvas,
91.4 x 76.2 cm (36 x 30 in.)

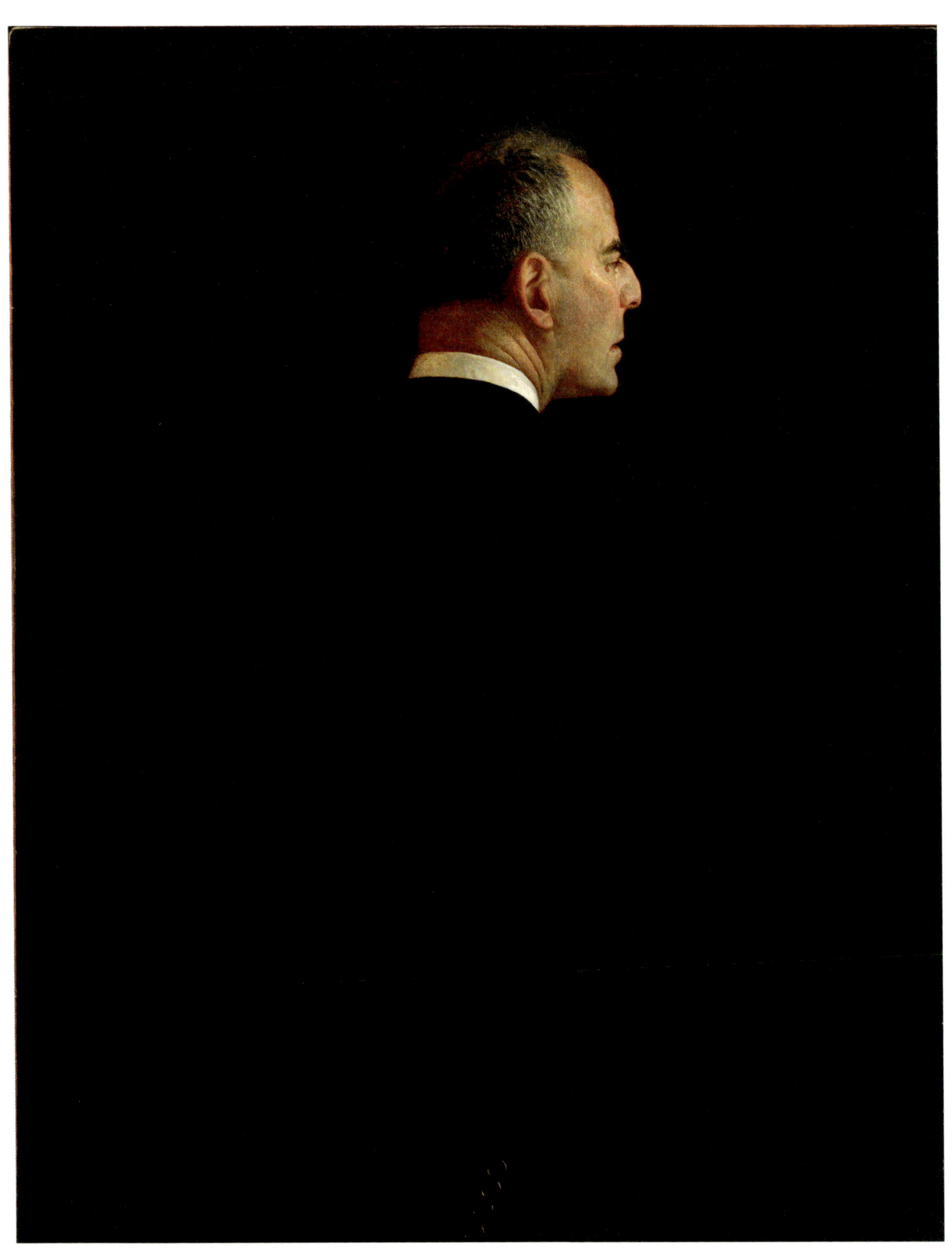

12. *Portrait of Lincoln Kirstein*, 1965. Oil on canvas, 97.8 x 73.7 cm (38½ x 29 in.)

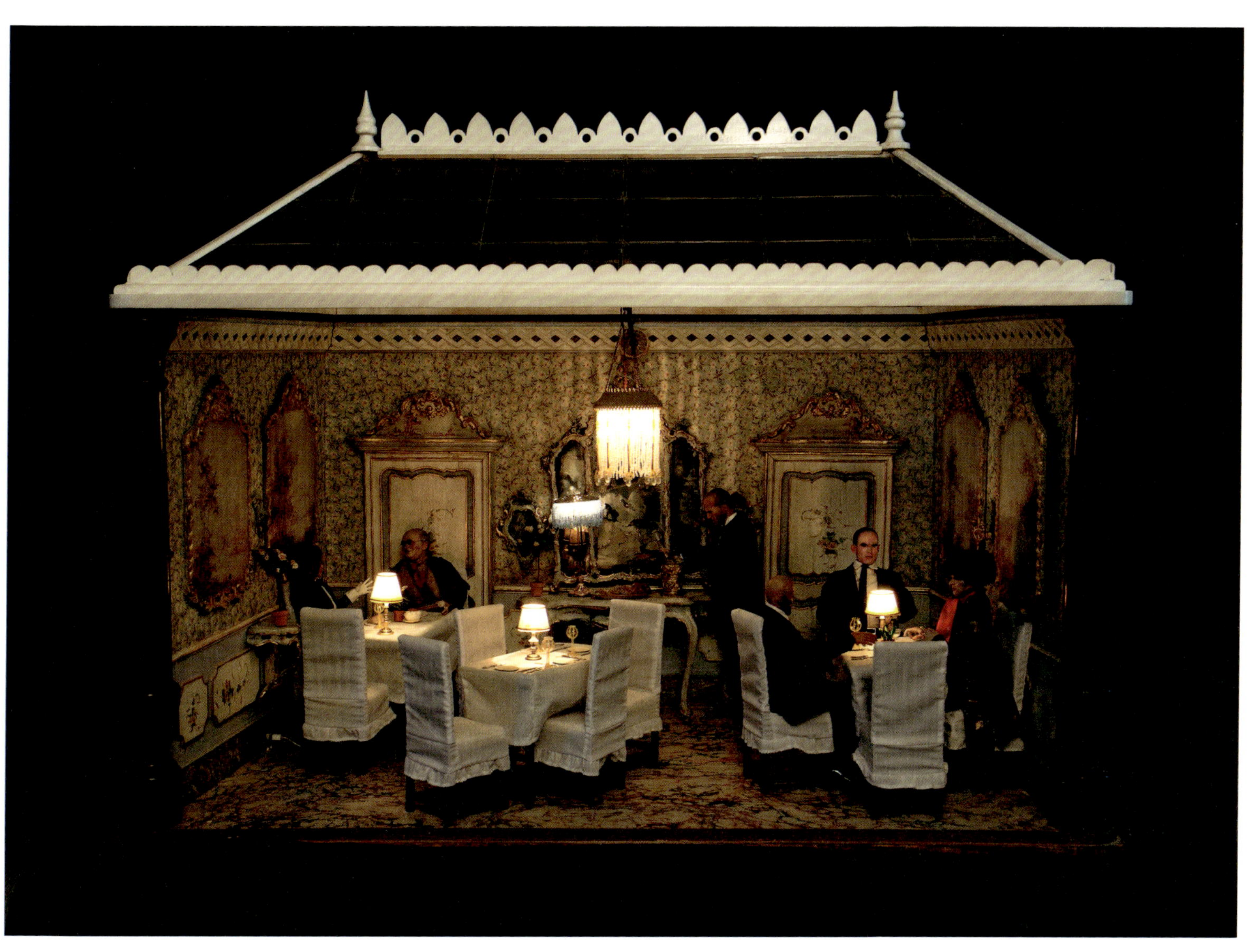

13. *La Côte Basque*, 2013. Combined media, assemblage, 76.2 x 101.6 x 53.3 cm (30 x 40 x 21 in.)

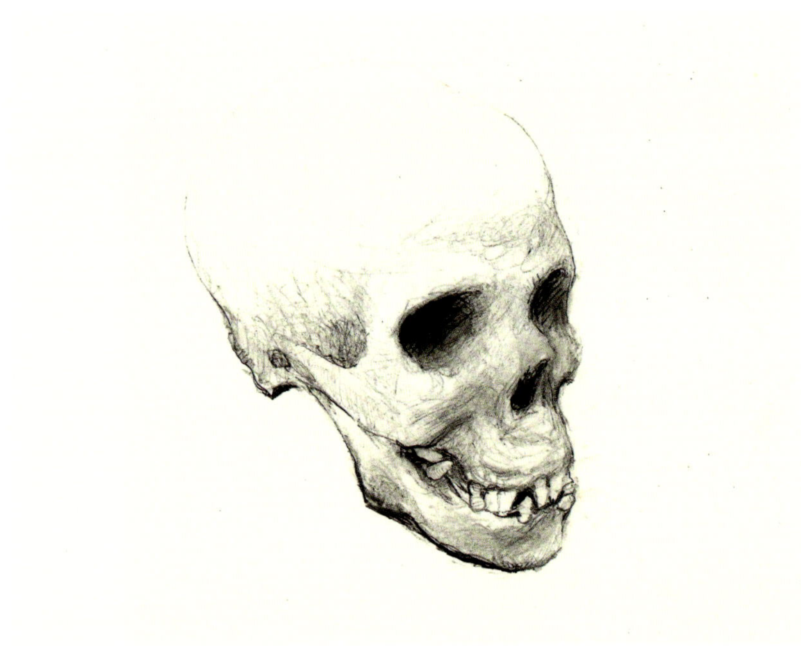

14. *Skull* (detail), 1965. Graphite on paper, 27.9 x 35.6 cm (11 x 14 in.)

15. *Five Hands*, 1965. Graphite on paper,27.9 x 35.6 cm (11 x 14 in.)

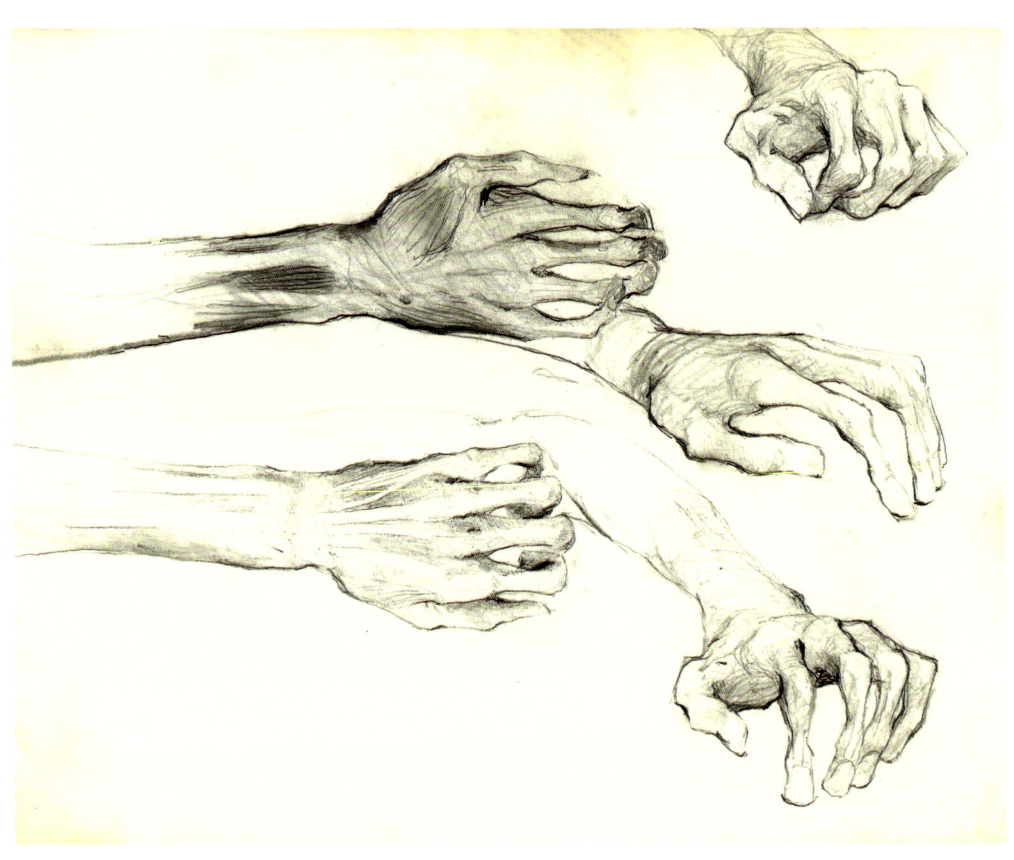

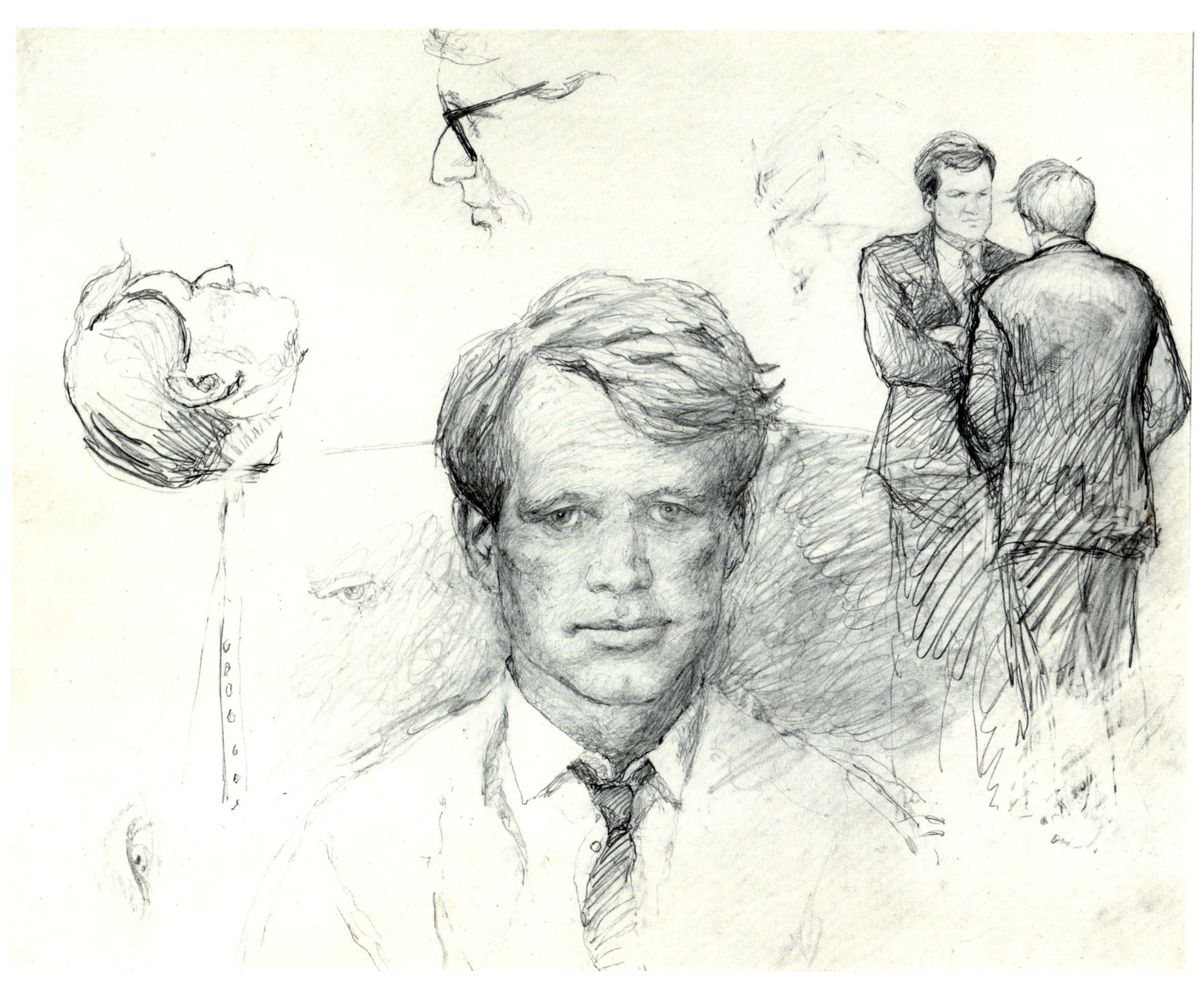

16. *Senator Robert F. Kennedy and Senator Edward M. Kennedy*, 1966. Graphite on paper, 26.7 x 34.3 cm (10½ x 13½ in.)

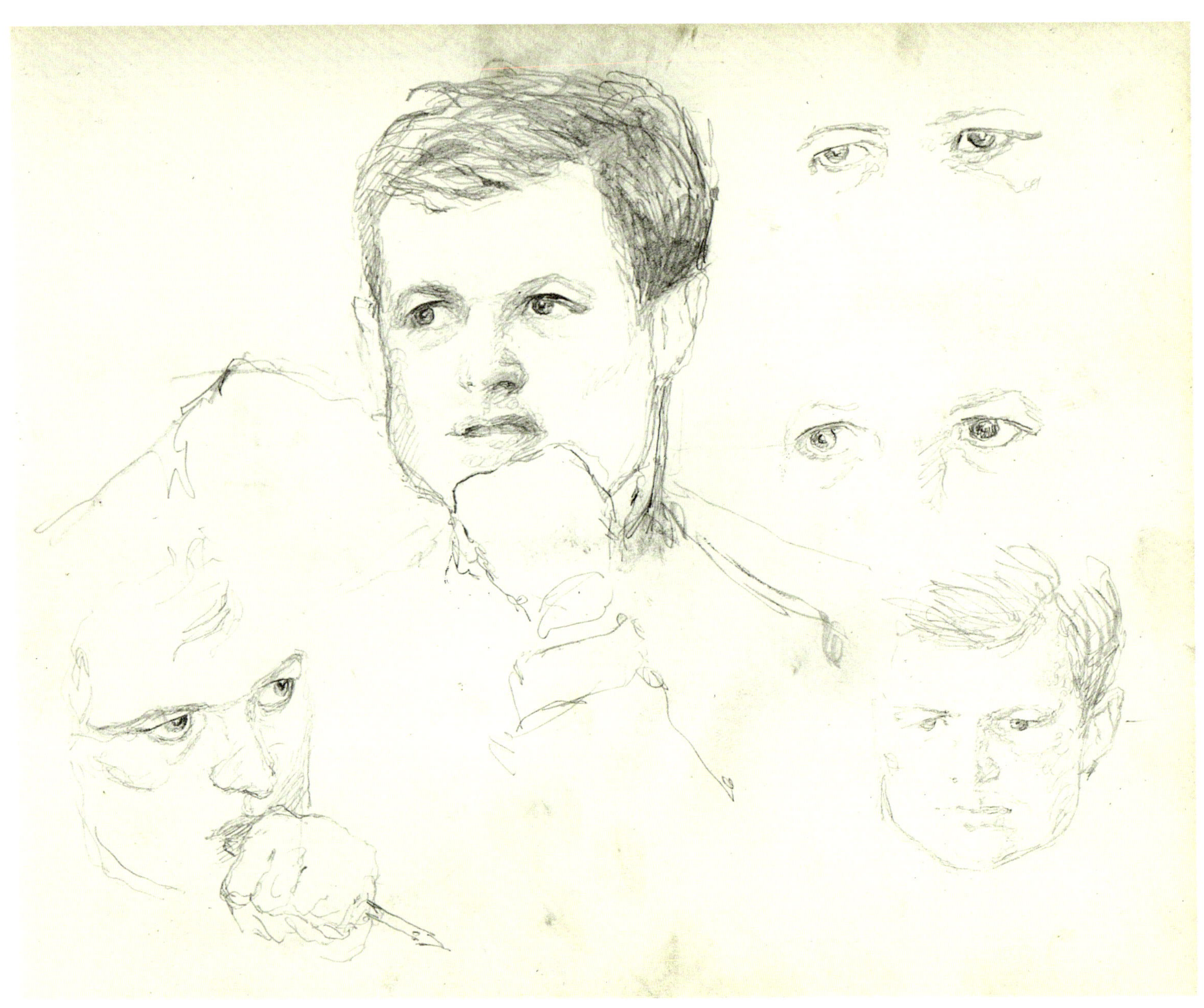

17. *Senator Edward M. Kennedy's Eyes*, 1966. Graphite on paper, 27.9 x 33.7 cm (11 x 13¼ in.)

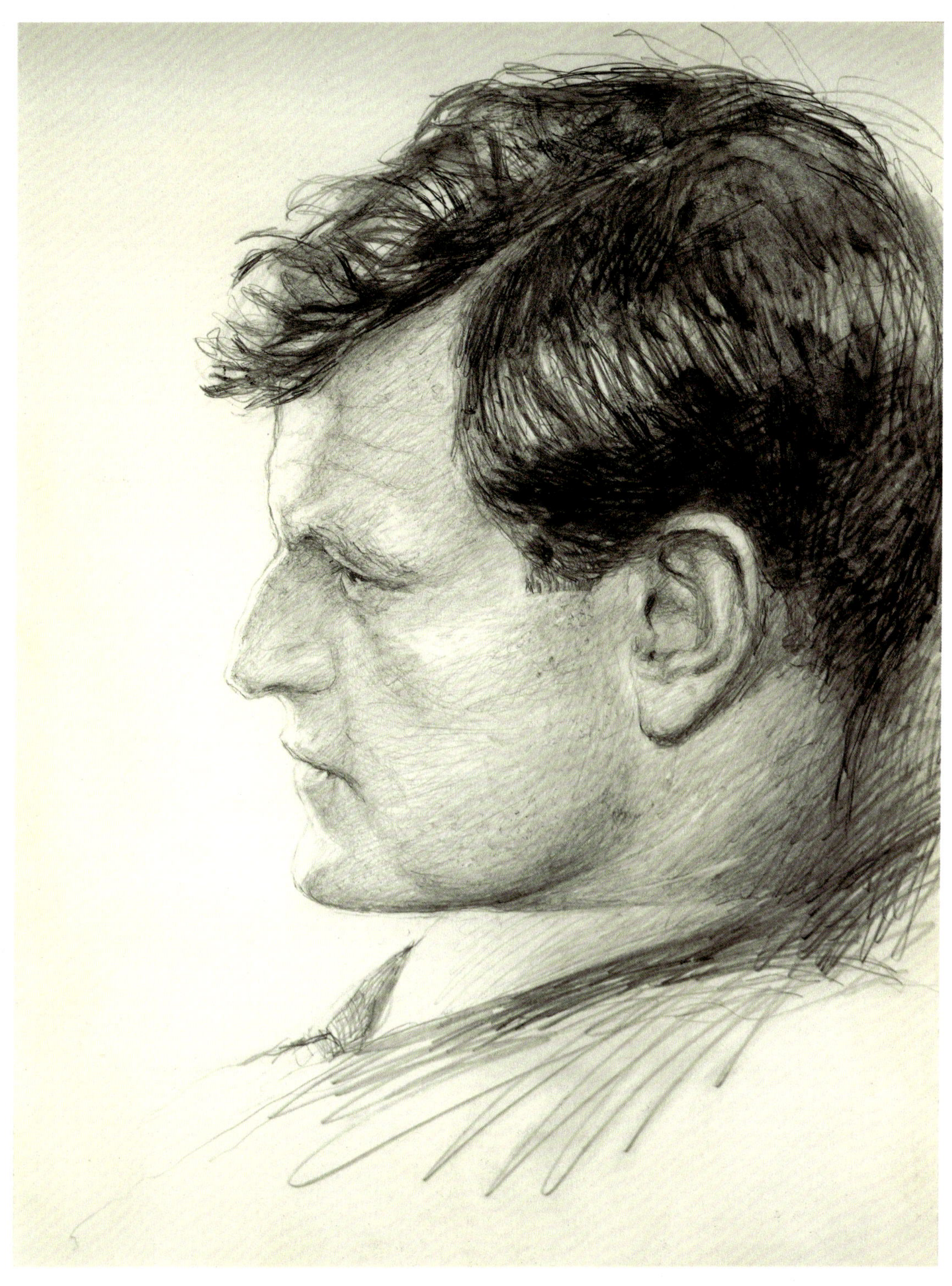

18. *Senator Edward M. Kennedy*, 1966. Graphite on paper, 35.6 x 27.9 cm (14 x 11 in.)

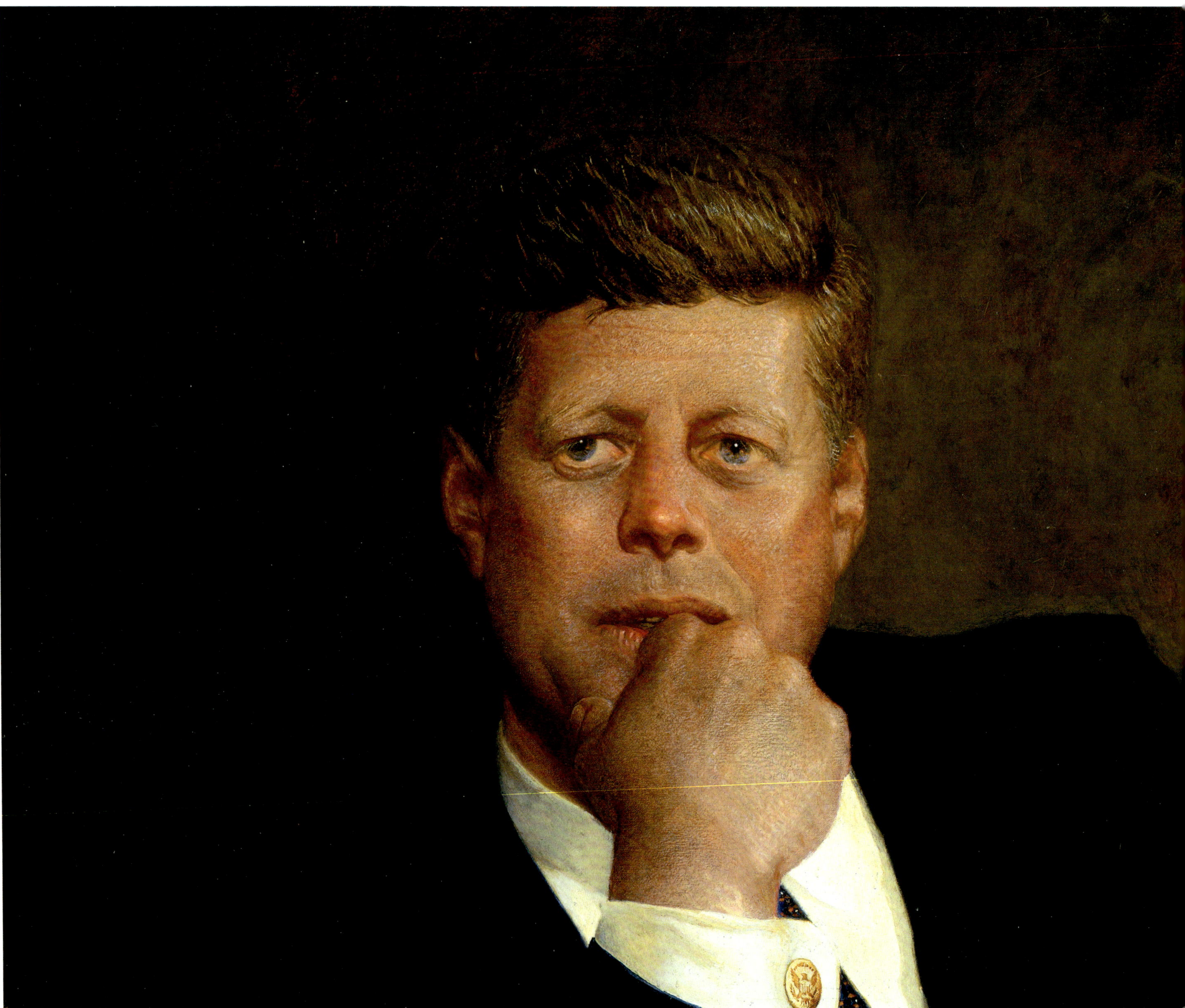

19. *Portrait of John F. Kennedy*, 1967. Oil on canvas, 40.6 x 73.7 cm (16 x 29 in.)

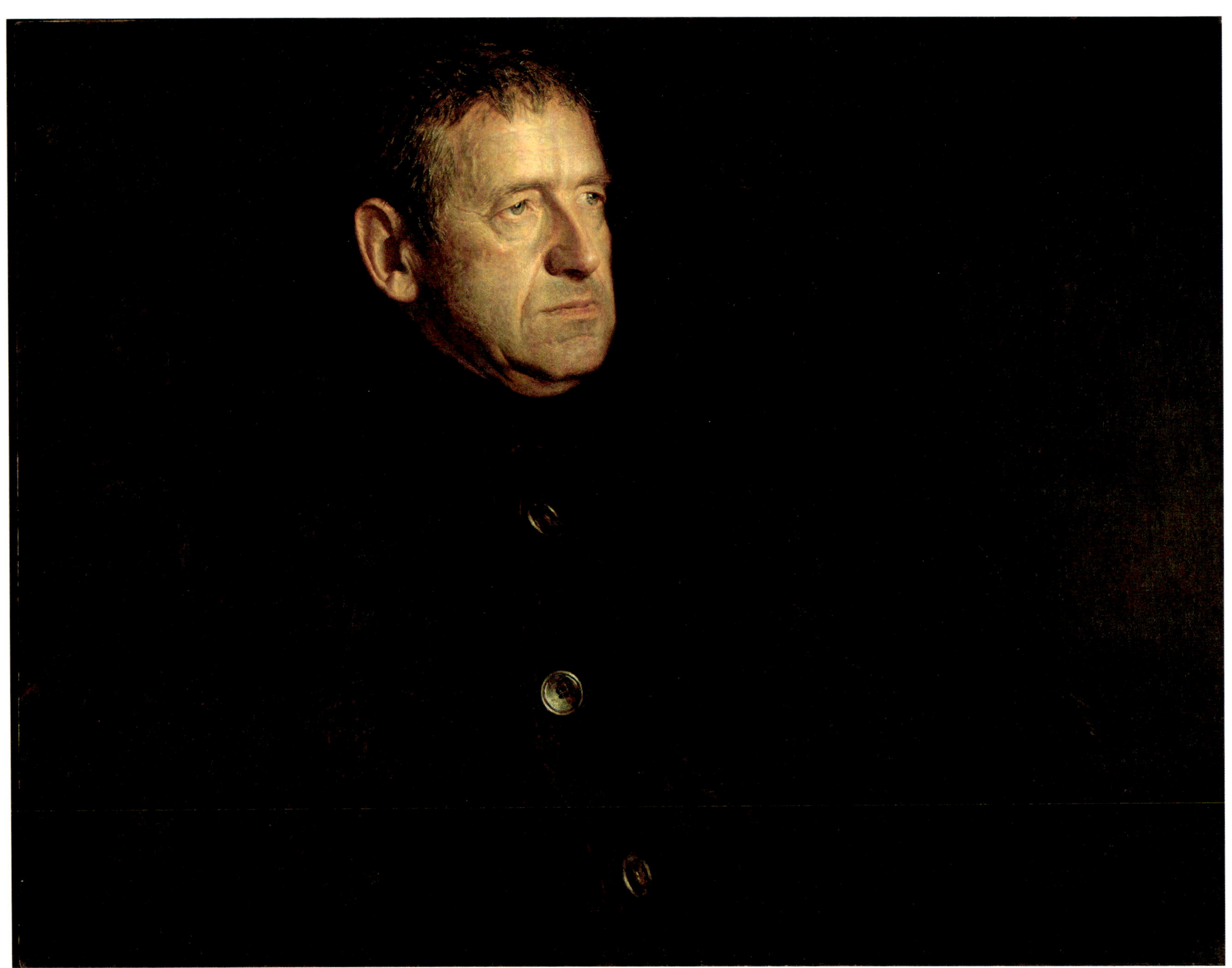

20. *Portrait of Andrew Wyeth*, 1969. Oil on canvas, 61 x 81.3 cm (24 x 32 in.)

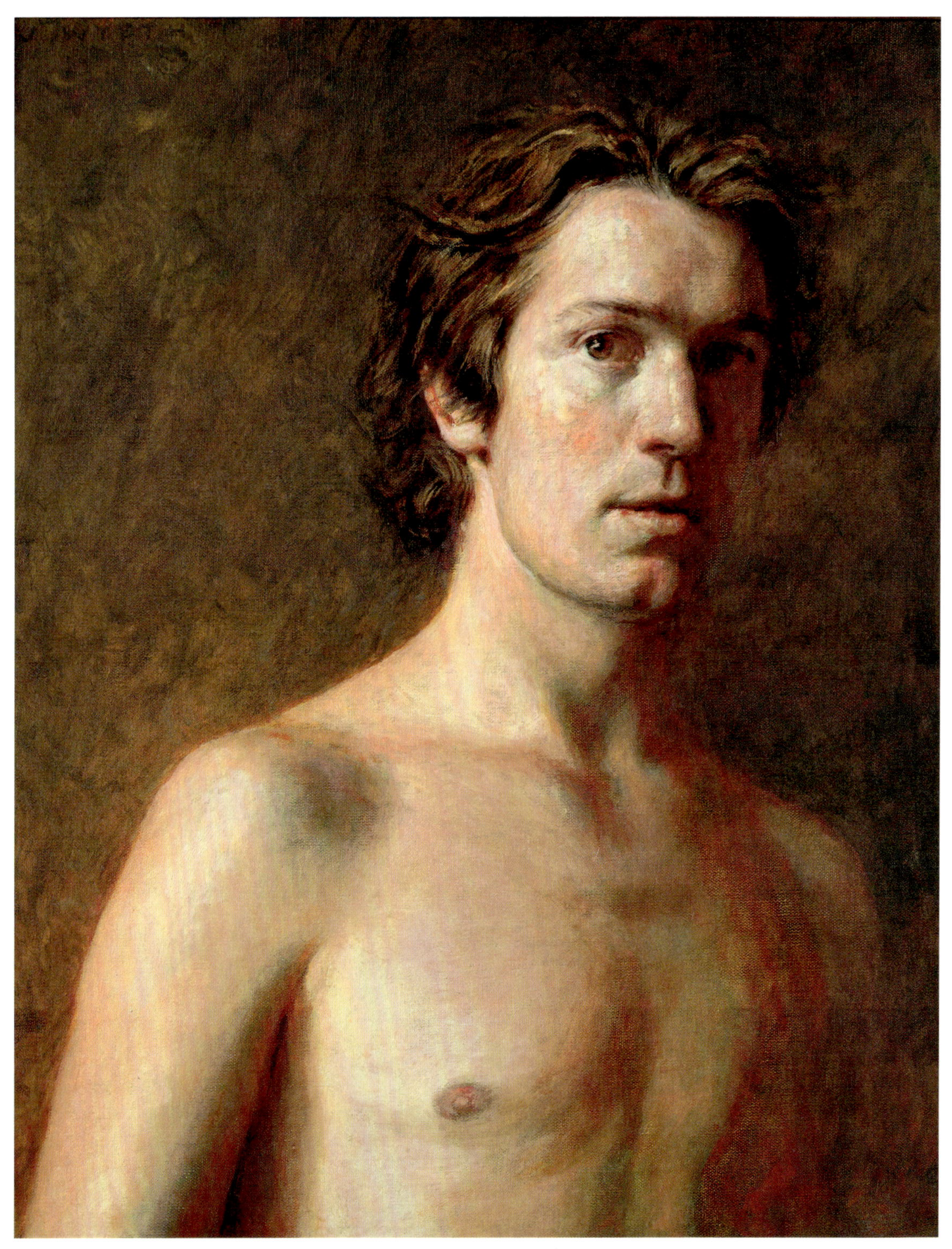

21. *Self-Portrait*, about 1969. Oil on canvas, 61.6 x 51.1 cm (24¼ x 20⅛ in.)

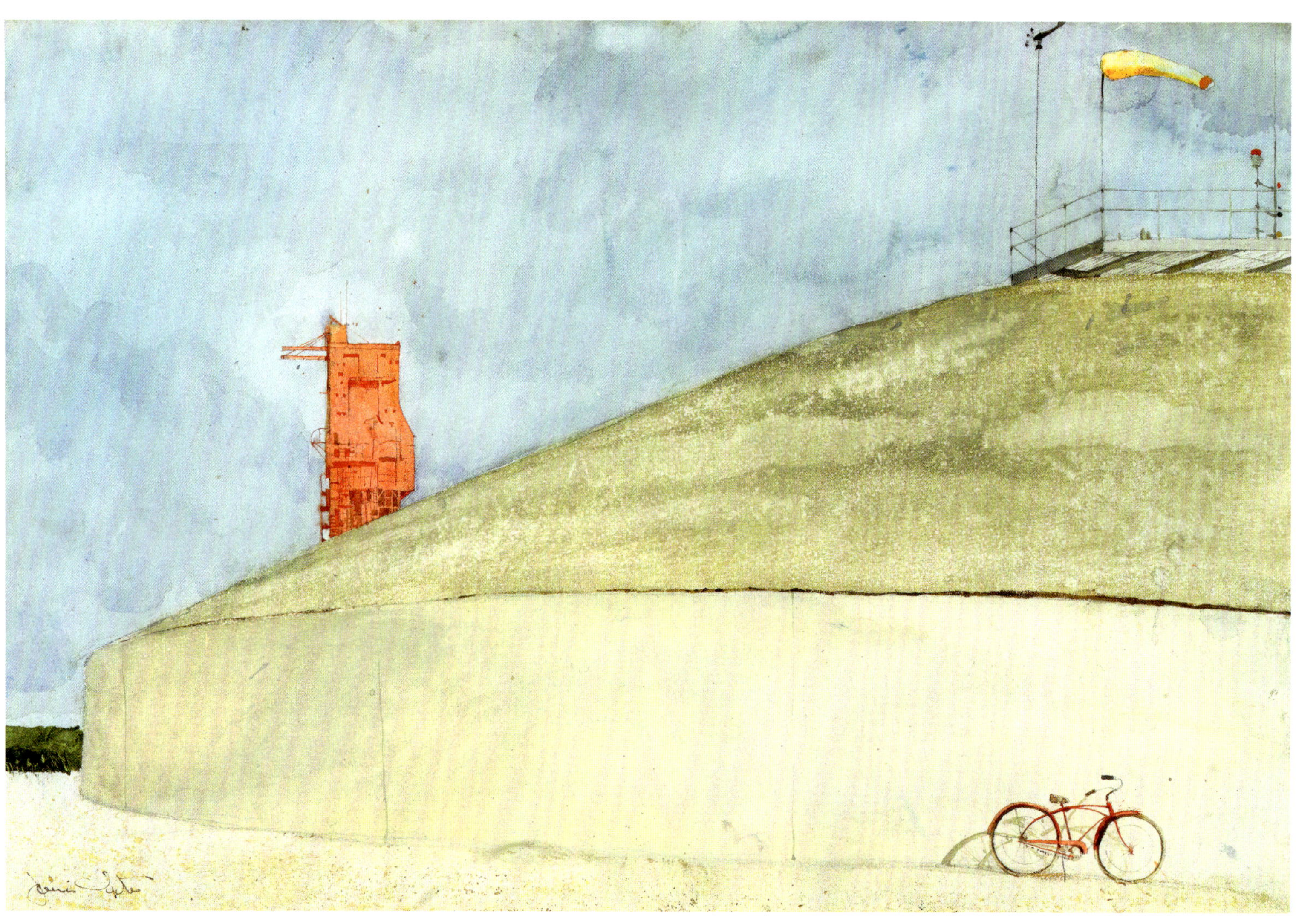

22. *Gemini Launch Pad*, 1969. Watercolor on watercolor paper, 68.6 x 86.4 cm (27 x 34 in.)

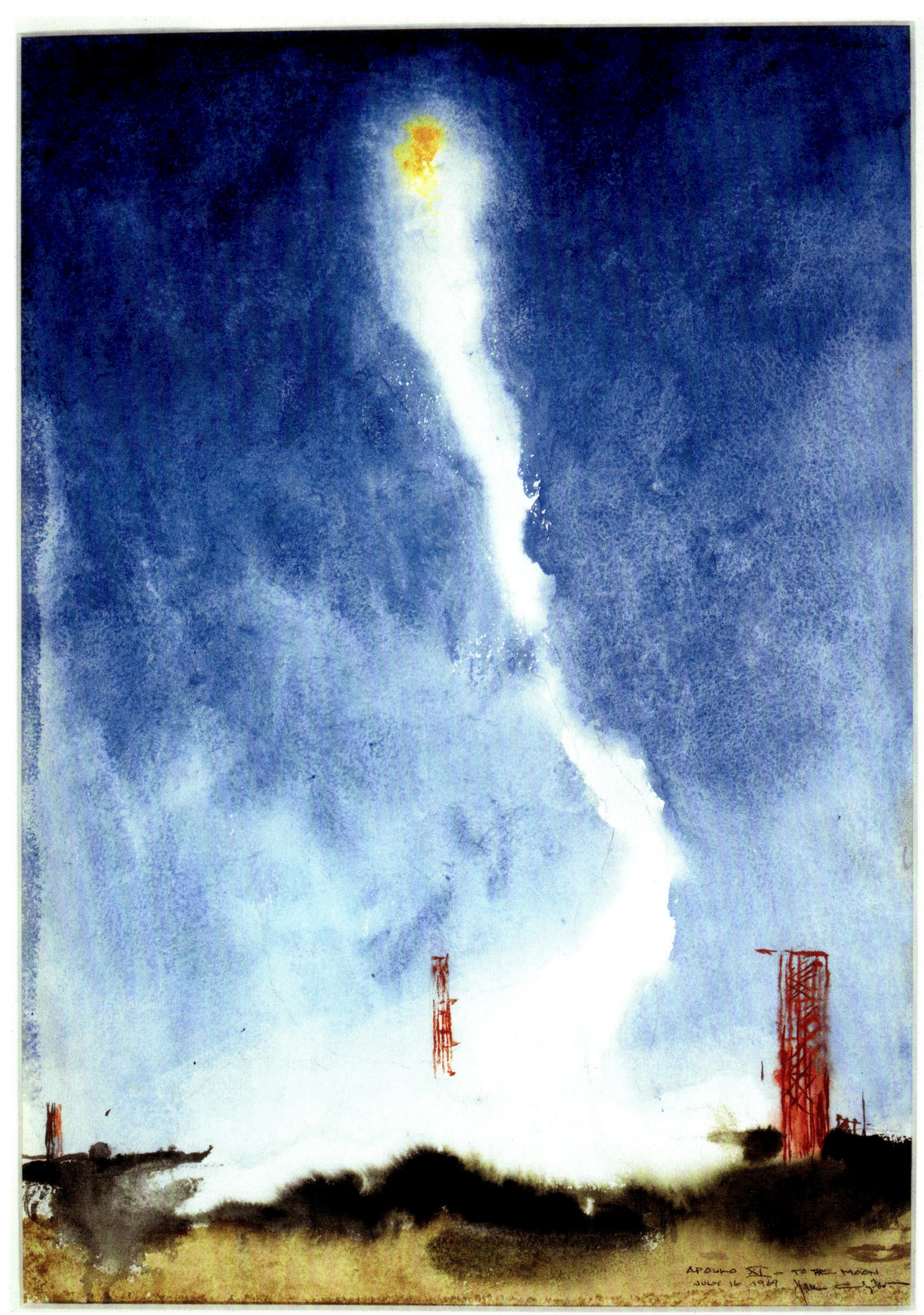

23. *Apollo XI—To the Moon, July 16, 1969*, 1969. Watercolor on Twinrocker handmade paper, 71.1 x 52.1 cm (28 x 20½ in.)

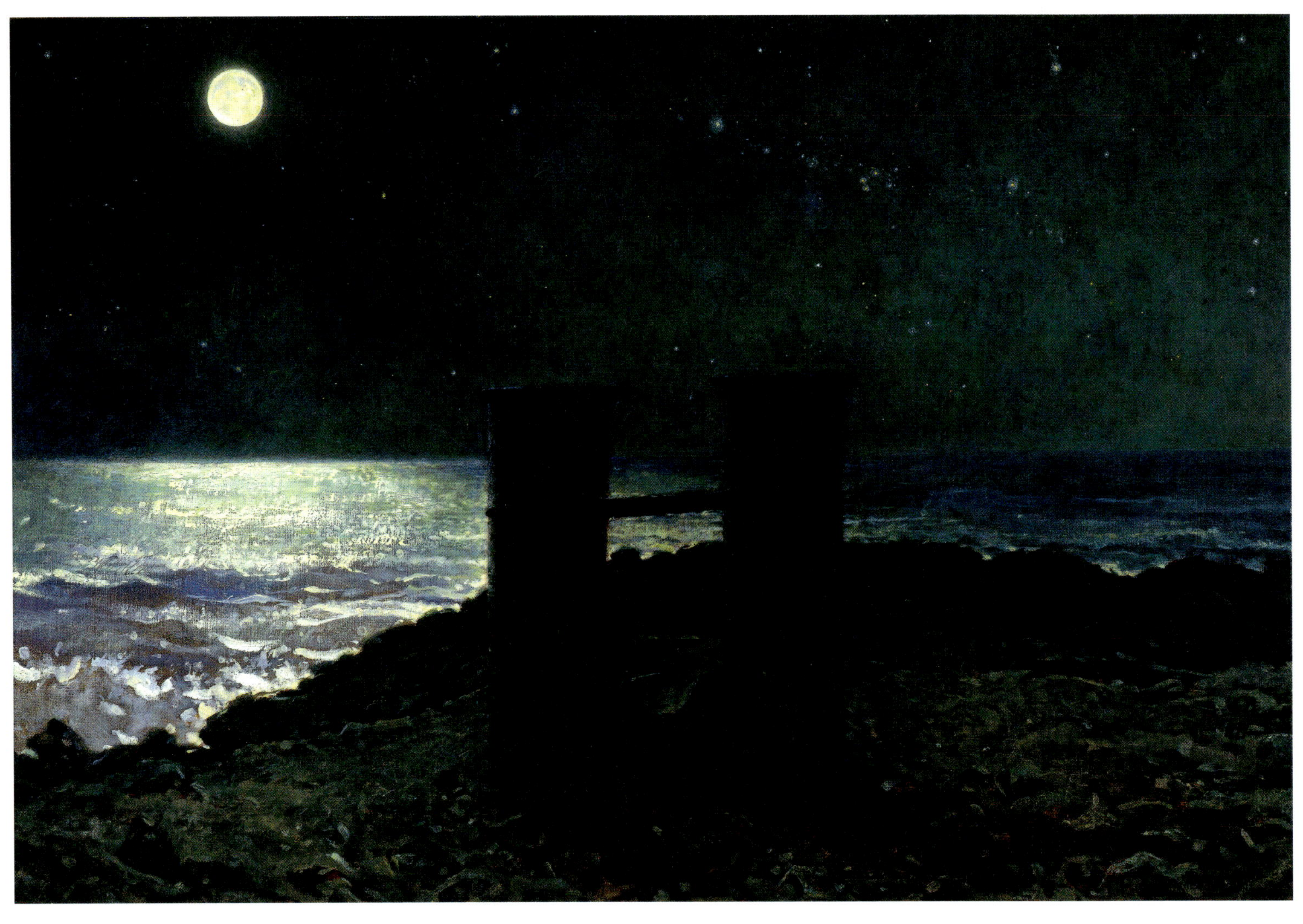

24. *Moon Landing*, 1969. Oil on canvas, 73.7 x 109.2 cm (29 x 43 in.)

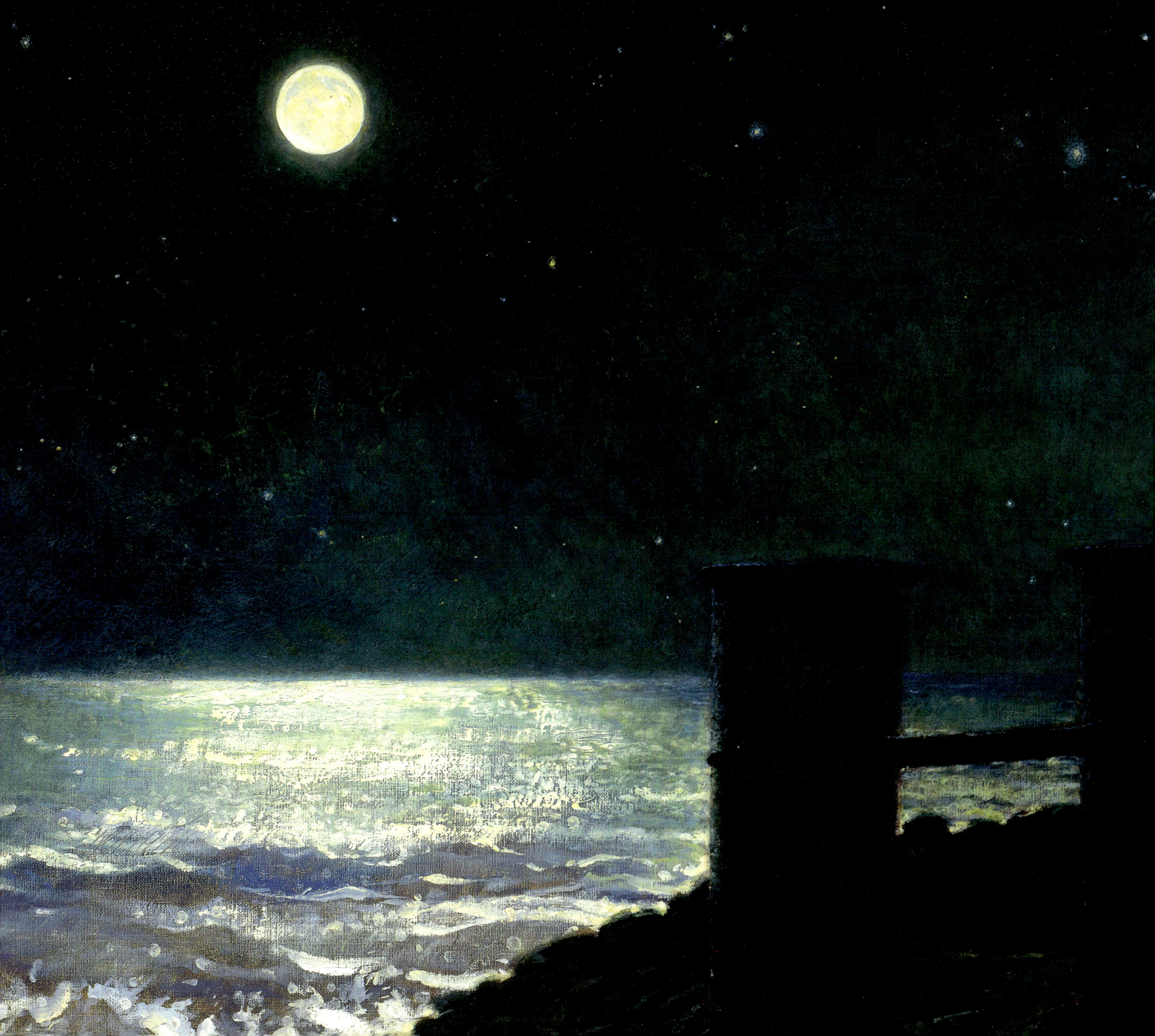

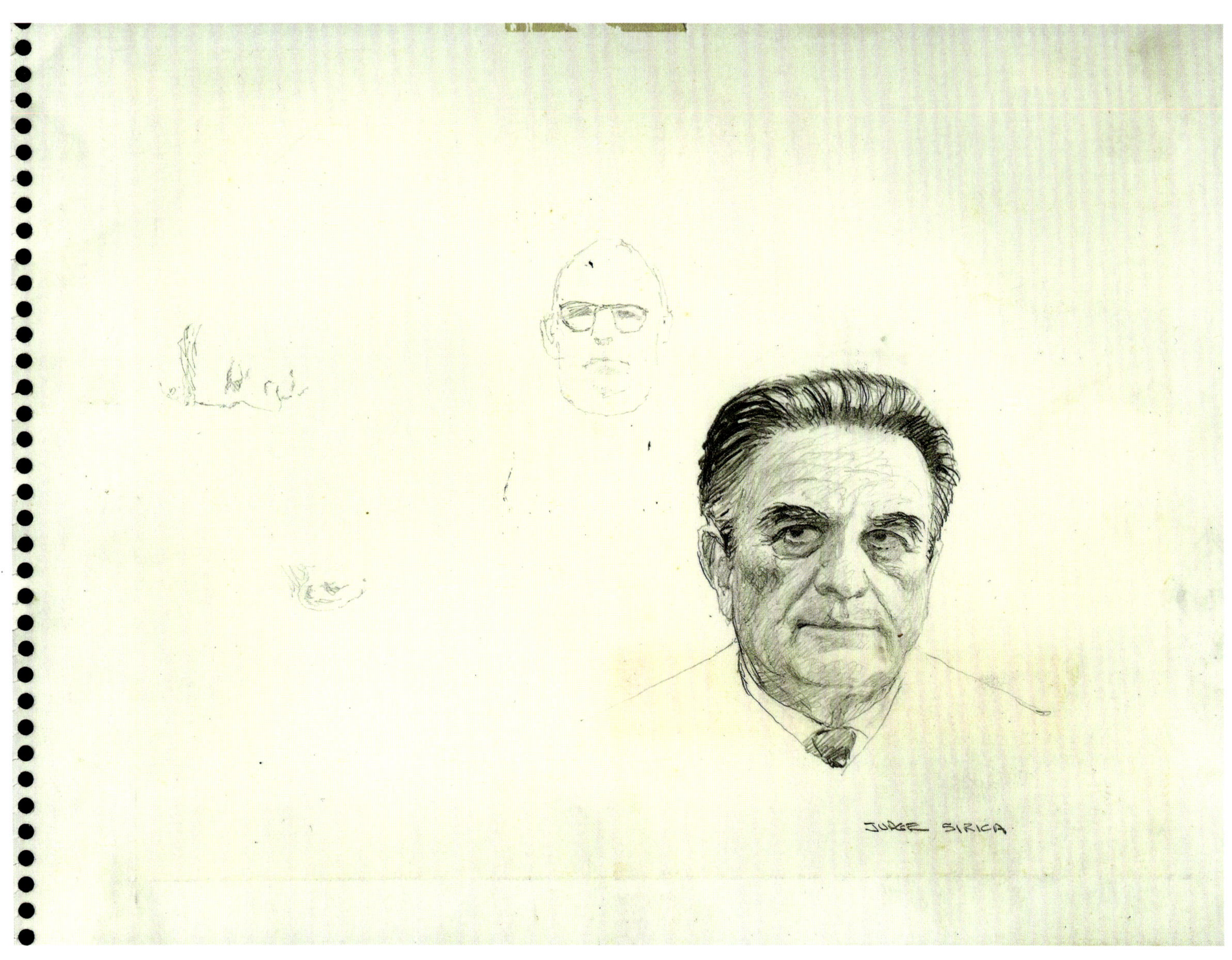

25. *Judge John Sirica*, 1974. Graphite on paper, 27.9 x 35.6 cm (11 x 14 in.)

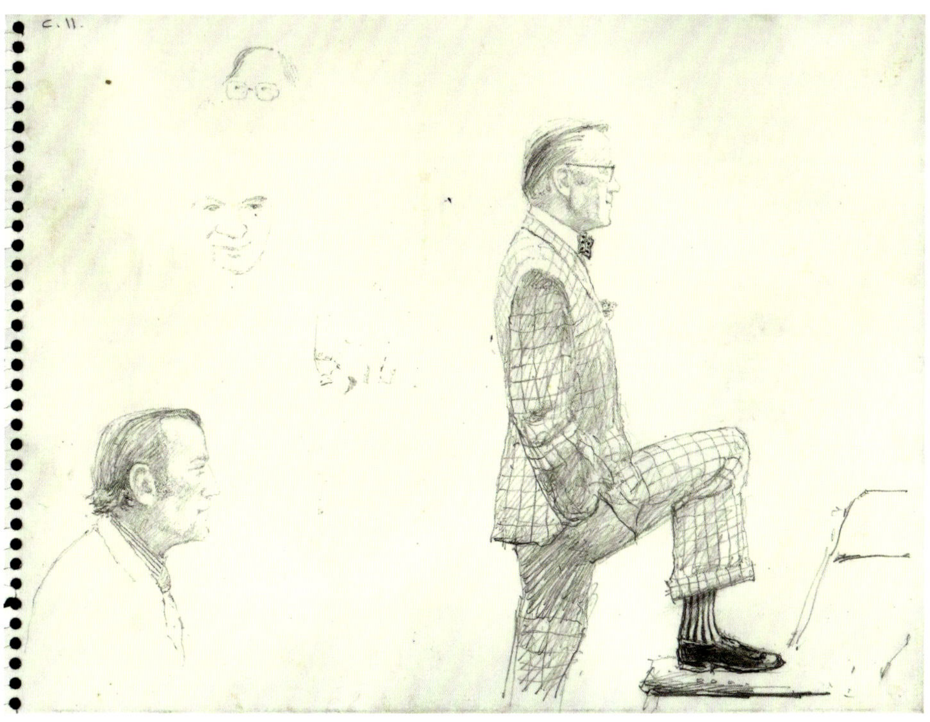

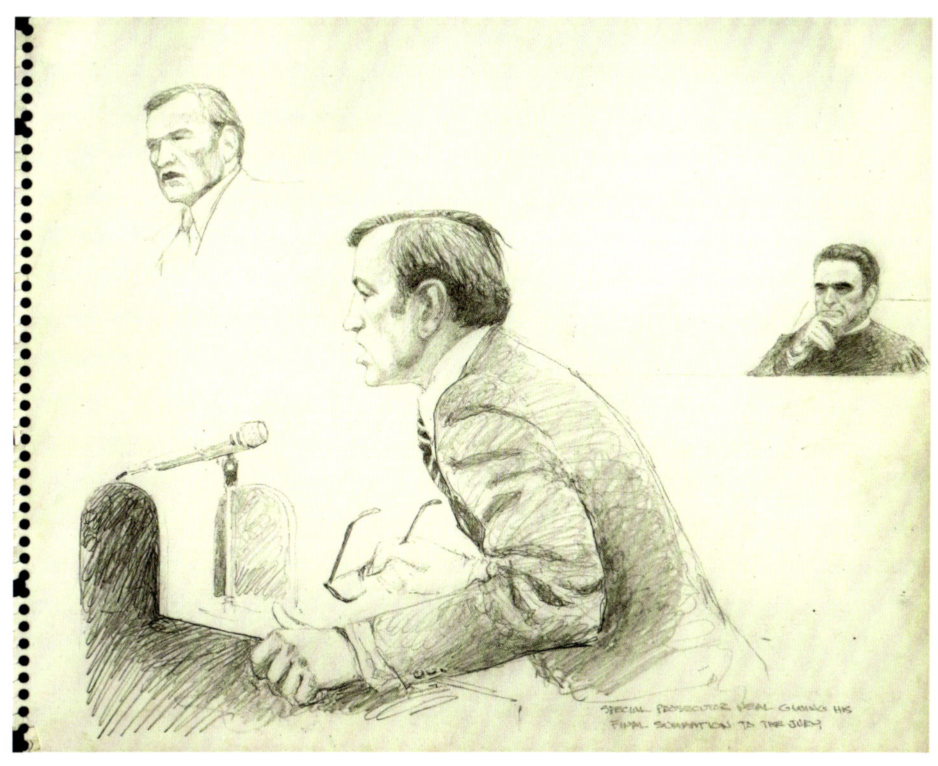

26. *Albert Jenner*, 1974. Graphite on paper, 27.9 x 35.6 cm (11 x 14 in.)

27. *Special Prosecutor James Neal Tries to Impeach John Ehrlichman's Prior Testimony*, 1974. Graphite on paper, 27.9 x 35.6 cm (11 x 14 in.)

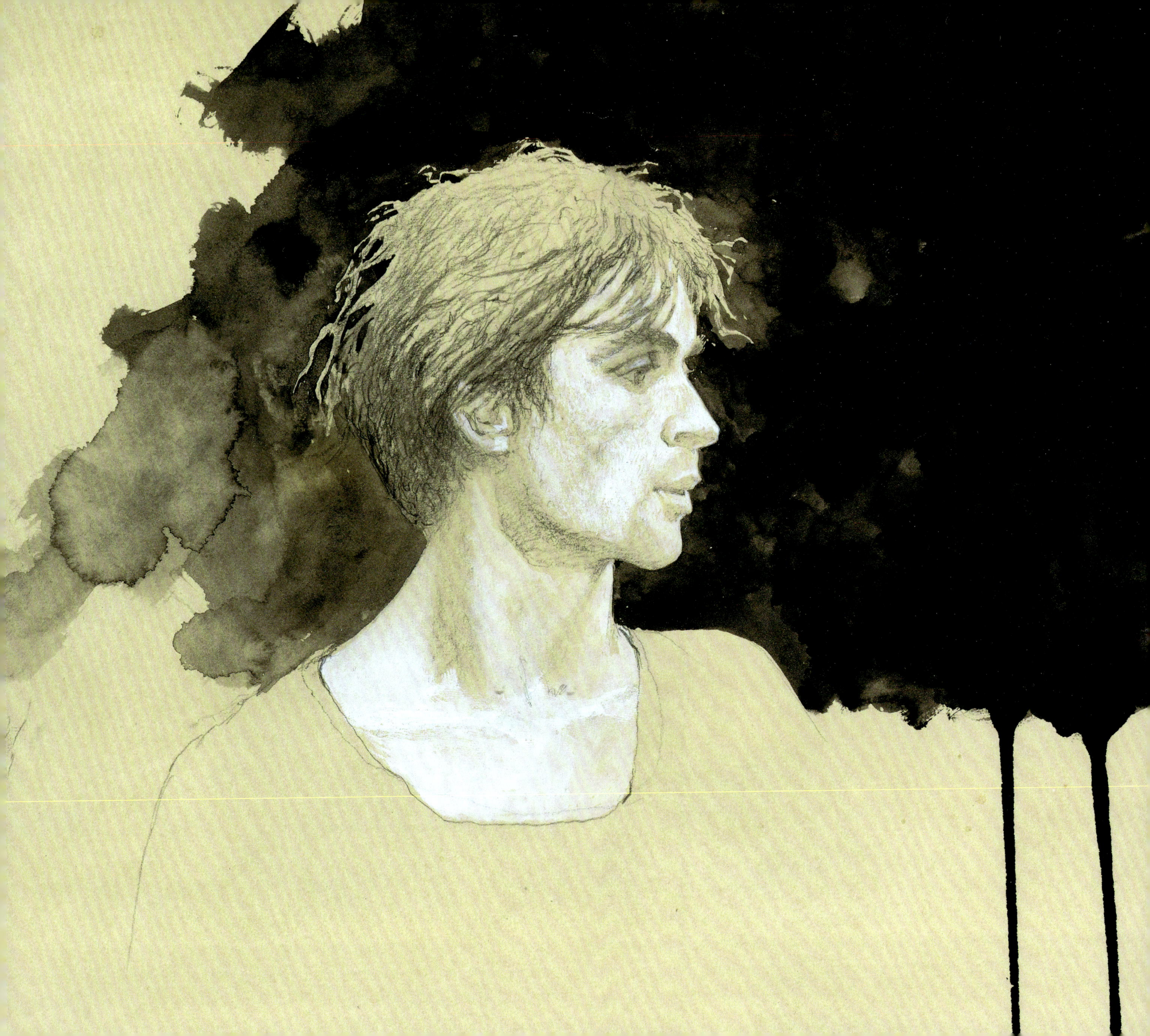

New York and the Factory

After the Watergate experience, Wyeth dove back into the New York art world with renewed vigor, strengthening his ties with Andy Warhol by entering into a portrait exchange that would lead to a joint exhibition at the Coe Kerr Gallery in 1976. Warhol's operation at the Factory, initially located in a former hat factory on East 47th Street that he used as a studio for producing his particular form of assembly-line Pop Art, was a world that was about as far as one could get from rural Chadds Ford. By 1973 the Factory had moved to 860 Broadway, on the north side of Union Square, where it continued to buzz as the epicenter of Warhol's artistic productions, happenings, and parties that went on around the clock. These events attracted "more and more real stars of the day, including Judy Garland, Tennessee Williams, Jim Morrison, Cecil Beaton, the Rolling Stones, most of Swinging London, even some of the Park Avenue swells Andy loved to lure into his version of high society."[1]

Wyeth later painted and constructed from memory the scenes he encountered there in the 1970s. Fred Hughes, an elegant dandy from Houston who liked to claim that he was "deeply superficial," played the role of Factory art impresario, handling sales of Warhol's paintings.[2] In *Fred Hughes and Andy Warhol* he appears nattily dressed, striking a nonchalant pose; his left hand is thrust casually in his pocket, while his right hand holds a lighted cigarette vertically, a fashionable acolyte's candle raised to illuminate Warhol, who is seated just below him. Warhol leans forward, eagerly listening as he clutches the ever-present tape recorder that enabled him to play his favorite role of detached voyeur and interviewer. Above Warhol's head, the amusing absurdity of an enormous proboscis interjects, from the taxidermy moose head that reappears in the tableau vivant of *Factory Dining Room*, along with an erotically charged Pre-Raphaelite painting by David Forrester Wilson, *The Wind* (n.d.). There Warhol and Hughes pass the time glued to the television, accompanied by their companion, Catherine Guinness, and surrounded by Andy's colorful collection of Fiestaware and an impressive array of liquor bottles, all gleaming under an elegant chandelier.

Warhol and Wyeth had been introduced by Peter Beard in the mid-1960s. When the two decided to paint each other's portraits in 1975, Warhol was at the height of his fame-seeking celebrity, and Jamie Wyeth, approaching the age of thirty, with his first exhibition at Knoedler's nearly a decade behind him, was still making his way in the New York art world. Wyeth had been drawn to Warhol's earlier work on view in the New York art galleries for some time: "It was very interesting to me, [in] the beginning of the pop-art movement, because it was the only sort of movement that had roots in the type of painting that I do, which is representational painting. . . . I thought that the Brillo boxes and the soup cans of Warhol's had a certain power to them. Warhol had taken the actual object, not really messed around with it or abstracted it in any way and it had a certain vitality. Why abstract the object if the object is what hits you?"[3]

The tradition of artists' exchanging portraits in friendship or to mark a period of collaboration includes such well-known European examples as those between Vincent van Gogh and Paul Gauguin, and Gauguin and Émile Bernard, and in the United

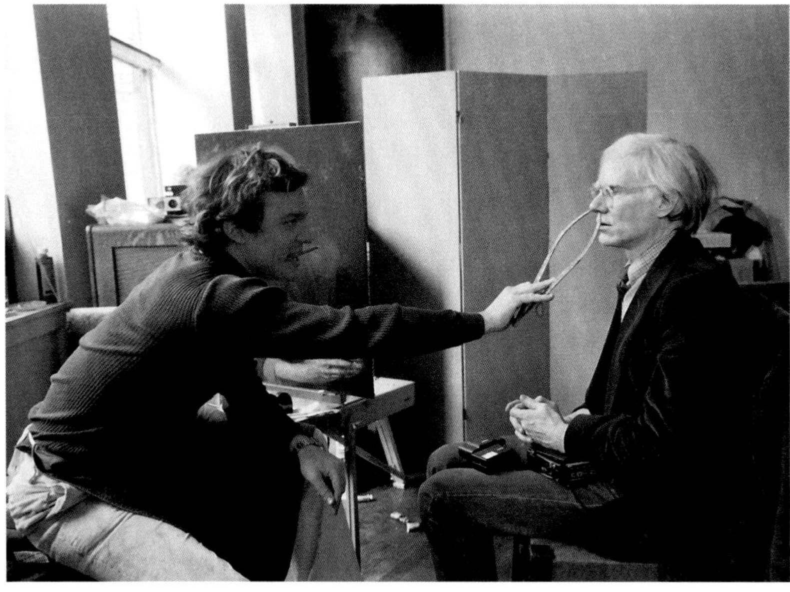

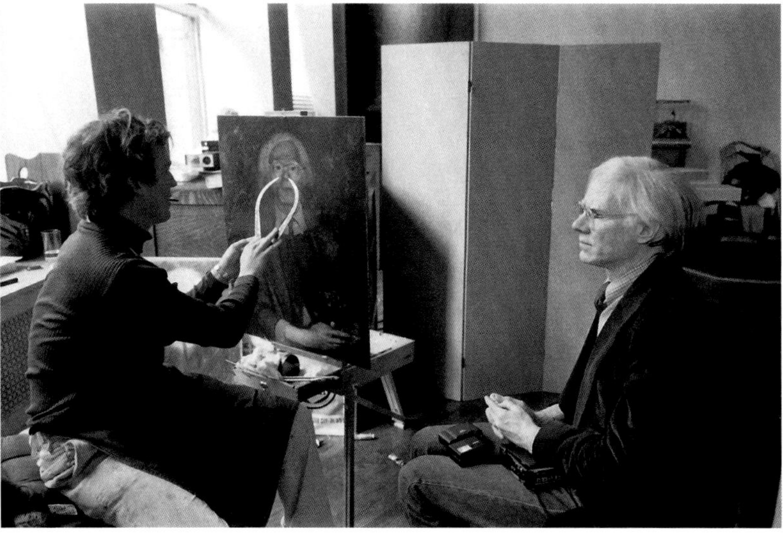

Fig. 12. Stanley Tretick (1921–1999)
Jamie Wyeth Measuring Andy Warhol with Calipers
about 1976

Fig. 13. Stanley Tretick (1921–1999)
Jamie Wyeth Placing Calipers on the Portrait of Andy Warhol
about 1976

States, honoring their close friendship in Boston, John Singer Sargent and Dennis Miller Bunker. Warhol himself painted portraits of Philip Johnson (1972), Man Ray (1974), and David Hockney (1974), and also exchanged portraits with Jean-Michel Basquiat (about 1982).[4]

The Warhol-Wyeth portrait exchange seems to have been a modern form of a Faustian pact struck for mutual exploitation. Warhol was a master at playing the role of detached impresario of the Factory and was known to draw in young talent, like Wyeth and, later, Basquiat, to supply new ideas and direction.[5] So adept was Warhol at sucking the creative juices out of other artists and into his own work that the former Factory groupie Bianca Jagger dubbed him a vampire.[6] Younger associates called Warhol "Drella," a hybrid of Dracula and Cinderella, for his ability to alter an artist's reputation overnight.[7]

During Wyeth's and Basquiat's stints at the Factory, Warhol began his series of "piss paintings," or, as they were known in Warhol's more highfalutin terminology, "oxidation paintings."[8] A tongue-in-cheek adaptation of Jackson Pollock's iconic drip paintings, successful piss paintings involved Factory artists, associates, and hangers-on urinating on canvases primed with copper-laced pigments that oxidized to greens and browns as the urine dried. Although various men contributed to the oxidation process, the resulting compositions are attributed solely to Warhol. Wyeth wryly portrays Warhol working on the piss paintings as an observer, gripping his beloved miniature dachshund, Archie, against his hip (cat. 30). Warhol's involvement was more cerebral, as the artist's diaries document the explicit instructions he relayed to his assistant, Ronnie Cutrone, directing the appropriate working routine each morning that would produce the best color combinations.[9]

For Jamie Wyeth, a public portrait exchange with Andy Warhol had the potential to bring attention to his immersive method of painting a portrait at a time when critics hotly favored more conceptual and painterly forms. Lincoln Kirstein's bold assertion that Wyeth, at the age of twenty, was the "finest American portrait painter since the death of John Singer Sargent," had helped to fan the flames of the New York press, which was unstinting in its disdain for the young artist's work.[10] In return, Wyeth combined his intensely crafted portraiture in the Renaissance mode of oil painting on panel with Warhol's celebrity branding through Polaroid images silkscreened onto canvas for maximum combustion.

What did Warhol stand to gain in the bargain? Certainly the portrait exchange could pump some new artistic blood into the Factory. Warhol professed admiration for Wyeth's technique: "I love his work. I always wished I could paint like him."[11] Unfailingly drawn to the glitterati and the accoutrements of their wealth, Warhol was undoubtedly attracted by what he perceived as Wyeth's social and artistic lineage, as well as what he described as his "cuteness,"[12] which he desired to capture in the portraits.

Whatever the artists' motivations, sparks flew as critics relished the opportunity to dissect the wildly different portraits that Wyeth and Warhol made of each other. Hilton Kramer considered the exchange a male version of Beauty and the Beast.[13] Some noted that Warhol expressed his painterly qualities in the image of Jamie Wyeth as a matinee idol, or the ironic image of the home-schooled artist, as "archetypal American as a high-school yearbook heartthrob, clearly the handsomest boy in the class, and not, as Warhol had thought of himself, the ugliest."[14]

For his part, Wyeth described his head-on pose for Warhol, a reprise of his earlier, controversial portrait of Helen Taussig, as a "deer in the headlights."[15] The phrase suggests Wyeth was shining the ever-present klieg lights of filmmaking and celebrity watching at the Factory onto Warhol himself. It also conveys a sense of menacing power, and Wyeth seems to have enjoyed making the older, more established artist squirm: "Well, he wasn't pretty to look at, you know, which fascinated me. He kept saying that I was using too much pimple color. He'd keep looking at my palette and he'd say, 'Why do you have this pimple color here?' But, he knew what I was doing."[16] Warhol was extremely self-conscious about his pasty skin, which suffered from frequent bouts of acne owing to a childhood disease, and he resorted to wearing a carefully styled wig to distract people from his face.[17] Yet Wyeth brought all his tools and skills to bear on Warhol's every pore, blemish, and strand of hair. His immersive form of representation, dismissed by some as the "university president treatment,"[18] quietly smashed to smithereens the popular perception of the image-conscious Warhol, who also just happened to be one of the most famous artists in the United States.

Since the early 1960s, Warhol had based his portraiture on photographs reproduced in newspapers or on instant photographs of his subjects. Jamie Wyeth described Warhol's contribution to portraiture as merely a "click" of the Polaroid on which the image was based, a comment that highlighted his deliberate method of creating a portrait through a prodigious series of studies and preparatory drawings. "Where painting portraits and photography differ is that photographs are really the instant of the moment, and painting, particularly the way I work in portraits, is a distillation of many moods, many sides of a person. Actually it's a culmination of all his moods; certain days he's happy, certain days he's excited, unexcited. . . . I can't work with photographs because to me painting is interpretive, and it is ultimately my interpretation, as close as I can get to the subject. I feel if I'm tied down with a camera or a photograph, it's just uncomfortable."[19]

Typical of the early stages of Wyeth's working method are looser drawings with looping arcs. Others are more finished, as in the case of *Andy Warhol—Facing Left (Study #2)* and *Andy's Feet*. Wyeth initially depicted the feet as part of a full-length study, but as a tribute to Warhol's planned series of celebrity feet paintings, he ultimately gave the work to Warhol as a token of their portrait exchange, figuratively and quite literally cutting him off at the knees.[20]

Wyeth's flirtation with celebrity manifested itself in another pairing of polar opposites that enabled him to develop artistically. The year 1977 found Wyeth simultaneously devoting himself to portraying the greatest bodybuilder of the day, Arnold Schwarzenegger, Mr. Universe and seven-time Mr. Olympia, as well as the star of the documentary film *Pumping Iron* (1977), and the greatest dancer of the ballet world, Rudolf Nureyev. Both were tremendous athletes known for their aesthetic physiques. Schwarzenegger himself describes the process of bodybuilding as sculpting, akin to performance art: "A bodybuilder who looks in the mirror is not looking at himself, he's looking at his body. He's looking at an object, he's not connecting it as part of him; he's just seeing how that left deltoid looks compared with the right one, and let's see how his biceps work. [You] have to criticize your body, and if you're attached to it you get emotional about it and get blind. [You're] much too easy on yourself instead of take [*sic*] yourself away and say, 'This is something I'm building,'—you know, like a piece of sculpture."[21]

In *Portrait of Arnold Schwarzenegger*, Wyeth pushes the powerfully sculpted torso to the foreground by draping the background with a piece of white fabric. This is not just any fabric, but clearly white linen that retains crisply demarcated, rectangular folds with tell-tale, diamond-shaped creases at each of the vertices, bearing the distinct appearance of having being mechanically pressed at one of the East Side Chinese-owned laundries then located near Wyeth's apartment. Schwarzenegger holds up an arm to capture our gaze, as he stands his ground in front of the sheet that diffuses the light from the window and enhances the appearance of his eye-popping physique. The use of the sheet, while certainly practical, recalls the great American trompe l'oeil of a female nude, Raphaelle Peale's *Venus Rising from the Sea, A Deception* (1822, Nelson-Atkins Museum of Art). Peale cleverly reveals only the woman's arm and feet; the rest of her body is hidden by a casually draped white cloth slung over a rope that teases us into believing we could easily lift it away to uncover Venus. Instead of retreating into the shadows, as Wyeth did in his *Self-Portrait* (see cat. 21), Schwarzenegger stands firmly before the sheet, welcoming the flood of daylight that washes over him, mapping the swelling contours of his body. His features have the set expression of a classical statue, as he casts his gaze on the massive biceps and surrounding muscles, the detached creator of his award-winning musculature, objective body sculptor, and unabashed star of the show.

This portrait is the most "Pop" of Wyeth's paintings inspired by his experiences with Warhol. The classic bodybuilder pose struck by Schwarzenegger is ingrained in popular culture, from images of the circus strong man to cartoons of Popeye the Sailor Man. The term Pop Art itself is associated with Richard Hamilton's classic collage, *Just What Is It That Makes Today's Homes So Different, So Appealing* (1956, Kunsthalle Tübingen), which depicts a bodybuilder working out at home holding a Tootsie Pop instead of a barbell.[22] The posing of a heroic nude in front of a linen drape turns on its head the tradition of American trompe l'oeil painting in the form of Peale's nude concealed and revealed by a curtain. And, at the time of the painting, Schwarzenegger himself was very much a commercial commodity, having successfully defended his Mr. Olympia title and being well on his way to rocketing into the stratosphere of movie stardom.

To create his portrait of Rudolf Nureyev, Wyeth immersed himself in the dancer's world, watching him rehearse and perform from both sides of the curtain, all the while recording countless minute details of the artist's body and image over the course of a year and a half. Wyeth had met Nureyev in 1974 and knew of his volatile portrait sitting at the Factory, when Nureyev crumpled up Warhol's Polaroid photographs in a fierce rage.[23] Nonetheless, he persuaded the star to pose for him in 1977 (fig. 14).[24] In the Nureyev sketchbooks we discover Wyeth working in the manner of traditional approaches to anatomy, measuring each and every part of his body to the point that the subject declared, "You could make me suit!" (cat. 41).[25] Wyeth's reliance on calipers demonstrates the remarkable zeal with which he attempted to pin down this challenging and complex personality, who was described by many, including the artist, as a force of nature, a creature half man, half beast, a Russian firebird.[26] Wyeth stated: "What attracted me was Nureyev's physicality, that peasant force. He is very aware of his animal nature—he has this marvelous energy, and he is always moving, always on stage. He is as strange off the dance stage as on."[27]

Fig. 14. *Portrait of Rudolf Nureyev*, 1977
Oil on canvas
114.9 x 102.9 cm (45¼ x 40½ in.)

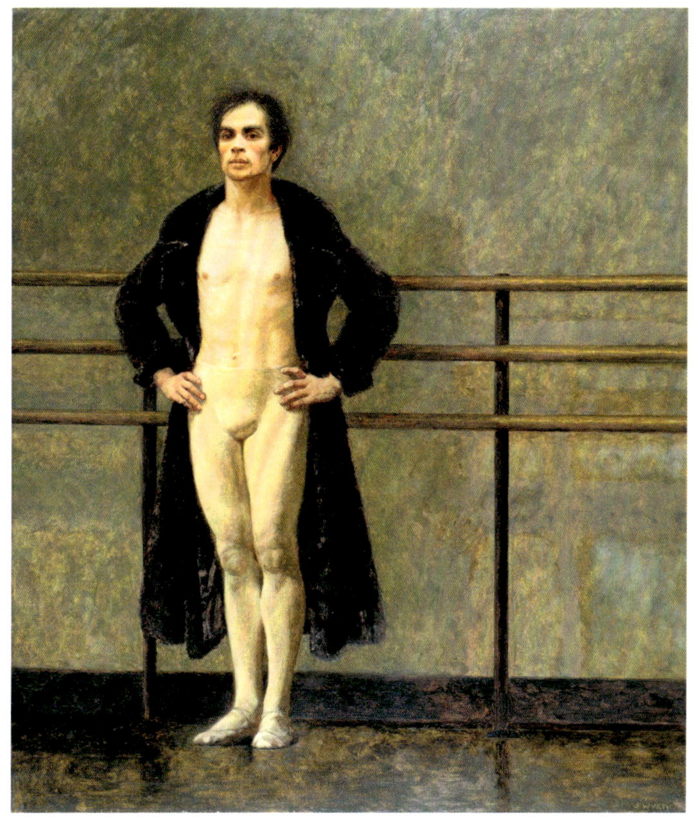

And yet Wyeth is unable or unwilling to capture something ineffable about Nureyev as a performer. In the combined media compositions from the Nureyev series, the dancer often appears more squat on canvas than photographs of him suggest, or static, as depicted taking a bow after a performance in *Curtain Call* (2001, Brandywine River Museum of Art). When Wyeth returned later to the subject in a series from 2001 (Nureyev had died in 1993), he depicts Nureyev as Don Quixote in a standing pose signaling the dramatic finish to a dance sequence that is consistent with conventional images of male dancers (cat. 38).[28] In this instance Wyeth invigorates the composition by placing the dancer against an egg-yolk-yellow backdrop that recalls one of N. C. Wyeth's signature effects, used to offset dramatic scenes of pirates storming across the landscape in *Treasure Island* (fig. 15). Nureyev's pose conveys a sense of flair, while the large, dark shadow projecting behind him, enlivened by nervous strokes of graphite and the rough-and-tumble manner in which Wyeth animates the background, together infuse the sheet with palpable, physical energy. He further heightens the effect by layering on lighter white and yellow paint from Nureyev's collar down the edge of his left arm in a gesture that transforms the elaborate gold embroidery on the costume into liquid gold that spills down the dancer's sleeve. Here Wyeth expresses in abstract terms that quality of Nureyev's ephemeral performance, reaching back into his repertoire of dramatic figural action as played out in his grandfather's illustrations to evoke the dynamism of Nureyev's line danced on stage.

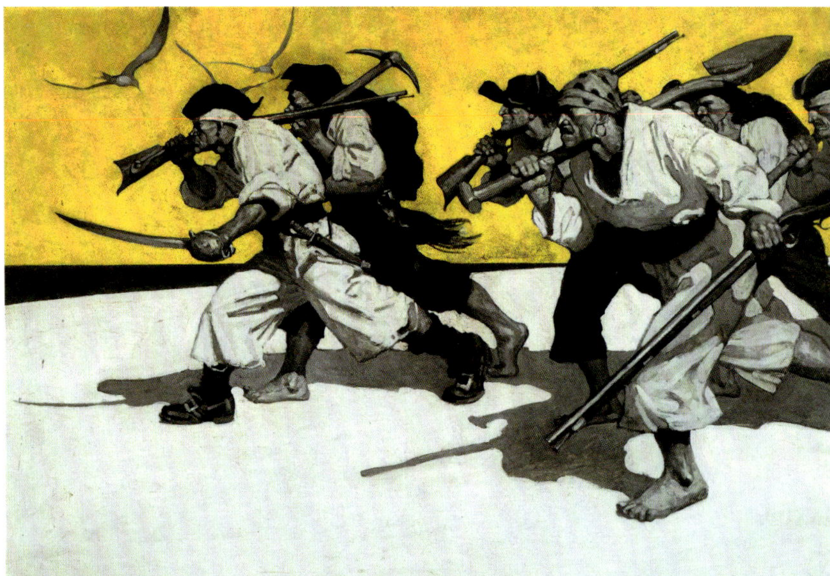

Fig. 15. N. C. Wyeth (1882–1945)
Treasure Island, 1911
Oil on canvas
83.2 x 119.7 cm (32¾ x 47⅛ in.)

When we meet Nureyev again in another of Wyeth's later portrayals, he appears in full stage makeup, which he routinely chose to wear as he left the theater (cat. 37). The drama of the dancer, in a flourish reminiscent of Henri de Toulouse-Lautrec's portrait of the great French café singer Aristide Bruant, is expressed by the tremendous sweep of a scarf in deep violet, a color found at the opposite side of the color wheel from the liquid gold seen in *Nureyev—Don Quixote* and yet one that is also closely associated with the brilliant oils of N. C. Wyeth, including those from Jamie Wyeth's collection.

Winslow Homer felt that his black-and-white chalk drawings of the 1880s were among his best work, and Wyeth himself demonstrates in the case of Nureyev that he finds the greatest expression of the dancer's artistry in his drawings of the dancer's head and torso from the original 1977 series, compositions that resemble seventeenth-century Dutch portraits, also known as *tronies* (a seventeenth-century Dutch word for face), for their intense study of human emotions visible in facial expressions. In those contexts, Wyeth gives himself free rein to express the complexity of Nureyev's personality and movement, as in the study with black wash background (cat. 39). Defining this particular composition are two parallel drips that the artists allowed to trail off with remarkable control. Together with the seriousness of Nureyev's expression, these drips could be seen as black tears, slowly creeping their way to the lower edge of the sheet. Compare these trails of tears with a small cluster of tiny drops punctuating the open area of the sheet just off to the left of Nureyev's head. In the cluster of four, one drop is larger than the others, and another drop appears just above the group, singled out for our attention. Wyeth inserts Nureyev's face again, drawn faintly below the blots, looking down, an invitation for us to look down as well. These small drops are created by the artist's manipulation of gravity by holding ink above the paper and physically letting go to make a mark on the horizontal surface below. That physical sense of letting go is just how Nureyev achieved his own, ineffable form of dance in relation to the dance floor. This cluster of drops could be seen as the visual equivalent of short, jabbing steps, culminating in a large leap above the rest, suggested by the drop separated from the others.

Wyeth maintains a sense of executing his drawings within a highly controlled, carefully paced format that ultimately frees him, allowing him to experiment with various combinations of technique, tone, and mood. In *Profile, in Fur, Nureyev (Study #9)*, the dancer's face appears against a mass of turbulent brushstrokes of white paint that suggest storm clouds or a blinding snowstorm from which the star takes cover under his black fur. These drawings show Wyeth giving freely of himself to express the exuberance of this highly complex and accomplished dancer in a way that brings to mind earlier American painters, such as John Singer Sargent, who had explored the possibilities of representing other forms of artistic expression, whether music or dance, in visual terms (see, for example, *El Jaleo*, 1882, Isabella Stewart Gardner Museum). In *Rosina—Capri* (1879, Crystal Bridges Museum of American Art), Sargent offsets the dancer's silhouette against the sky, executing rhythmic control as he moves the paint across the canvas from left to right, emphasizing the angle of the dancer's upraised arms and the slant of her torso. Like the musician practicing scales or the dancer repeating steps, both Sargent and Wyeth rehearse strokes and motifs until the movements of the brush or pencil become effortless and merge with the unconscious mind.

Nude Three-Quarter Figure, Nureyev (Study #18) is, in many ways, a capstone of Wyeth's experience at the Factory. Both Warhol and Wyeth ultimately derive their greatest strength when they are able to play off the superficial sensibilities of Pop Art. When Wyeth depicted Nureyev in the nude, he would certainly have been aware that Warhol had begun working on his series *Torsos* and *Sex Parts* (1977–1982). Warhol snapped thousands of close-up Polaroid photographs of male genitalia to create his *Sex Parts* prints, which he intended for private collectors, as opposed to museums, which suggests he was well aware of how the images would be received. Wyeth's frontal portrayal of Nureyev, although the dancer appeared nearly nude in many contemporary performances, would have been similarly provocative then, and, over time, continued to elicit a certain frisson at institutions wary of displaying a male nude.[29]

The ghostly quality of the figure, rendered largely in white watercolor and gouache on toned paper of the sort that Wyeth used for many of the Nureyev studies, reveals a technique that hovers between the past and the present. *Nude Three-Quarter Figure* combines an elegant, refined sense of touch recalling Old Master drawing styles and the loose, nervous agitation of more contemporary drawing techniques that capture contours by approximation, the gap between outlines energizing and defining the form. The elusiveness of this particular portrayal is distinctly a product of Wyeth's technique, the deft and deliberate result of hundreds of hours of observing the dancer's body in action. The artist noted that he undertook the nude in an effort to become even closer to Nureyev.[30] Unlike the tentative *Self-Portrait*, this nude exhibits a quiet confidence, as suggested by the classic pose of a dominant male, firmly planting his hands on his hips to call attention to the genitals. Wyeth is able to subtly and powerfully conjure this complex figure with only the lightest touches of graphite to suggest Nureyev's wildly untamed hair and luxuriant, nearly bovine eyelashes. The figure takes shape as the white mixture plays across his forehead and dances its way along the forms of Nureyev's body, piling up in the hollows of the collarbone, gliding over the pectorals, skipping over the rippling muscles of his abdomen, and finally streaming down as a glistening streak of perspiration on his right quadriceps. The intensity of the dancer's lowered gaze suggests that Nureyev is focusing on the performance, catching his breath before launching into another dance sequence. Nureyev's physique is completely objectified, rendered with as little emotion as possible, as a means of calling attention to the body as an instrument of artistic expression. And yet the figure also frankly exudes Nureyev's feral sexuality. Wyeth demonstrates impressive restraint in the pose, which does not engage with the viewer, and the manner in which the contours of the body gradually and steadily come into focus through the delicate dance Wyeth himself performs. By manipulating his physical pressure and shifting his touch by means of spidery graphite contours, white modeling, and exposed toned support below, Wyeth creates a visual pas de deux that merges his form with his memory of the dancer's own ephemeral artistry.

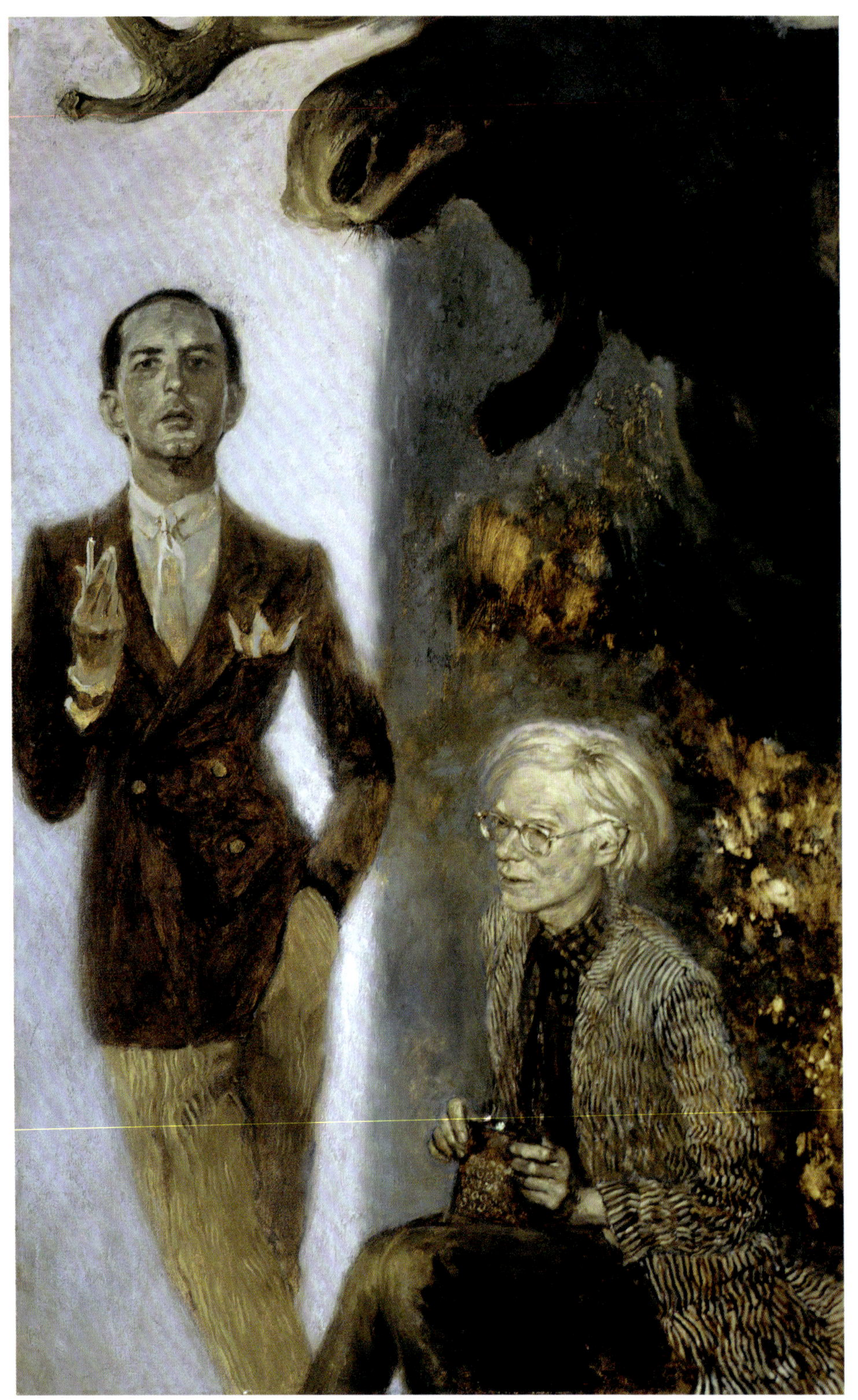

28. *Fred Hughes and Andy Warhol*, 2005.
Oil on canvas, 121.9 x 76.2 cm (48 x 30 in.)

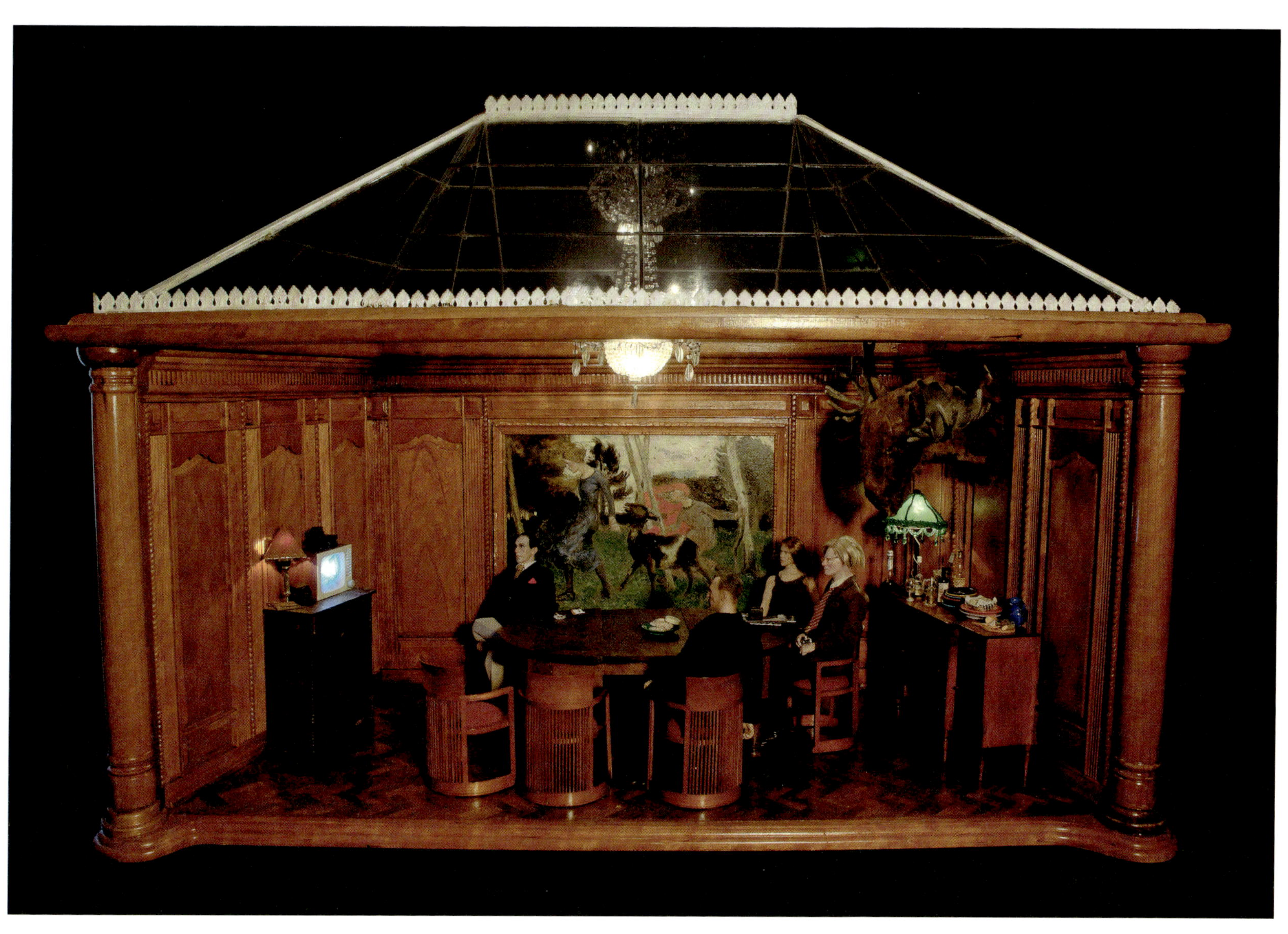

29. *Factory Dining Room*, 2013. Oil and combined media, assemblage, 109.2 x 78.7 x 55.9 cm (43 x 31 x 22 in.)

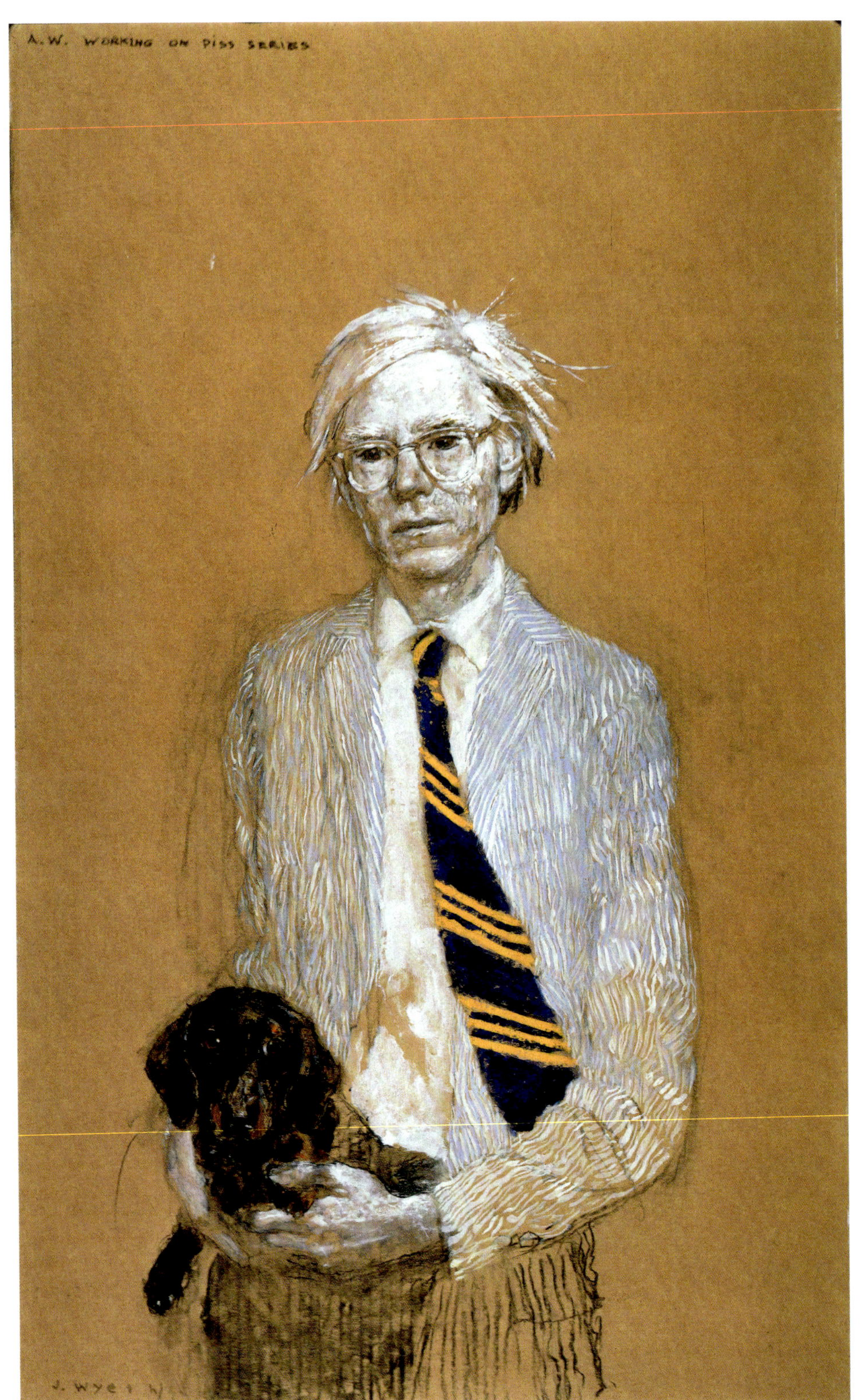

30. *A.W. Working on Piss Series*, 2007. Acrylic, oil, and watercolor on cardboard, 121.9 x 76.2 cm (48 x 30 in.)

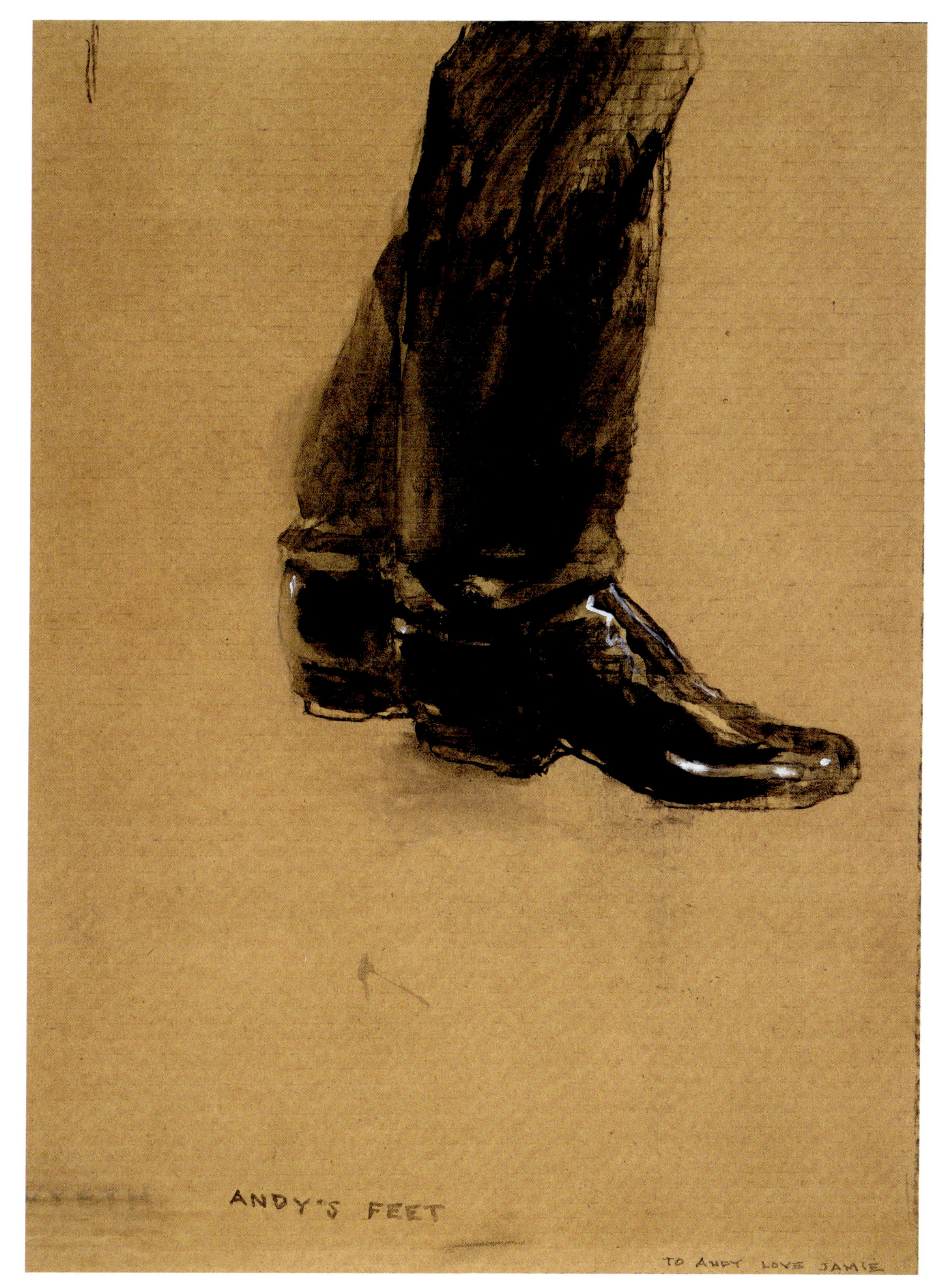

31. *Andy's Feet*, 1976. Charcoal, gouache, and watercolor on brown cardboard, 66 x 48.3 cm (26 x 19 in.)

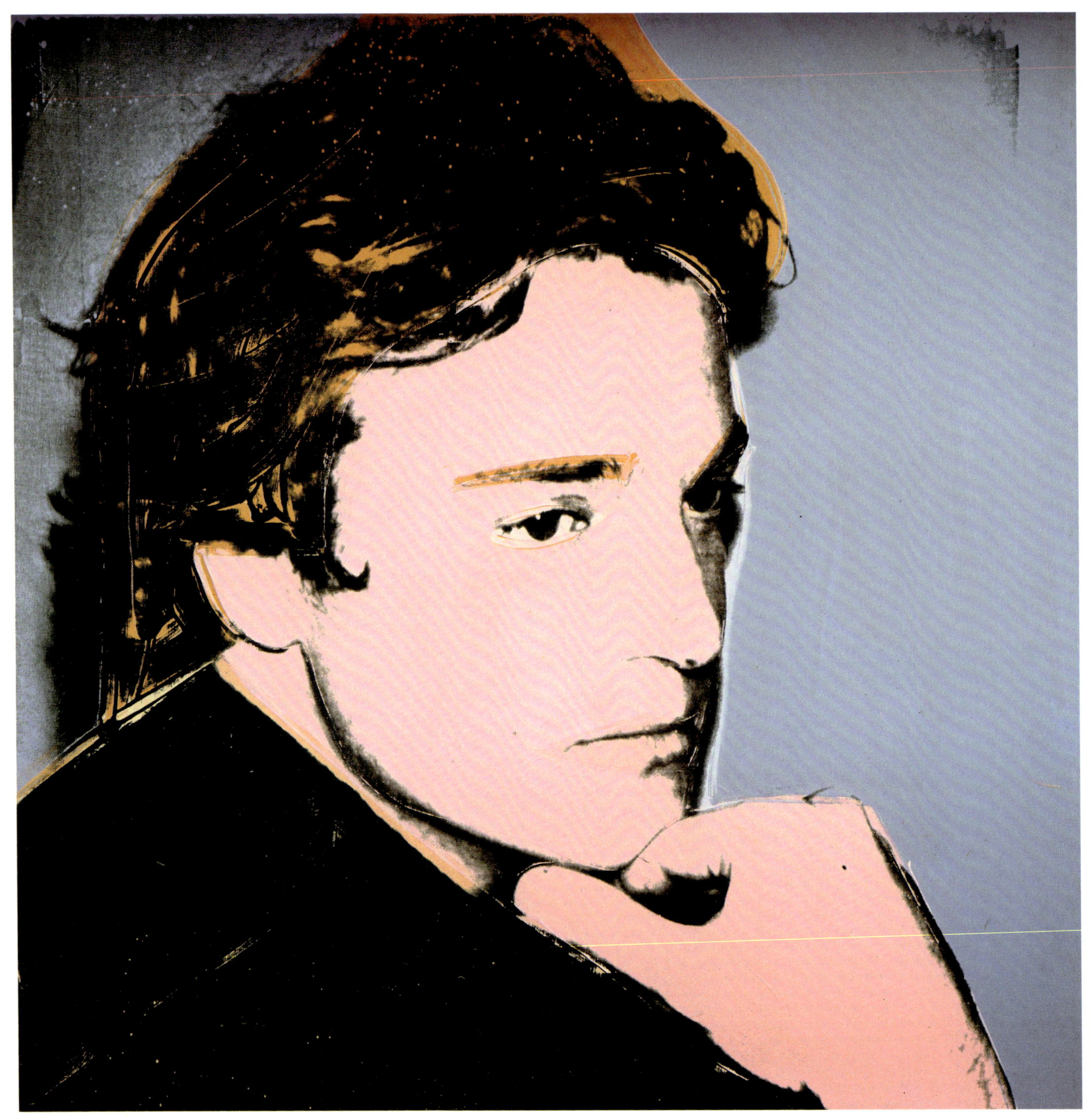

32. Andy Warhol (1928–1987), *Jamie Wyeth*, 1976. Oil on canvas, 101.6 x 101.6 cm (40 x 40 in.)

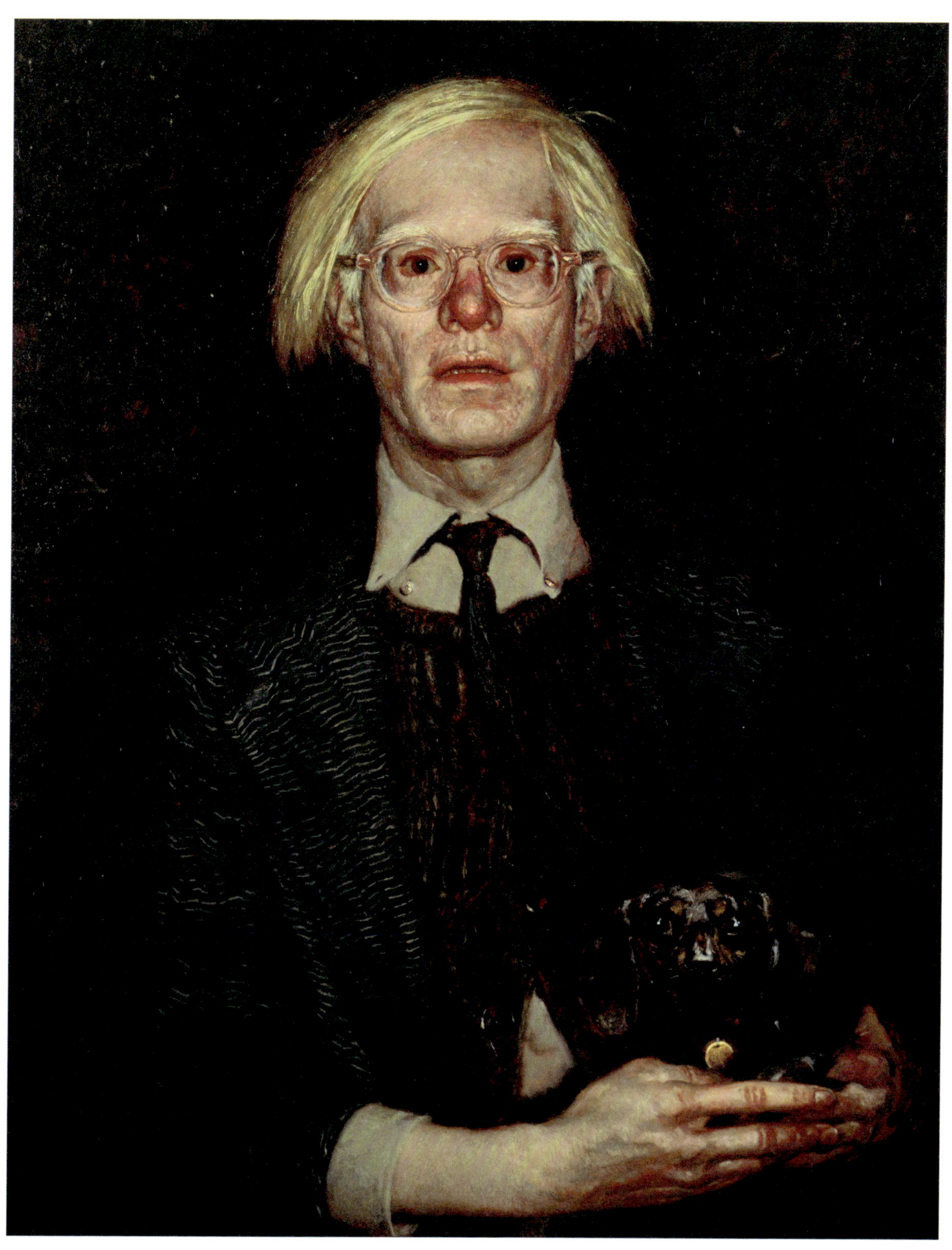

33. *Portrait of Andy Warhol*, 1976. Oil on gessoed panel, 76.2 x 61 cm (30 x 24 in.)

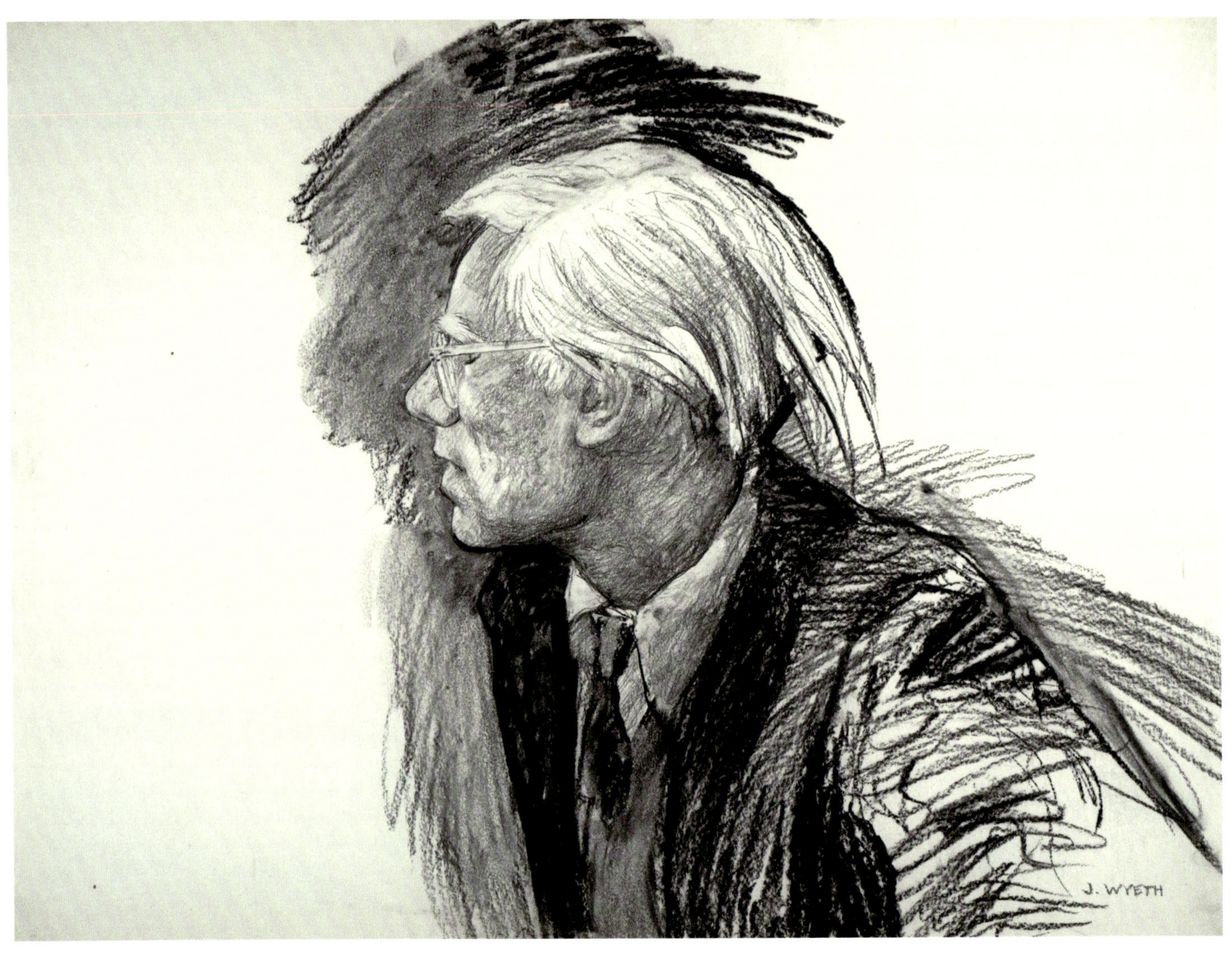

34. *Andy Warhol—Facing His Right (Study #15)*, 1976. Graphite on paper, 55.9 x 76.2 cm (22 x 30 in.)

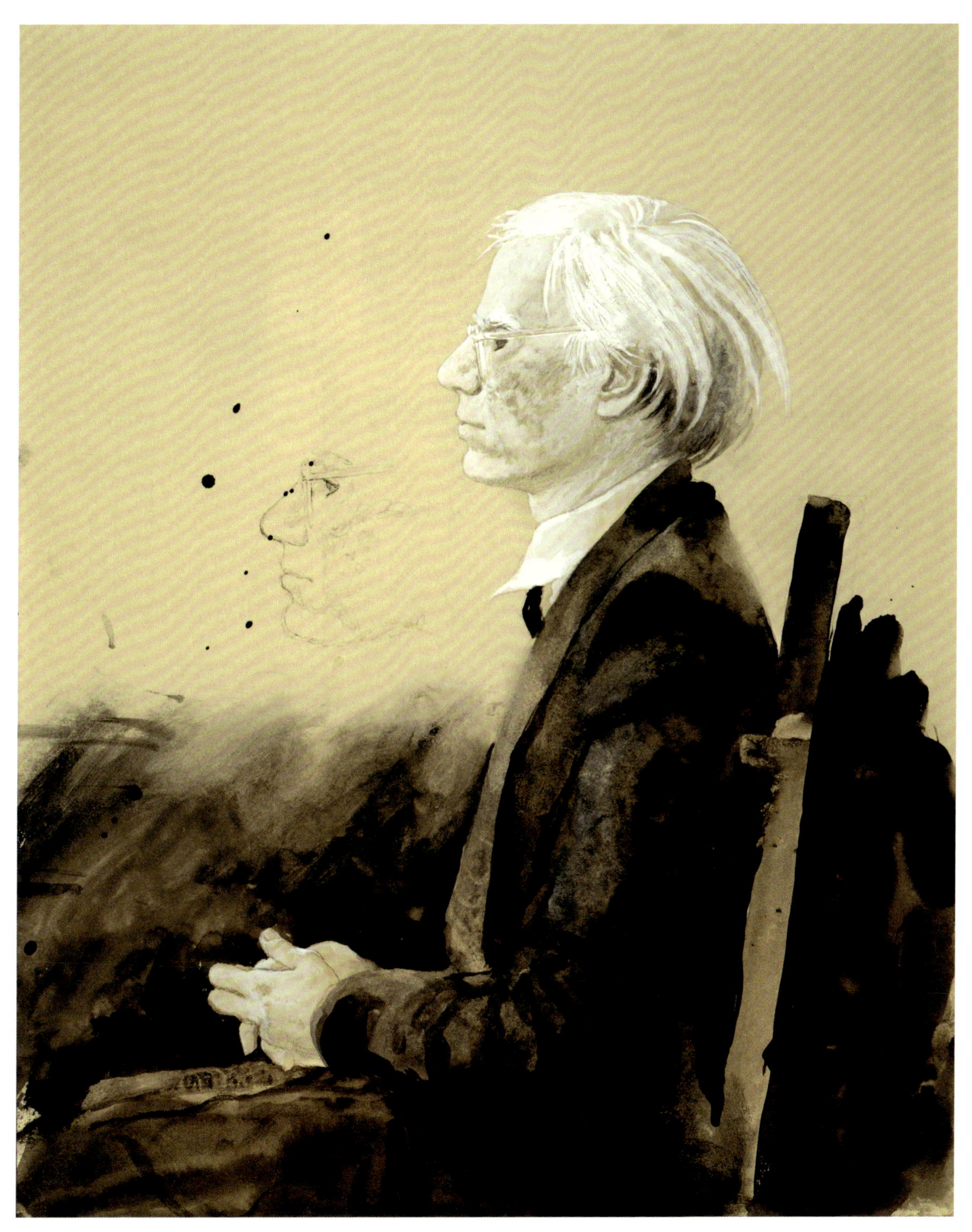

35. *Andy Warhol—Facing Left (Study #2)*, 1976. Graphite, India ink, and opaque white watercolor on board, 40.6 x 33.7 cm (16 x 13¼ in.)

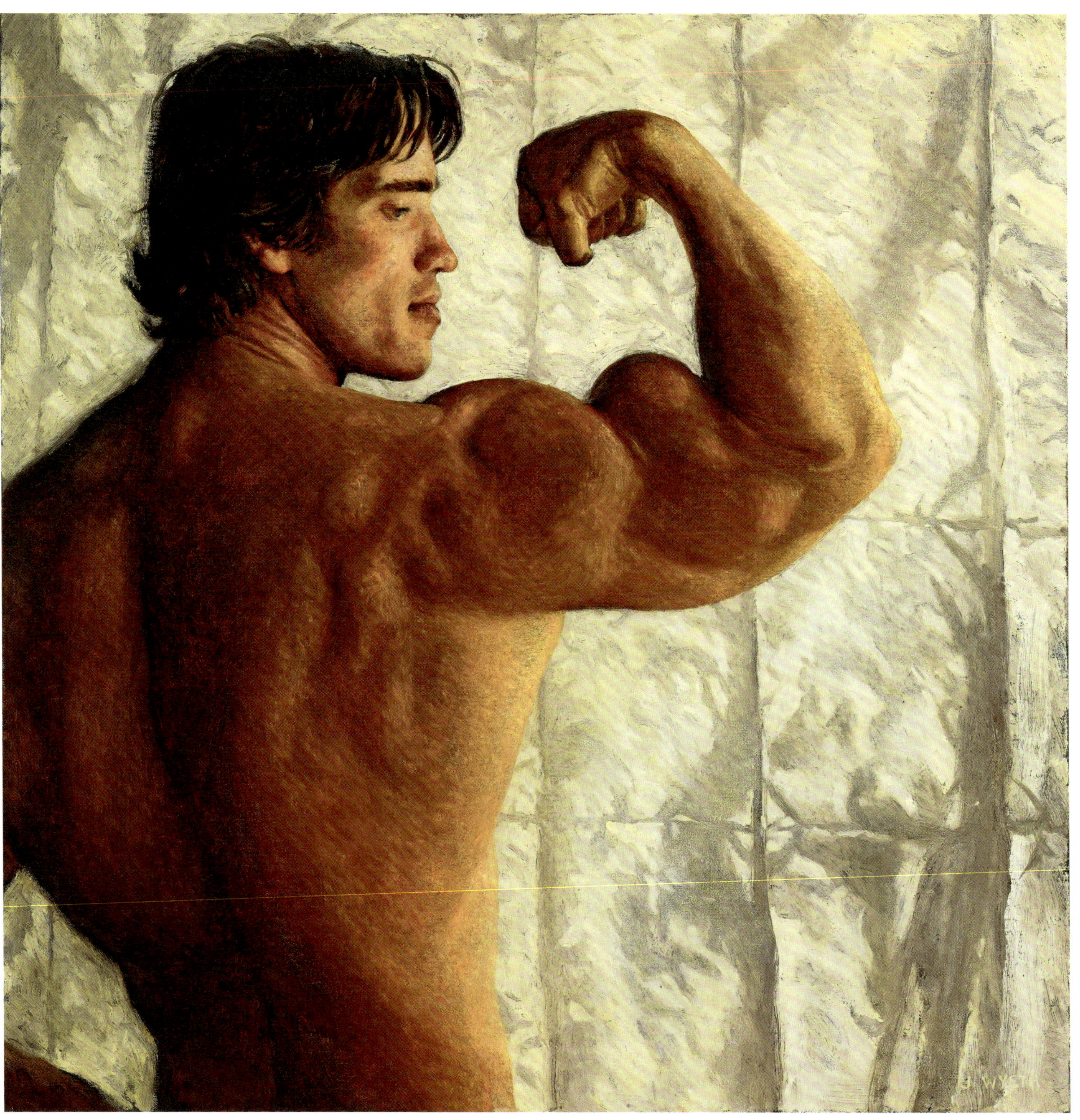

36. *Portrait of Arnold Schwarzenegger*, 1977. Oil on canvas, 83.8 x 83.8 cm (33 x 33 in.)

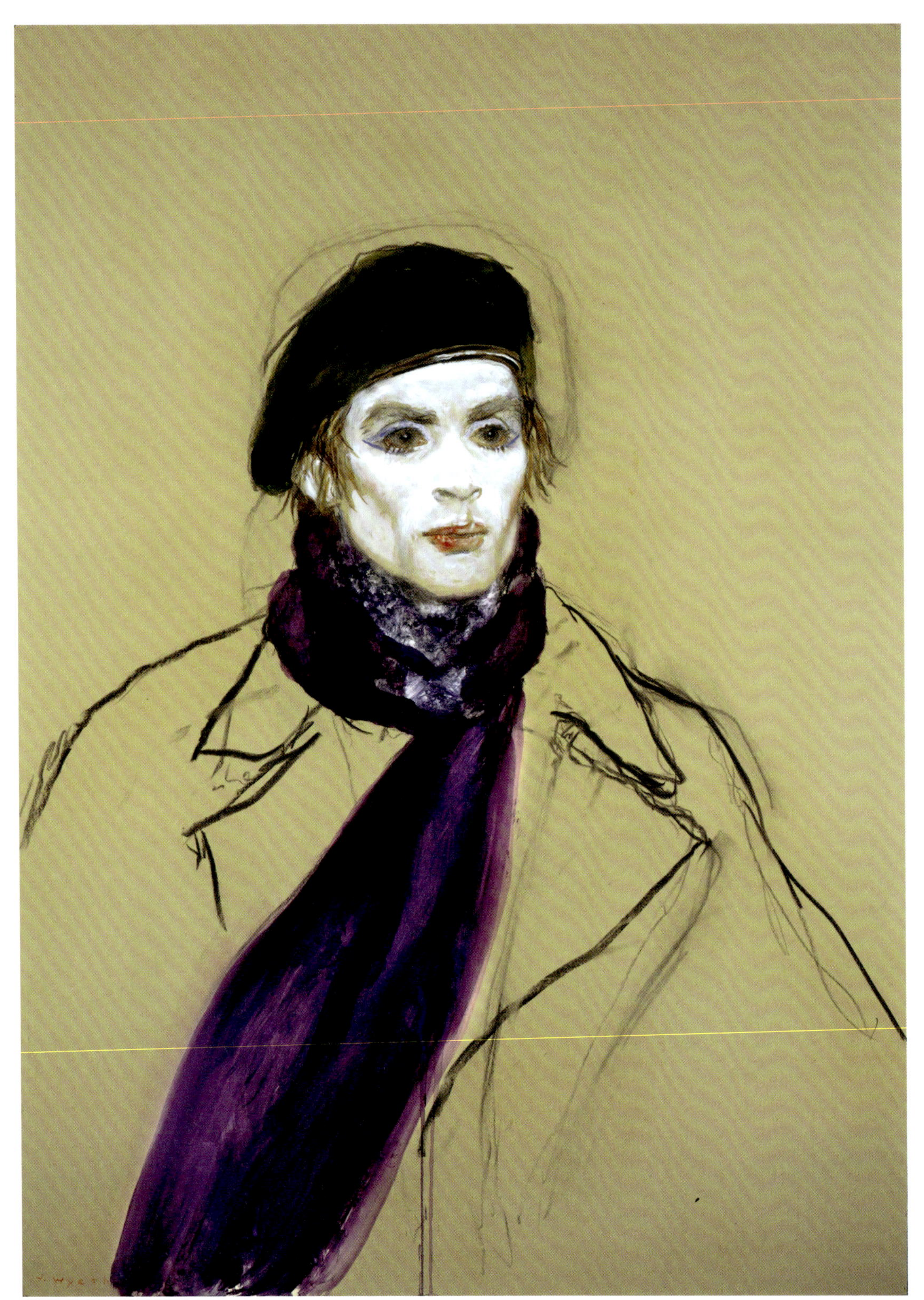

37. *Nureyev—Purple Scarf*, 2001. Graphite, gouache, and watercolor on toned rag board, 90.2 x 64.8 cm (35½ x 25½ in.)

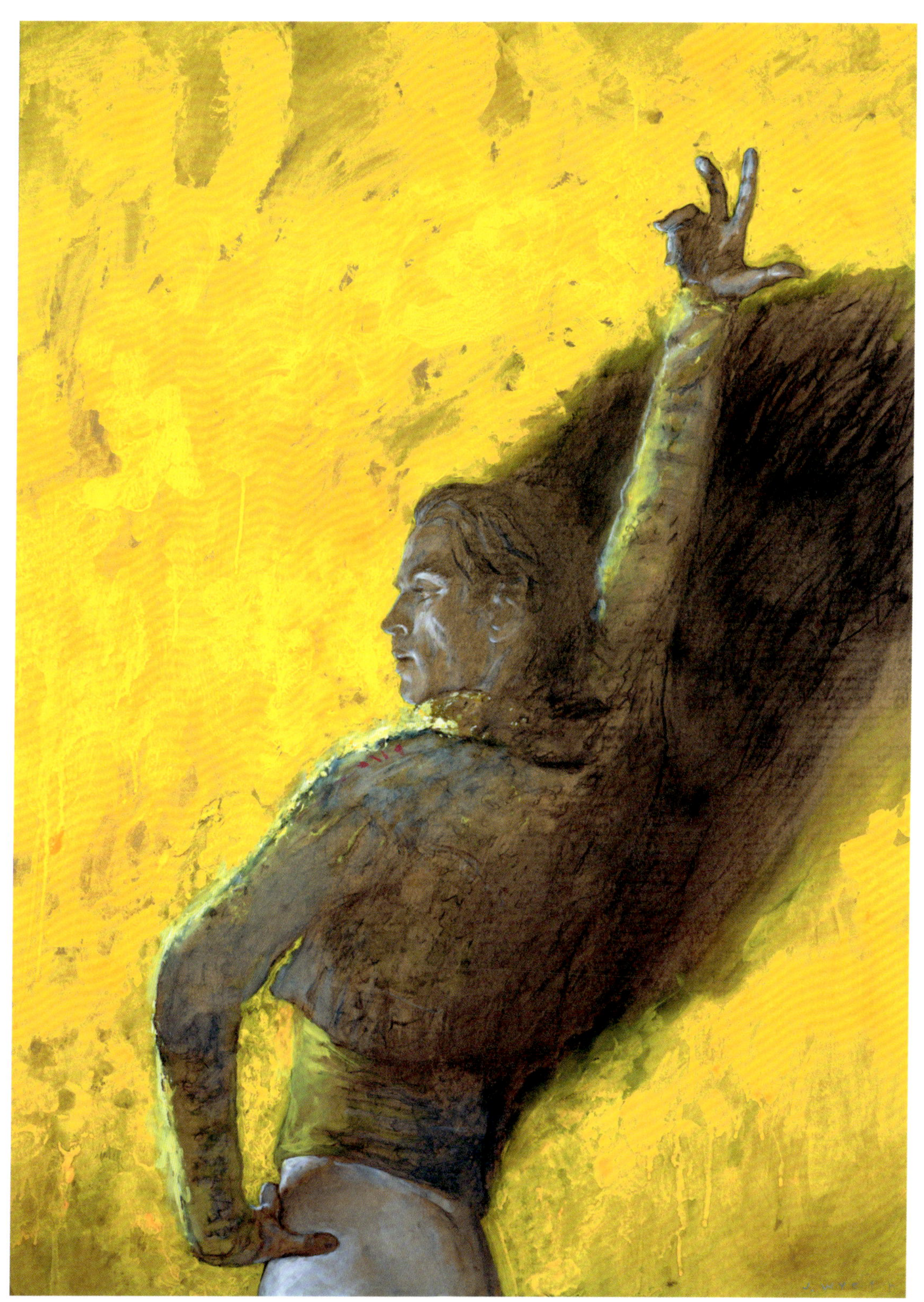

38. *Nureyev—Don Quixote—Yellow Background,* 2001. Graphite, gouache, and watercolor on cardboard, 121.3 x 91.4 cm (47¾ x 36 in.)

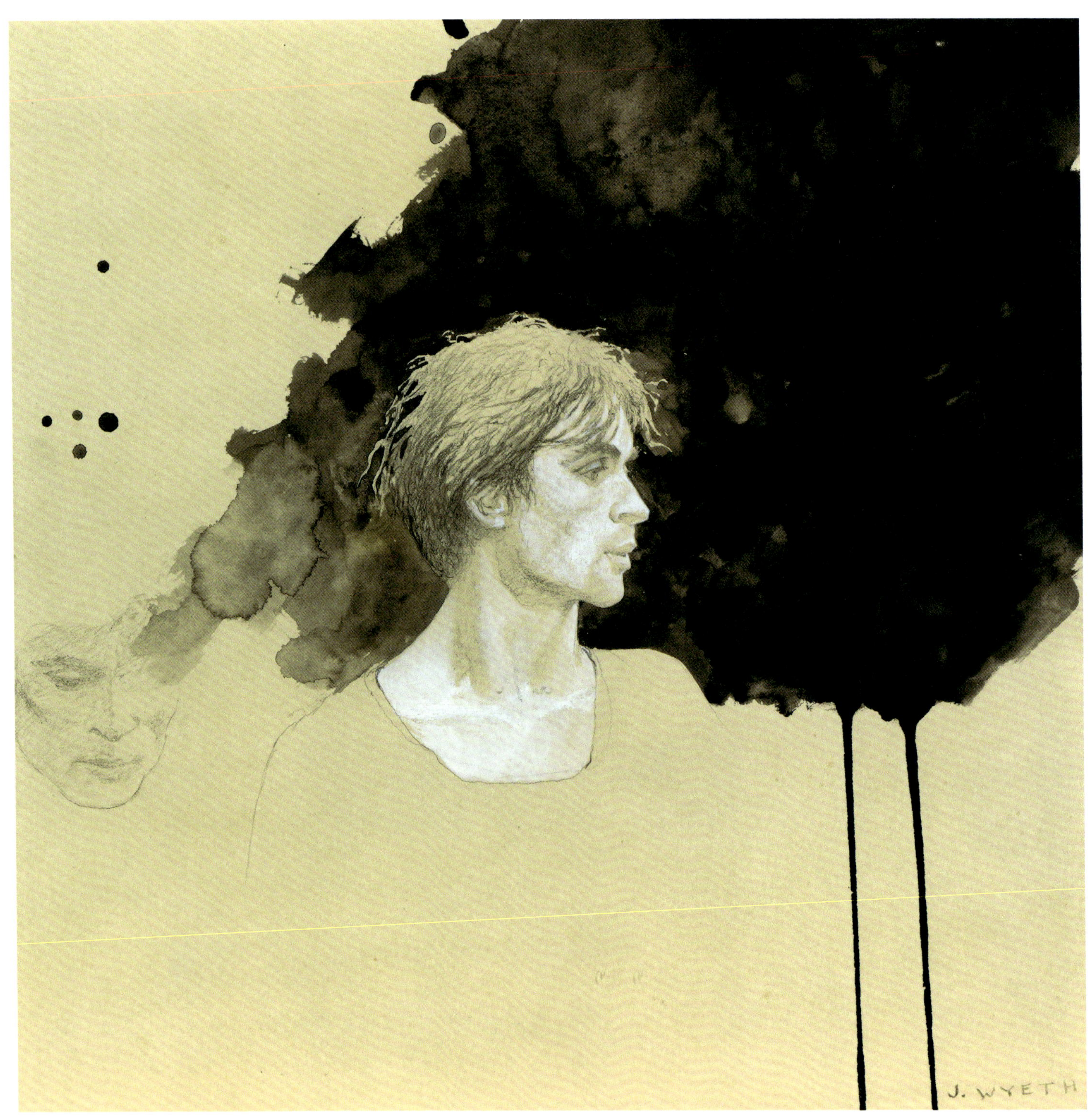

39. *Profile with Black Wash Background, Head, Nureyev (Study #23)*, 1977. Graphite, gouache, and watercolor on toned rag board, 52.7 x 54 cm (20¾ x 21¼ in.)

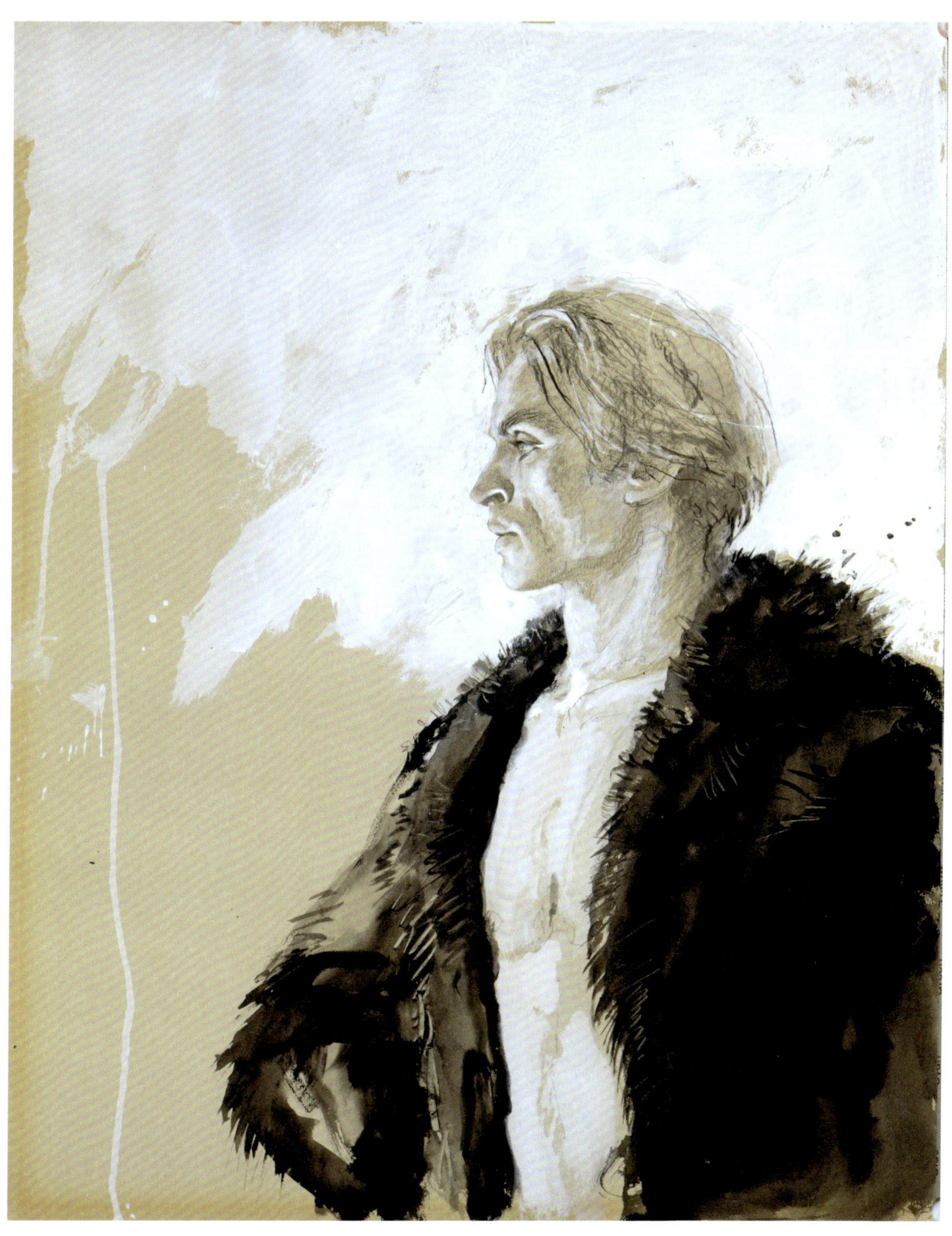

40. *Profile, in Fur, Nureyev (Study #9)*, 1977. Graphite, gouache, and watercolor on toned rag board, 50.8 x 40.6 cm (20 x 16 in.)

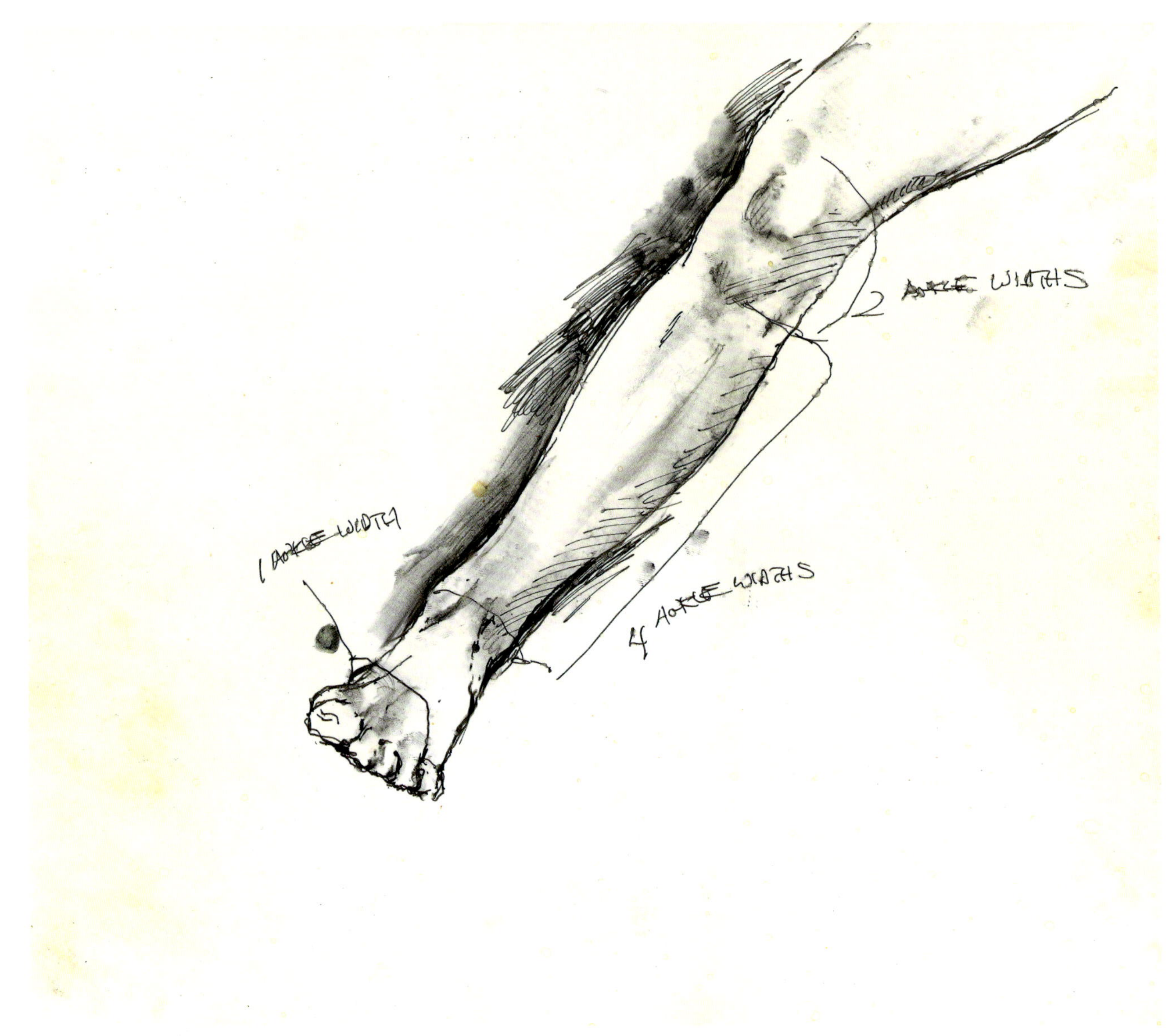

41. *Nureyev Sketchbook, Image N-31b*, 1977. Pen and ink on paper, 27.9 x 35.6 cm (11 x 14 in.)

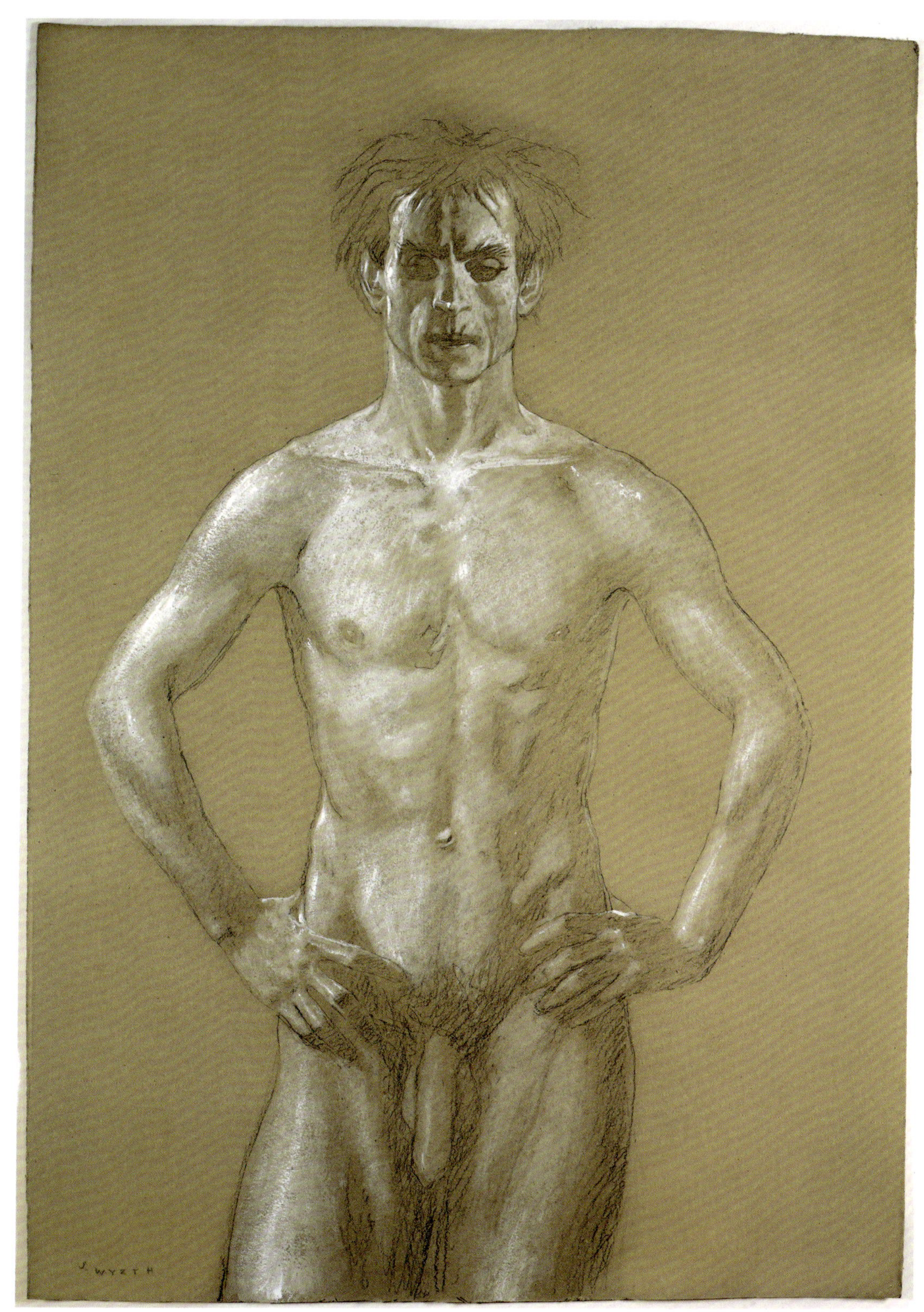

42. *Nude Three-Quarter Figure, Nureyev (Study #18)*, 1977 (finished in 1993). Graphite, charcoal, watercolor, and gouache on toned rag paper, 121.9 x 87.6 cm (48 x 34½ in.)

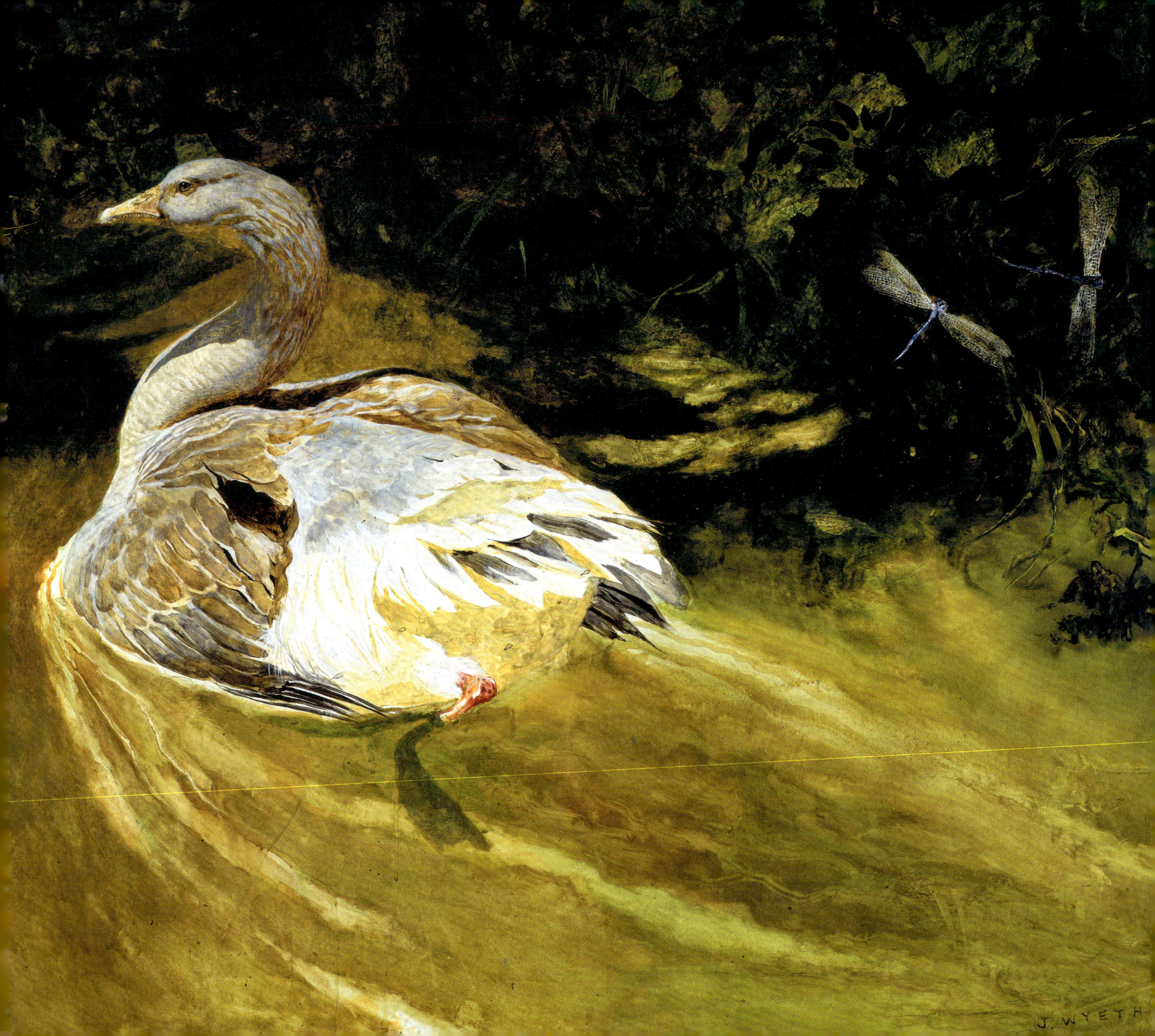
J. WYETH

Brandywine

At the time of the Warhol-Wyeth portrait exchange, Wyeth observed that, to him, Warhol was the epitome of New York City.[1] To absorb and assimilate all the heady experiences of Warhol's Factory, as well as the glittering realms of Kirstein's and Nureyev's circles, Wyeth often retreated to and recharged at his farm near Wilmington, Delaware, close by his childhood home in Chadds Ford, Pennsylvania, both nestled in the valley surrounding the Brandywine River. His first studio space was a far cry from the goings-on at the Factory. Instead of being surrounded by celebrities, socialites, drag queens, and round-the-clock parties, Wyeth painted his early portraits—*Portrait of Shorty*, *Draft Age*, and *Portrait of John F. Kennedy*—within a narrow sliver of the generous anteroom outside his father's studio at the Wyeths' first home. He claims he was absorbed in his own world there, while his famous father was often at work on the other side of the door, accompanied by loud strains of Sibelius. It is no wonder that Jamie Wyeth expressed ambivalence toward his identity in his early *Self-Portrait* (see cat. 21), as well as in *Pumpkinhead—Self-Portrait*, painted after he had established his own studio at Point Lookout Farm.

In *Pumpkinhead—Self-Portrait*, he poses himself just off-center in a flat, tree-lined field strewn with autumn foliage. The artist stands costumed in a black jacket that is clearly too small for him, as his bare wrists extend awkwardly below his cuffs. Hands at his sides, he gives the impression of posing dutifully, if somewhat shyly and self-consciously, as a young child would for yet another family photograph. That he has cut off his feet at the bottom edge further enhances the impression of an amateur photographer snapping away at a reluctant subject. Rather than painting his own head, he has made the surreal substitution of a carved jack-o'-lantern, which nearly fills the distance between his broad shoulders. The slanted eyes and jagged mouth both grin and leer at us, with an expression that hovers between playful and off-putting. It is a strange image, recalling the Headless Horseman from Washington Irving's tales, or the freakishly realist portrait photographs of Diane Arbus, whom Wyeth noted as an inspiration for the composition.[2] With his feet and head hidden from view, Wyeth suspends himself somewhere in front of and yet not firmly planted within the Brandywine landscape, and he effectively sets himself apart as "other" by obscuring his identity with a jack-o'-lantern. And yet, given the long-standing Wyeth family tradition of donning costumes, especially at Halloween, his self-portrait as Pumpkinhead situates him squarely within the realm of both amusing and terrifying others from behind masks.[3]

More than a decade earlier, the thirteen-year-old Wyeth climbed to the top of a tower high above his parents' second Chadds Ford home to paint a scene of a weathervane extending above the spidery winter tree line (cat. 45).[4] The young artist focuses our attention on specific details of the vane, highlighting the directional with a capital N indicating true north. In case we missed it, he calls further attention with the abstract shape of the feather quill just above the N. And, oddly positioned above and off to the upper right corner, the finial flourish of the vane takes the shape of a star. Even this early, Wyeth seems to assert that he will follow his own true north with the guiding star of

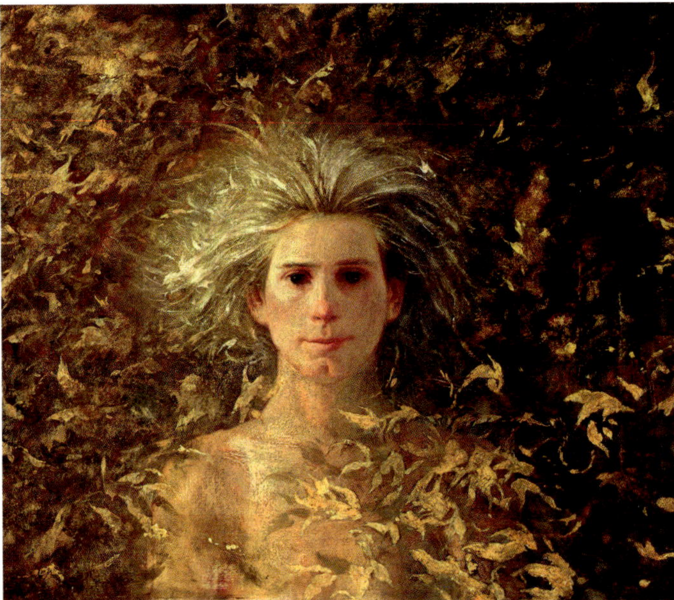

Fig. 16. *Phyllis Mills*, 1967
Oil on canvas
50.8 x 61 cm (20 x 24 in.)

his own vision. An impressive rendition of "Look, Ma (and Pa), no hands," the composition astounded his parents, who could not figure out how he was able to capture the scene.

In another early painting of Chadds Ford, *Lime Bag*, Wyeth explores one of the cozy, enclosed interiors that would characterize many of his Brandywine compositions. There, within the rich, chocolaty browns of a barn, a bag of white lime has been ripped open, spilling its brilliant contents onto the floor.[5] The deep stone window recesses recall the many images of the nearby Kuerner farm painted by Andrew Wyeth, and yet the animation of the crumpled brown paper bag injects Jamie Wyeth's personality into the barn scape. Lime is frequently used to improve the quality of the soil and for mixing up the lime-based paint most commonly known as whitewash. Within the context of Andrew Wyeth's famously pristine interiors painted at the Kuerners', a bag of lime illuminating a darkened interior signals that Jamie Wyeth is heading in his own direction, one that paints the essence of the lime in its basic form—before it has been transformed into the gleaming surfaces of his father's paintings.

The surrounding landscapes of Chadds Ford and the Brandywine River Valley are a gift to any artist: gentle hillsides and fields of rich, tilled soil, snaking stone walls, trees affording majestic canopies, paddock fences that stretch over hill and dale like unending musical staffs for a chorus of birdsongs, all wrapped up by a sparkling ribbon of river. The region historically supported agriculture, mills, and the manufacture of gunpowder, and it is home today to those drawn to the elegant country lifestyle established by the du Pont family and its many descendants. The Wyeths are based at Point Lookout Farm, home to a host of horses, domesticated farm animals, and family pets—many of whom have taken star turns in Jamie Wyeth's paintings over the years.

Phyllis Mills, a descendant of the du Ponts, became Wyeth's dominant female muse beginning in the late 1960s; they married in 1968. His first impression of Phyllis is of a woman surrounded by nature, as rendered in various iterations of *Phyllis Mills* (fig. 16). The initial series of drawings depicts her face and later extends to her bare torso, discreetly cut off at her breasts, and interlaces her flowing locks of hair with leaves and more abstracted foliage that recall the classical myth of Daphne, turned into a tree as she fled the god Apollo. This may also be a poignant reference to the devastating automobile accident Phyllis had suffered at the age of twenty-one, in which she broke her neck and was left unable to walk without crutches; she later acquired a motorized scooter that enabled her to dart about the farm, at times accompanied by her cigar and favorite dog, while frugally swiping holly for her holiday decorations (cat. 48). Early sketches for *Phyllis Mills* may also have been inspired by Sandro Botticelli's *La Primavera*, a painting that Wyeth himself greatly admired.[6] A detail of the figure of Flora, her head and neck adorned with flowers and leaves, appeared in the form of a poster that hung prominently in the Andrew Wyeth home, which also served as Jamie Wyeth's studio when he was painting this work.

Following those initial sketches and painting, Jamie Wyeth's first finished portrait of Phyllis Wyeth, *And Then Into the Deep Gorge*, casts her as the determined protagonist in a dramatic driving scene set deep in the woods. Phyllis Wyeth had been a champion equestrian, and after her accident she took up carriage driving as a way of combining her passion for horses with a practical means of getting out and about Wilmington. In 1975, when Jamie Wyeth embarked on this scene of his wife driving, the sport was virtually unknown in the United States beyond the Brandywine River Valley and a few other communities that could support it. In earlier centuries, when carriages were a common mode of transportation, the subject of coaching captured the imagination of artists and challenged them by requiring a sophisticated understanding of anatomy, both human and equine, as well as of how those forms are rendered in motion.

Wyeth created three scenes of Phyllis Wyeth driving her teams of Connemara ponies and later her horses. *And Then Into the Deep Gorge* submerges her within an overgrown landscape, creating an ominous mood that suggests a mysterious tale unfolding before our eyes. When asked about this composition, Phyllis Wyeth replied that she never liked how her husband had painted her blouse wide open in the front and recalled that, at the time, she was intently focused on practicing driving over the most challenging features of the terrain to improve her timing for pony-cart competitions.[7] Jamie Wyeth noted that the ponies she raised and trained at Point Lookout Farm effectively became her legs. The awkward foreshortening that obscures the front half of the carriage may be his way of reimagining Phyllis Wyeth as one of the mythical female centaurs perhaps best known for frolicking in Walt Disney's movie *Fantasia*.[8] The deep woods setting, combined with the steep incline that she is intently traversing and the fairy-tale title, suggests imminent danger. According to Jamie Wyeth, though, the gorge opened up onto an expanse of bluebells that grew deep in the woods, and thus Phyllis Wyeth, intent on training for competition, is also on a direct course to reach a hidden place of great natural beauty.

Driving a cart or coach with multiple ponies or horses at top speed may appear easy, but since the vehicles are easily toppled, it is inherently risky, especially for someone with paralyzed legs. Yet in *And Then Into the Deep Gorge* Phyllis Wyeth appears vital, physical, sensual, and determined to pursue her own course through the landscape. Her contrast with the disfigured body reclining on the hillside of Andrew Wyeth's *Christina's World* is striking.[9] Early in their courtship, Phyllis Wyeth recalled, Jamie had taken her to see Christina Olson at the Olson farm in Maine and had pointed out the pile of newspapers that Christina used to relieve herself in a corner of the house.[10] Phyllis's response was that she intended to live life independently, and, as the driving paintings depict, she has gone on to demand a great deal of herself physically and mentally while pursuing her own path.

Jamie Wyeth subsequently immersed himself in the physical challenges of driving by riding in the pony cart behind Phyllis, an experience he renders in *Connemara*. Just as he had earlier plunged into the worlds of John F. Kennedy and Rudolf Nureyev, Wyeth attempted to get as close as possible to becoming the driver himself, an approach that was common to many American artists seeking verisimilitude, including Winslow Homer and Newell Convers Wyeth.[11] Wyeth undoubtedly knew Mary Cassatt's painting *A Woman and a Girl Driving*, in which the central figure appears in pink, just as Phyllis and Christina Olson did (fig. 17). And yet, Cassatt's image is far more introspective, juxtaposing girlhood and womanhood. Jamie Wyeth renders the fabric rippling across Phyllis's fitted jacket in a way that Cassatt does in various paintings such as *Tea* (1879, Museum of Fine Arts, Boston), a detail she depicts to convey a sense of active, independent American women seen from a distance. But Wyeth contrasts Phyllis's coat, seen from behind as it stretches tautly across her ramrod-straight back, with the spiky fur of the Jack Russell terrier seated beside her, leaning into the turn. Taken together, the scene thrusts the viewer into the experience of hurtling through space in a rapidly moving pony cart, traversing the winding carriage trails of Brandywine.

In the last and largest of Wyeth's scenes of his wife driving, *Connemara Four*, she appears in the upper right corner, farthest removed from the central focus of the composition. Dressed somberly in brown tweed, she sits atop a massive coach at the reins of a team of horses that require great skill to manage, as indicated by the two liveried grooms seen from the back, one wearing a pigtail, the other bending over behind and mostly obscured by the first. This monumental composition, inspired by the spectacle of a modern-day carriage competition that the Wyeths attended in Newport, Rhode Island, responds primarily to the external trappings of the sport, which requires great fortitude on the part of the driver. The horses appear eager and alert, and the artist sensitively distinguishes their varied temperaments. Against these expressive equine faces that peer out from between their blinders, Phyllis Wyeth appears distant and wistful.[12]

Connemara Four shares some affinity in scale and ambition with Thomas Eakins's *A May Morning in the Park (The Fairman Rogers Four-in-Hand)* (1879–1880, Philadelphia Museum of Art), a major composition that was inspired by Eakins's exhaustive study of trotting horses in motion as documented by Eadweard Muybridge's stop-action photography.[13] Yet Eakins's resulting composition is distinctly static, and, of Wyeth's three coaching images, *Connemara Four* is the only one in which he portrays the carriage at rest. He may have understood intuitively that Phyllis's days of active carriage driving were waning.[14]

In one of Wyeth's most striking figural compositions painted in Wilmington, *Twins*, the artist poses his young models on two similar, although distinctly different early American ladder-back chairs that are closely associated with the cache of important American furniture assembled at the Winterthur Museum and in other collections in the area. The artist recalled meeting the identical twins in a local market in Chadds Ford, drawn to their contrasting appearances, "one with wild flowing hair and the other with corn rows in her hair."[15] Wyeth's composition invites us to scan back and forth, comparing the different personalities of the two girls, who wear identical frothy, white lace dresses. The girl at the left appears wide-eyed, intently focused on an image we cannot see; her sister, at the right, appears more withdrawn, self-contained, nuanced. He also contrasts the height of the chairs, the shapes of the finials atop them, and the varying curves of the splats that resemble enormous thrones. The ribbons of the wood splats effectively create rippled white banners that undulate over the girls' heads, evoking a call-and-response of negative space created by the white surface of the paper and the positive space defined by the resonant browns of the wood. Wyeth pairs these two sets of twins, one human, one handmade, to explore the realms of the real and the ideal, creating an intriguing image that shows the artist multiplying his form of realism by a power of two.

Mirror imaging also appears in depicted reflections in water that inspire contemplation and encourage intense looking. *Brandywine Spiders* portrays a profusion of roots lining the clear water of the river. The spiders, exposed tree roots and branches stripped bare in their winter guise, are arranged in four clusters, above and below the waterline, a richly intertwined composition of theme and variations that suggests the abstract forms of musical fugues or inventions of point and counterpoint. *Dragonflies* takes us right onto the surface of the river and, like Winslow Homer's *The Mink Pond* (1891, Harvard Art Museums/Fogg Museum), explores the dynamic interplay of reflections above and below the water. The glinting light on the surface of the water flickers off wings, whether tiny and gossamer of the insect variety or the plush, soft feathers of the local waterfowl. Reflections of a dismembered flag appear in *Patriot's Barn*, an image that evokes the nation's loss and disillusionment following the events of September 11, 2001. Here Wyeth sets off the still water that pools

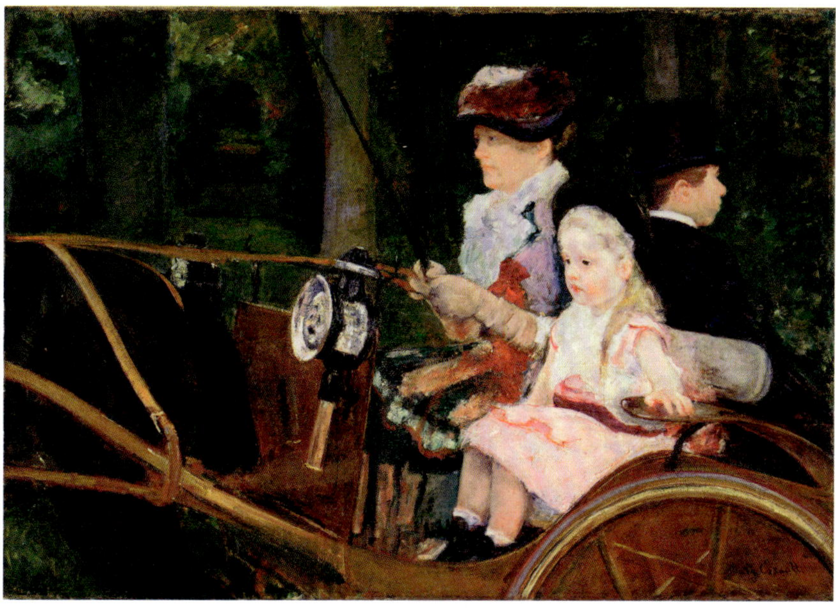

Fig. 17. Mary Stevenson Cassatt
(1844–1926)
A Woman and a Girl Driving, 1881
Oil on canvas
89.7 x 130.5 cm (35 5/16 x 51 3/8 in.)

in the foreground with a dark stretch of hillside. The reflection of the flag in the water is cut off at the bottom edge by a narrow, dark band that resembles a black mourning ribbon traditionally worn to signify the loss of a family member. Several of the reflected flag's stars and stripes are obscured by the encroaching landscape, preventing it from unfurling its full glory as a vivid symbol of our nation's freedoms.

Within the realms of Point Lookout Farm, the parade of animals Wyeth portrays at his home, studio, and barns, like those described in a favorite childhood storybook, *The Wind in the Willows*, have distinct personalities and do all but talk. Wyeth finds beauty in the smallest creatures, such as the purple martin in *Dragonfly*. The surface of the elegant dragonfly wings held gingerly in the martin's beak appears fragile and iridescent yet as durable as an eggshell with its jewellike appearance of enamel on copper, an effect achieved by mixing essence of pearl into the pigment.

While *Dragonfly* focuses our attention on a single martin's gesture of delicately holding onto an insect before devouring it, *Birds' House* presents a flock of seemingly sophisticated martins that are eagerly seeking plush accommodations in an elegant high-rise decorated like an imaginary castle with dentil moldings, gables, and turrets all outlined in cherry red. Den-den, the massive sow depicted nearly life-size in *Portrait of Pig* (see fig. 7), forged such a close relationship with the artist that she would pose quite happily for him if he played music for her, and we frequently find Wyeth drawing or painting his pet pigs with gusto. In an illustration for the children's book *The Stray*, Wyeth's pigs live it up over a jolly round of beers, exuding a devil-may-care swagger, as large hams curing on meat hooks hang ominously overhead (cat. 57). Wyeth's golden Labrador retriever, Kleberg, is the star of a charming portrait also set inside one of the Point Lookout Farm buildings, posed in front of a shelf on which the artist has lined up his most important and inspirational books (cat. 65).[16] Kleberg sits next to a massive woven beehive, these two mounds, one animal, one straw, a striking comparison of animate and inanimate forms. For his portrait Kleberg dutifully allowed Wyeth to paint a black circle around his eye so that he would resemble the mascot from *The Little Rascals* movies: the artist's dog literally becomes the artist's canvas, as well as the subject reimagined on the artist's canvas.

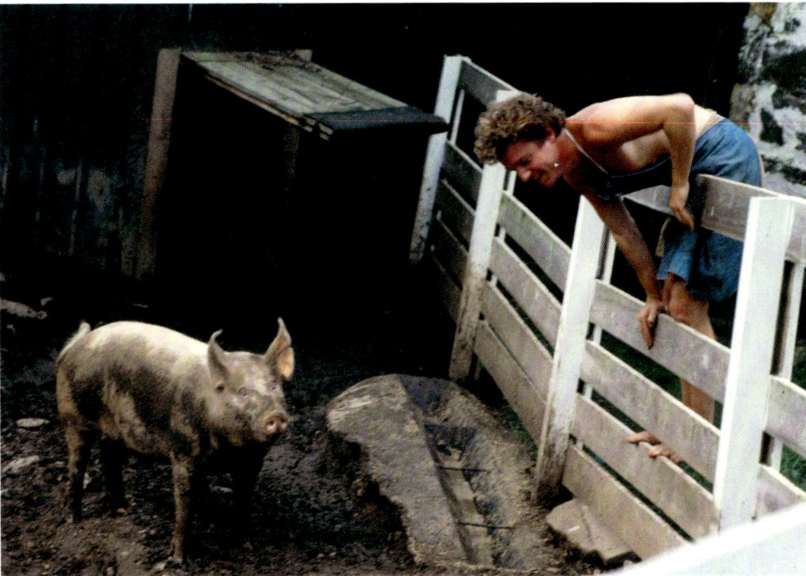

Fig. 18. Henrietta Alexander (born in 1958)
Jamie and His Pig, Frank Fowler, 1981.
Color photograph
20.3 x 25.4 cm (8 x 10 in.)

Diminutive Christmas cards portray another side of Wyeth's personality and a dog's life on the farm. In two intimate scenes of Phyllis asleep in bed, one favorite dog reveals a Jekyll-and-Hyde personality. In one scene, Ziggy's swelling stomach, hindquarters, and paws, gently curving against the pillow and Phyllis's head, nestle around her in a comforting, protective pose (cat. 59). In *Christmas Morning 2006*, her furry friend has been transformed into a furry fiend, snarling at the three adorable puppies that dare, bright and early, to peek their eager, elvish faces up over the edge of the bed.

In more recent years, the birds and beasts of Point Lookout Farm have been captured with brilliantly oscillating Day-Glo colors in compositions such as *Barn Owls, Immature* and *Goat Tree*. The acidic, tooth-grinding palettes of these more recent works initially put us on edge, yet they ultimately invigorate the canvases with the sense that Point Lookout Farm is teeming with new life and the brilliant greens and yellows of springtime. The baby owls pose sweetly as they hide themselves behind a beam to avoid becoming a delicacy for a bird of prey, so they can grow up to indulge their own appetites with passing pigeons. In a scene of barnyard humor, goats with guilty expressions—whether emerging from an amorous adventure or just nibbling at spring shoots—comically poke their heads out from behind a large tree.[17]

Wyeth's portrayal of the laying hens and roosters of Point Lookout Farm nesting and strutting before an array of packing boxes in *10 W 30* and *Cornflakes* may be an ironic response to Andy Warhol's silkscreened grocery boxes.[18] Wyeth is certainly game to spar with the Pop Art concept of a simple, printed carton that appears roughed-up on the outside and the pristine white box of Leo Castelli's New York gallery, where he first saw Warhol's Brillo boxes on display. In *Cornflakes* a live rooster seemingly strides off the commercial packaging in all his cockscombed glory, bringing to life the popular brand symbol, which Wyeth has cleverly hidden by folding down the box top.

It is *Bale*, however, that magically brings together the artist's intense immersion in the natural world with the commercialism of Warhol's Pop Art. Wyeth remakes the bale of hay through the process of painting, grounding the concept of Pop Art in the abstract realm of American folk art by way of Warhol and their shared respect for the object presented without abstraction.

Warhol produced, with the help of his assistants, many silk-screened replicas of the Brillo and Campbell's Tomato Juice boxes; Wyeth, on his own terms, replicates again and again an intentional stacking up of paint strokes that are carefully ordered in such a way that they become the two-dimensional expression of a real bale of hay. For folk artists who are oblivious to academic conventions of rendering objects in perspective, the process of "making" an object from the mind's eye triumphs; as artists become more aware of conventions, they become more adept at "matching" an object's appearance.[19] The folk-art quality of *Bale* emerges early on in Wyeth's working process. One of the extant studies reveals that Wyeth initially worked on a wood support with very thin pigment, allowing the undulating patterns of the grain to show through beneath his strokes of paint, much as folk painters would have incorporated wood grain into the decorative surface of a piece of furniture or a painting. The finished version of *Bale* hovers somewhere between folk art, in terms of remaking the hay bale, and contemporary styles of Abstract Expressionism or op art, when the individual strokes of paint are viewed close up. Wyeth envisions the cut ends of the hollow grasses as tiny circular orbs of color—perhaps a riff on the Benday dots of commercial printing that appear in Roy Lichtenstein's Pop Art compositions. The artist noted that while he worked on the painting, he witnessed a solar eclipse that he hoped to capture, and, indeed, the outermost strands of hay seem to glisten magically. The repeated pattern of tiny bull's-eyes could also be seen as diminutive penumbras around the sun as painted by Rockwell Kent in scenes of Monhegan.[20] *Bale*, Wyeth believes, is perhaps the closest he has come to presenting an abstract form as a finished work, noting that the composition works just as well if seen upside down.[21]

A hay bale made of grass grown on Point Lookout Farm is about as elaborate a rectangular box as anyone could find to paint, and it is about as far away as one could possibly get from an ordinary cardboard box of Brillo that Warhol asked a studio assistant to run down to Gristede's market to buy.[22] Both Warhol and Wyeth were actively engaged in the intense practice of making their objects appear real through the process of replication, for Warhol in the technique of commercial silkscreen, and for Wyeth by meticulously rendering each strand of hay with a brush. Their mutual fascination with the role of the object in their art exudes a sense of sheer joy in making objects that was expressed by nineteenth-century American folk artists who worked in urban contexts, as well as rural and itinerant ones. It is not surprising that both Wyeth and Warhol found inspiration in their own collections of American folk art. Warhol collected carved cigar store Indians, as well as simple painted furniture and toys.[23] Wyeth himself owns an extensive and varied collection of handmade objects, including a carved eagle by Henry Bellamy (a gift from his mother, who had earlier acquired objects and archives from the Bellamy studio); many sailors' valentines (intricate shadow-box designs formed by small seashells), which he replicated in the form of frames for his works (see *Sea Star*, cat. 88); elaborately constructed birdhouses; furnishings; and even a floor painted by the nineteenth-century folk artist Rufus Porter.

Birds described in Pliny's ancient competition between the realist masters of painting Zeuxis and Parrhasius may not swoop down to perch on *Bale* (although they might be tempted), but Wyeth recounted a story of the remarkable verisimilitude of the painting when a farmer saw the canvas in his studio. After spending considerable time examining it, he turned back to Wyeth and said, "I see you've got a John Deere."[24] As Wyeth tells it, the farmer knew which model baler had been used to shape this particular bale of hay. Whether the story is based on actual fact or is just plain, pure malarkey from Wyeth country, the artist demonstrates a remarkable ability to spin the proverbial straw (or hay) into gold, even leaving behind a strand or two in the paint. *Bale*, while seemingly a simple, run-of-the mill rectangular solid that he could have drawn as an exercise under the watchful eye of his aunt Carolyn, is here transformed into a composition that is distinctly American. Wyeth takes as his point of departure the American folk artists who taught themselves to paint, often while eking out their living as farmers, and gives his humble subject a heightened sense of realism that American artists from colonial times to the present have explored in rendering the possibilities of "making" versus "matching" objects on canvas.

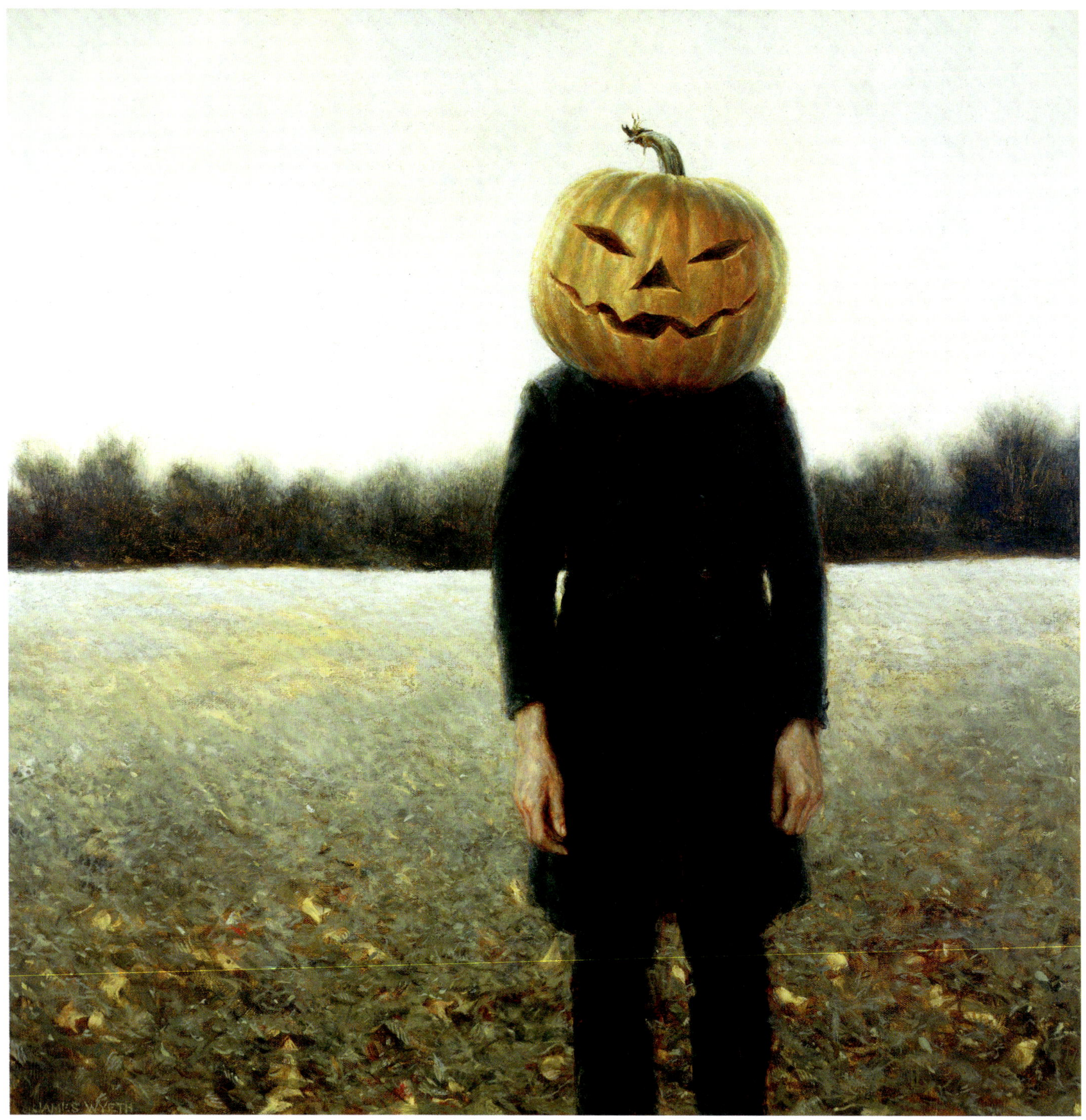

43. *Pumpkinhead—Self-Portrait*, 1972. Oil on canvas, 76.2 x 76.2 cm (30 x 30 in.)

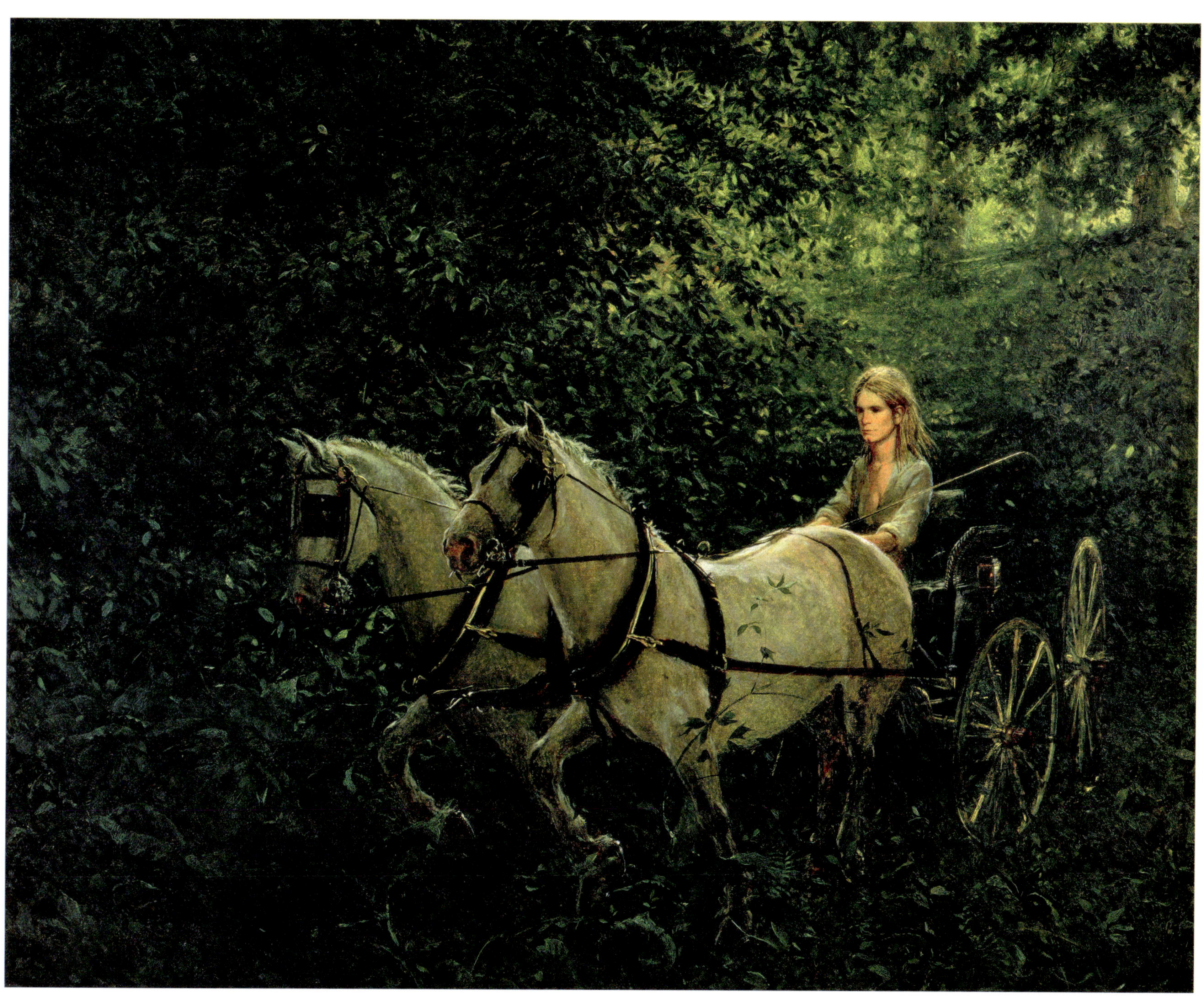

44. *And Then Into the Deep Gorge*, 1975. Oil on canvas, 91.4 x 116.8 cm (36 x 46 in.)

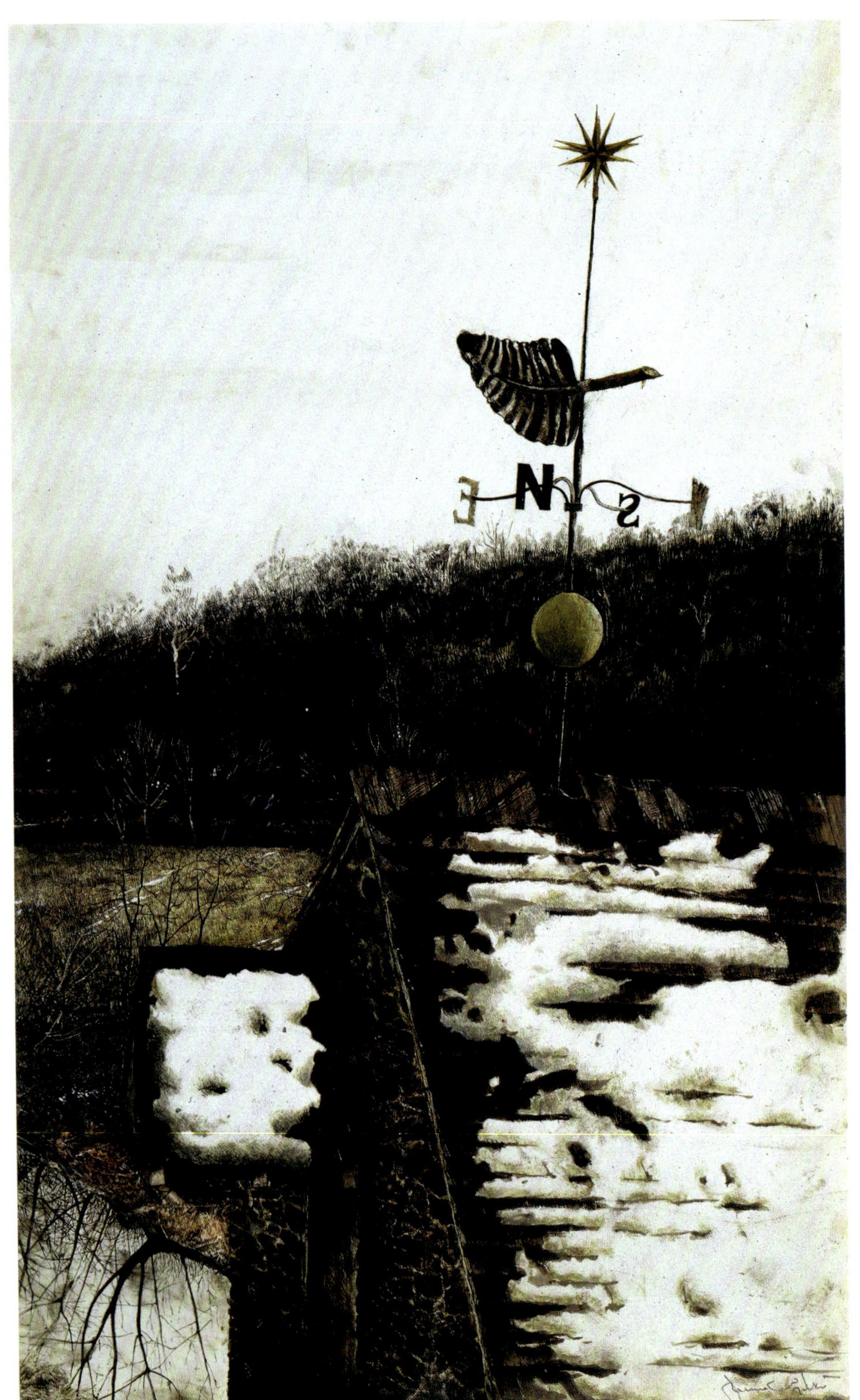

45. *The Weathervane*, 1959. Watercolor on Strathmore paper, 56.5 x 35.6 cm (22¼ x 14 in.)

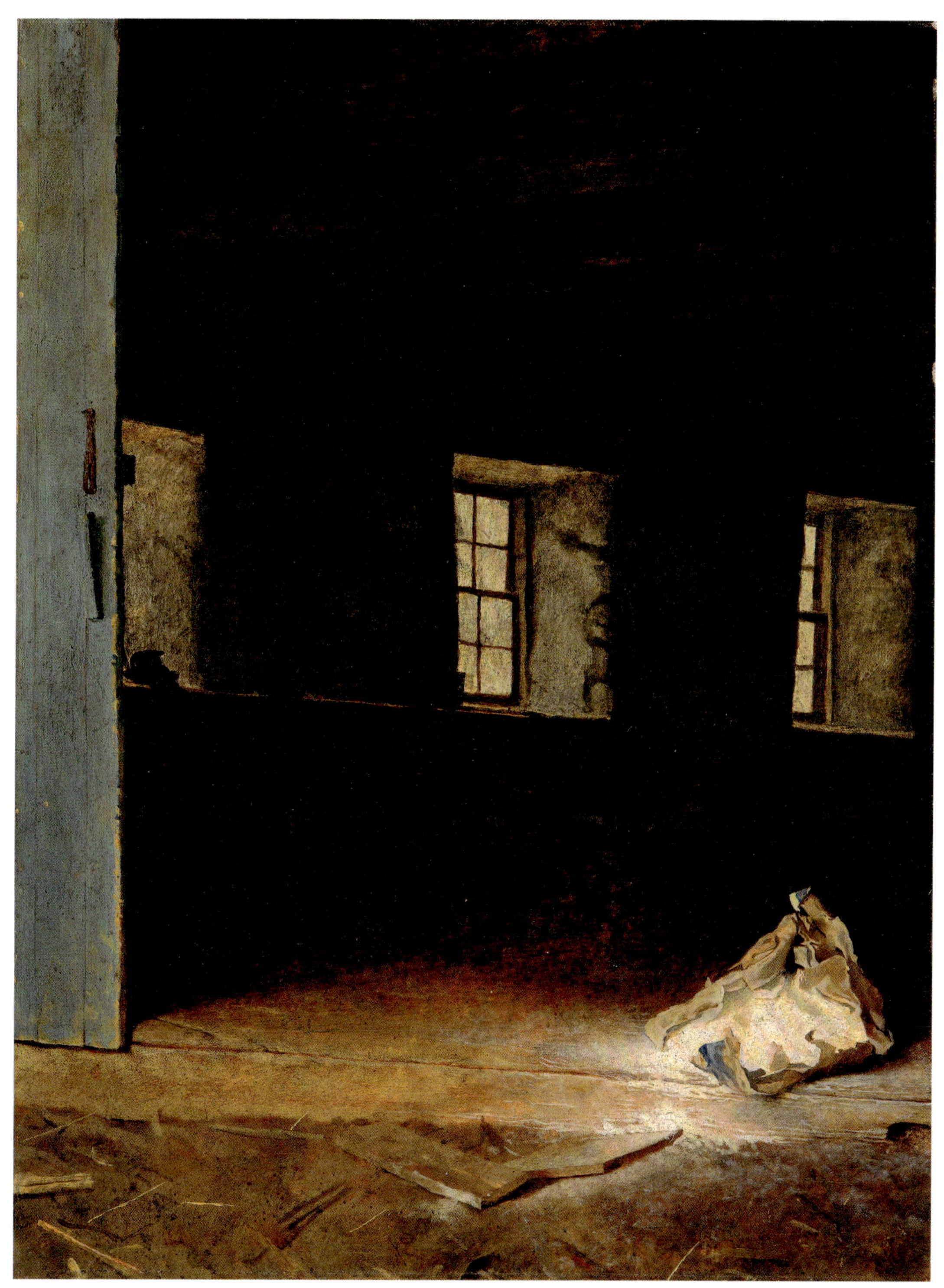

46. *Lime Bag*, 1964.Oil on board, 40.6 x 31.1 cm (16 x 12¼ in.)

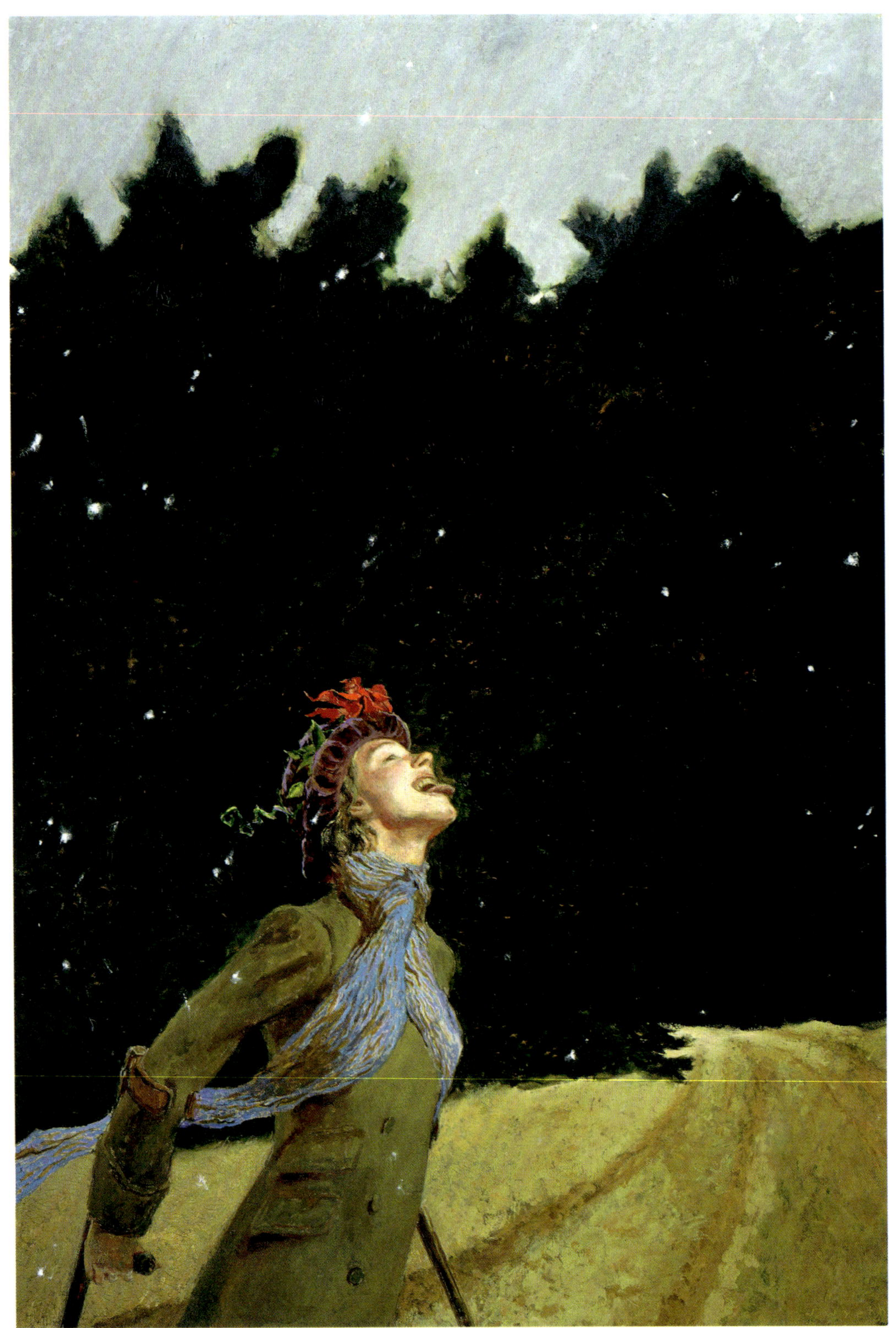

47. *Catching Snowflakes*, 2004. Watercolor and gouache on toned rag board, 101.6 x 71.1 cm (40 x 28 in.)

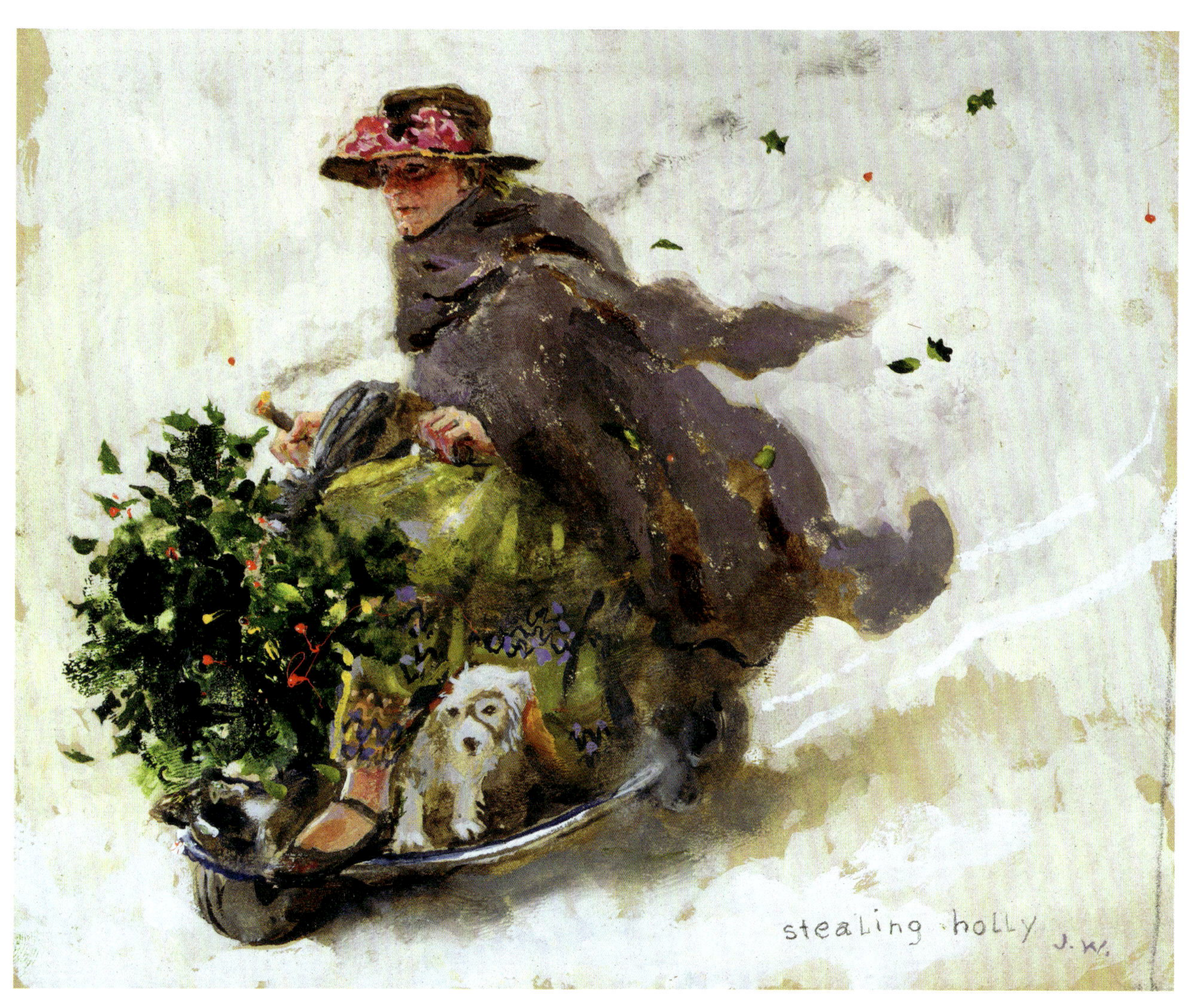

48. *Stealing Holly*, 2004. Watercolor and gouache on toned rag board, 14.6 x 18.1 cm (5¾ x 7⅛ in.)

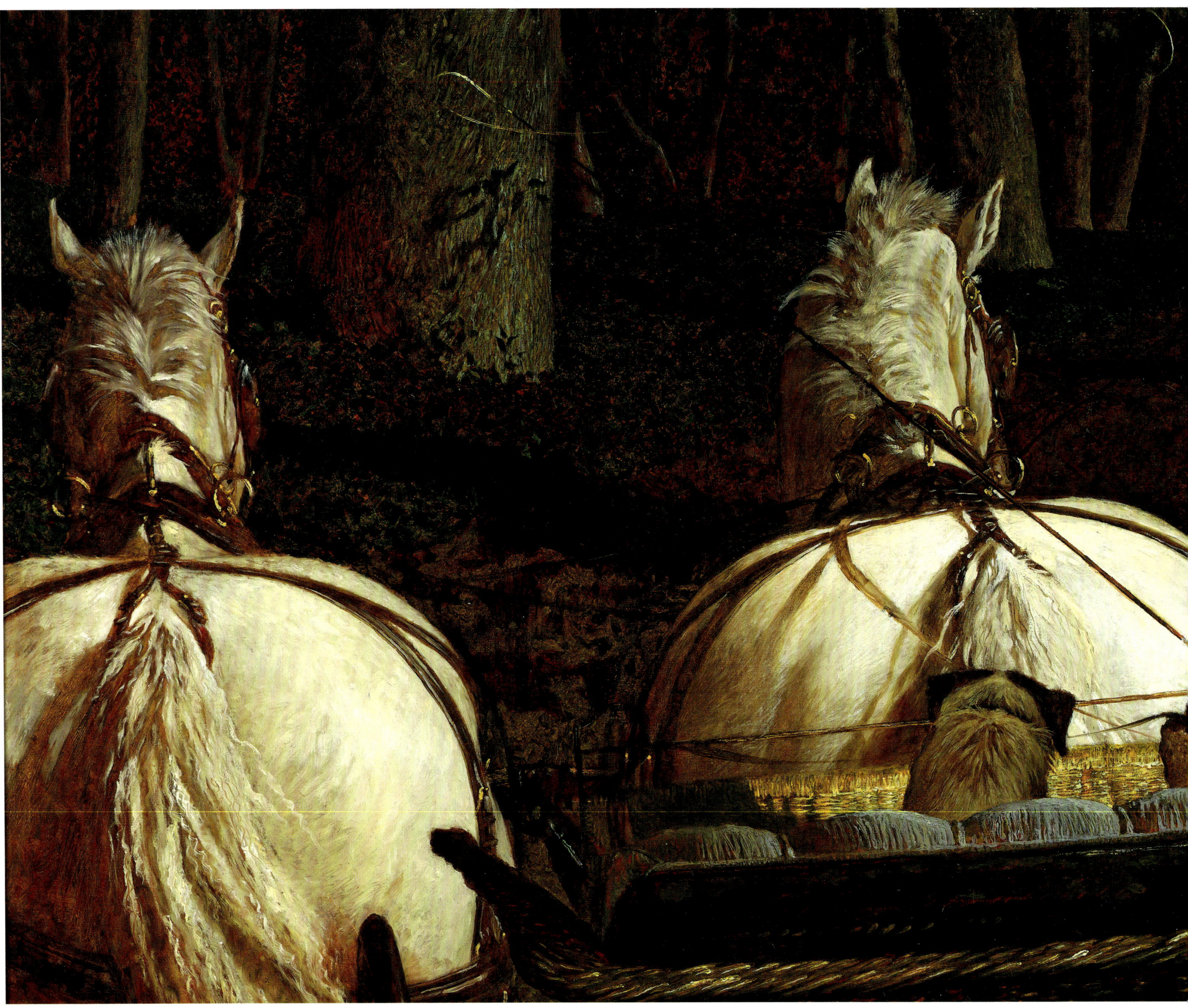

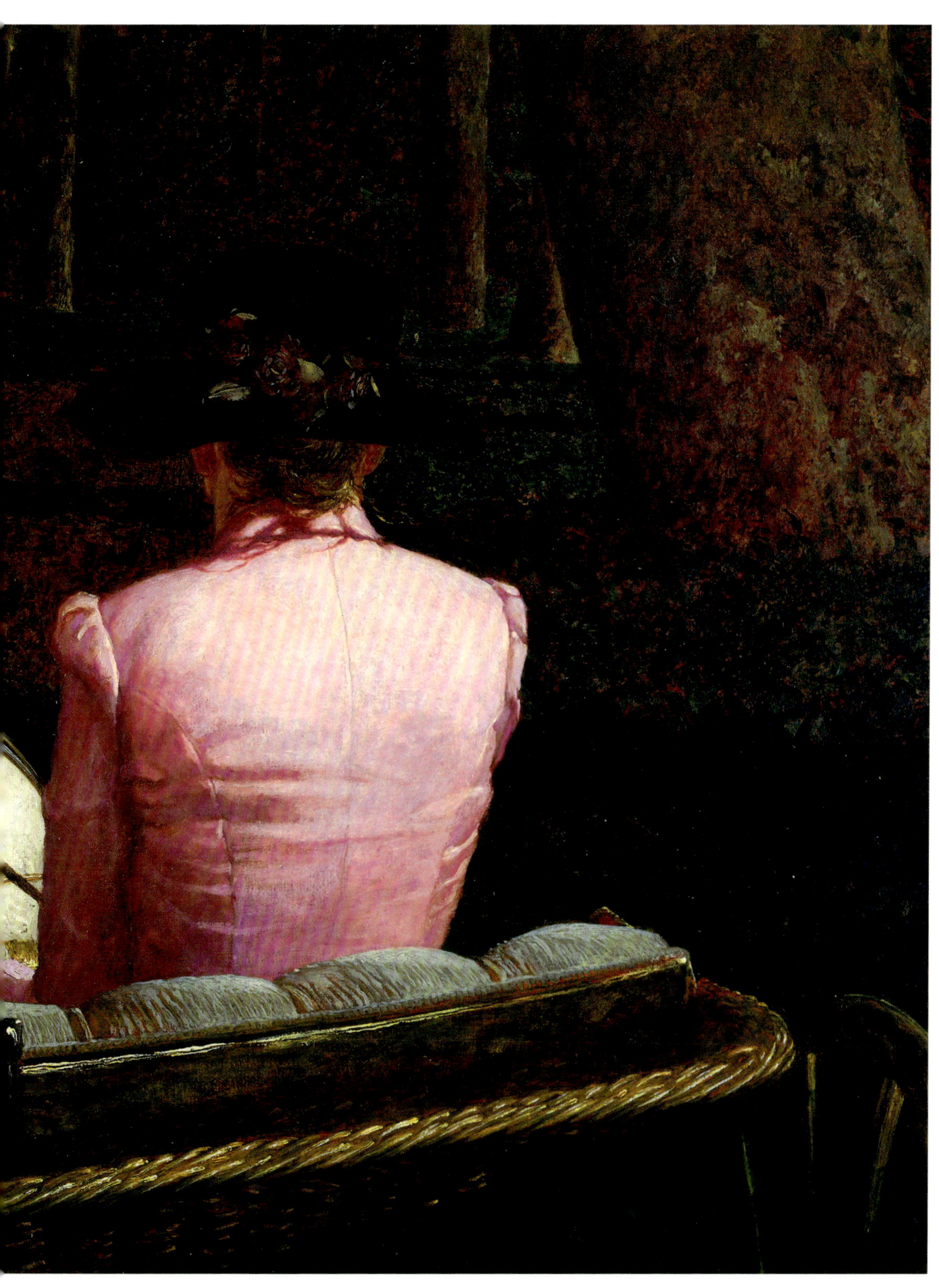

49. *Connemara*, 1987. Oil on canvas, 94 x 185.4 cm (37 x 73 in.)

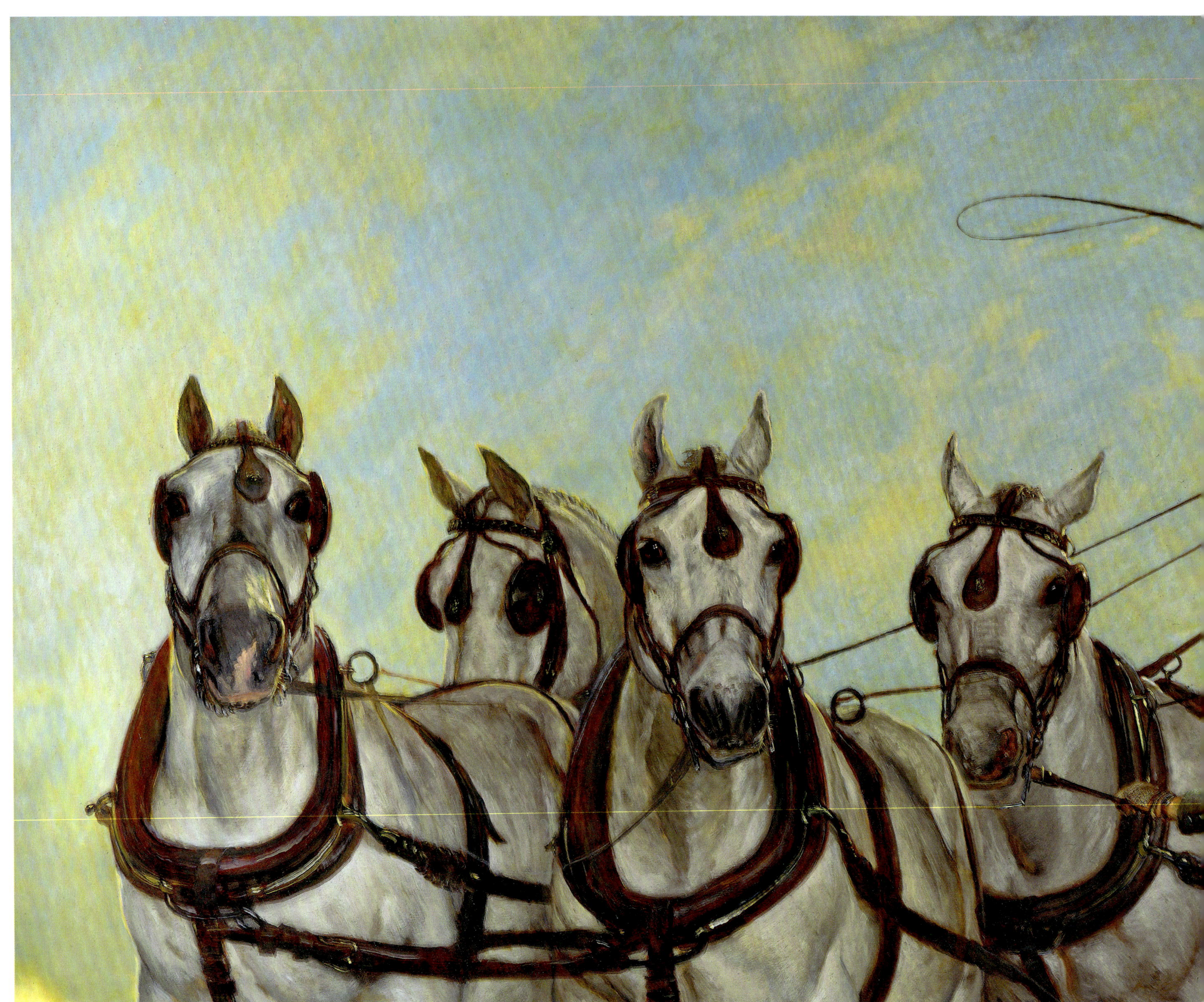

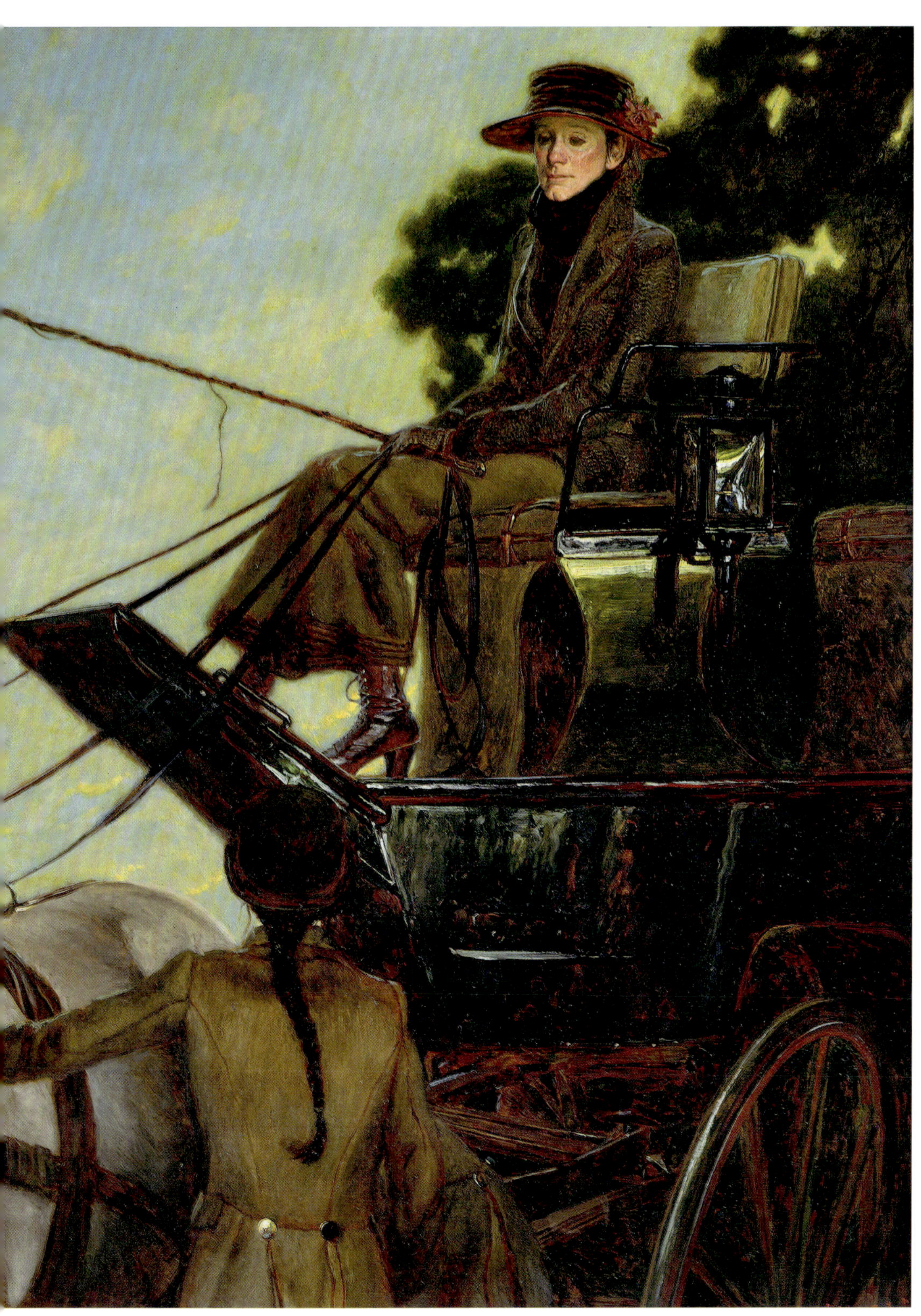

50. *Connemara Four*, 1991. Oil on panel, 121.9 x 243.8 cm (48 x 96 in.)

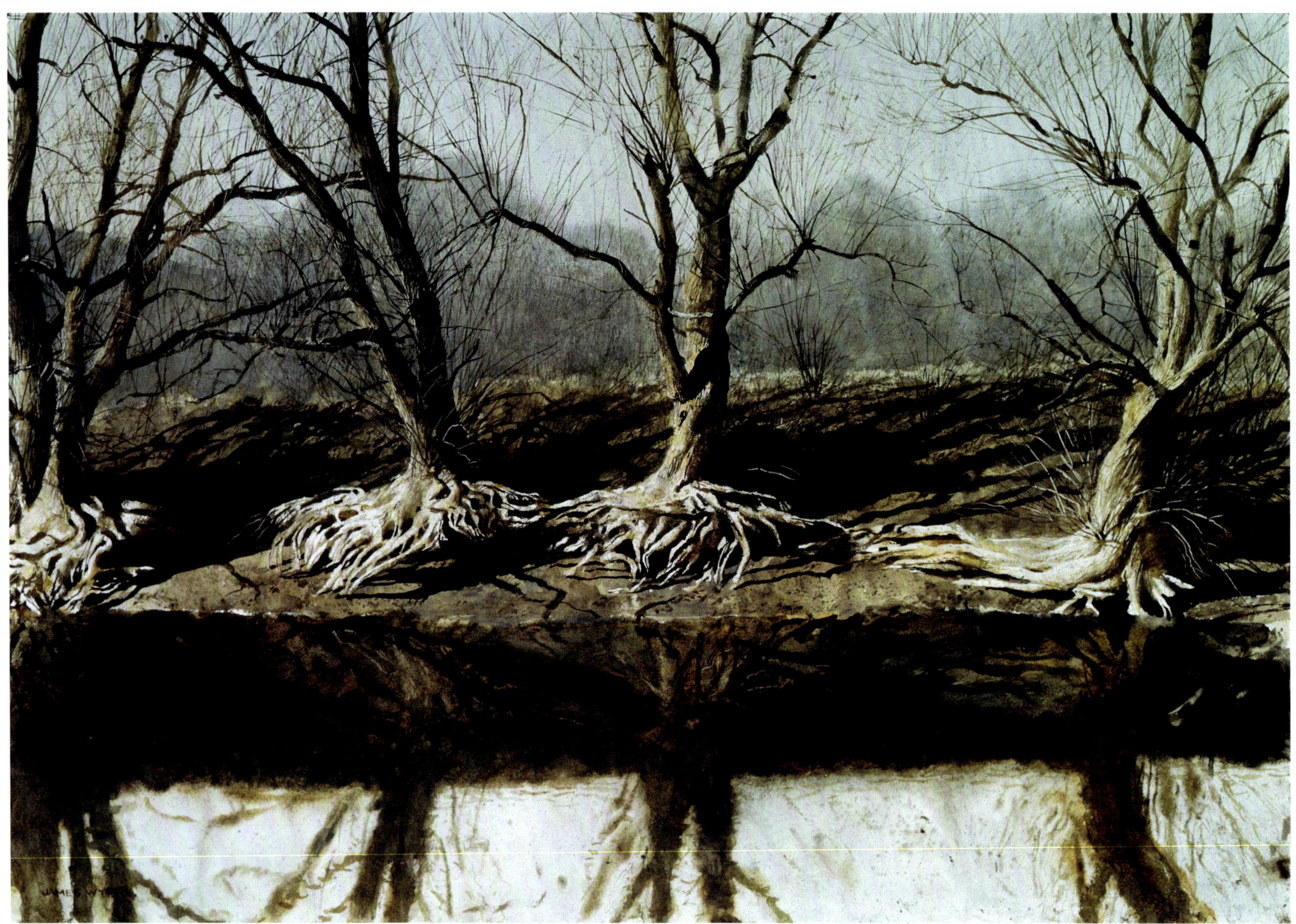

51. *Brandywine Spiders*, 1973. Watercolor on Strathmore plate-finish paper, 63.5 x 89.5 cm (25 x 35¼ in.)

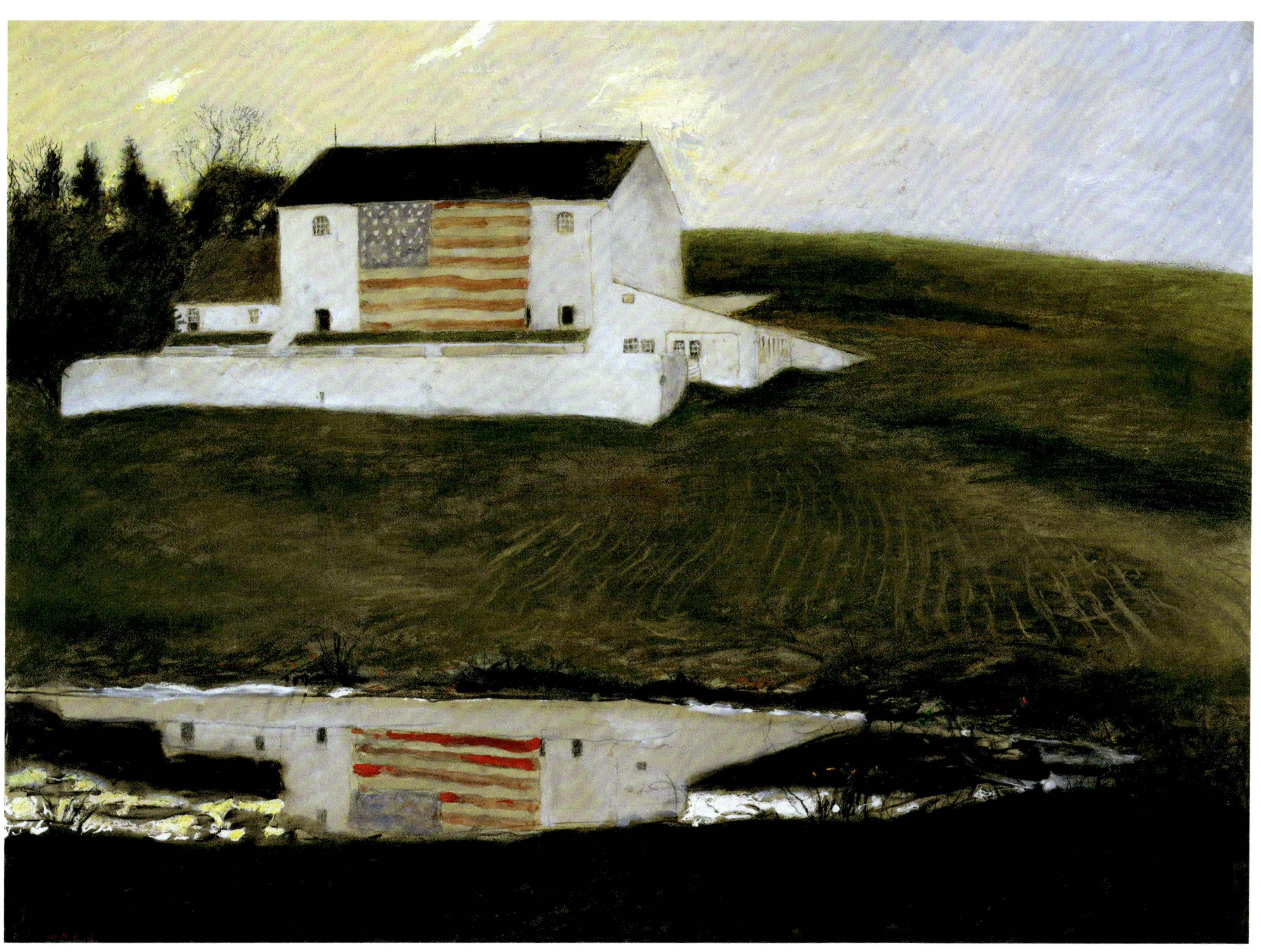

52. *Patriot's Barn*, 2001. Watercolor, gouache, and pastel on toned rag board, 66.7 x 99 cm (26¼ x 39 in.)

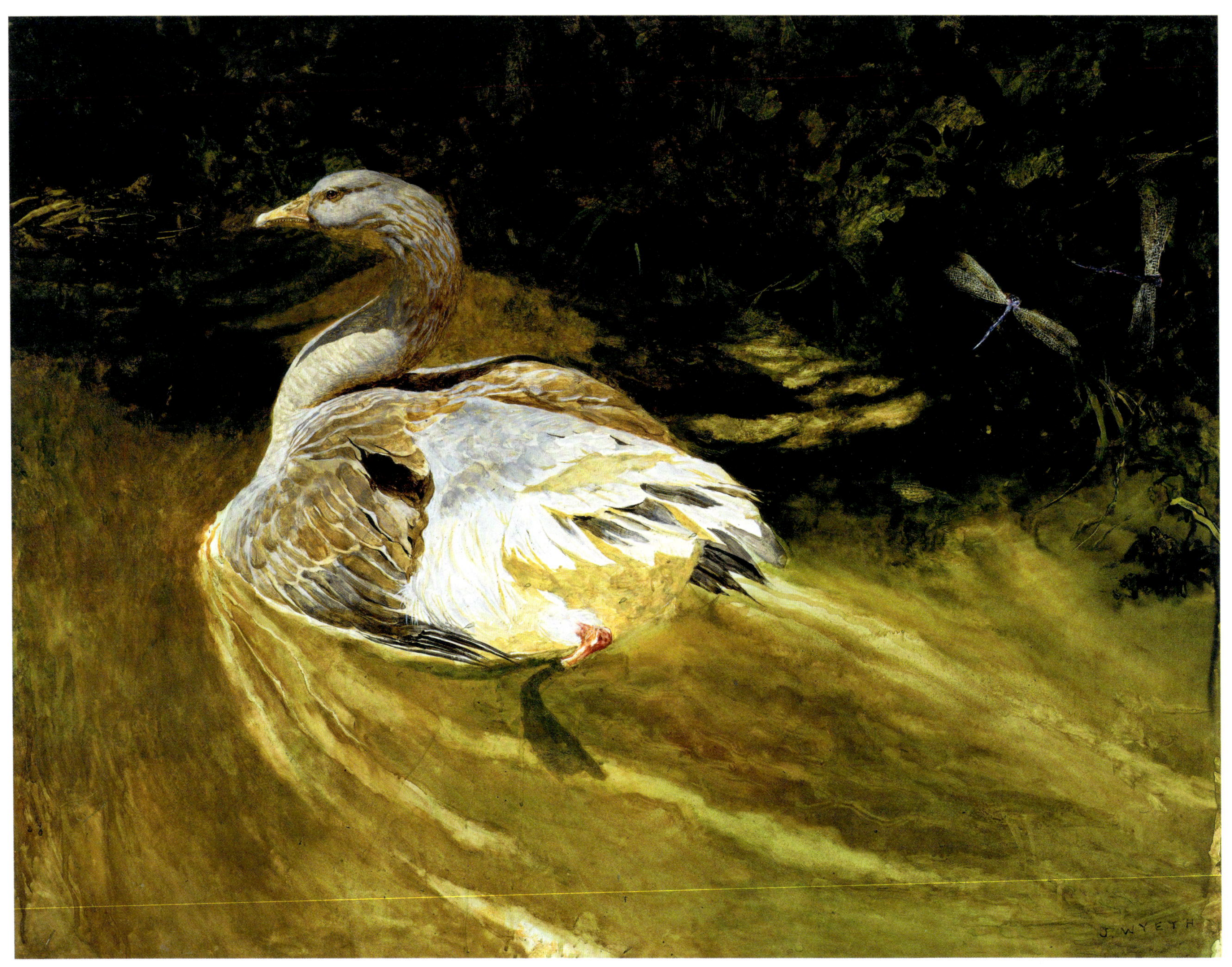

53. *Dragonflies*, 1986. Watercolor on three-ply Strathmore paper, 76.2 x 101.6 cm (30 x 40 in.)

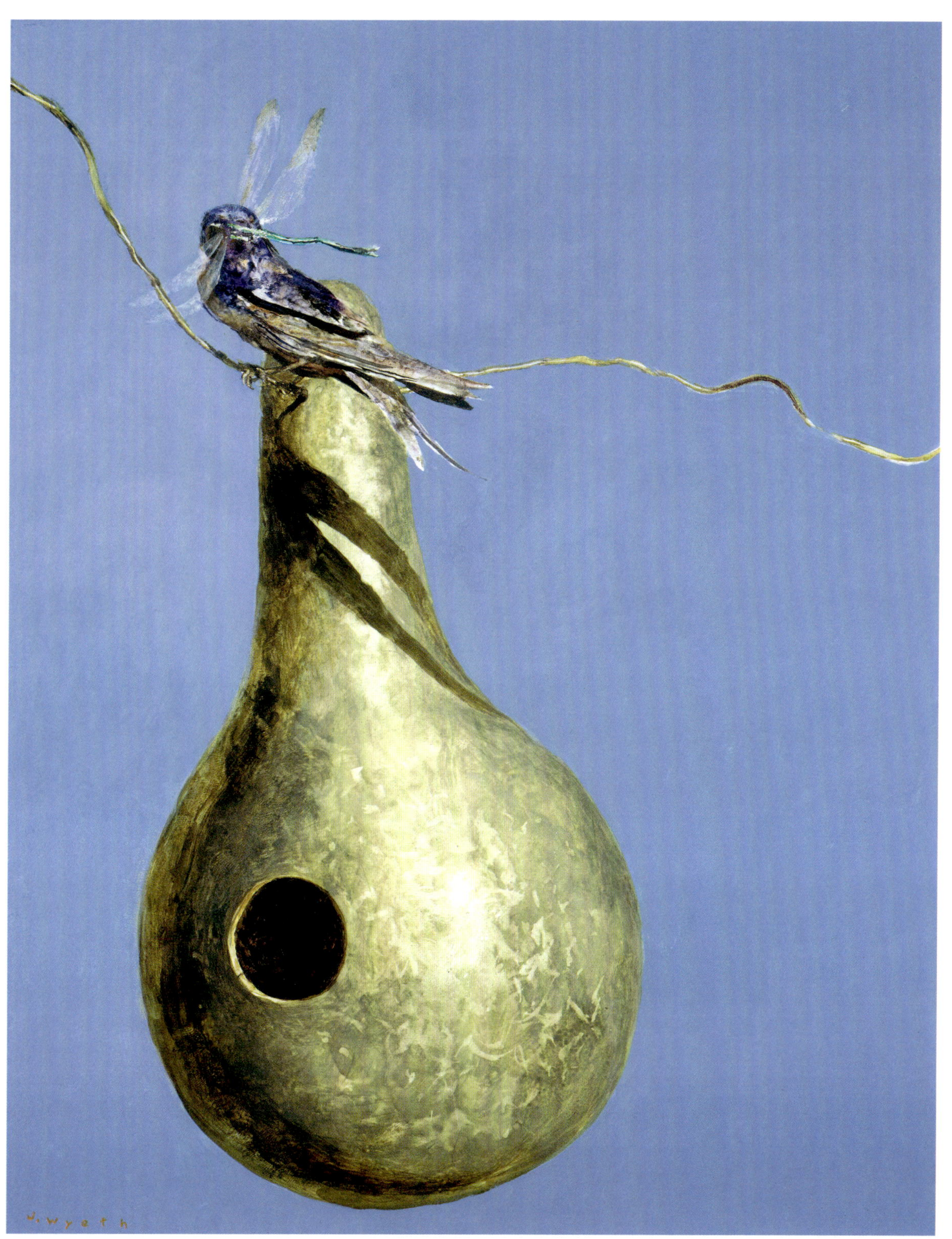

54. *Dragonfly*, 1994. Essence of pearl, gouache, varnish, and watercolor on Strathmore paper, 49.5 x 39.4 cm (19½ x 15½ in.)

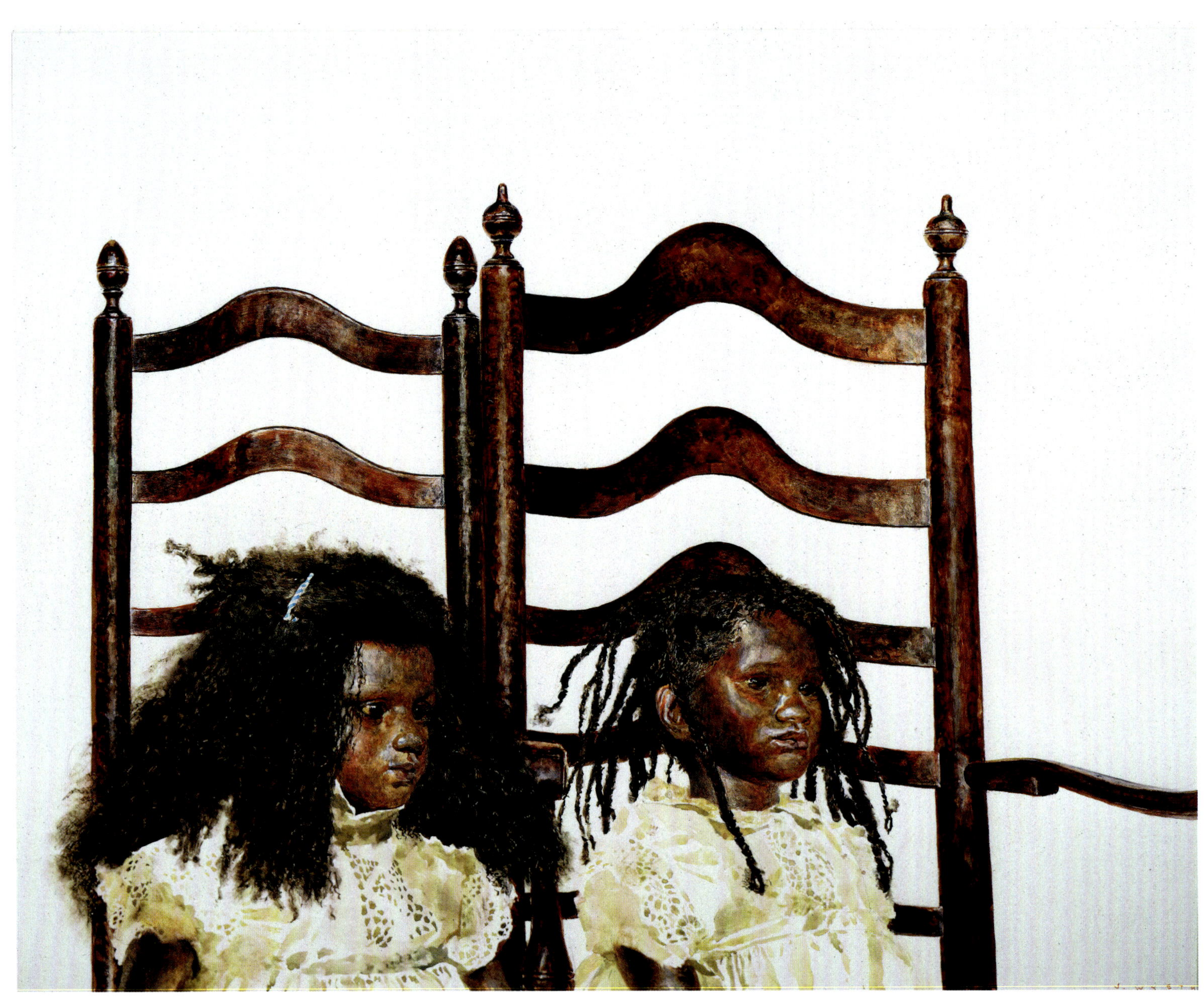

55. *Twins*, 1990. Watercolor on three-ply Strathmore paper, 58.4 x 73.7 cm (23 x 29 in.)

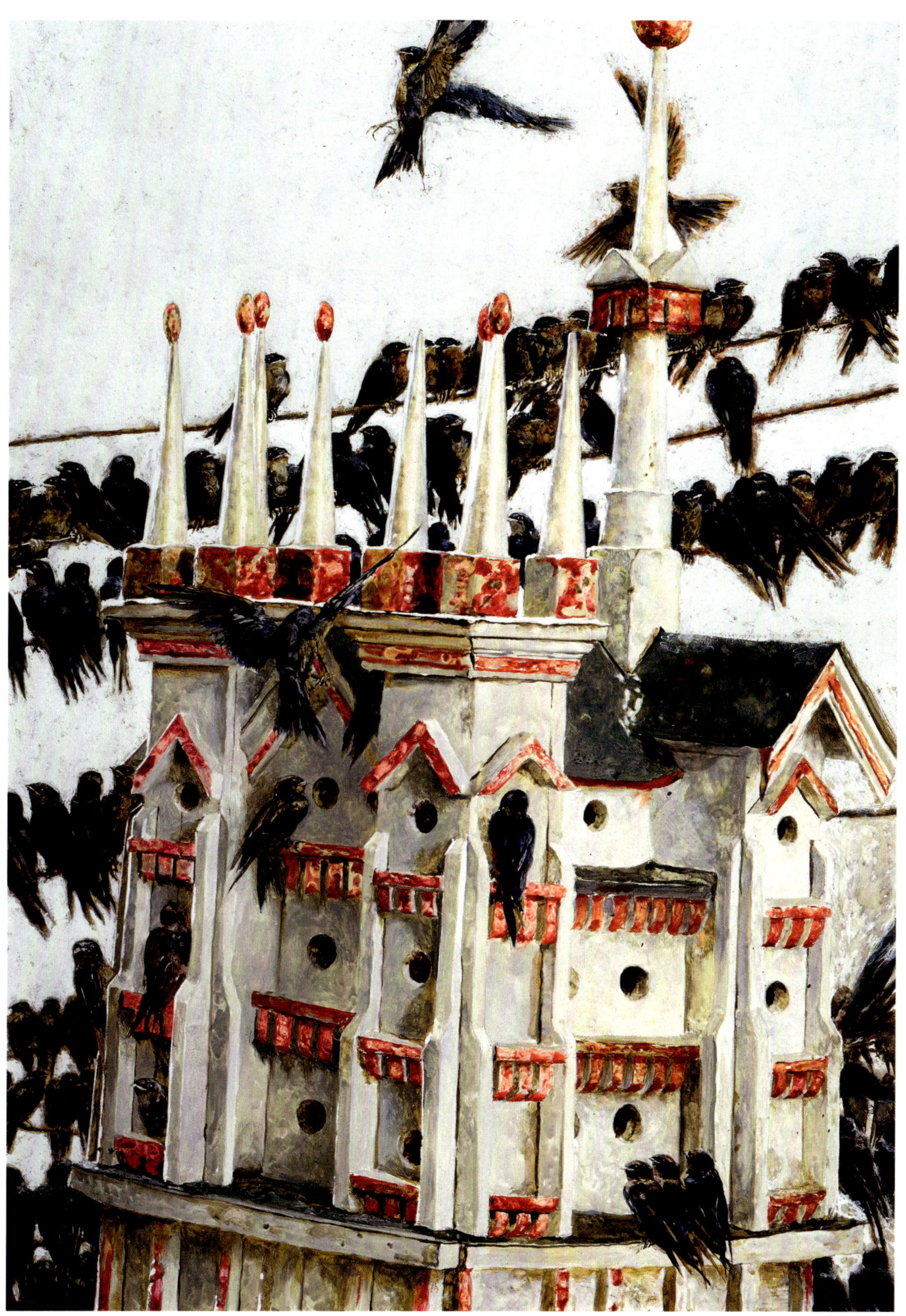

56. *Birds' House*, 1989. Varnish and watercolor on white Strathmore paper, 76.8 x 54.6 cm (30¼ x 21½ in.)

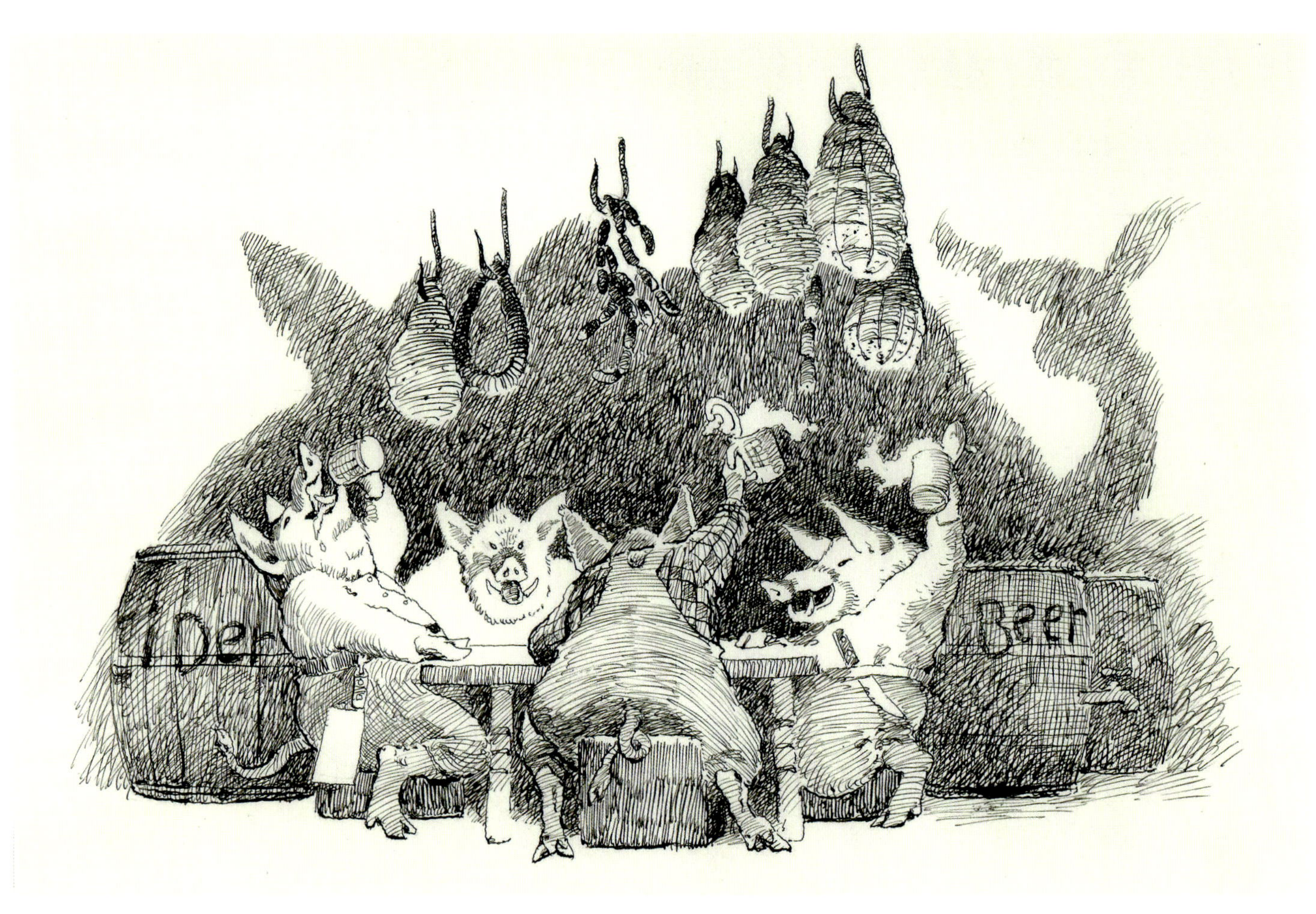

57. "They were seated around tables, roaring with laughter, drinking mugs of beer,"
1979. Pen and ink and watercolor on rag paper, 16.5 x 25.4 cm (6½ x 10 in.)

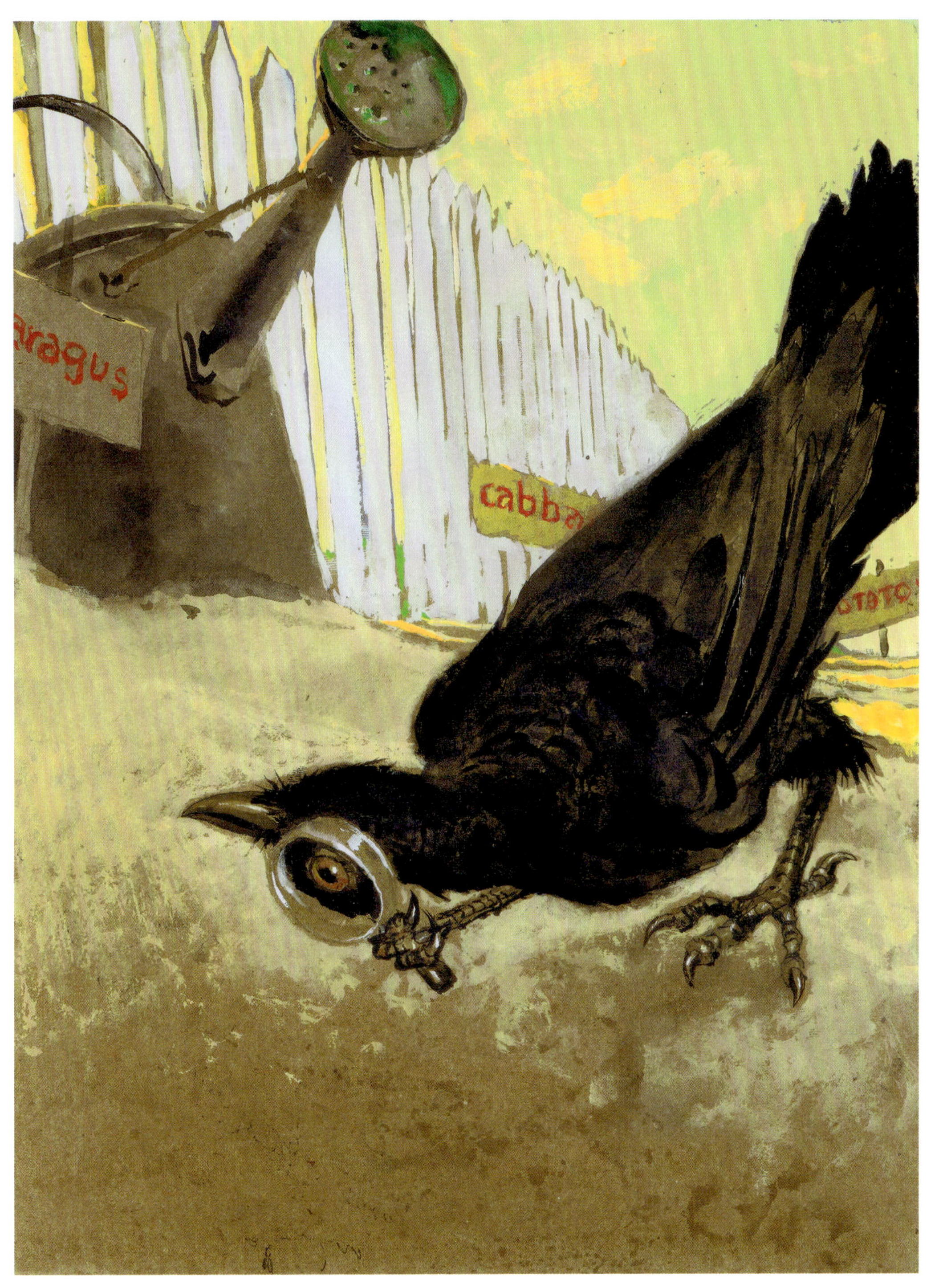

58. “Too late, he chirped, after he carefully studied the ground,” 1996.
Gouache and watercolor on toned rag board, 31.8 x 24.1 cm (12½ x 9½ in.)

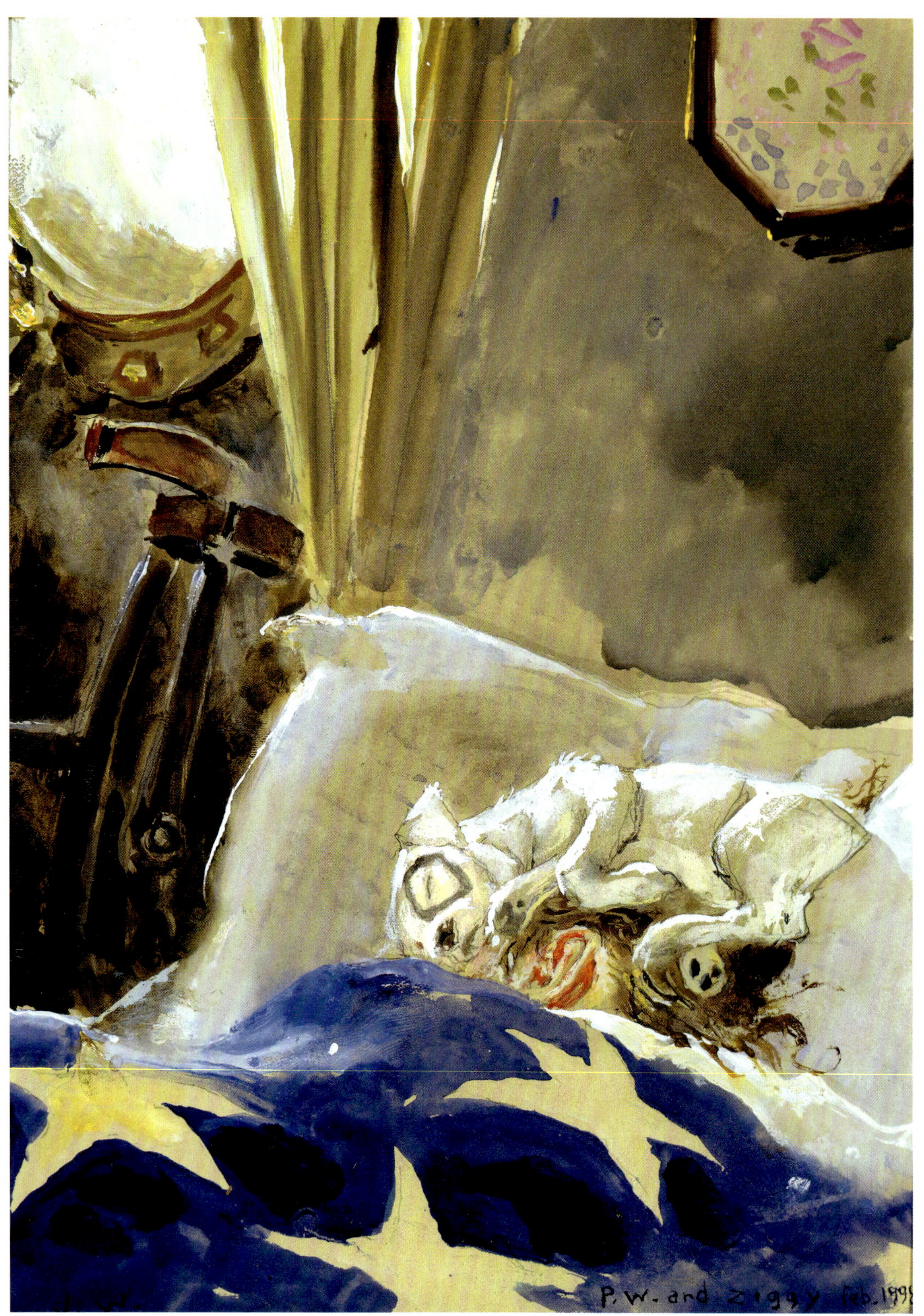

59. *P.W. and Ziggy*, 1998. Watercolor and gouache on toned rag board, 33 x 24.8 cm (13 x 9¾ in.)

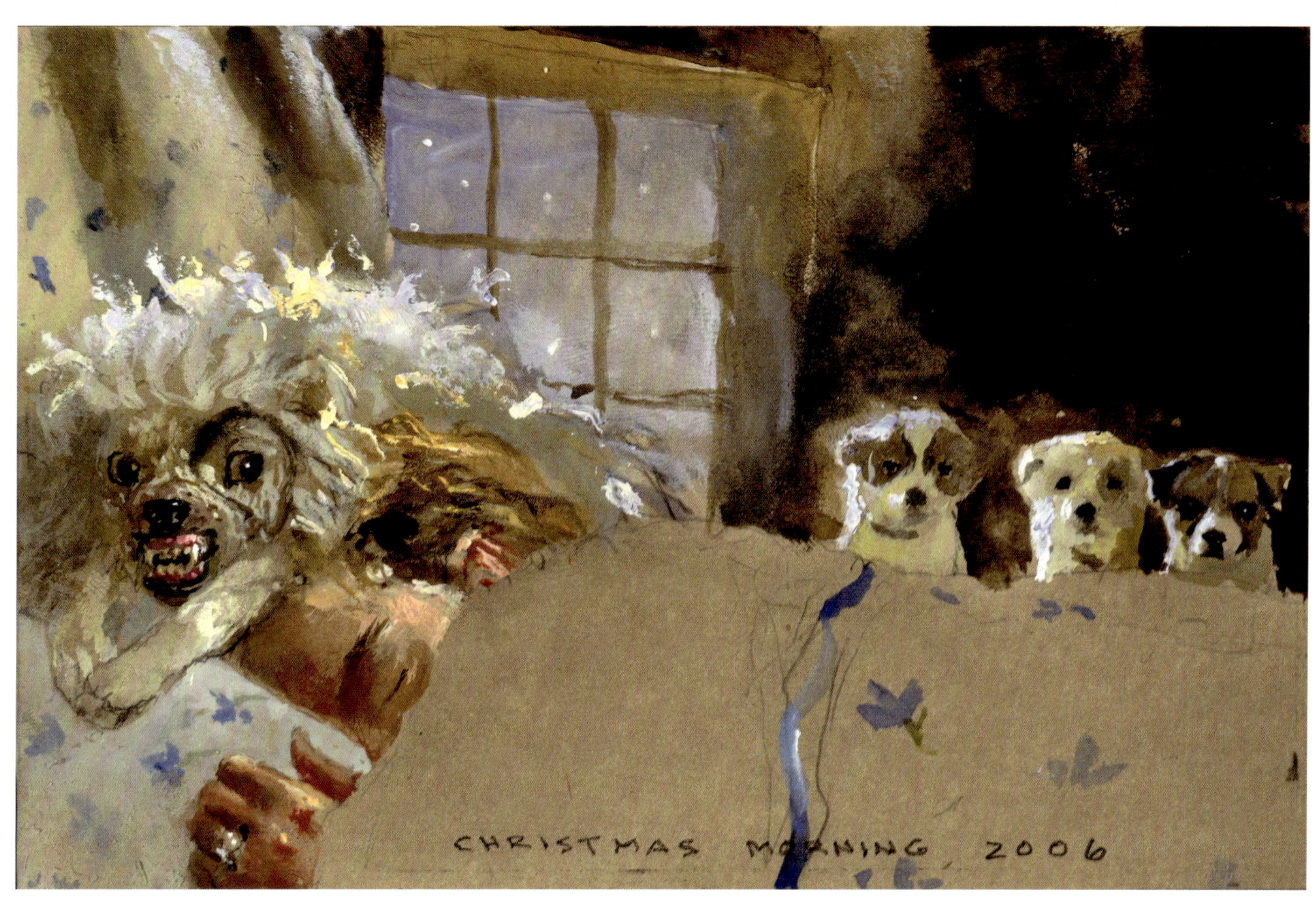

60. *Christmas Morning 2006*, 2006. Watercolor and gouache on toned rag board, 13.7 x 21 cm (5⅜ x 8¼ in.)

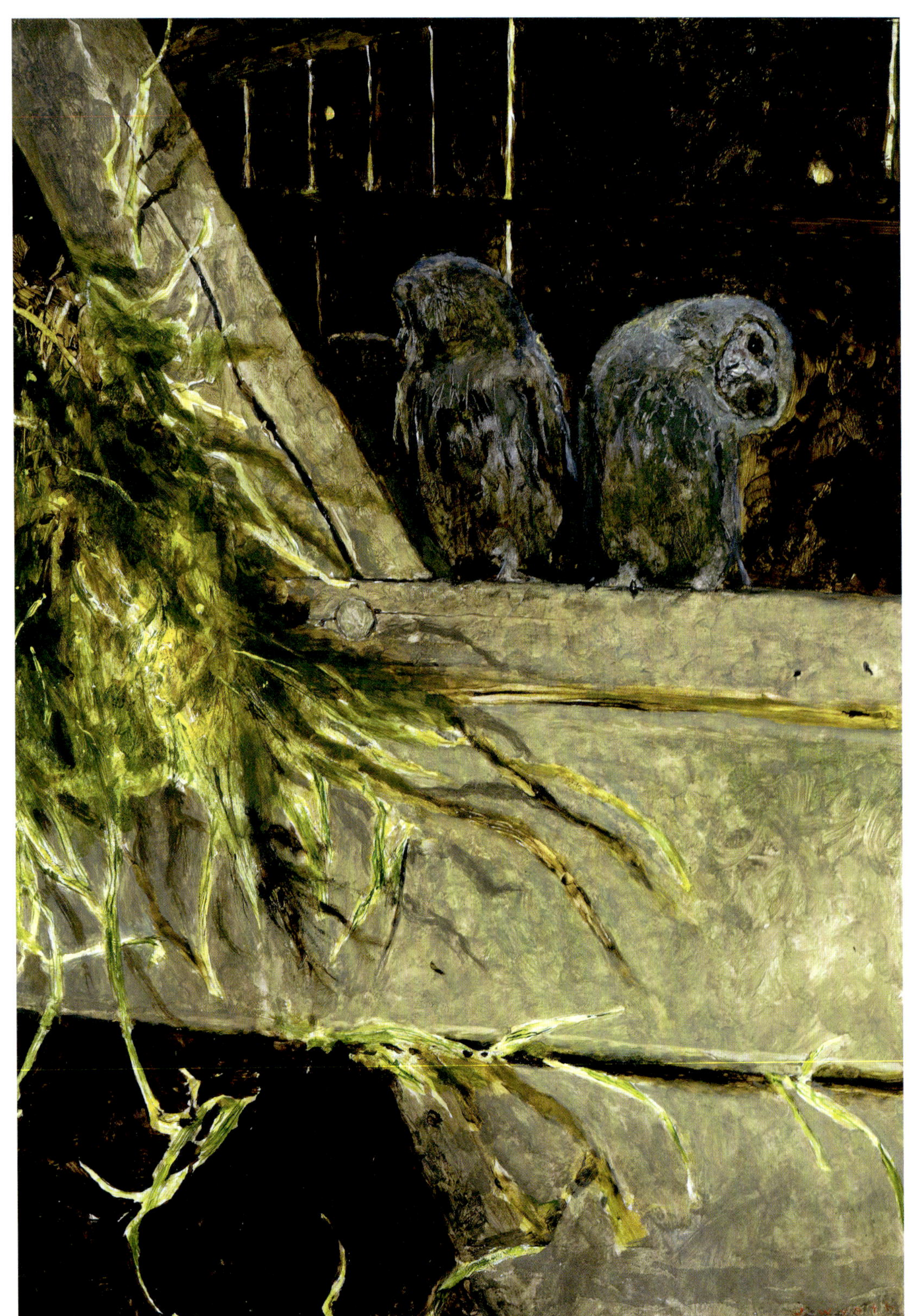

61. *Barn Owls, Immature*, 2006.
Watercolor and gouache on Strathmore paper, 89.9 x 64.8 cm (35⅜ x 25½ in.)

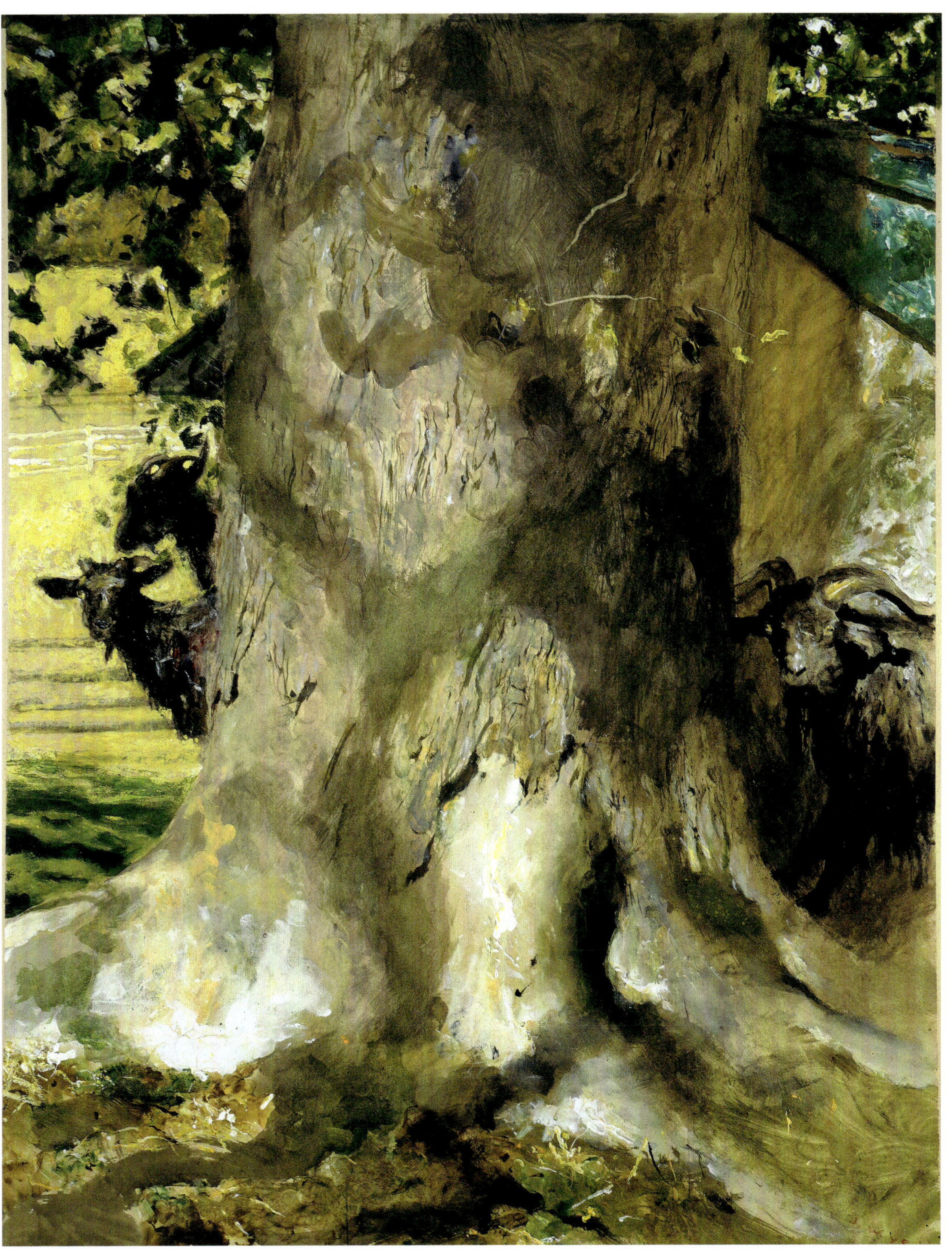

62. *Goat Tree*, 2006. Watercolor and gesso on toned rag board, 90.1 x 69.9 cm (35½ x 27½ in.)

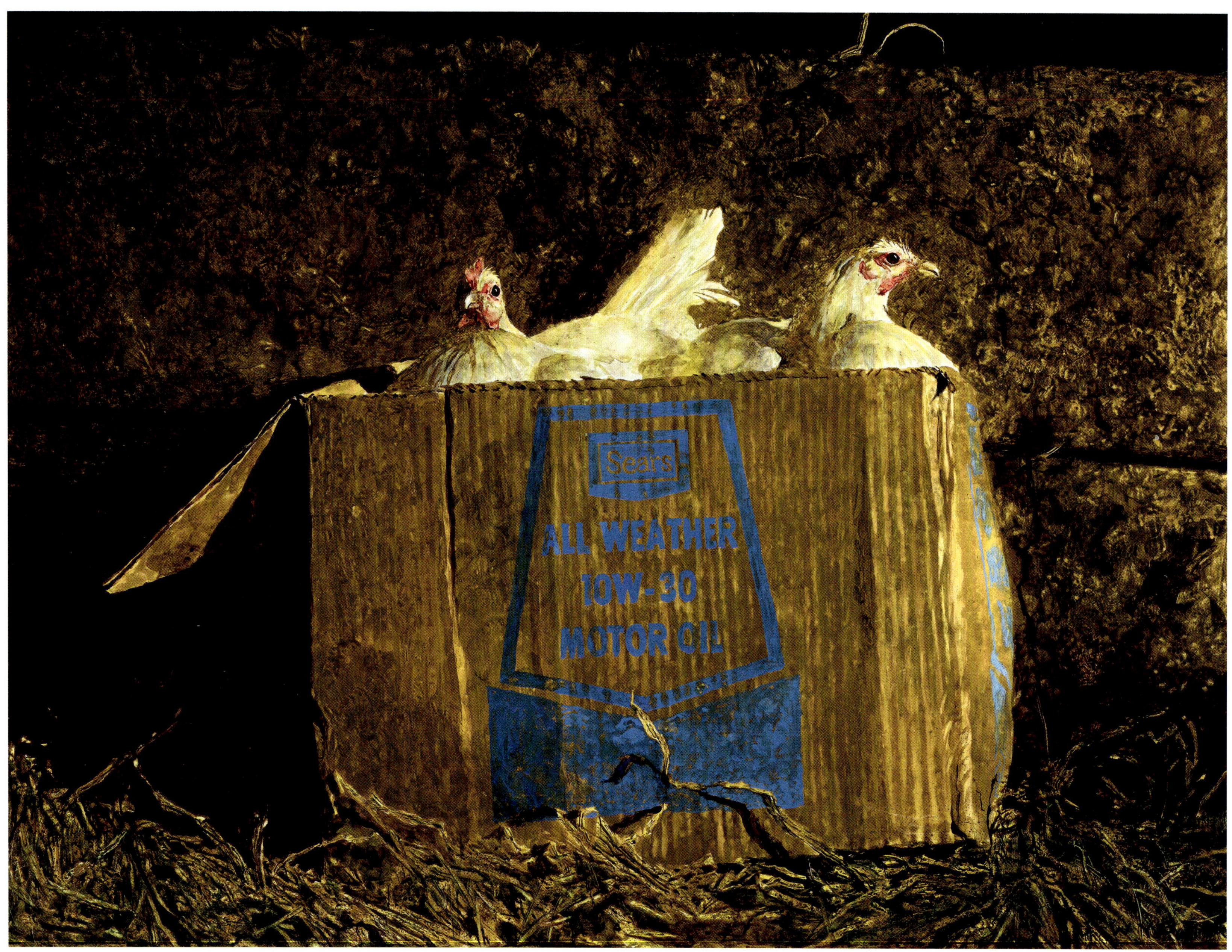

63. *10 W 30*, 1981. Watercolor and varnish on white Strathmore rag paper, 58.4 x 78.7 cm (23 x 31 in.)

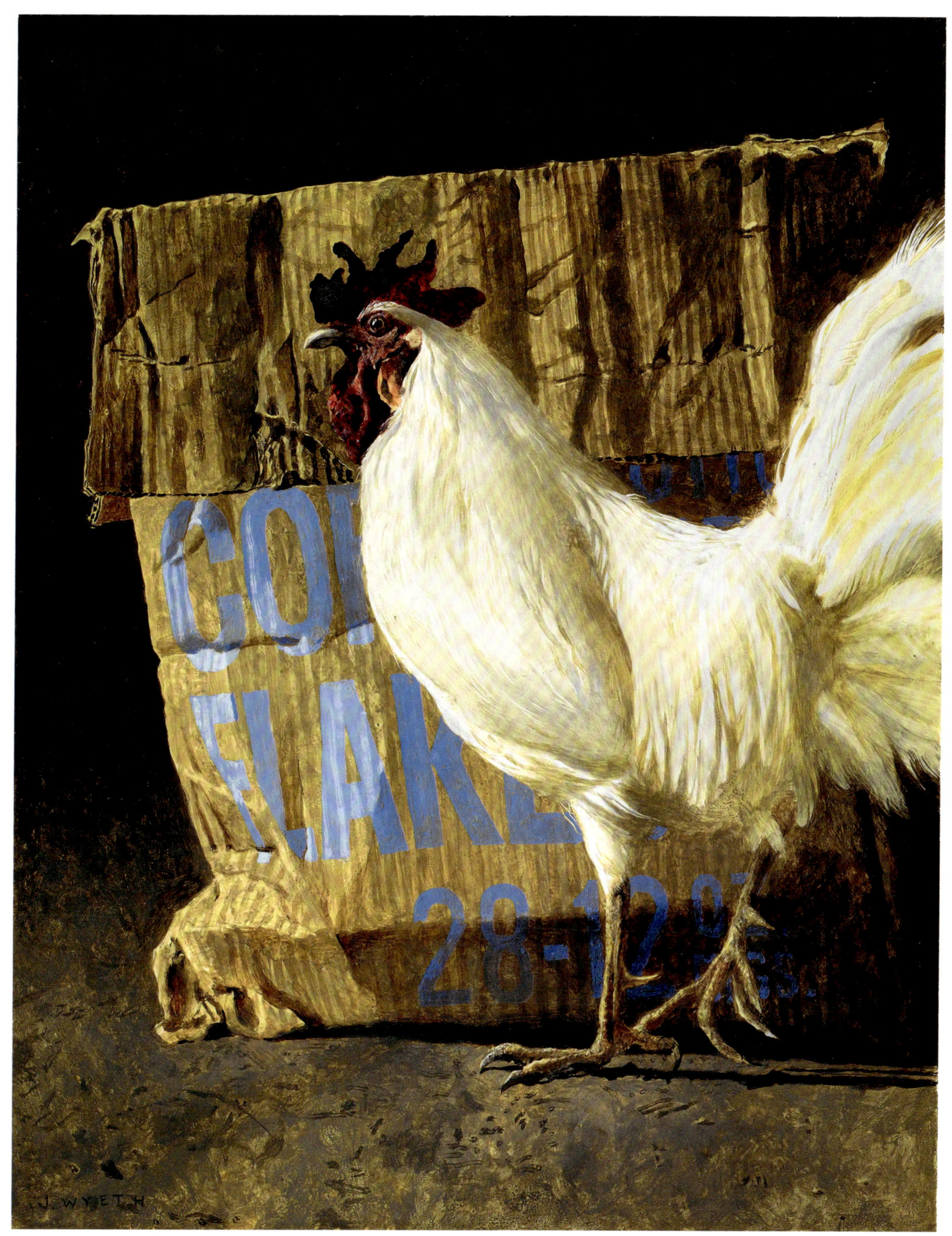

64. *Cornflakes*, 1985. Watercolor and varnish on white Strathmore rag paper, 71.1 x 55.9 cm (28 x 22 in.)

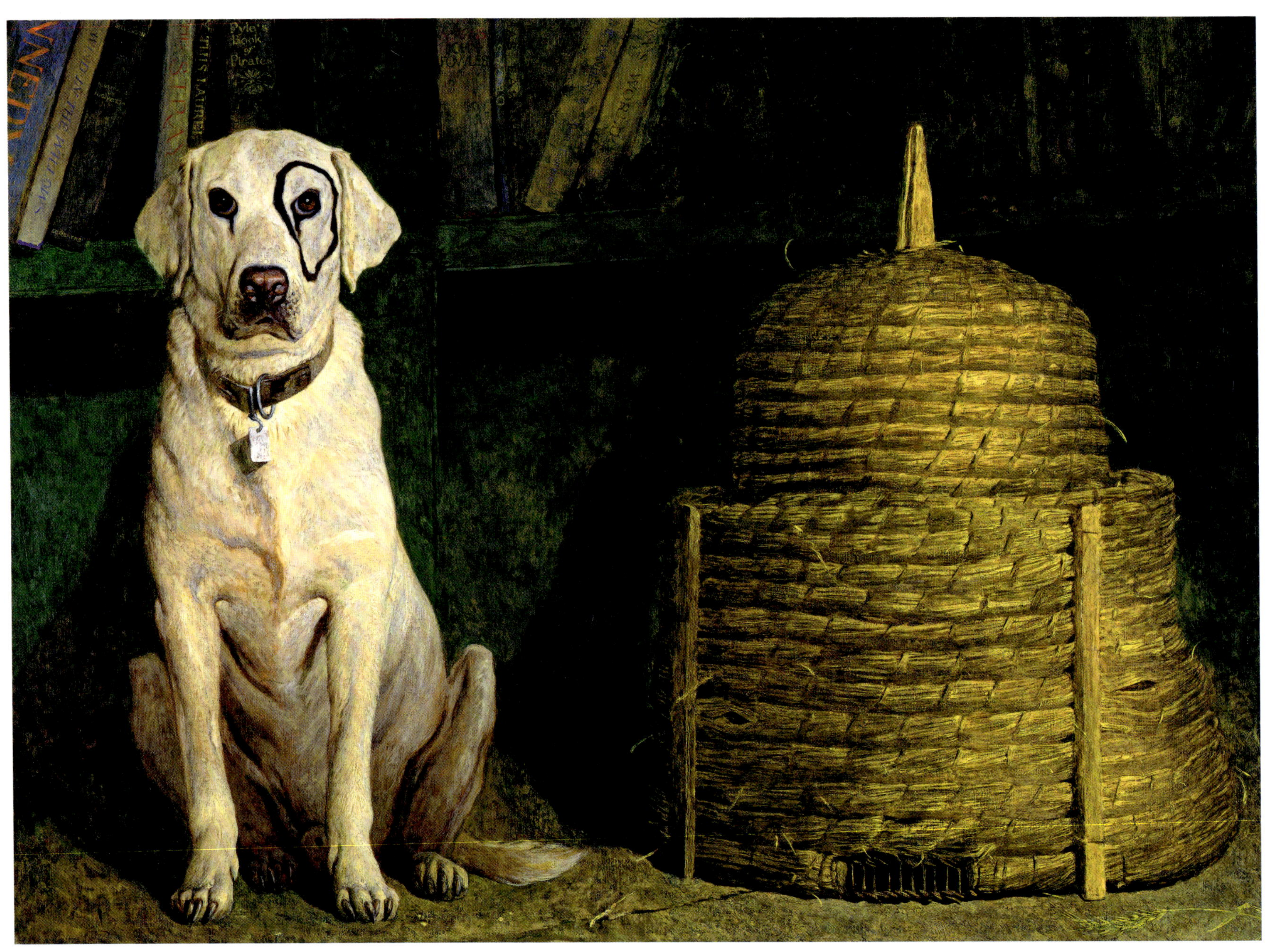

65. *Kleberg*, 1984. Oil on canvas, 77.5 x 108 cm (30½ x 42½ in.)

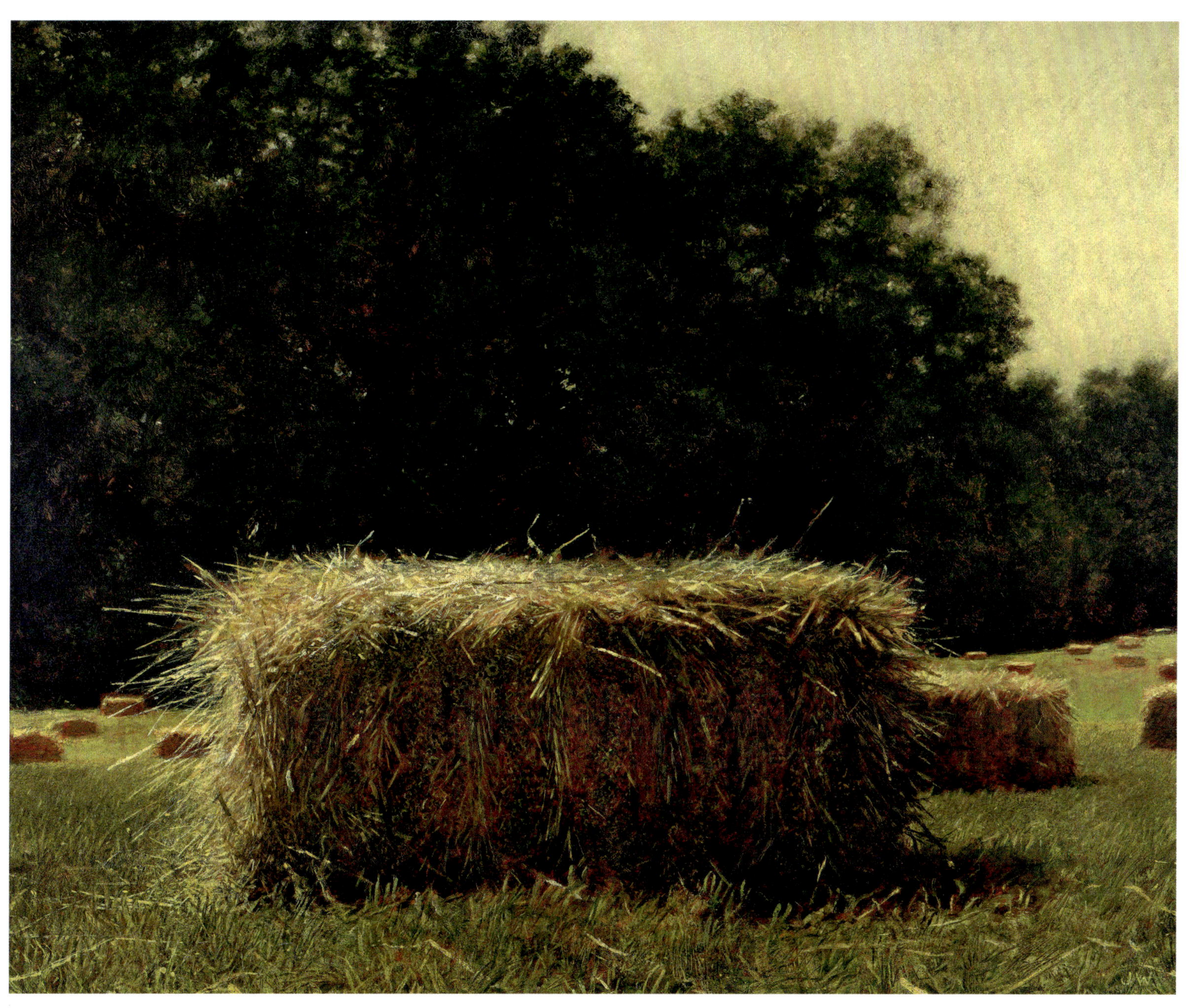

66. *Bale*, 1972. Oil on canvas, 72.4 x 88.9 cm (28½ x 35 in.)

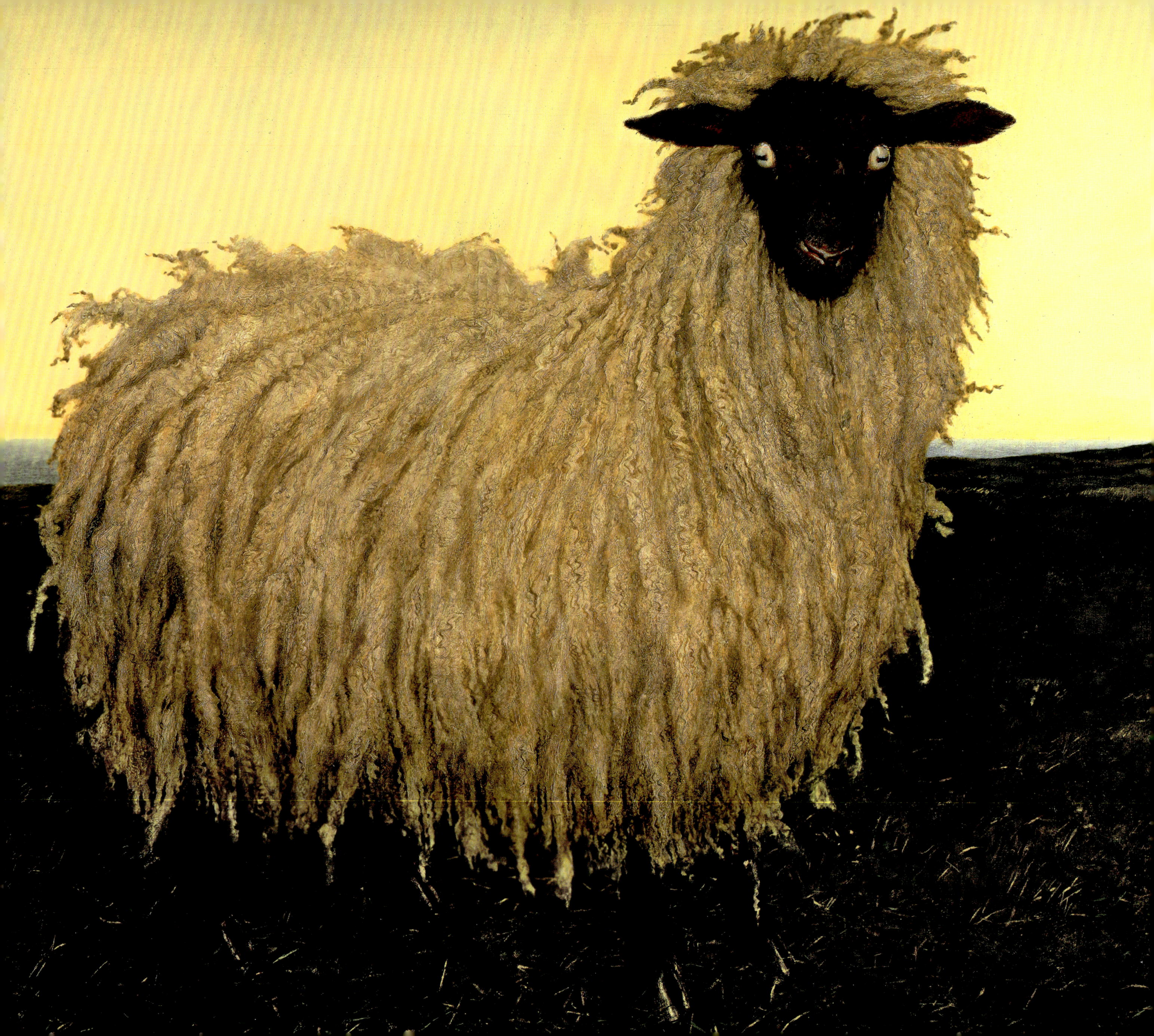

Maine

Wyeth's Brandywine River Valley paintings would seem to play well with the pastoral strains of Ludwig van Beethoven's Sixth Symphony; in the artist's own words, the Maine island of Monhegan, where he has had a studio since 1968, conjures up the drama of Richard Wagner's *Ring* cycle, for which we can easily imagine swooping gulls performing the *Flight of the Valkyries*. His portrayals of Maine exude nature in the raw, often at the edge of the sea, with the surf and the power of the ocean ever present even when absent from his images. As the artist himself describes it, "The danger with Maine is that it is so anecdotal and emblematic in terms of pot buoys, pretty houses, pretty lobster traps—'quaint' things. Maine is not that way. Maine has a lot of edge, a lot of angst. In particular, islands, the part I know of Maine from having lived on them."[1] The New England transcendentalist Henry David Thoreau, who was such a significant figure for all three generations of Wyeths, wrote eloquently about his explorations of the wilderness near Mount Katahdin in *The Maine Woods*, which he visited while based at his beloved, more bucolic Walden Pond in Concord, Massachusetts. The Maine woods as described by Thoreau evoke that sense of rawness and awe on the edge of wilderness that embodies the experience of the terrifying and the sublime found in nature, which emerges in many of Wyeth's images of Maine.

Those untamed, feral qualities of Maine come across vividly in paintings of one of Wyeth's muses there, Orca Bates, a boy born to parents who lived on Manana, the island just off Monhegan. In *Orca*, Wyeth meets the harshness of Maine's seafaring heritage head-on by posing the model in front of a looming array of whaling implements, perhaps inspired by his given name, which is also a species of killer whale distinguished by its dramatic black-and-white markings. Orca stands stiffly, wearing a trim jacket that resembles a nineteenth-century military costume, with a neat row of brass buttons marching down its front. His stance echoes the sharp triangular barbs of the harpoons, as he holds his arms straight at his sides with his fingers pressed together so firmly they resemble fins. His hair extends to his shoulders, his angled jaw, echoed in the whaling implements behind him, and his lean physique swathed in a unisex jacket make him appear androgynous, as he does in several other paintings, including *Screen Door to the Sea* (1994, Farnsworth Art Museum) and *Portrait of Orca Bates* (1989, Farnsworth Art Museum).

That same year, Wyeth posed Orca Bates seated nude on a seaman's chest, in a painting that seems straightforward upon first glance but upon reflection captures his subject with an unexpected, searing bite (cat. 68). Orca sits at attention, his bony rear end perched uncomfortably on the hard edge of a massive seaman's chest, certainly large enough to have served for a burial at sea. His hair appears wet, and the whale jaw behind him conjures up the biblical story of Jonah being swallowed whole by a whale. This particular whale jaw was a gift to the artist from his wife, and he had some years earlier painted Phyllis seated on a sofa beneath the jagged bone, facing us, in *Whale*. In that composition the whale teeth cast increasingly larger and more sinister shadows on the simple clapboard wall as they extend from left to right. In this scene, the jawbone appears to close in on Bates's thin legs as the whale teeth rip through the composition horizontally, passing directly behind the boy's bare abdomen. Wyeth effectively and unforgettably holds the defenseless prey in a visual grip between whale jaw and chest, pinned down like a butterfly in a naturalist's shadowbox, a specimen he clearly labels in red letters: Orca Bates. The artist seems to be holding on to Orca for dear life, as the boy embodies that fleeting sense of feminine masculinity on the cusp of adolescence, between the worlds of childhood and manhood.

Outside the studio, Wyeth's Maine often features the distinctive vernacular architecture of the region, especially as he returns again and again to buildings on the islands he inhabits, Monhegan and Southern. On Monhegan, Wyeth lives and works in the former home of Rockwell Kent's mother, which Kent designed and helped build (cat. 72). Wyeth considers Kent a Monhegan mentor and muse; with the proceeds of sales from his first public exhibition at Knoedler's, Wyeth acquired Kent House, as well as his first Kent oil painting. Since then he has assembled the foremost collection of Monhegan paintings and drawings created during Kent's various visits to the island between 1905 and 1910, and later from 1947 to 1953.[2]

Kent initially arrived on Monhegan in June 1905 at the age of twenty-three, primed by his architectural studies at Columbia and Robert Henri's evening life classes at the New York School of Art, and intent on making his way as an artist. He supported himself by working at various odd jobs, including drilling wells, carpentry, lobstering, and emptying privies—physical labors that fueled his desire to paint fiercely and intensely. As he observed of his life on Monhegan during that first visit, "Between and after days of work with maul and drill, with hammer and nails or at the oars, on days it blew too hard at sea, on Sundays, I was painting; painting with a fervor born, as I have said, of my close contact with the sea and soil, and deepened by the reverence that the whole universe imposed."[3]

Kent's early education at Horace Mann School in New York City bestowed on him a reverence for manual work and a respect for craftsmanship, which he considered fundamental "to the practices of all arts."[4] As he eloquently observed, "What joy there is in making things. In beating red-hot iron into useful, often lovely shapes; in making patterns, moulding them in sand, in casting them with molten metal, in turning them on a lathe to the precision that their use demands; in fashioning from a stick in wood a penholder, itself a means towards the fashioning of words to give substantial form to thought; to transmute paint to mountains, seas, and depths of space; to flesh and blood."[5] Wyeth's architectural rendering of Kent's buildings shows their maker's attraction to well-made details.

After building a cottage for himself, among the early structures Kent added to Monhegan's coastline were the Jenny Houses, the first on the island to be equipped with running water and modern plumbing, in 1907.[6] Built side by side, the boxy buildings were intended to mirror each other, as they do in Wyeth's early watercolor *Twin Houses*. Dividing his watercolor paper into wide stripes of brilliant green grass and pale sky seamed together by a thin ribbon of inky blue Monhegan water, Wyeth pushes the two solid clapboard buildings to the left and right edges of the paper, thus opening at the center a void that draws our eye far out to sea. The resulting composition becomes a visual game of back-and-forth. If we enter the scene as Western viewers at the left, following along the horizontal clapboards, we are interrupted by window openings of different shapes, some of which are dressed up with green shutters. Heading down the stairs, which Wyeth has graciously illuminated for us with brilliant white, we step down into the flats, and we cannot but be intrigued to follow the path across the grass and up the steps on the other side. And there, as we head up the gray staircase, we discover that the windows, though similar in shape, lack shutters. The darker clapboards seem more menacing, and the edge of the building at the far right is darkened by woolly vines creeping up its side.

Kent considered these two houses a blight on the island, but they capture our attention from Wyeth's perspective, seemingly the outward expression of the two different personalities that reside therein. The two structures may reflect Kent's own observations of his personality as a young artist who arrived in his early twenties and found himself attracted to a young, simple island woman, despite his efforts to maintain the propriety of what he described in his autobiography as "his better self."[7] Whether the twin houses allude to Kent's split personality, Wyeth has clearly designated one as the reflection of domesticity, all prim and proper, while the other expresses the darker, wilder, untamed sides of human nature, sprouting visibly into a tangle of foliage that thwarts our ability to perceive the plumb line of the building's right edge.

In the oil of the house that Kent subsequently built for his mother at Lobster Cove, on the southern tip of the island, the building—now Wyeth's studio—appears perched high above the viewer at the top of an formidable expanse of rocky coastline (cat. 72). The composition effectively places Kent and all that he represents on Monhegan at a seemingly unattainable distance. By situating his studio nearly at the center of the composition, silhouetted against clear blue sky, Wyeth focuses our attention on the sharp edges of the gabled roof and sides. The prominence of the Kent House in the Maine landscape recalls Winslow Homer's view of his own Maine studio at Prout's Neck, seen through a veil of fog (*The Artist's Studio in an Afternoon Fog*, 1894, Memorial Art Gallery, University of Rochester). Homer's scene is mysterious; its long, loose strokes of paint in the right foreground play before our eyes to suggest water, foam, and glistening rock in rapid succession as they congeal and dissolve. In Wyeth's composition an array of strokes with varying shapes and thicknesses create a looming pile of sharp rocks. The artist's chosen angle forces us to confront the placement and erect posture of the Kent House in such a forbidding setting.

The fruits of Kent's physical labor both building and painting on Monhegan set a high standard for Wyeth that the younger artist celebrates by rendering each rock and board—of "clear, straight-grained, seasoned spruce"— in his painting of Kent House. When the two artists later corresponded about Wyeth's purchase of Kent's painting, *Rocks, Monhegan*, as well as the Kent House, Kent recounted the gutsy decision he made in siting the building, against the better judgments of Monheganers, but according to his own keen observations of where the green grass grew right up to where the waves could lick the shoreline.[8]

Architecture on the mainland captures Wyeth's attention in *Head Tide—Maine*, where he explores the balance of proportions in the facade of a church with two symmetrical fan windows. The composition is a study in contrasts, the openings in the white clapboard set off by the darkened pines, golden light, and snow-covered landscape. And yet, without the top of the steeple visible, the building seems oddly planar and abstract, floating as though rendered on a theatrical flat that could be whisked up into the fly space of a stage in the blink of an eye.

On Southern Island, where Jamie Wyeth first painted in his youth, and where he now lives and works, he often depicts the landscape and a distinctive concatenation of buildings, including a rare surviving bell tower accompanying a lighthouse and keeper's residence (cat. 74). In an early rendering, the bell tower looms overhead, rushing into perspective toward the top edge of the sheet like a fantastic beanstalk stretching into the sky. Seen from below, the bell appears about to fall on top of us, or, at the least, sound an alarm loud enough to deafen us as it warns ships off the nearby ledge.

Thirty years later, the Southern Island Lighthouse becomes the quintessential Maine backdrop for Wyeth's intensely rendered purple iris rising up in the foreground (cat. 75). The smooth cylinder of painted brick supporting the lighthouse's beacon and the carefully delineated horizontal clapboards of the adjoining residence provide a pleasingly creamy mixture of proportions and textures that enhances the brilliant green blades of grass and softly curving iris petals unfurling themselves to full effect. The flowers present themselves shyly at first in the blossom at left, and then more boldly at right, as a mature iris pushes itself above the blades of grass, flaunting its sensual curves against the milky-white building.

Another decade later, in *A Murder of Crows*, Wyeth renders the winter landscape with the mesmerizing lavender hues that N. C. Wyeth so frequently favored in the reflected light of his snowscapes. The Southern Island Lighthouse and the bell tower are pushed out to the edges of this tightly shaped vertical canvas, a reprise with distinct variation on Wyeth's scene of the Monhegan *Twin Houses*, placed at the edge of the horizontal sheet. Rather than drawing our eye out to sea, the two structures are linked by the black shapes of crows taking flight from the darkened woods. The bare brush in the foreground is speckled with red berries, and the shape of another crow appears severed by the lower left edge. The winter sky is brilliant blue and streaming with undulating white cumulus clouds, but the birds are jarring—as are the more sinister crows that bear down on a snowbound fox in Winslow Homer's monumental winter landscape *Fox Hunt* (1893, Pennsylvania Academy of the Fine Arts), a painting that Jamie Wyeth admires.

The Southern Island bell tower doorway also serves as the triumphal archway for a celebration of Phyllis Wyeth's recovery from major surgery on her back. In *Southern Light* she stands erect with the help of a crutch and the rope banister, framed above by a gentle curve and on either side by doorjambs adorned by an array of deeply carved stars. Although Phyllis Wyeth had feared that she might never see Southern Island again after the surgery, she was able to return there to recuperate. Here she exudes an ethereal quality. In his own words, Jamie Wyeth hoped the portrait would capture her fragility as well as her triumph at having been able to sustain the ordeal, which he expressed through the eerie colors of the turbulent sea visible through the window behind her.[9] Outside, the warm sunlight illuminates her face, highlighting the clapboards that radiate on either side of her. The light magnifies the significance of her first step outdoors, as her right arm, grasping a crutch, casts a large shadow that echoes the curve of the archway. Poised at a portal between darkness and light, death and life, Phyllis appears as a modern-day version of the slender, elegant Gothic jamb figures on French cathedral doorways, lit from within by grace and radiating divine joy.

The clarity of Maine's autumn light is a perfect foil for Wyeth's fascination with pumpkins, a subject that appears in one of his earliest childhood drawings.[10] Dating from his productive year following the portrait exchange with Warhol at the Factory, *Pumpkin Shadow* draws us in with an image of a seemingly simple still life that when held up to the light casts a menacing silhouette.[11] Against a screen of pine trees that Wyeth frequently strings along the backgrounds of his Maine scenes to render a shallow space, he plops down on his watercolor paper a nearly perfect, brilliant orange pumpkin, with firm, deeply ridged skin that contrasts with the roughly textured and creviced granite ledge that it is perched on. The scene could be interpreted as a contemporary visual expression of Henry David Thoreau's well-known observation from *Walden* that he "would rather sit on a pumpkin and have it all to myself than be crowded on a velvet cushion."[12] Warhol's red velvet couch at the Factory certainly was that crowded cushion, but on Monhegan, where this scene was painted, Wyeth has the pumpkin all to himself—at least in the off-season.[13] The tension between those two worlds comes across in this image, between the transformation of the real object and its cast shadow. In the bright light, the appealing roundness of the pumpkin becomes a distorted, stretched oval that is divided by the long shadow formed by a deep gouge in the rock. And, if that were not enough to grab our attention, Wyeth highlights the phallic shape of the pumpkin's stem, mutating the fibrous tendrils of the pumpkin vine into formidable spikes the size and shape of pickaxes.

The pumpkins hurtling from *The Headlands of Monhegan Island, Maine* are also at once appealing and disturbing. The lush quality of the oil paint laid on with gusto draws us into a disorienting scene of resonant orbs flying out over the brilliant ultramarine blue sea. They are grinning at us both right side up and upside down, and they initially resemble balloons that are playfully suspended for our visual delight—that is, until we notice the looming dark shadow at the lower edge and witness pumpkin flesh smashed into pieces against the rocks. High on the cliffs to the upper right edge of the composition, Wyeth renders the jagged shapes of Monheganers crowded together on the Headlands to perform a post-Halloween ritual of casting jack-o'-lanterns into the sea. The composition is carefully observed and bizarrely surreal. The brilliant palette is intensely real, and the scene depicted both sinister and fun, much like the pagan rituals of Halloween that have been transformed into the annual American carnival. Wyeth imagines a place that holds all these traditions in suspension, a magical trick worthy of the best of Halloween treats.

In *Walden* Thoreau lives alone at the edge of a pond, whereas in *The Maine Woods* he climbs to the summit of Mount Katahdin, one of the highest points in the Northeast. Those two perspectives, one at the waterline and the other a vantage point that offers panoramic views, also distinguish themselves in Jamie Wyeth's contrasting images of the Brandywine River Valley and Maine. The reflections of *Brandywine Spiders*, *Dragonflies*, and *Patriot's Barn* all unfold near the waterline and ground level (see cats. 51–53). By contrast, several of Wyeth's scenes of Maine exploit an expansive perspective above or dramatically below the horizon. In *The Islander*, *Meteor Shower*, and *Wreck of the Polias*, Wyeth silhouettes his subjects against the horizon. *The Islander* depicts the fierce ram that wandered freely on Manana as an all-seeing, regal embodiment of untamed nature. His wool coat is lush with its wild curls, and the prominent profile of his muzzle and his curled horns make evident that this islander is a world apart from the goats that frolic around in *Goat Tree* on Point Lookout Farm (see cat. 62). The wild ram has even been described as a stand-in for the artist himself, who is fiercely dedicated to and protective of the world of Monhegan, which has been his touchstone since he was very young.[14]

Whereas the islander is master of all he surveys from the promontory of Manana, the direct gaze of the subject of *Portrait of Lady* is far more timid. The black-faced Hampshire sheep, her ears extending horizontally to mimic the background darkened by the afterglow of sunset, appears both comical and otherworldly. Her eyes gleam like two yellow glass marbles, and her woolly coat stands up off the surface of the canvas in a tour de force of paint laid on as though to replicate in three dimensions each curly lock. Imagined in 1968, when peace, love, and fringe were all the rage, along with shag carpeting and dreadlocks, Wyeth's answer to the fashion of the times takes the shape of a single sheep silhouetted against two broad bands of color. Although Lady is rooted in the earth, her head seems separate from her body, with her face floating before her like a mask. Her engaging black face invites us to think about what life and the landscape might look like from the perspective of a sheep—not just any sheep, but this very inquisitive personality named Lady, who quite regally poses for us in the barren and beautiful setting that surrounds her.

Meteor Shower is more sinister in mood, the sharply angled head of the costumed scarecrow resembling the scythe of the Grim Reaper against a night sky that is illuminated by moonlight and the arcs of streaming meteors. To achieve a sense of otherworldliness, Wyeth added ground pearl to his pigment, injecting a certain preciousness that enhances the foreboding quality of the menacing, beaked silhouette. The scarecrow wears a military jacket that appears in many Wyeth paintings, an allusion to a particular jacket that was originally given to N. C. Wyeth by his mentor, Howard Pyle.[15] The off-kilter tilt of the scarecrow looming up in the foreground belongs to the larger body of work that has been recently identified by Joyce Hill Stoner as part of the Wyeth family signature perspective of vertigo. The nocturnal setting, the juxtaposition of a looming face against a distant sea, and the ominous,

Fig. 19. Winslow Homer (1836–1910)
The Lookout—All's Well, 1896
Oil on canvas
101.28 x 76.52 cm (39⅞ x 30⅛ in.)

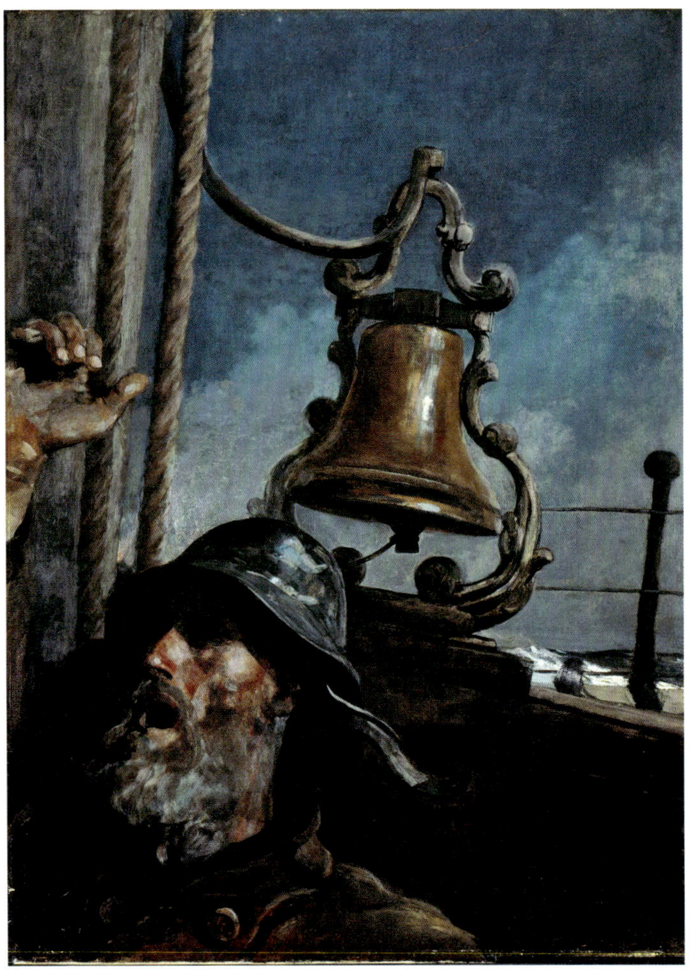

canting foreground on which the viewer struggles to find footing recall the night watch of Winslow Homer's *The Lookout—All's Well* (fig. 19). The lighthouse beam nearly dead center suggests that all may be well if only there is a way to traverse the eerily moonlit rocks and sea to get there, and yet the ominous scarecrow would be right at home in the setting of a horror story or screenplay by the Maine author Stephen King.

In *Wreck of the Polias* a large propeller from a massive vessel that ran aground greets visitors from its current resting place on Southern Island atop a ledge. Here the bold, abstract form of the propeller carves away parts of the sky with curved petal shapes attached to a central stem that take on the appearance of a surreal flower. Like the subjects silhouetted above the horizon in *Meteor Shower* and *Kent House*, the propeller looms before us, sucking us into the image like an enormous turbine and dropping us into the center of the composition, where the visual effect of the scene emerges with dynamic energy unleashed by a carefully constructed centrifuge. Just right of center, Wyeth depicts his diminutive Jack Russell terriers with all their gamine appeal. They perch on the ledge casually, seemingly undaunted by the edginess that falls into their surroundings like a guillotine. One turn of the propeller blade would easily slice these Jacks in two; Wyeth poses one dog beneath the curve of the blade, severed like a taxidermy head mounted to a backboard, and the other sits with his back nearly touching it, unaware of the possibility of becoming at any moment the next mounted specimen.

Wyeth's dogs, especially his Jack Russell terriers, have been loyal companions for adventures on land and sea. They are vividly portrayed in two smaller, jewel-like paintings, *Thanks for Saving My Life* and *Homer.* In the first, the dog Tiller sits forlorn if relieved in a gleaming puddle of water, having been fished out of Tenants Harbor and resuscitated by quick action on the part of a nearby good Samaritan, Steve Ausplund.[16] Homer, a Jack Russell with the spiky fur known as a rough coat, seems to float magically above the ultramarine-blue waters of Maine, with the green sliver of

Southern Island peeking above the distant horizon. Homer's soulful expression presses toward the front of the picture plane, an invitation to all dog lovers to enjoy another finely painted portrait of the artist's best friend.

The death of a young girl's favorite dog, Sammy, is the subject of Wyeth's third illustrated book, which is set in Maine (cat. 87). The bubbles that Sammy chases along the beach belong to an august tradition of still life painting dating to the Renaissance, in which bubbles are a symbol of life's fragility. In the final scene, Wyeth reimagines the bubbles, set off against the pale blue Maine sky and water, as streaming puffs of white clouds that transform themselves into the shape of a dog rushing headlong toward heaven. The story of *Sammy in the Sky* and Wyeth's accompanying illustrations offer a bittersweet tribute to a beloved family pet; following Andrew Wyeth's death in January 2009, the illustration project may have offered a way to work through mourning a parent's death.

American films offer an enticingly rich context for Wyeth's portrayals of Maine, including Alfred Hitchcock's *The Birds* (1963), *Dolores Claiborne* (1995), based on a novel by Stephen King, and *Seven* (1995), all of which have a distinct cinematography and deadly undertone that play well with Wyeth's own compositions—and especially his major preoccupation with creating *Inferno, Monhegan* and *The Seven Deadly Sins*, between 2005 and 2008.[17] Wyeth spent much of his youth attending movies and drawing his favorite stars, becoming a James Bond fan as a teenager, and later regularly watching King Vidor's *The Big Parade* (1925) with his father in their studio.[18] While visiting the Metropolitan Museum of Art with Lincoln Kirstein, Wyeth noted that a medieval helmet reminded him of something he had seen in a Sergei Eisenstein film; Kirstein later shared with him the volumes of drawings and sketches the Russian director had given him as a token of thanks for the financial support that made Eisenstein's film *Thunder over Mexico* possible.[19] There was certainly a great deal of filmmaking happening in and around Warhol's Factory, and, more recently, Wyeth collaborated with Stephen King on creating concepts for an imaginary beast that stalks its unsuspecting victims in a television pilot, *Kingdom Hospital*, set in Maine, which aired in 2004.[20] To this day, the artist watches films as part of his morning routine, and he even produced a documentary film with the director and cameraman D'Arcy Marsh about the painting of *Inferno, Monhegan*.

The trajectory that culminates in the paintings and related studies of *The Seven Deadly Sins* and *Inferno, Monhegan* may be traced over the course of two and a half decades, beginning with the gigantic *Raven*, which the artist began on Monhegan and later returned to his Wilmington studio to finish. The picture measures five by six feet, giving ample room to render the beak and talons at the scale of a good-sized scimitar; this monstrous raven seems to have more in common with its carnivorous prehistoric ancestor, *Tyrannosaurus rex*, than with any of its modern-day descendants. A gull similar to the one that later becomes the model for *Anger* in *The Seven Deadly Sins* initially debuted in Wyeth's first retrospective of 1980, although his images of gulls reappear somewhat innocently in his work over subsequent decades—*Sea Star, Run*, and *Butterscotch, Gull, and Hot Fudge Sundae*.[21] All three of these paintings share an interest in the work of art as an assemblage of real elements. Of the three, *Sea Star* depicts a gull biting a starfish, a gesture that later reappears in *The Seven Deadly Sins*, but in this instance predator and prey are meticulously camouflaged within the shell- and pebble-strewn shore. Wyeth expands his world as imagined within the world of real objects by creating his very own artfully constructed frame in which an array of tiny shells are carefully laid in mosaic-like patterns inspired by traditional nineteenth-century sailors' valentines. The artistic nature of the construction, in which larger shells are grouped together to resemble the carved rosettes that appear in corners of picture frames, makes *Sea Star*, both painting and frame, a masterful composition.[22] Wyeth teases us by including so many real shells around an image of the beach that we seem

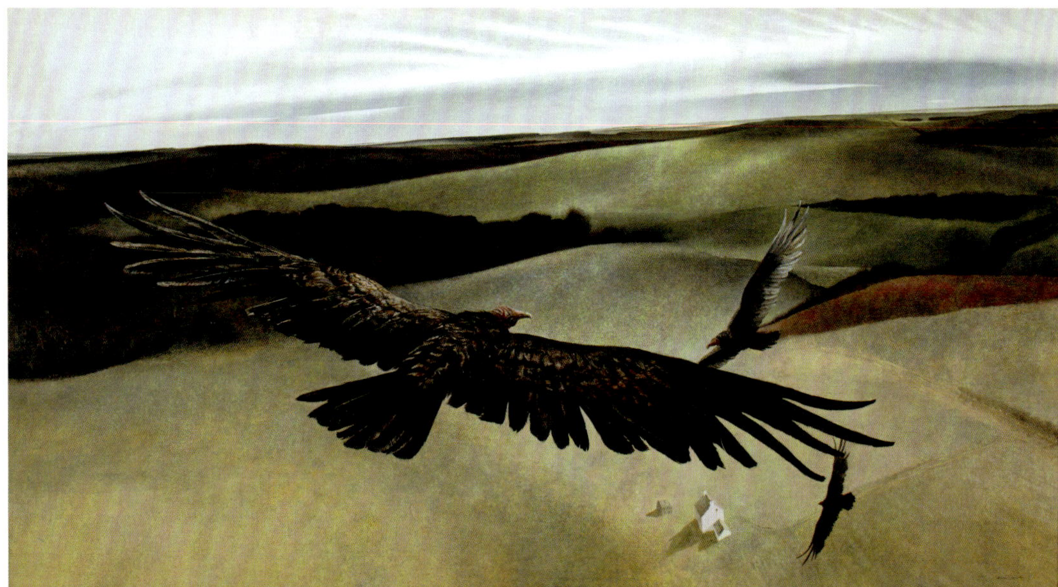

Fig. 20. Andrew Wyeth (1917–2009)
Soaring, 1942–50
Tempera on Masonite
121.9 x 221 cm (48 x 87 in.)

to be able to reach out and grab our own "sea star" as a souvenir. Though many artists go to great lengths to create sympathetic frames for their paintings, Wyeth's construction of the frame for *Sea Star* effectively places side by side the object he paints and the found objects he assembles, a visual collision of his skill at matching and making that mediates among the realms of folk art, found assemblage, and his own brand of realism.

In *Run* Wyeth appeals to our parental instincts, depicting a mother gull that fills half of the composition, while a young chick scurries away, presumably to escape some looming predator. Wyeth tries to distract our attention from the young bird's run for its life with an array of white streaks of paint beneath the brooding mother that initially—humorously—resemble bird droppings from a bird that definitely has the runs. The fate of the chick is a mystery. Wyeth attaches three small, unmatched letter tiles made of bone at the lower left corner. As we turn our heads to investigate, the letters spell out the chick's prophecy, "RUN," in mismatched fonts resembling those on a Ouija board. Drawing on his well-stocked toolbox of visual puns and games, Wyeth is ultimately playing with us, as we take in the composition and wonder whether the chick ultimately escapes.

In *Butterscotch, Gull, and Hot Fudge Sundae*, every dripping ooze of chocolate sauce, softly creased piping of vanilla-tinged whipped cream, and translucent glaze of Maraschino cherry becomes a feast for the eyes. The brilliant red cherry on top, reflecting the intense hue of artificial food coloring, is echoed by the red spot on the underside of the gull's beak—a detail that may leave us with quite a different taste in our mouths. Newly hatched herring gulls peck at the brilliant red spot on the mother's beak to solicit nourishment in the form of regurgitated food. As though to connect the red dots between the appetites of humans, gulls, and their myopic progeny, Wyeth suggests that we, too, might be moved to regurgitation if we were to eat as much ice cream with all the trimmings as he has placed before us. And, underscoring Wyeth's sense that our eyes are bigger than our stomachs, the artist has observed that the missing chunk of paper at the lower left looks as though someone has recently taken a bite out of the sheet.[23]

And then there is the unfolding of *The Seven Deadly Sins* in its full Sensurround experience. If we think in cinematic terms, the series could begin with *The Monhegan Island Schoolhouse*, in which seagulls appear static on the lawn beneath the Gothic Revival New England clapboard building that rises up toward the upper edge of the composition. The steep cant of the landscape and the severed roof of the schoolhouse immediately set the viewer on edge. Streaming across the clapboards of the white building and seeming to reach inside the windows are large shadows that suggest fingers, or even feathers of the sort that appear in the turkey vultures' wingtips in Andrew Wyeth's painting *Soaring* (fig. 20), and Jamie Wyeth's various images of turkey vultures based on a chick raised at Point Lookout Farm.[24] The presentation of the gabled schoolhouse high on the crest of the hill resembles the prominent position of the Bates home as seen from below at the edge of the highway in Hitchcock's film *Psycho* (1960). A scene of seagulls quietly and steadily stalking a simple schoolhouse with a belfry from Hitchcock's *The Birds* (1963) strikes a tone closer to that of *The Monhegan Island Schoolhouse*. The birds later appear in the film scattered across the grass in front of the house occupied by Tippi Hedren and her family, just as they dot the foreground of Wyeth's painting, in both instances calmly awaiting their prey. In *The Birds*, as in Wyeth's composition, the chilling quality of these images derives from tales and observations of seagulls behaving as killers, and, on Monhegan, the real-life experience of those who have witnessed gulls waiting patiently outside the schoolhouse ready to swoop down on their prey, the lunches of the island's children.

As Wyeth works his way through all the manifestations of *The Seven Deadly Sins*, we arrive at the full expression of his Maine experience in *Inferno, Monhegan*. Here the everyday that is overlooked meets the eye of the artist and is transformed into one of the largest and most panoramic scenes he has executed in recent years. Wyeth recalled how he came to imagine his surroundings on Monhegan through the visions of the Italian poet of the Middle Ages Dante Alighieri and the northern Renaissance painter Hieronymus Bosch. In the catalogue that accompanied an exhibition of *The Seven Deadly Sins*, Wyeth described how he had witnessed the scene he ultimately painted in *Inferno, Monhegan* over the course of several years: "To burn garbage on the island they created this moveable tank, an oil tank, they cut a hole in it and then put wheels on it. It would be taken to various beaches on the island . . . and this amazing child, a brother of Orca Bates of whom I did a series of paintings, was given the job to feed this thing. I remember when I first saw it I just about fainted. I mean, it was something out of Wagner." Wyeth focused on the irony of how others, new to the island, found the scene completely unremarkable: "It always kills me, you know, you see painters arriving with their easels and whatnot and they walked right by this. [It] stunk, and the gulls were streaking in and here is this angelic boy shoving garbage in with his oar. It was just like out of Dante. You couldn't have made it up."[25]

And Wyeth paints it in many ways as Everyman's nightmare: stoking the fires of hell for eternity while savage birds swirl, hover, and dive from above. Seen from behind, the skinny brother of Orca Bates hardly looks like a match for the work he has to do. Even without having seen the film Wyeth made while he painted *Inferno, Monhegan*, one can imagine the sound of gulls screeching, wings beating, the putrid smell of garbage and smoke, and fire and light glinting off the water. In this instance, Wyeth takes us right to the water's edge, and yet we are worlds apart from the contemplative, reflective nature of the Brandywine River. Instead, the artist offers us a dramatic ringside seat on the inner sanctum of Monhegan's form of hell.

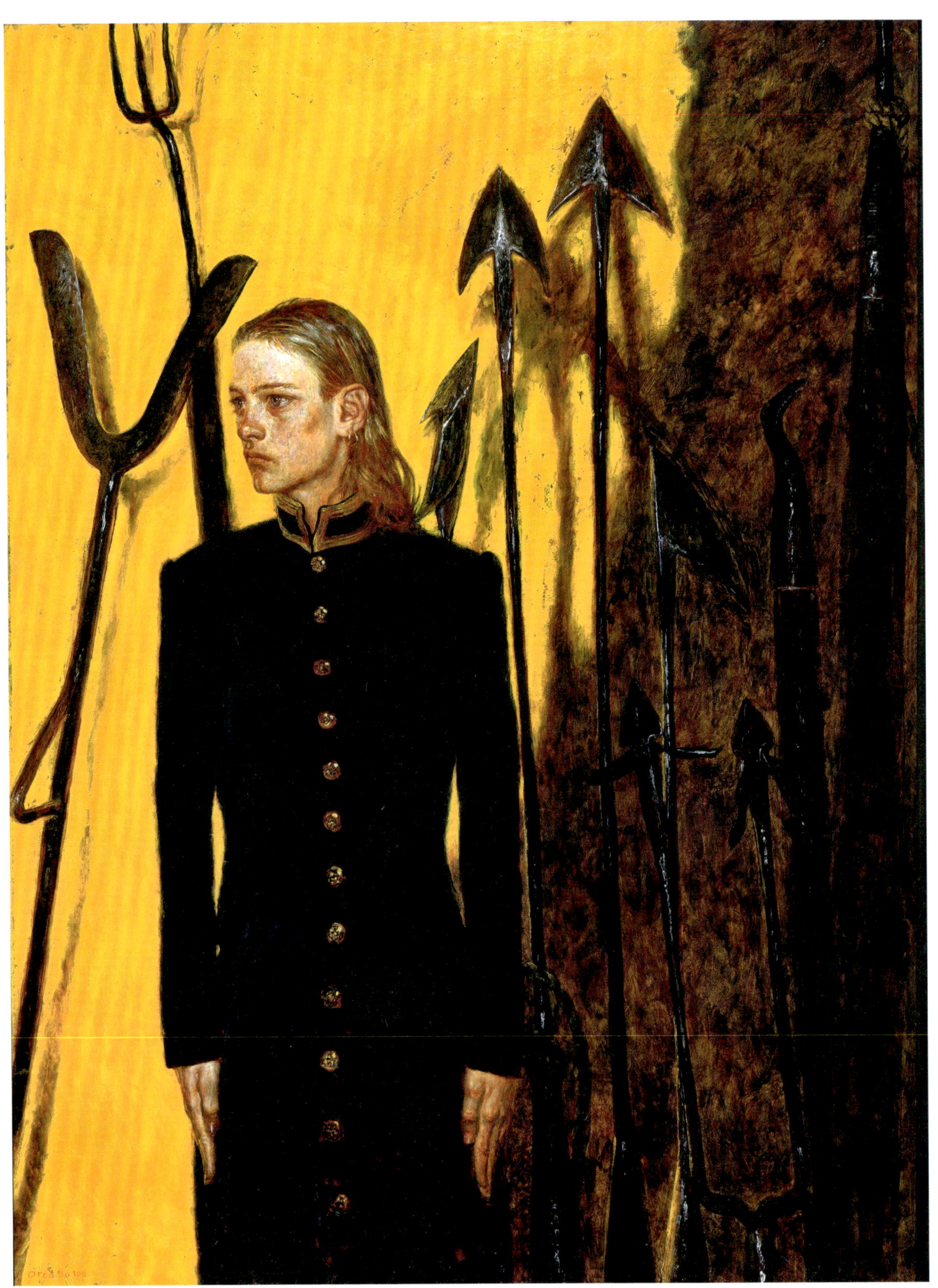

67. *Orca*, 1990. Oil on panel, 101.6 x 76.2 cm (40 x 30 in.)

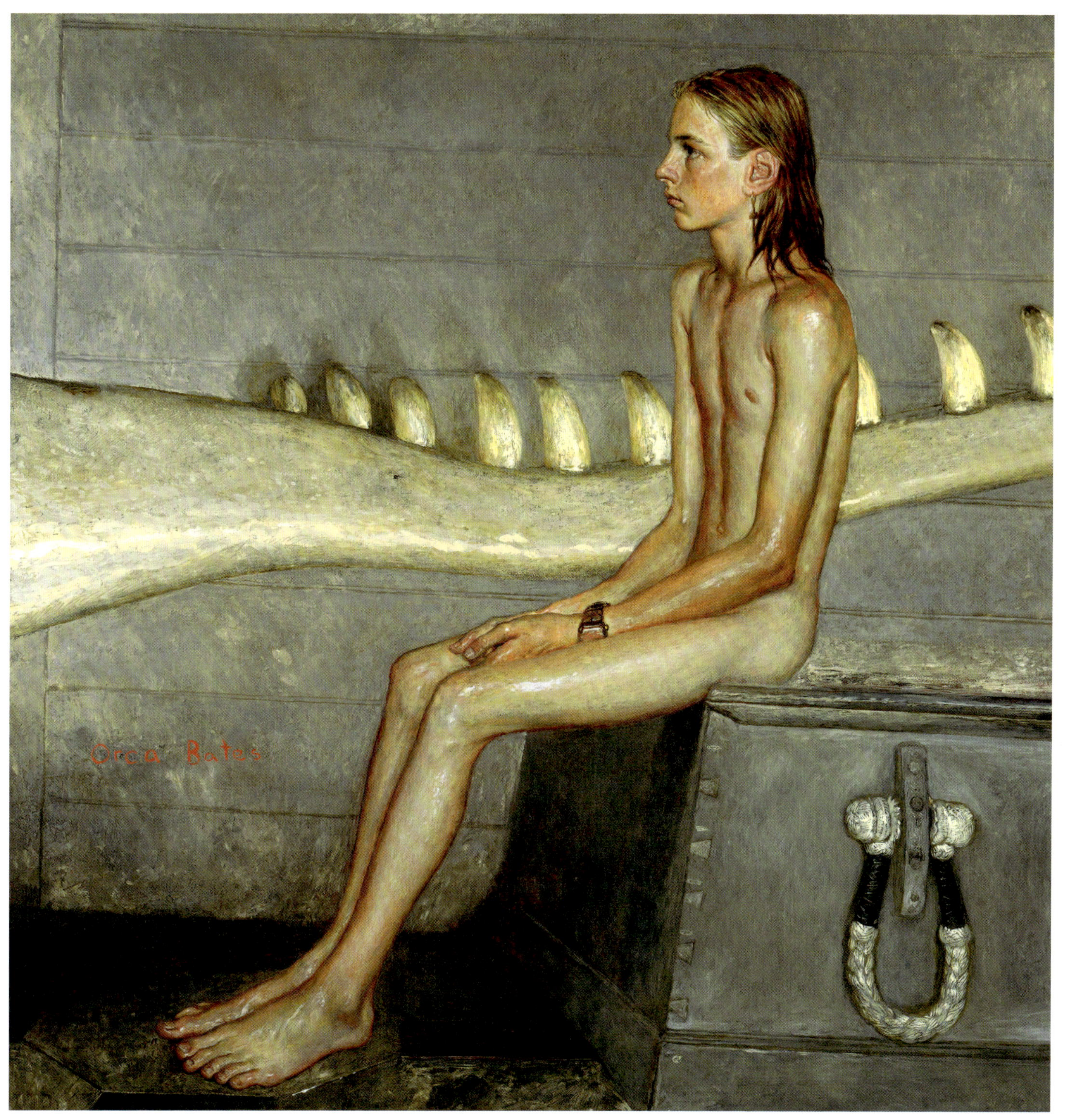

68. *Orca Bates*, 1990. Oil on panel, 101.6 x 101.6 cm (40 x 40 in.)

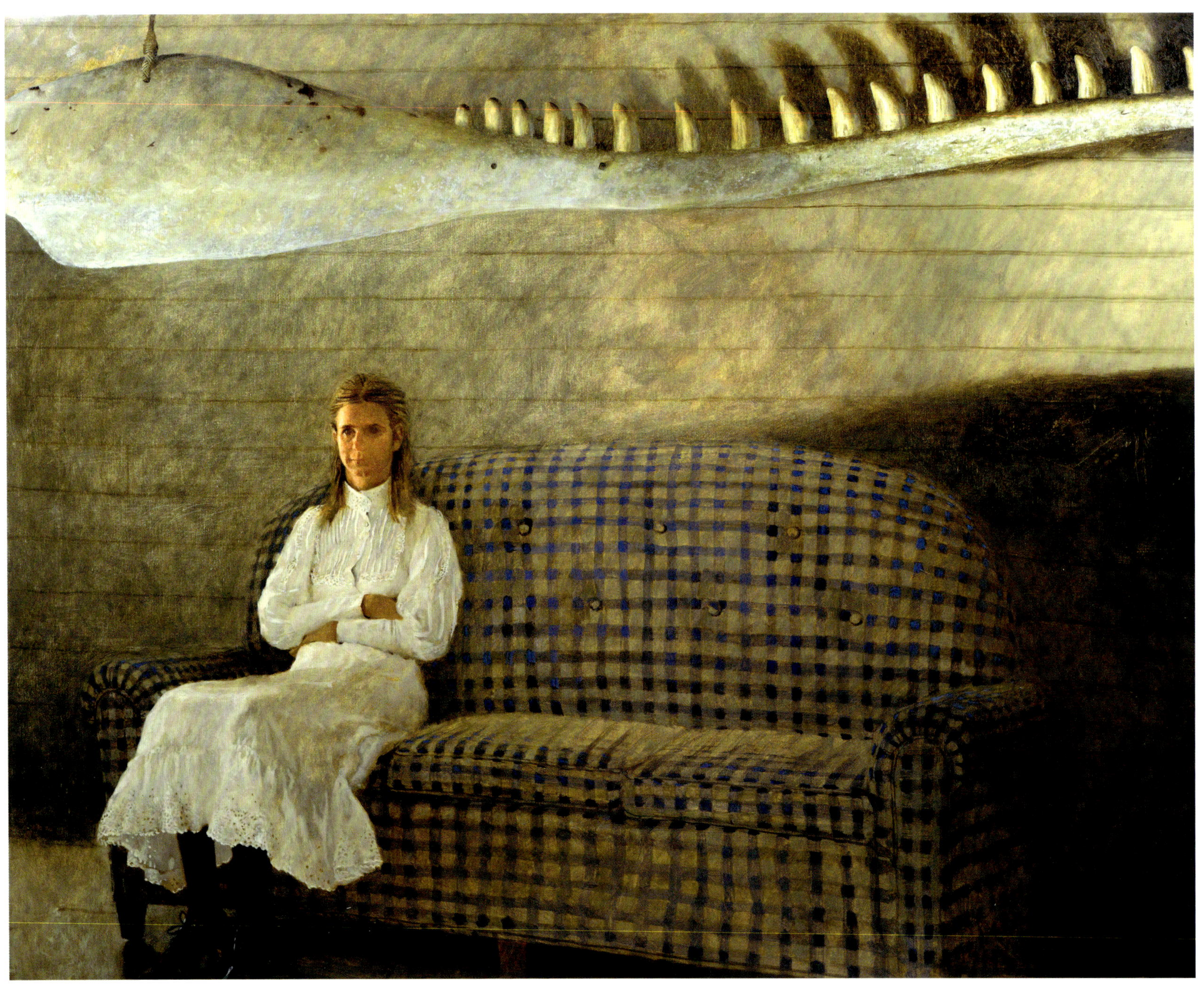

69. *Whale*, 1978. Oil on canvas, 91.4 x 116.8 cm (36 x 46 in.)

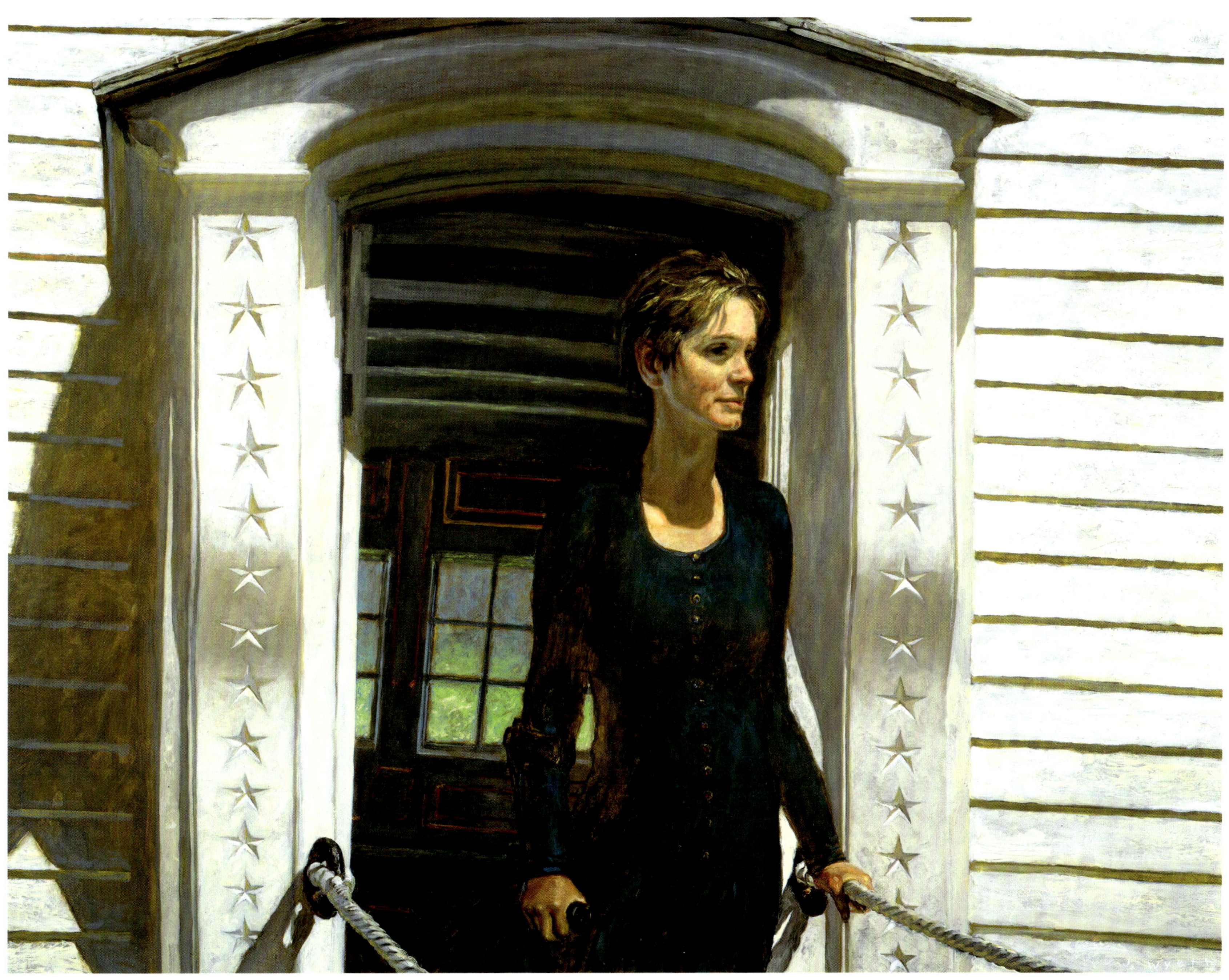

70. *Southern Light*, 1994. Enamel and oil on board, 91.4 x 122 cm (36 x 48 in.)

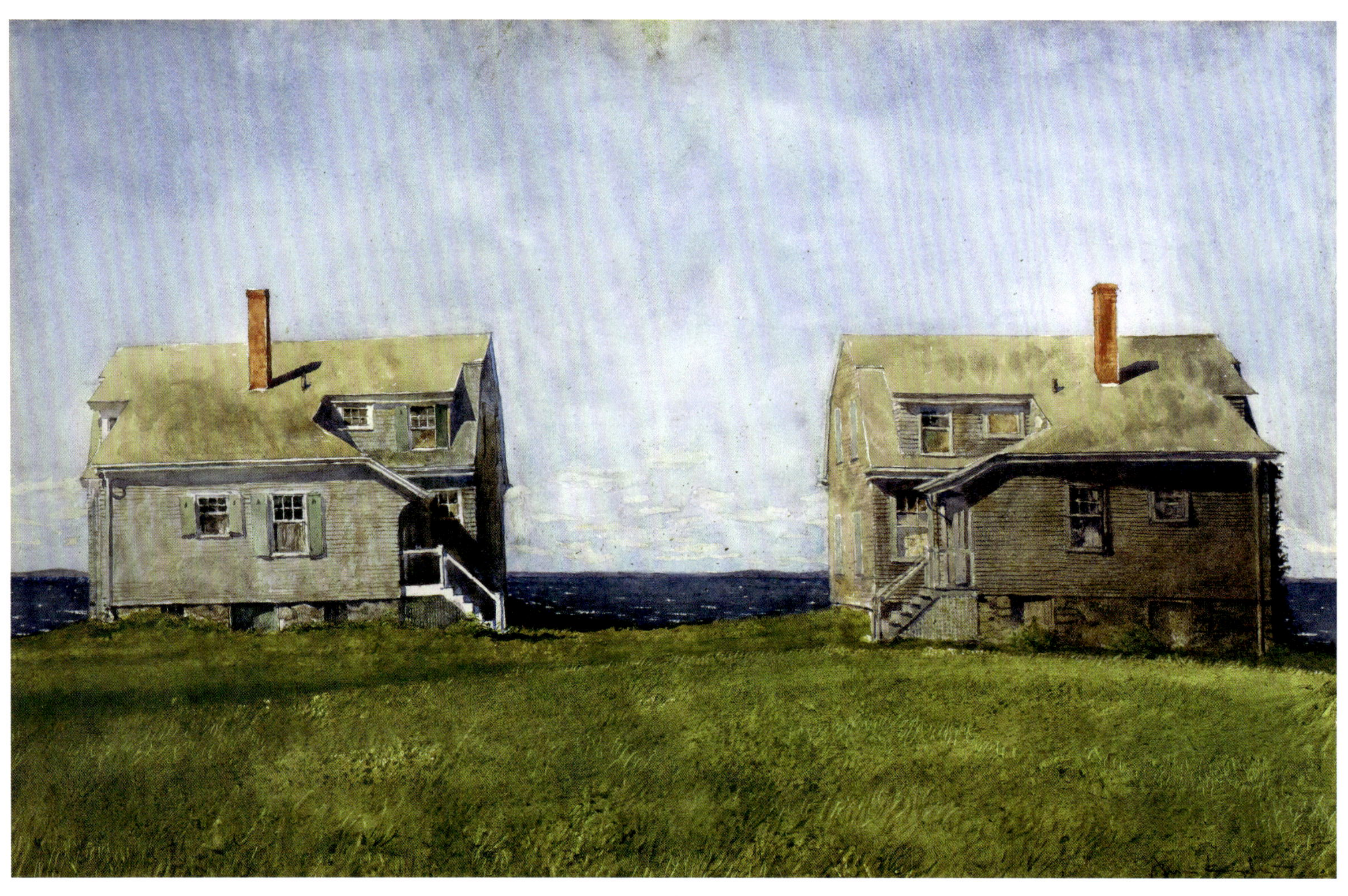

71. *Twin Houses*, 1969. Watercolor on watercolor paper, 48.3 x 76.2 cm (19 x 30 in.)

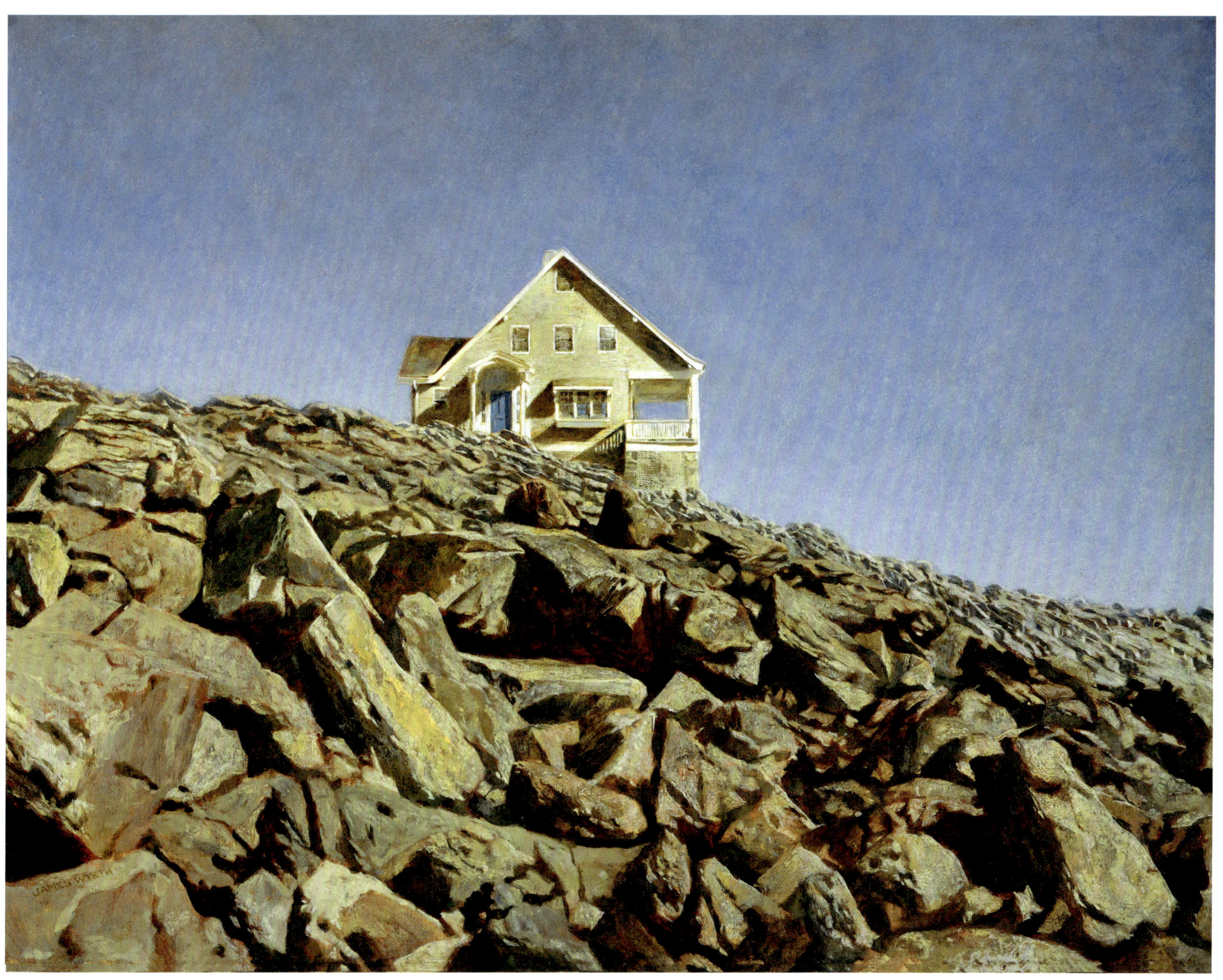

72. *Kent House*, 1972. Oil on canvas, 76.2 x 101.6 cm (30 x 40 in.)

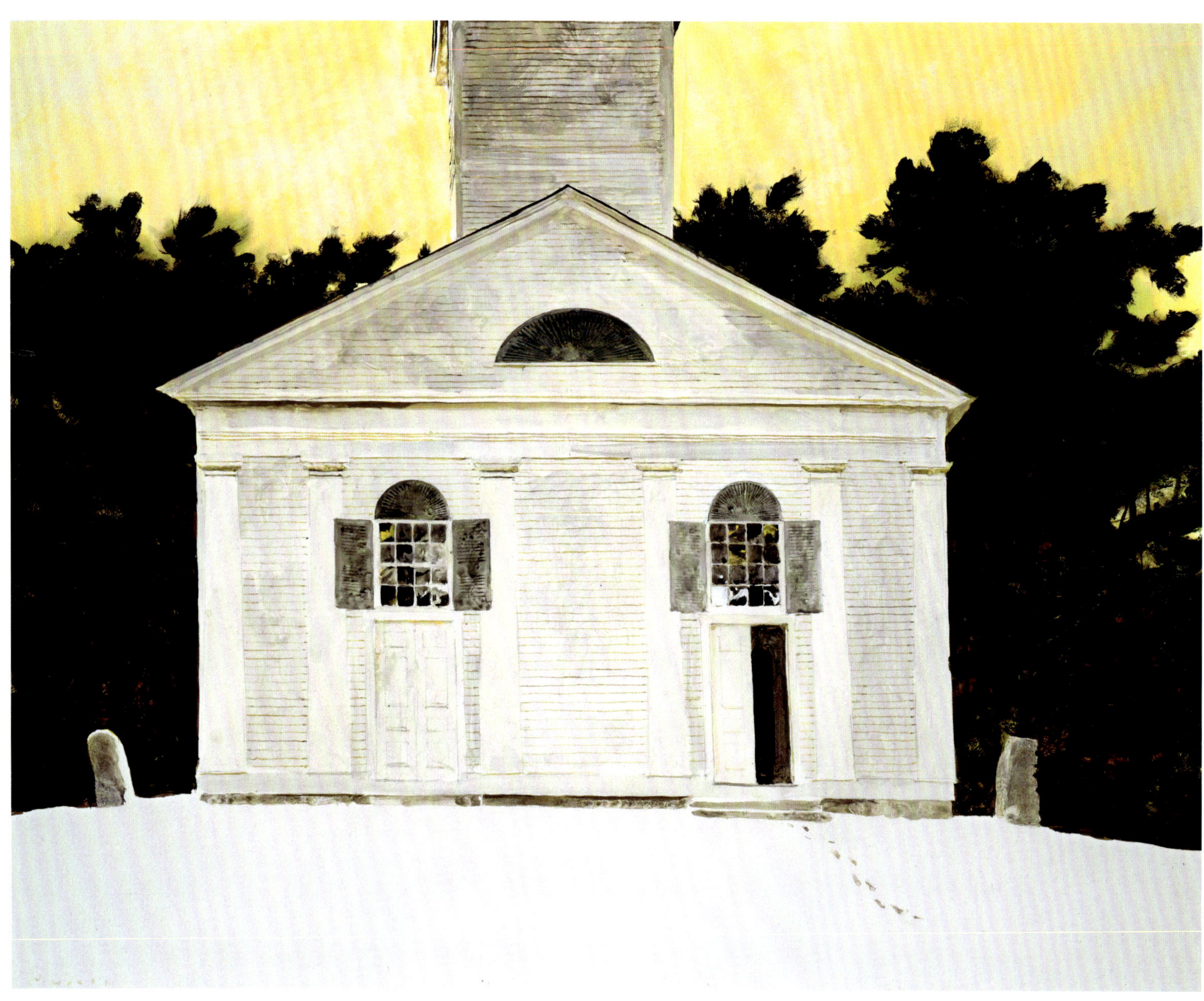

73. *Head Tide—Maine*, 1991. Watercolor on rag paper, 58.4 x 73.7 cm (23 x 29 in.)

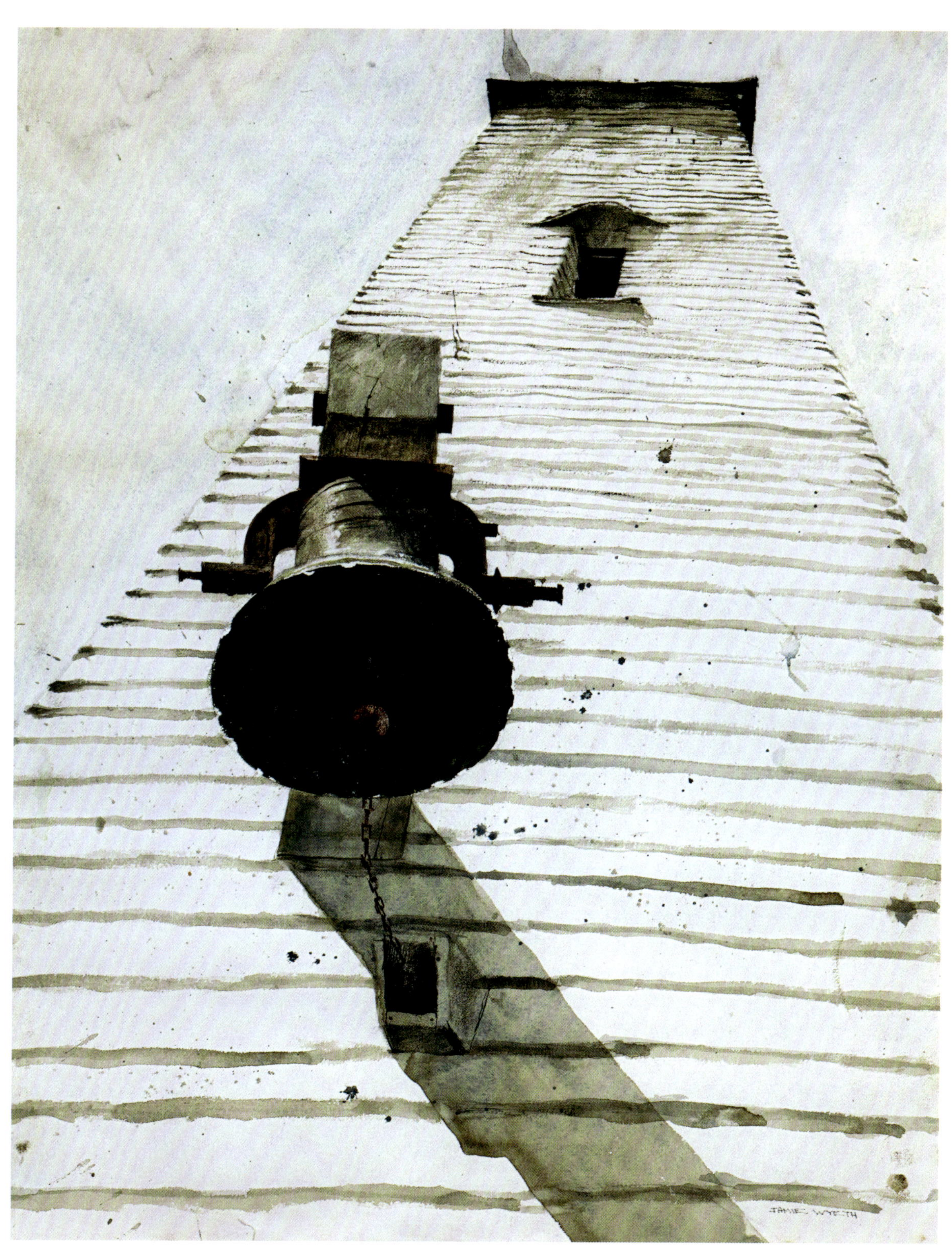

74. *Bell Tower*, 1963. Watercolor on paper, 58.4 x 47 cm (23 x 18½ in.)

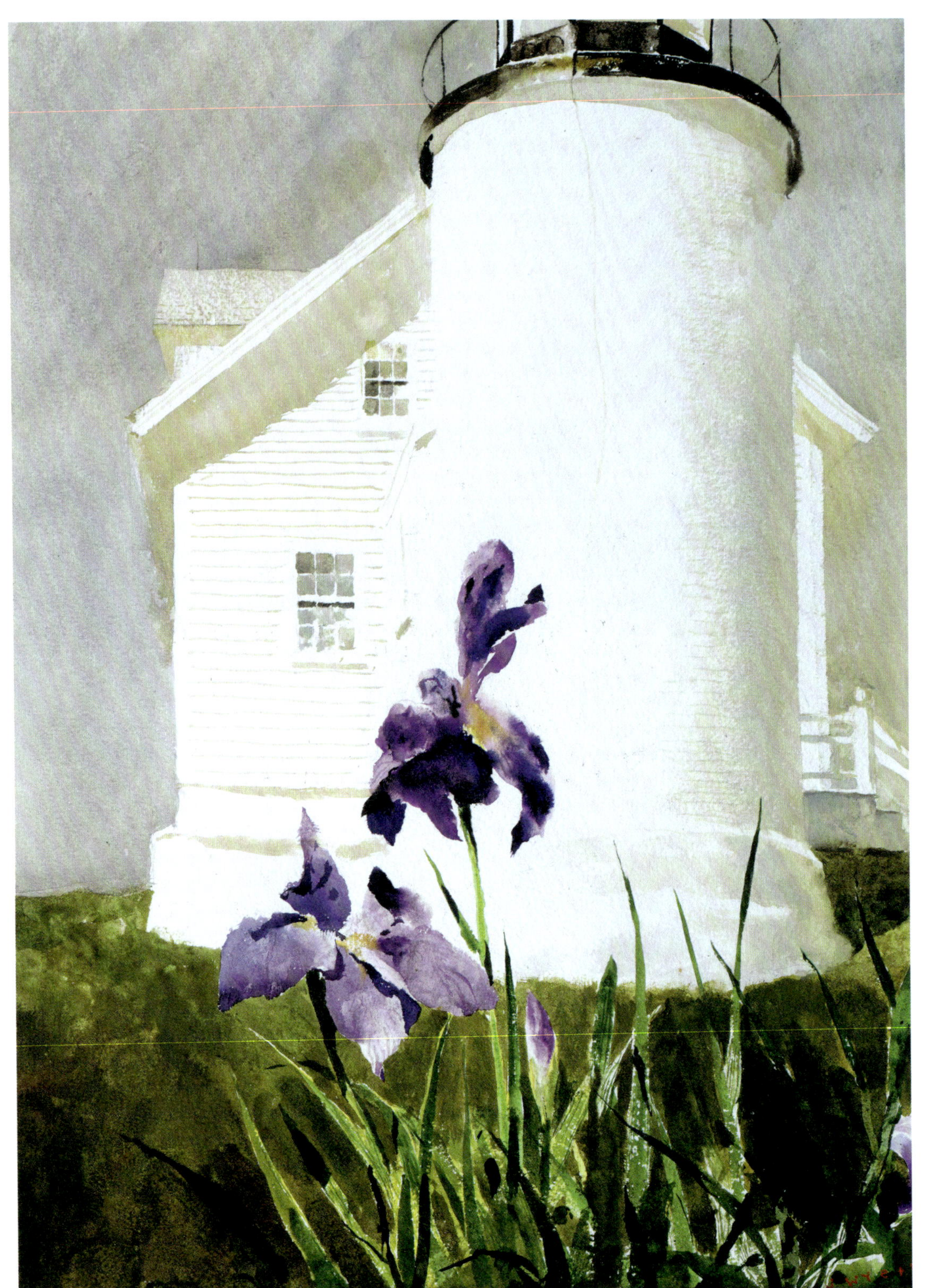

75. *Lighthouse Iris*, 1993. Gouache and watercolor on toned rag board, 71.1 x 53.3 cm (28 x 21 in.)

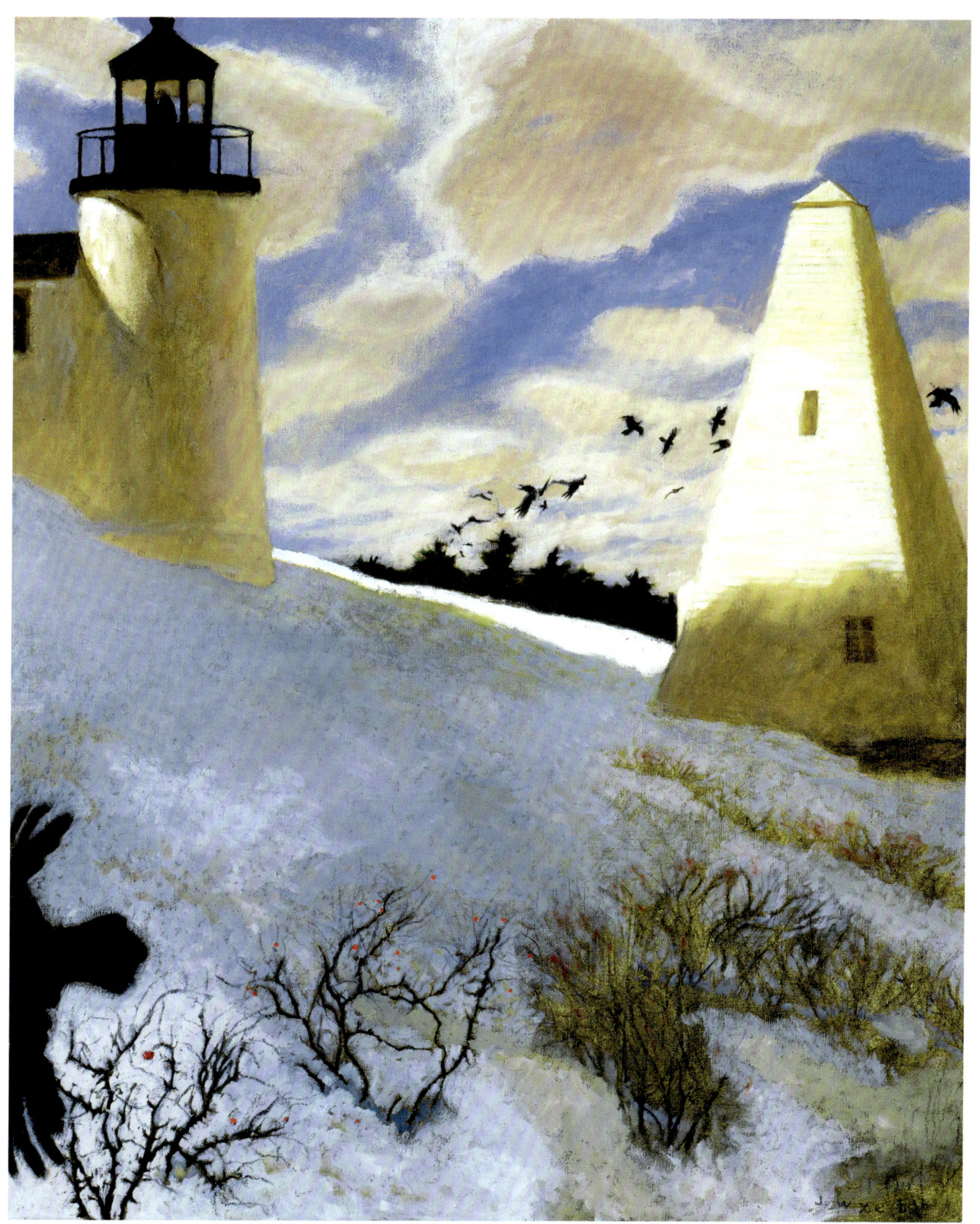

76. *A Murder of Crows*, 2003. Oil on canvas, 91.4 x 76.2 cm (36 x 30 in.)

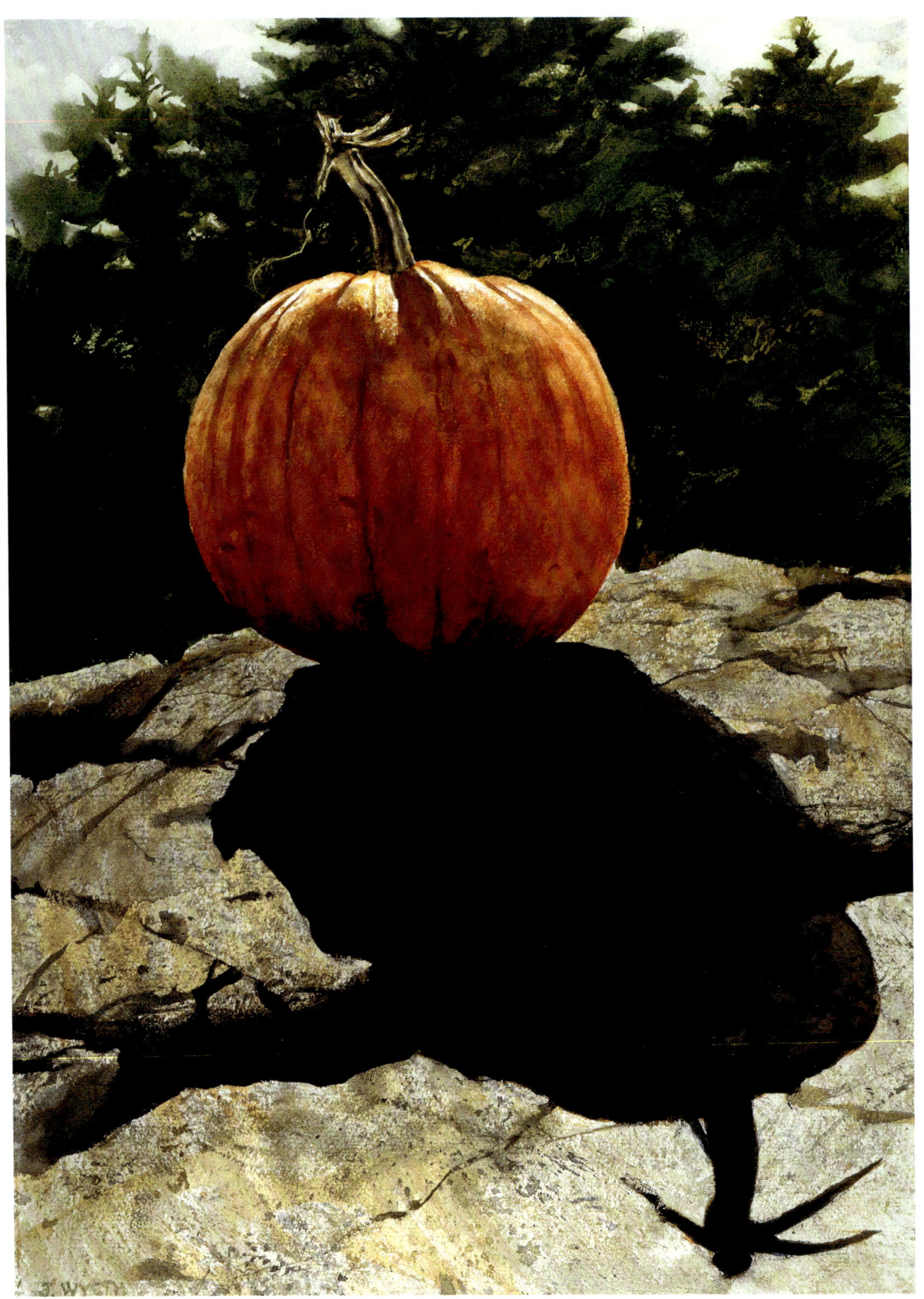

77. *Pumpkin Shadow*, 1977. Watercolor on paper, 76.2 x 54.6 cm (30 x 21½ in.)

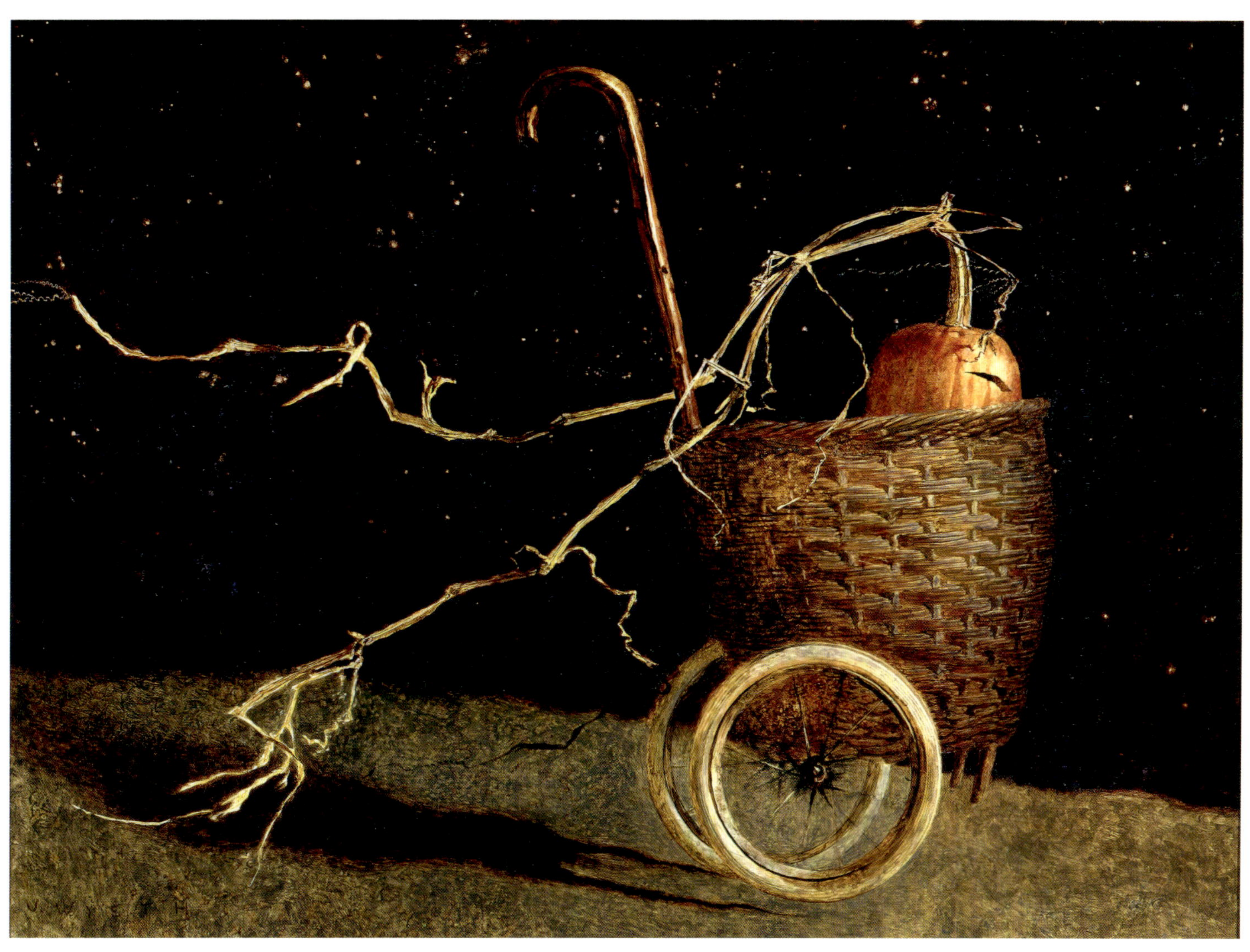

78. *Mischief Night*, 1986. Watercolor and varnish on Strathmore rag paper, 57.2 x 78.7 cm (22½ x 31 in.)

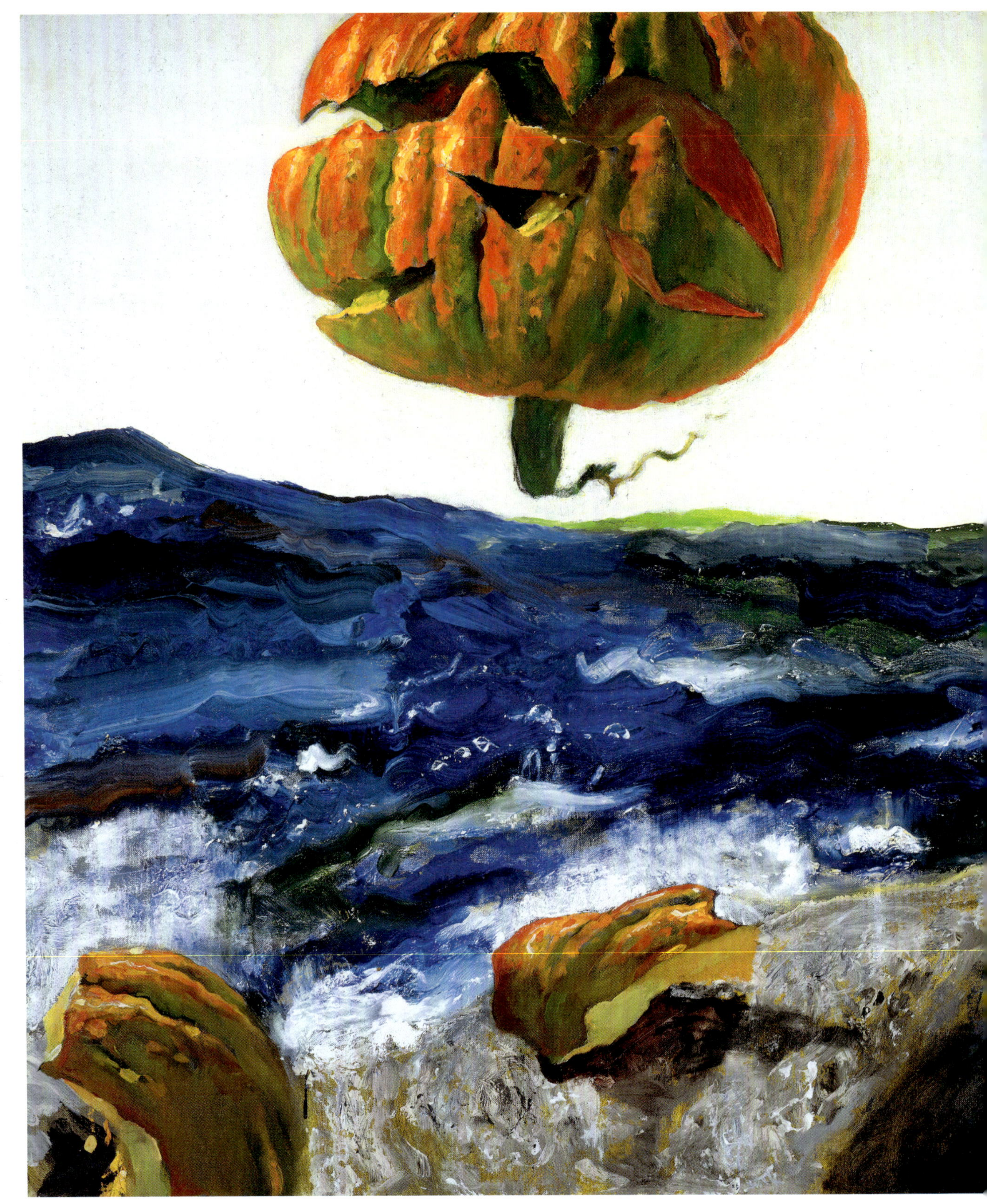

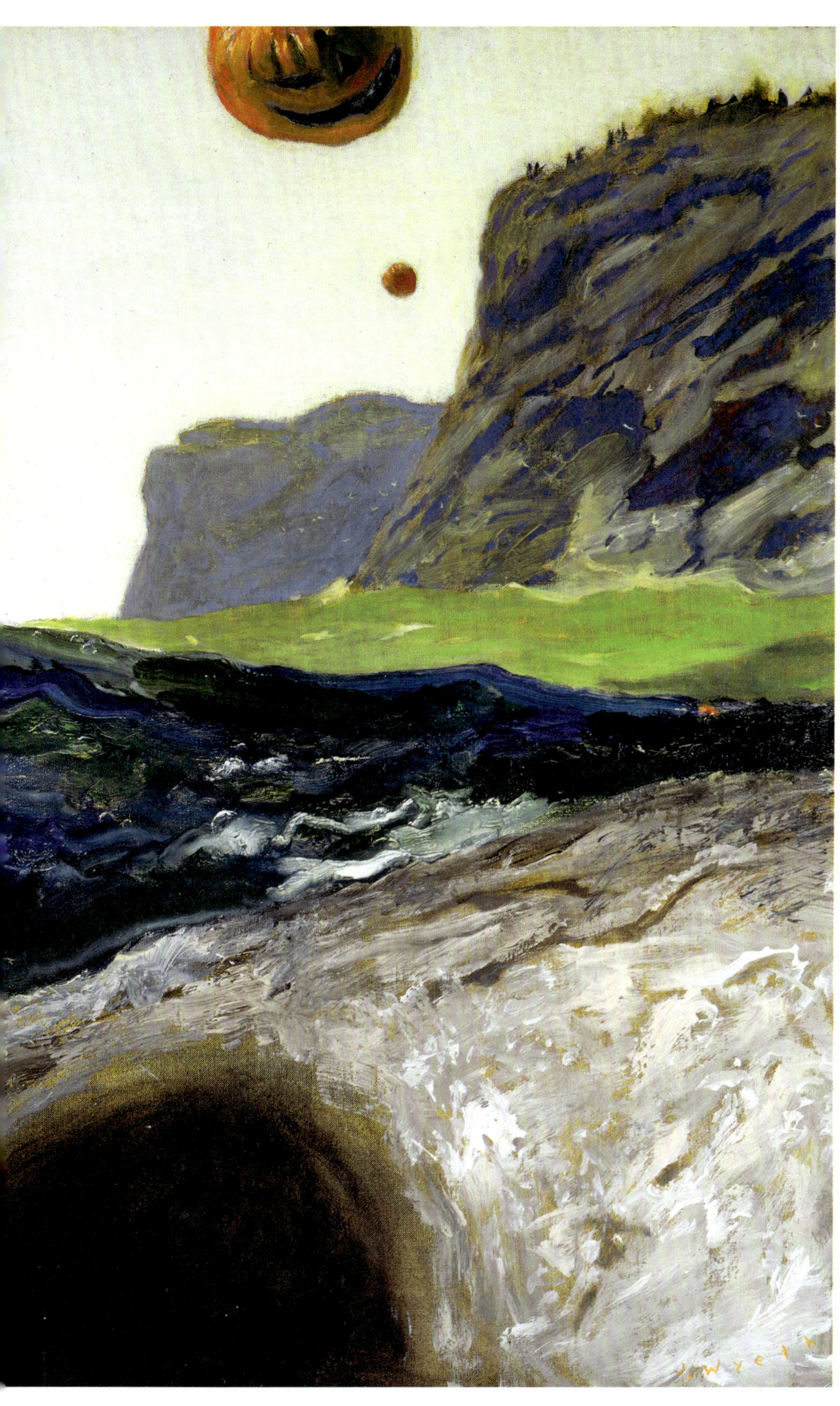

79. *The Headlands of Monhegan Island, Maine,* 2007. Oil on canvas, 101.6 x 152.4 cm (40 x 60 in.)

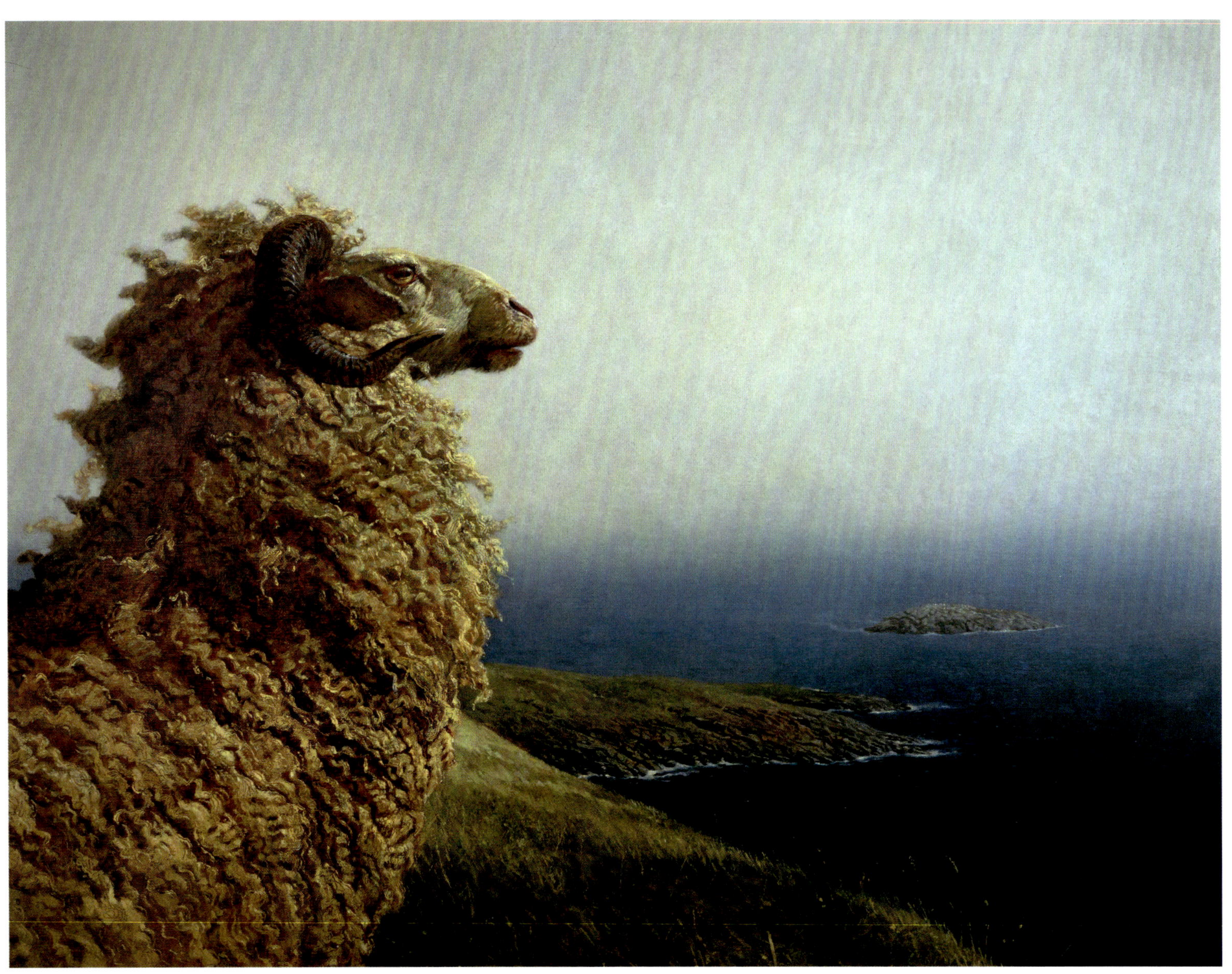

80. *The Islander*, 1975. Oil on canvas, 86.4 x 112.7 cm (34 x 44⅜ in.)

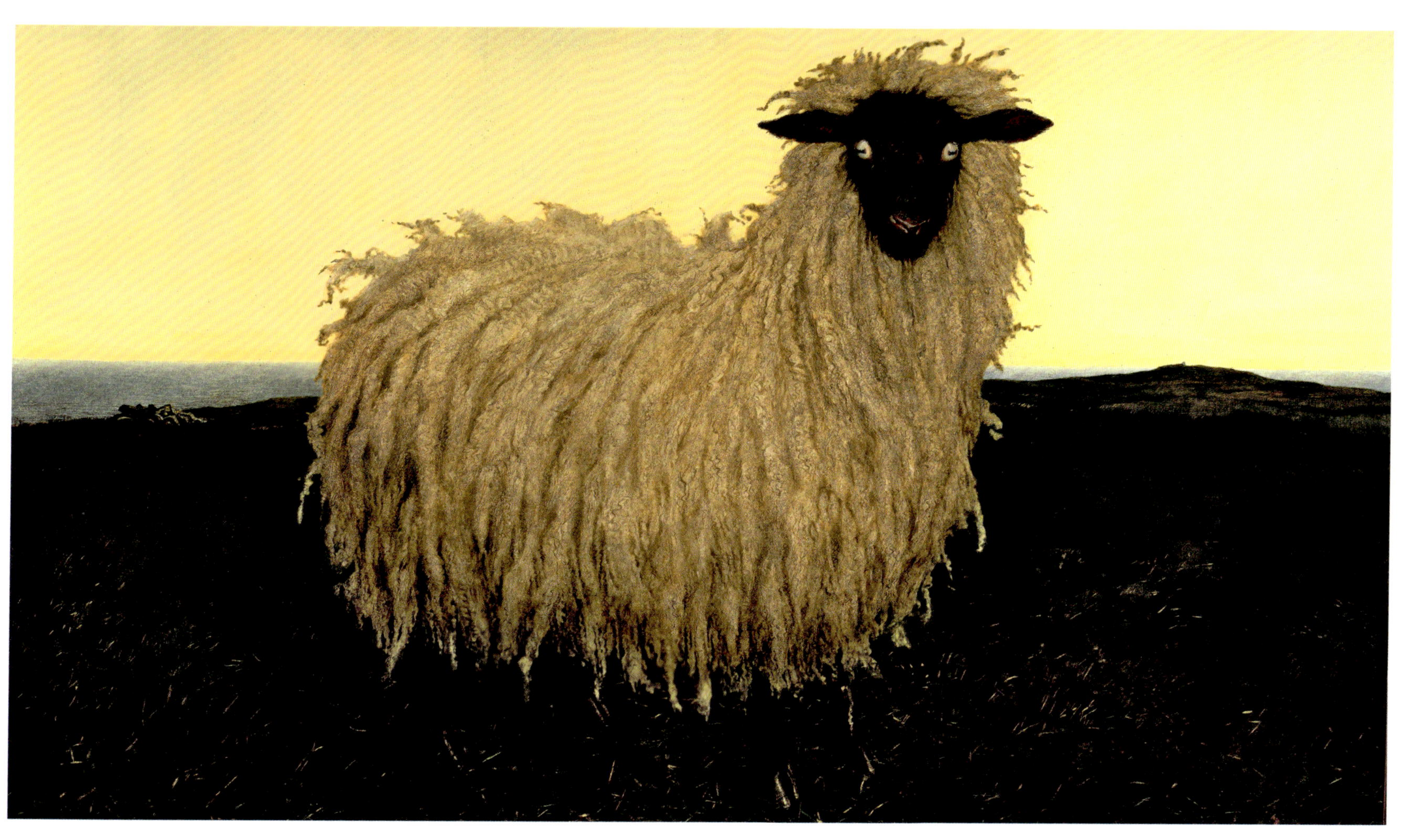

81. *Portrait of Lady*, 1968. Oil on canvas, 91.4 x 161.3 cm (36 x 63½ in.)

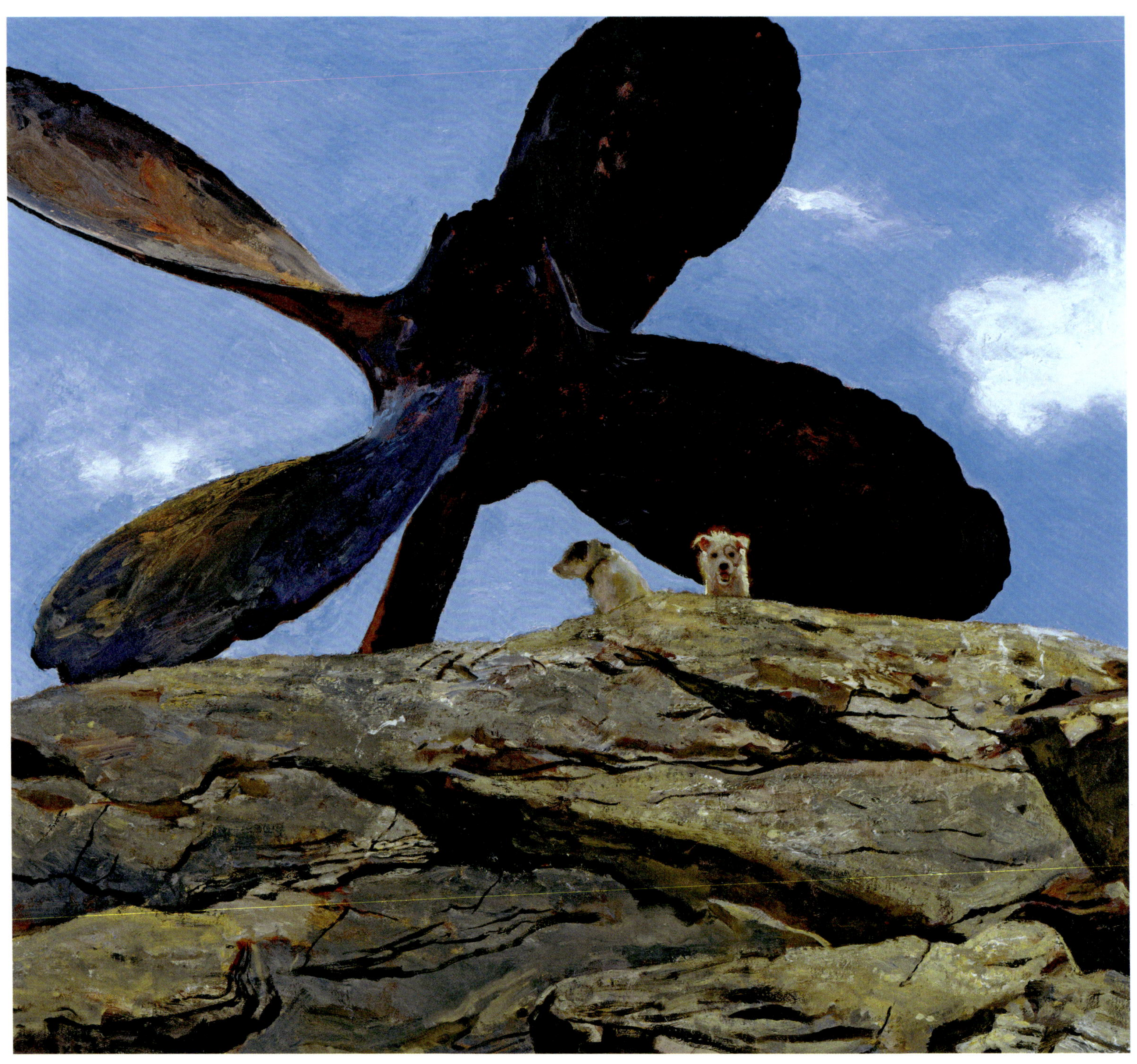

82. *Wreck of the Polias*, 2002. Oil on board, 70.5 x 78.7 cm (27¾ x 31 in.)

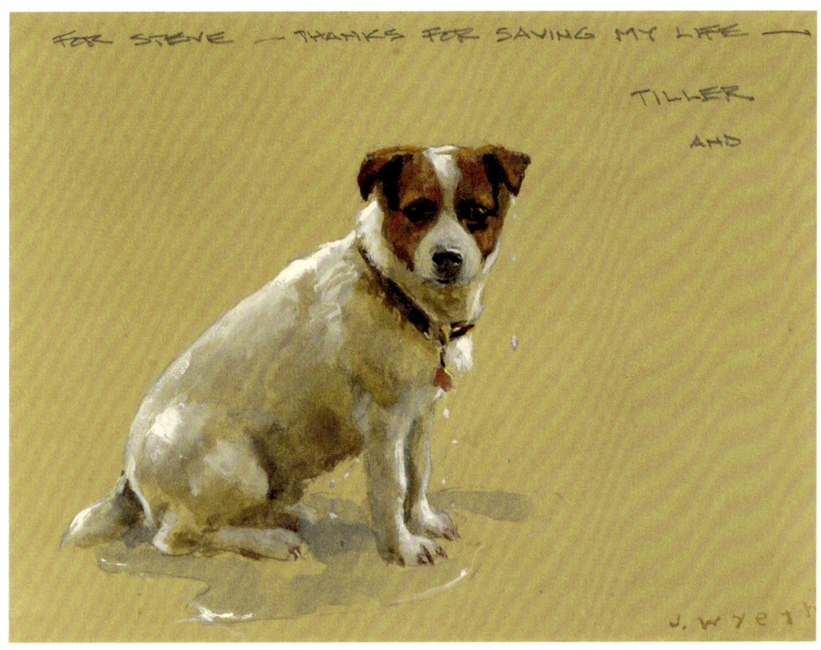

83. *Thanks for Saving My Life*, 2008. Watercolor and gouache on toned rag board, 17.5 x 20.6 cm ($6\frac{7}{8}$ x $8\frac{1}{8}$ in.)

84. *Homer*, 2003. Watercolor and gouache on toned rag board, 13.7 x 16.2 cm ($5\frac{3}{8}$ x $6\frac{3}{8}$ in.)

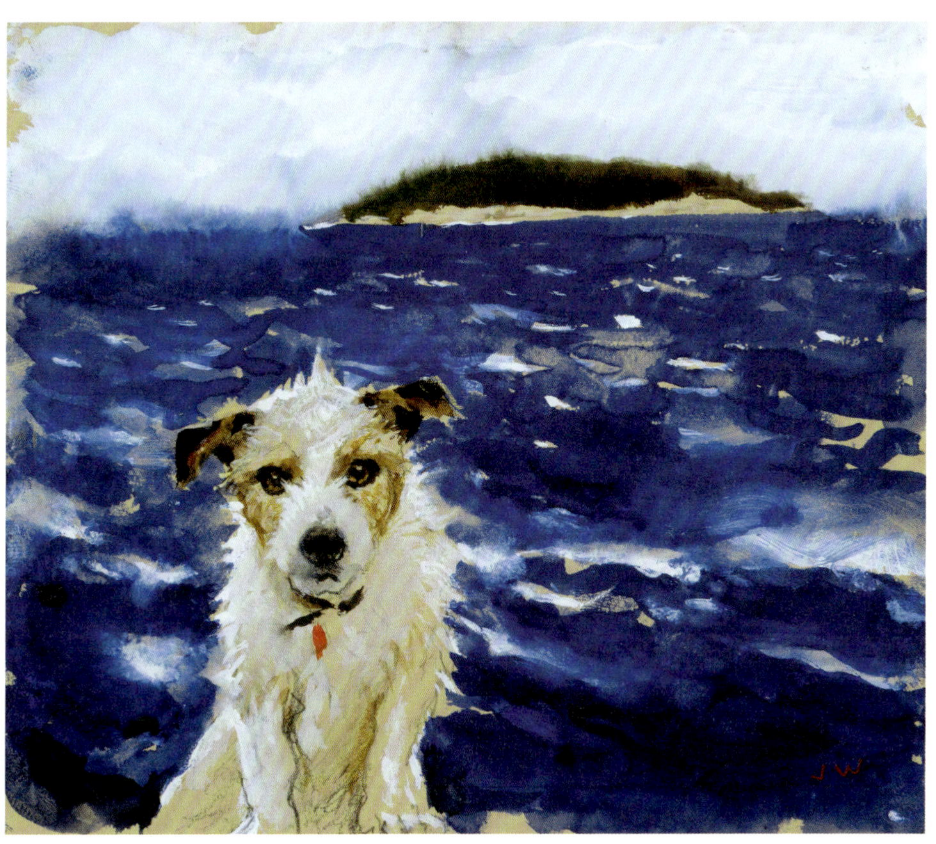

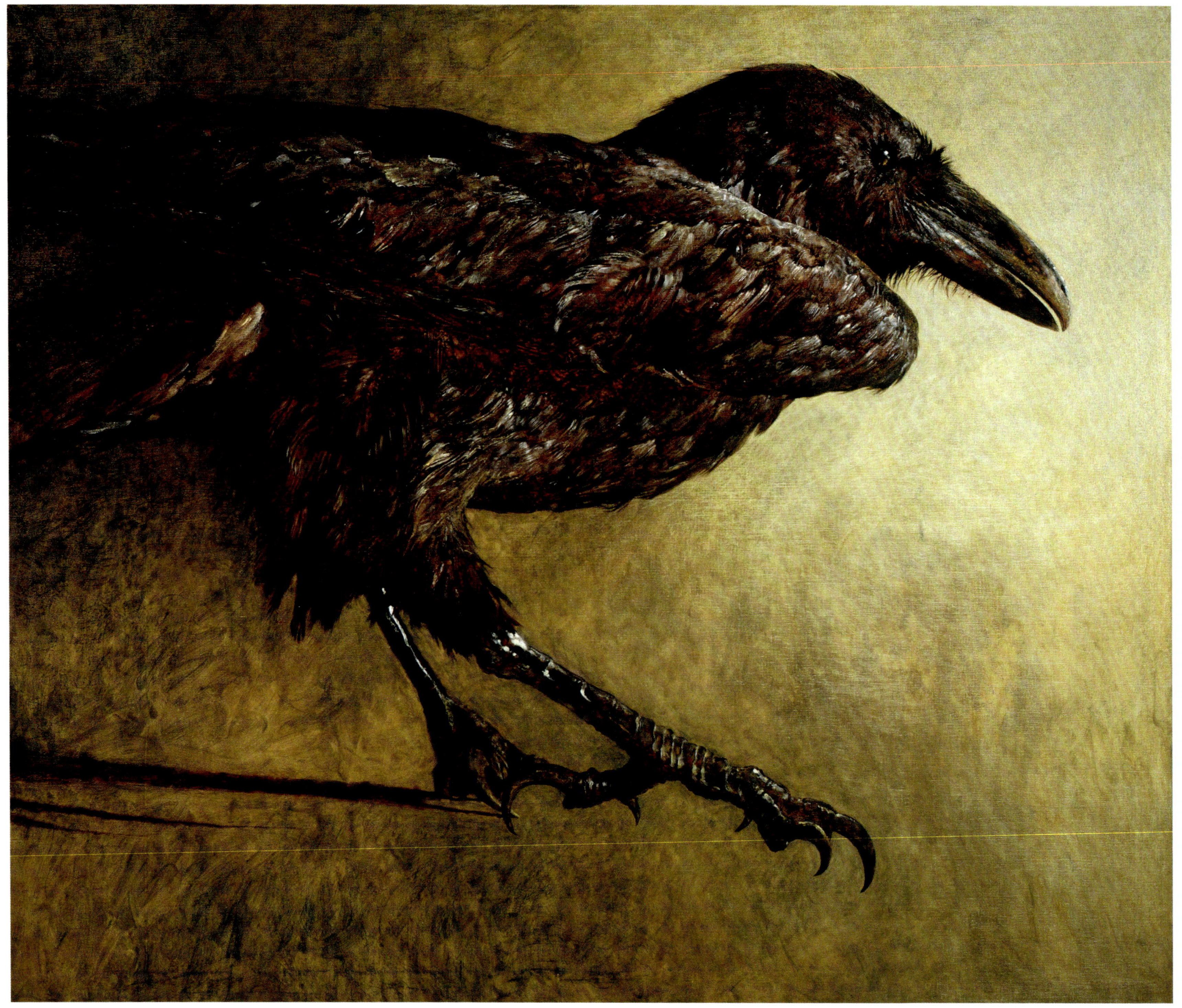

85. *Raven*, 1980. Oil on canvas, 152.4 x 182.9 cm (60 x 72 in.)

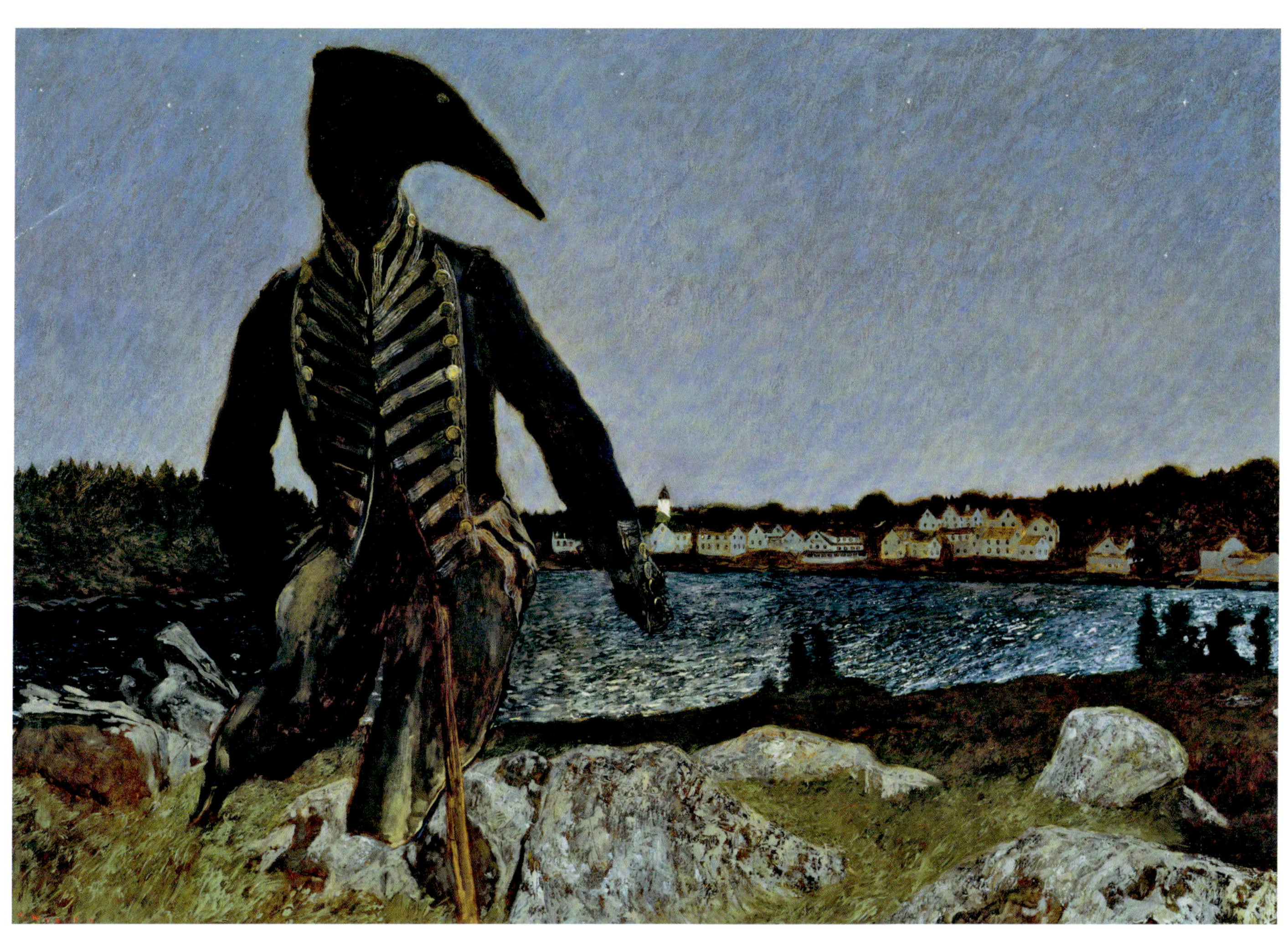

86. *Meteor Shower*, 1993. Oil and essence of pearl on panel, 83.8 x 121.9 cm (33 x 48 in.)

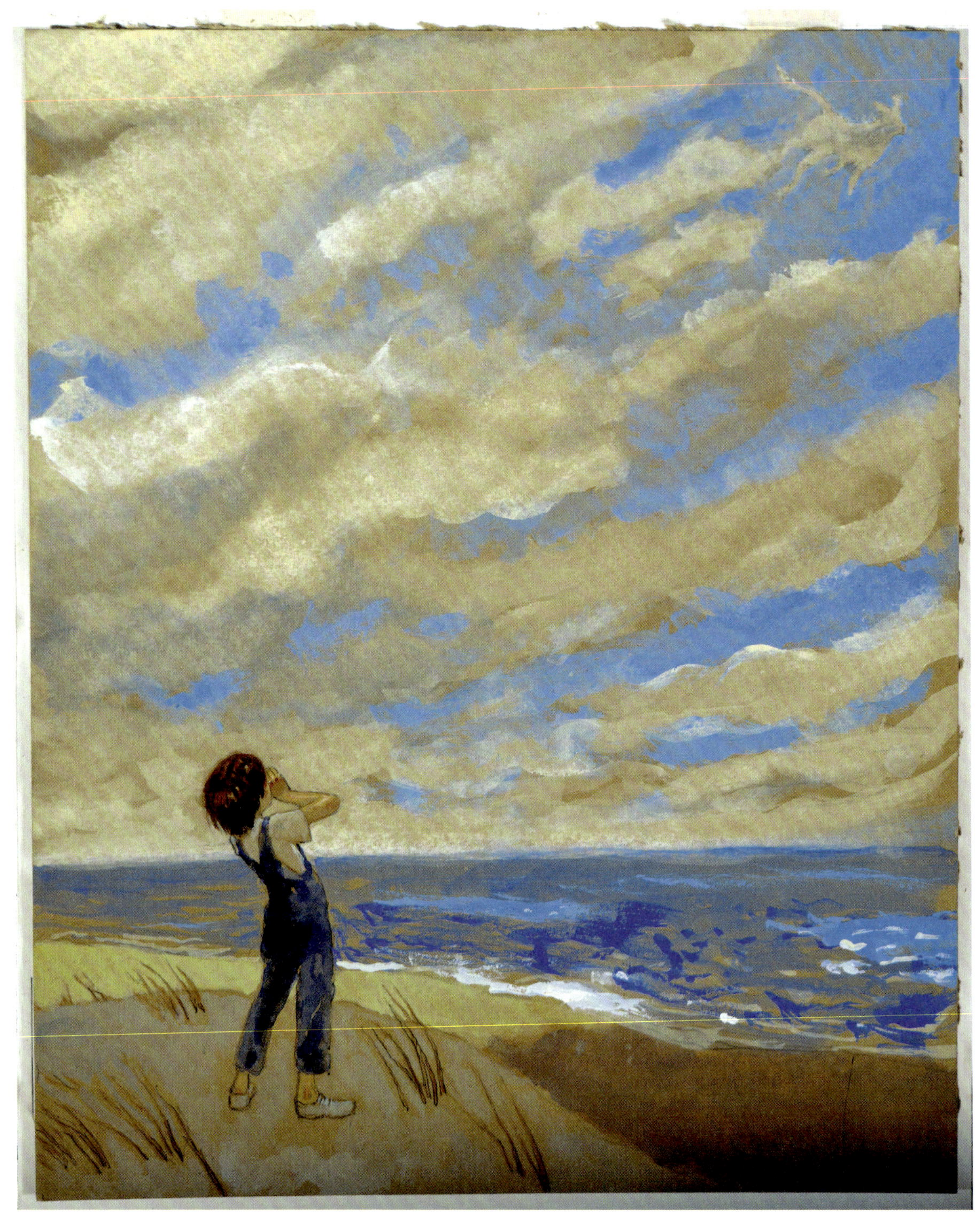

87. “I stared up at the sky and shouted, ‘I love you Sammy. You are still the best,’”
2011. Watercolor, pencil, and gouache on toned rag board, 30.5 x 25.4 cm (12 x 10 in.)

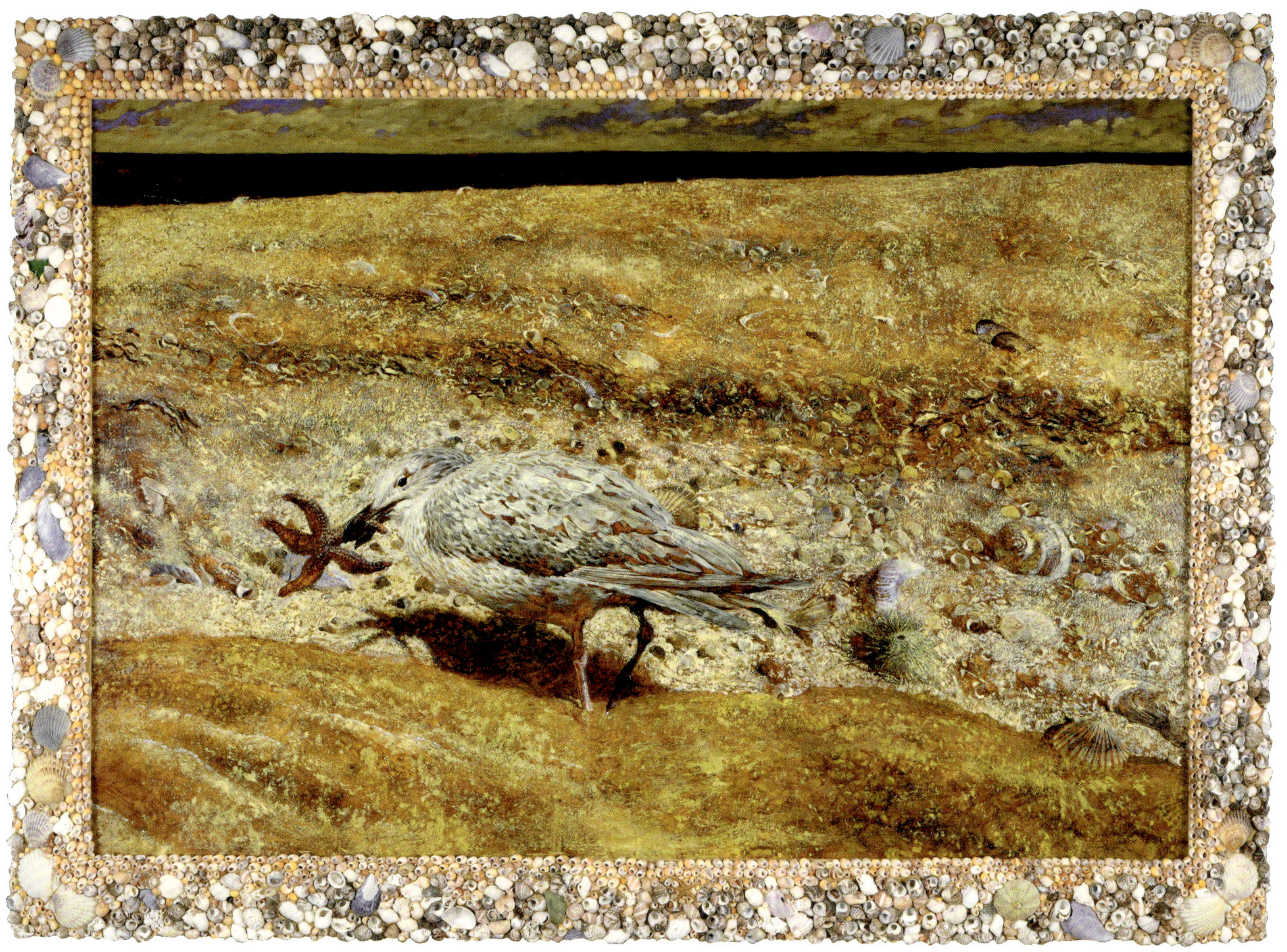

88. *Sea Star*, 1985. Oil on gessoed panel; frame of assembled found objects, 78.7 x 116.8 cm (31 x 46 in.)

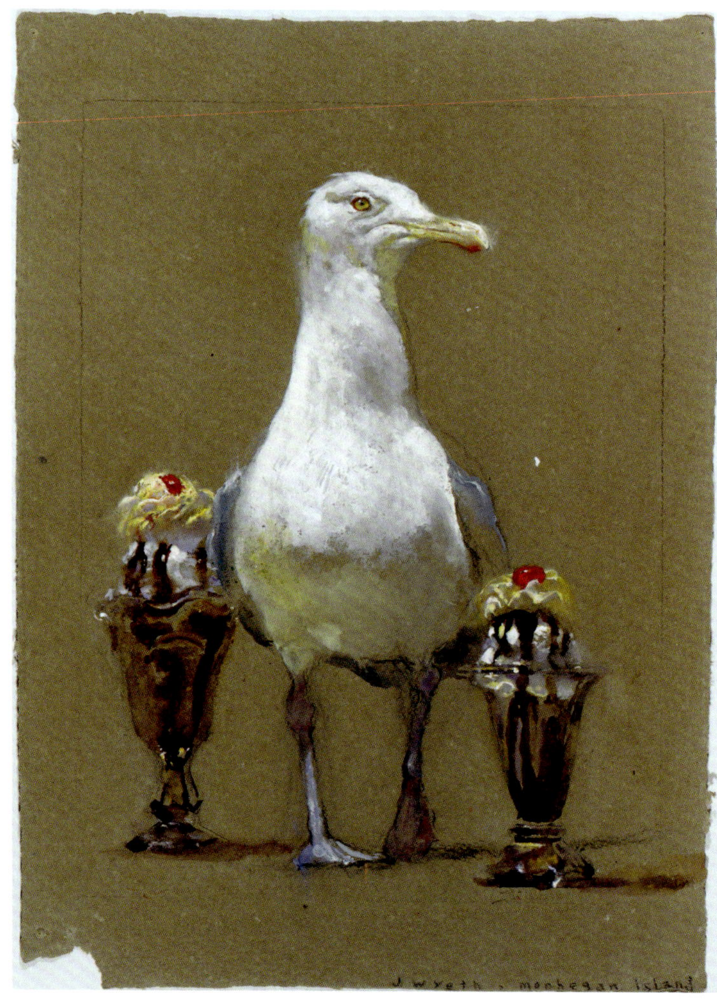

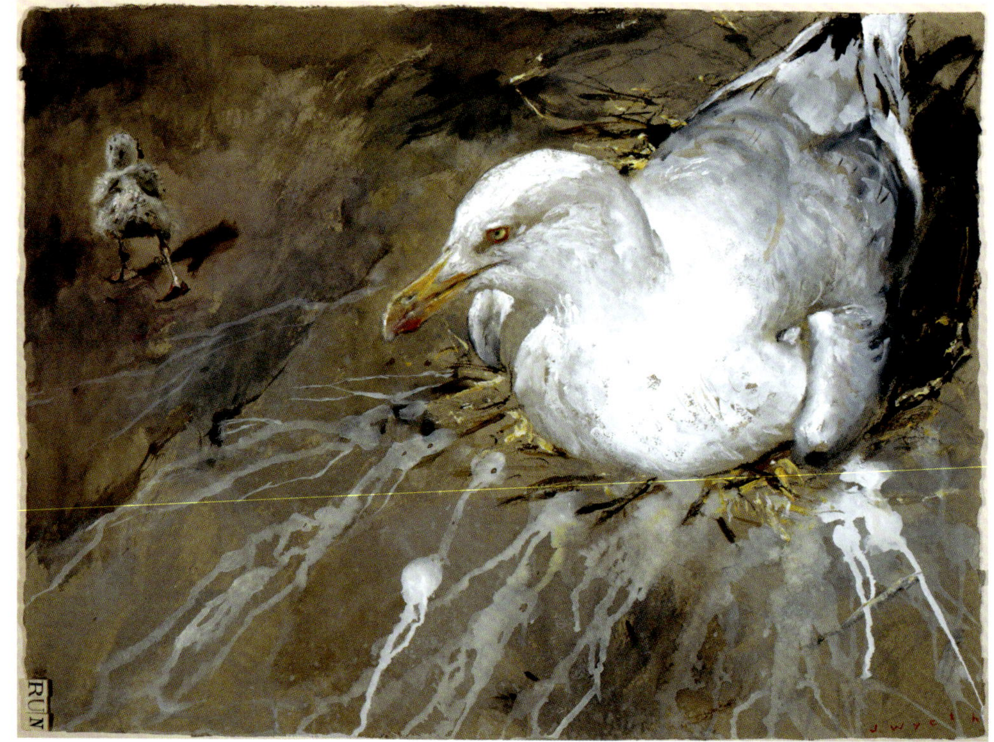

89. *Butterscotch, Gull, and Hot Fudge Sundae*, 2004. Watercolor and gouache on toned rag paper, 74.9 x 57.2 cm (29½ x 22½ in.)

90. *Run*, 1999. Watercolor, gouache, and bone on toned rag paper, 55.9 x 76.2 cm (22 x 30 in.)

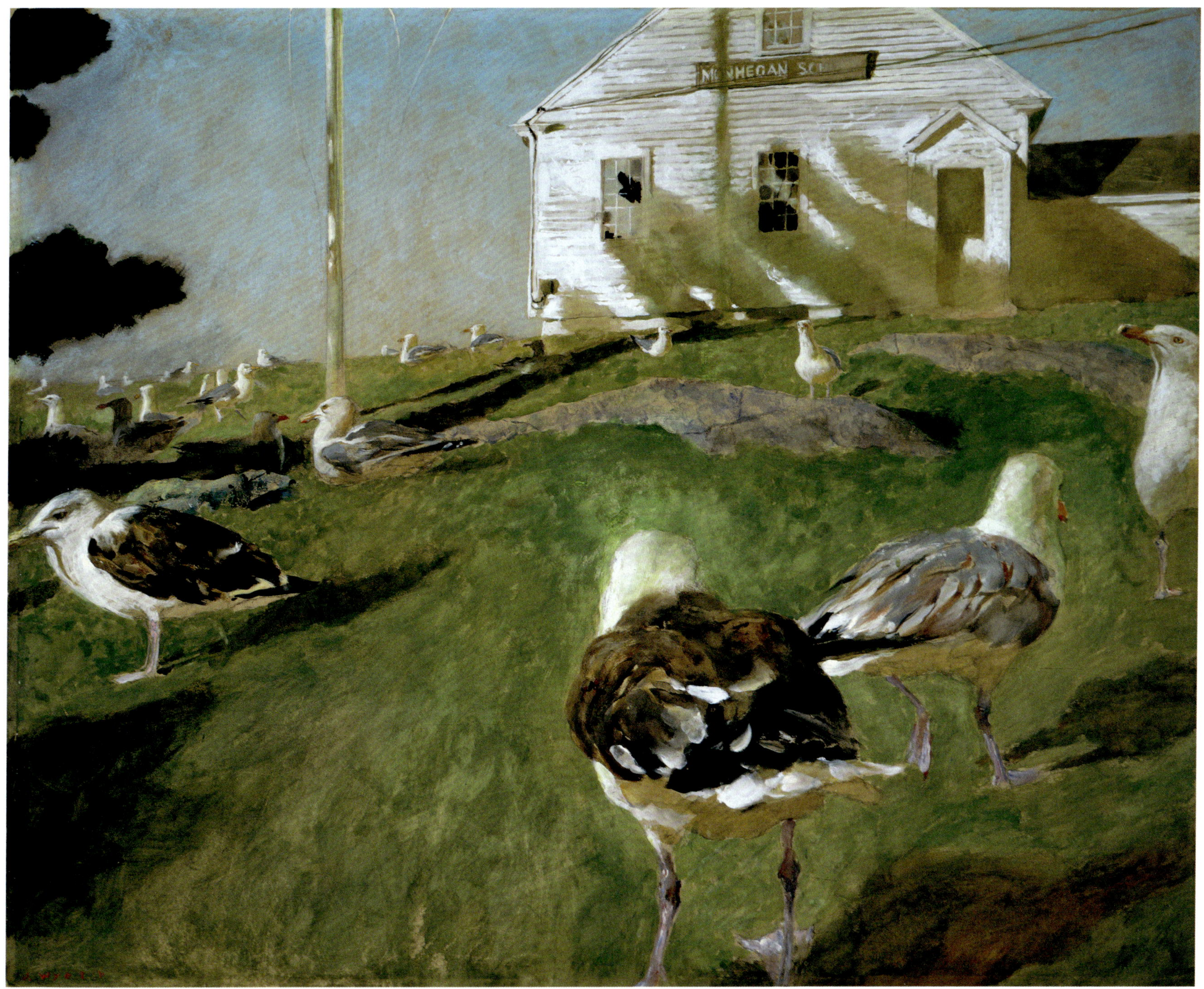

91. *The Monhegan Island Schoolhouse*, 2007. Gouache and watercolor on toned rag board, 81.3 x 101.6 cm (32 x 40 in.)

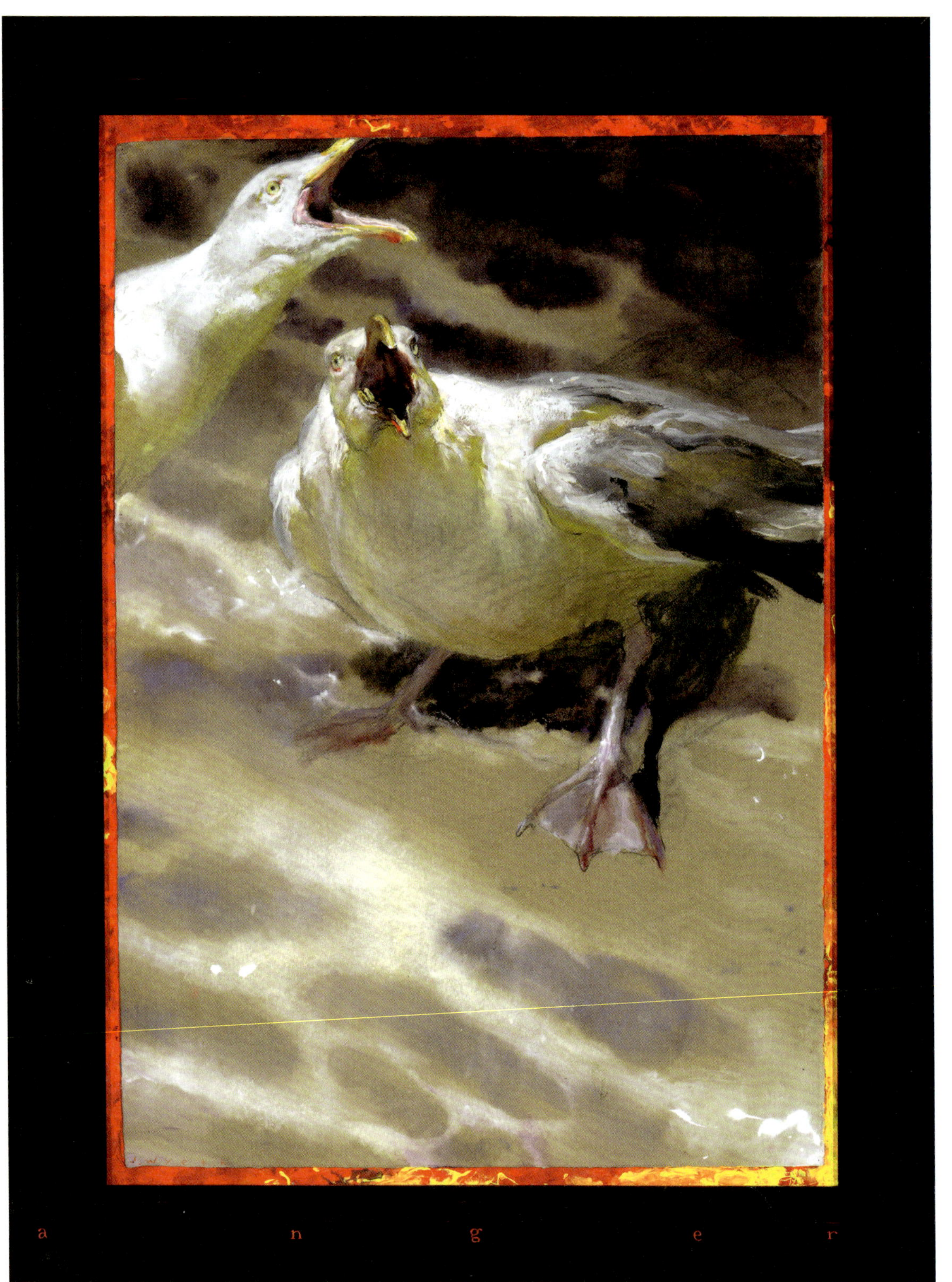

92. *Anger—The Seven Deadly Sins*, 2005. Watercolor and gouache on toned, handwoven rag paper mounted on archival board, 87.6 x 61.6 cm (34½ x 24¼ in.)

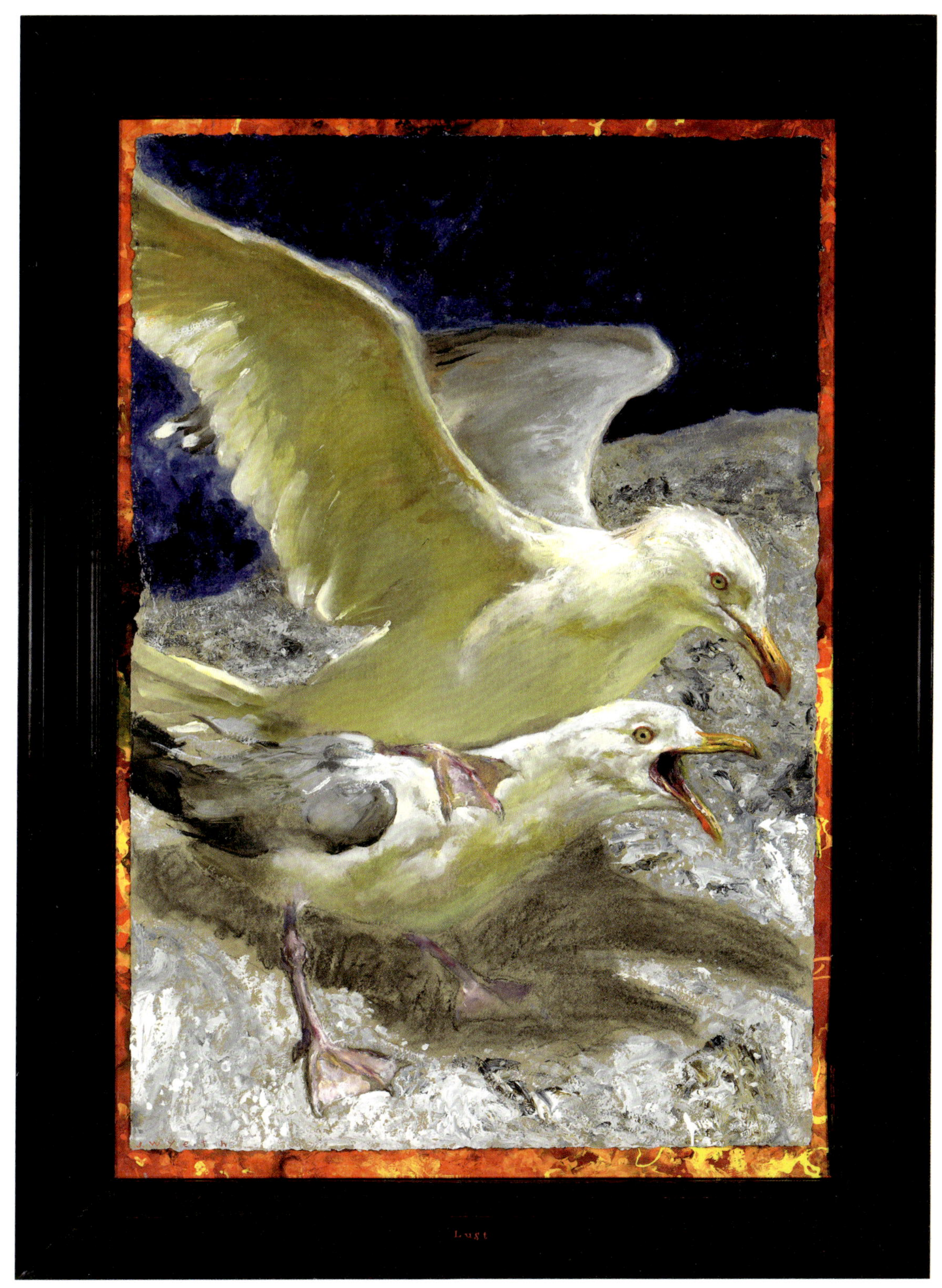

93. *Lust—The Seven Deadly Sins*, 2007. Watercolor and gouache on toned, hand-woven rag paper mounted on archival board, 87.6 x 61.6 cm (34½ x 24¼ in.)

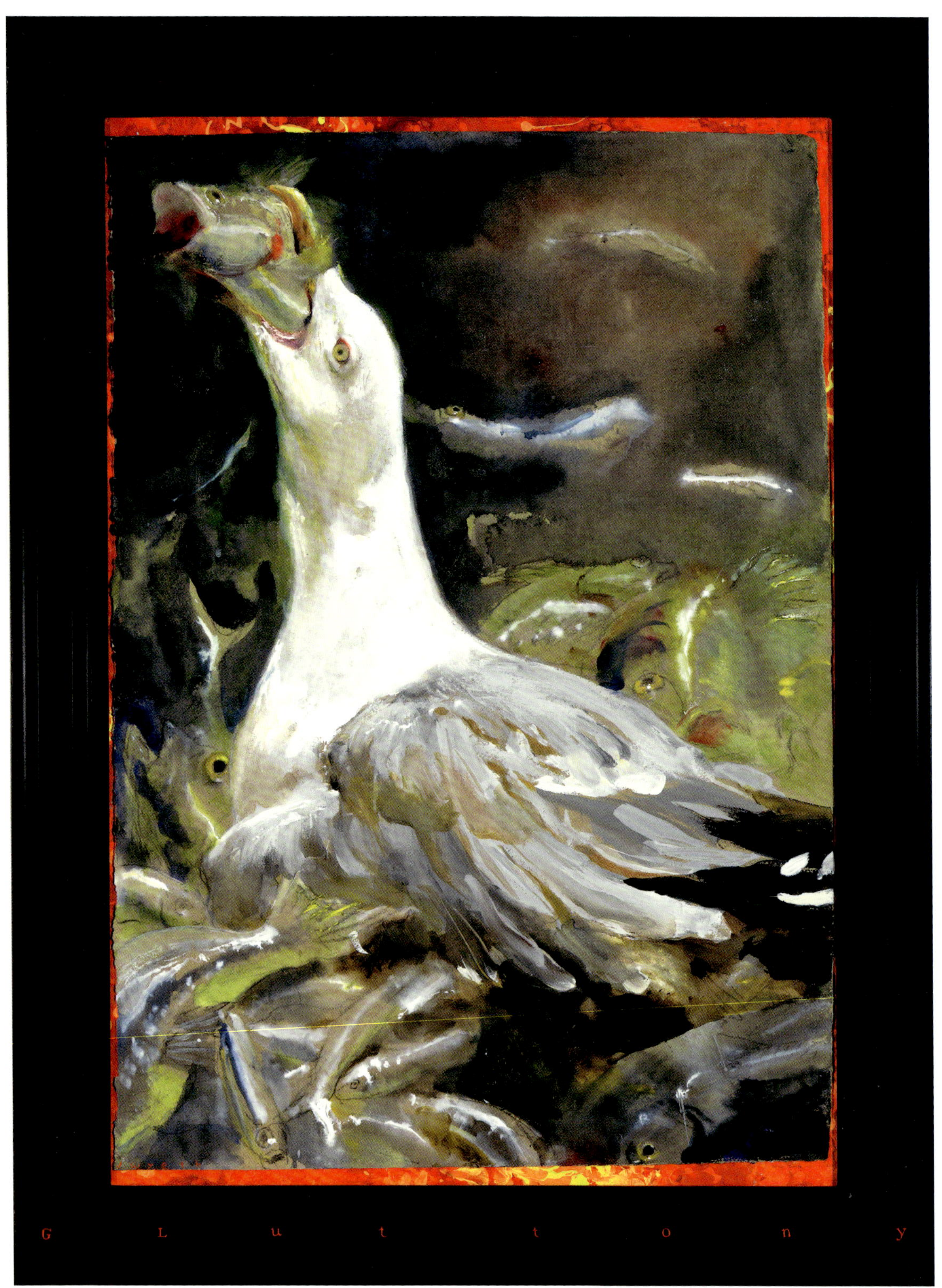

94. *Gluttony—The Seven Deadly Sins*, 2005. Watercolor and gouache on toned, hand-woven rag paper mounted on archival board, 87.6 x 61.6 cm (34½ x 24¼ in.)

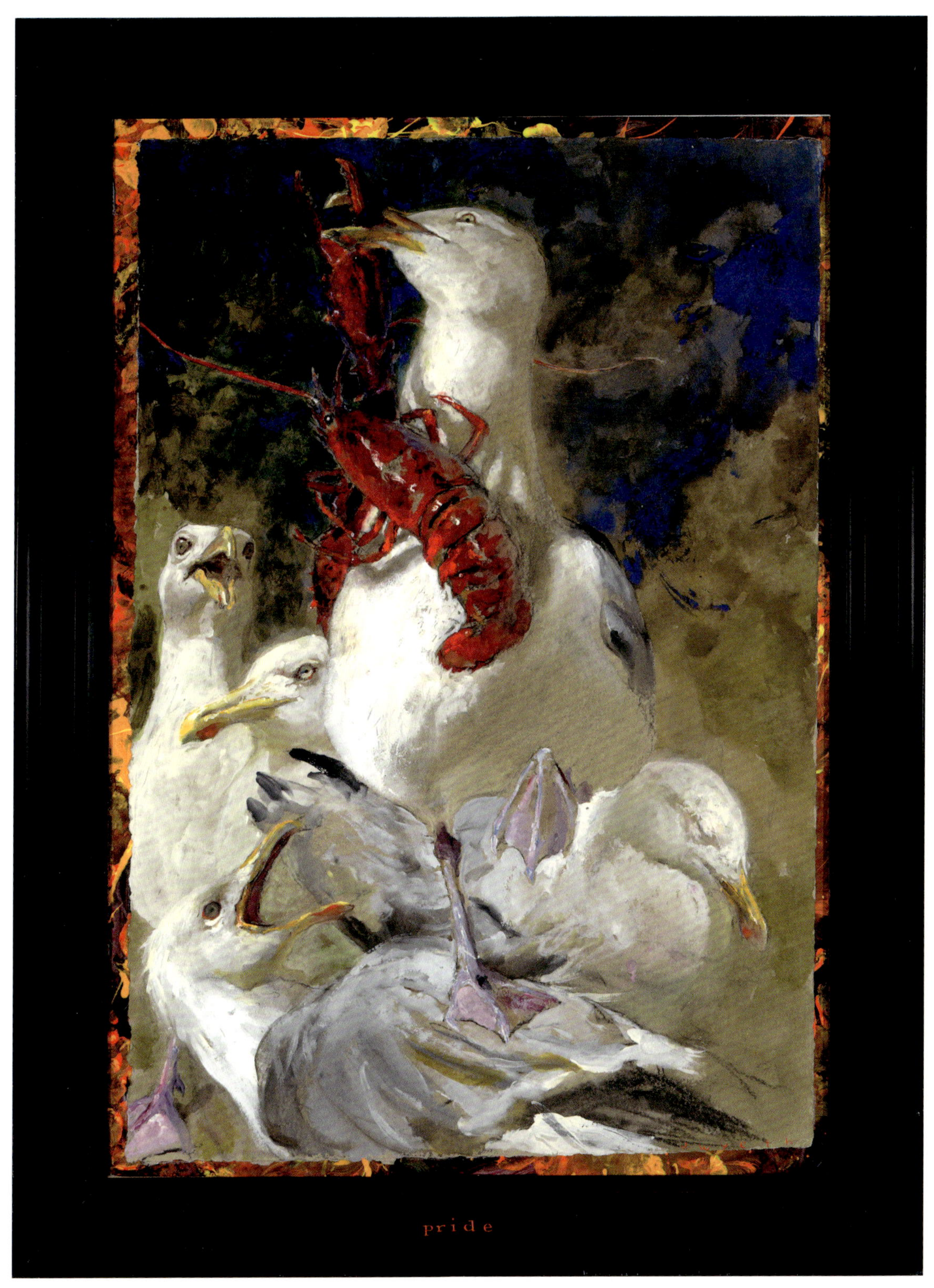

95. *Pride—The Seven Deadly Sins*, 2008. Watercolor and gouache on toned, hand-woven rag paper mounted on archival board, 87.6 x 61.6 cm (34½ x 24¼ in.)

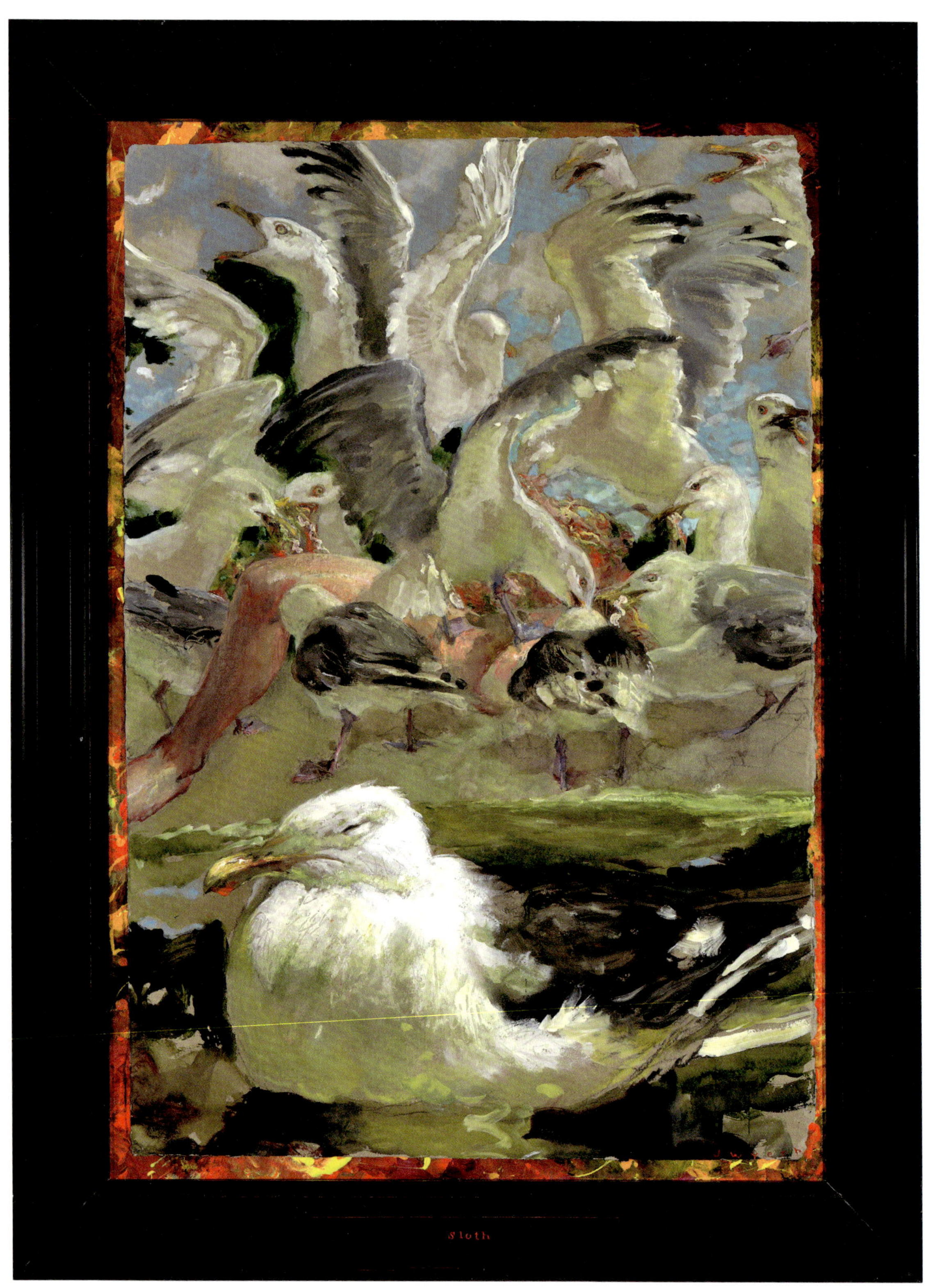

96. *Sloth—The Seven Deadly Sins*, 2007. Watercolor and gouache on toned, hand-woven rag paper mounted on archival board, 87.6 x 61.6 cm (34½ x 24¼ in.)

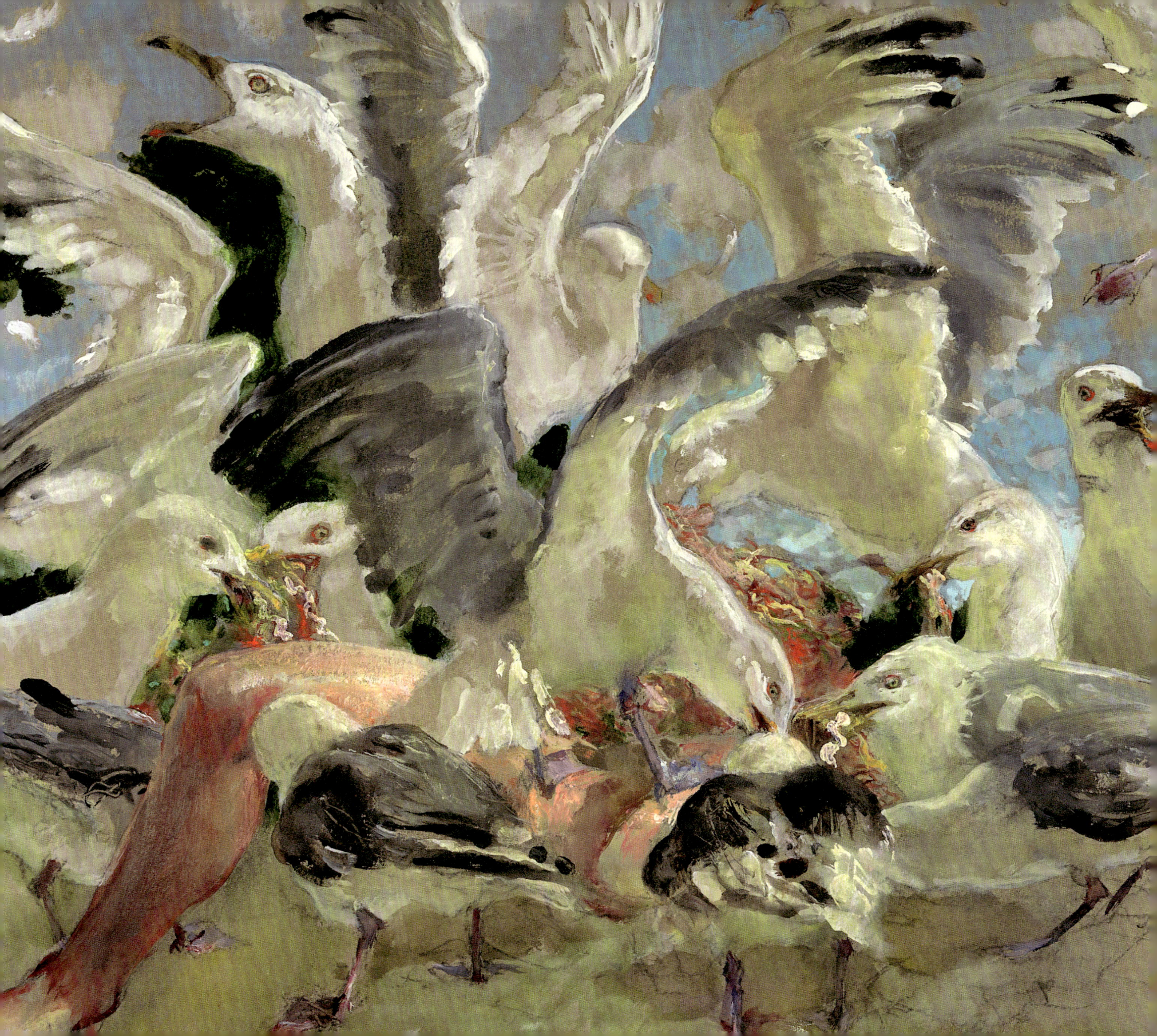

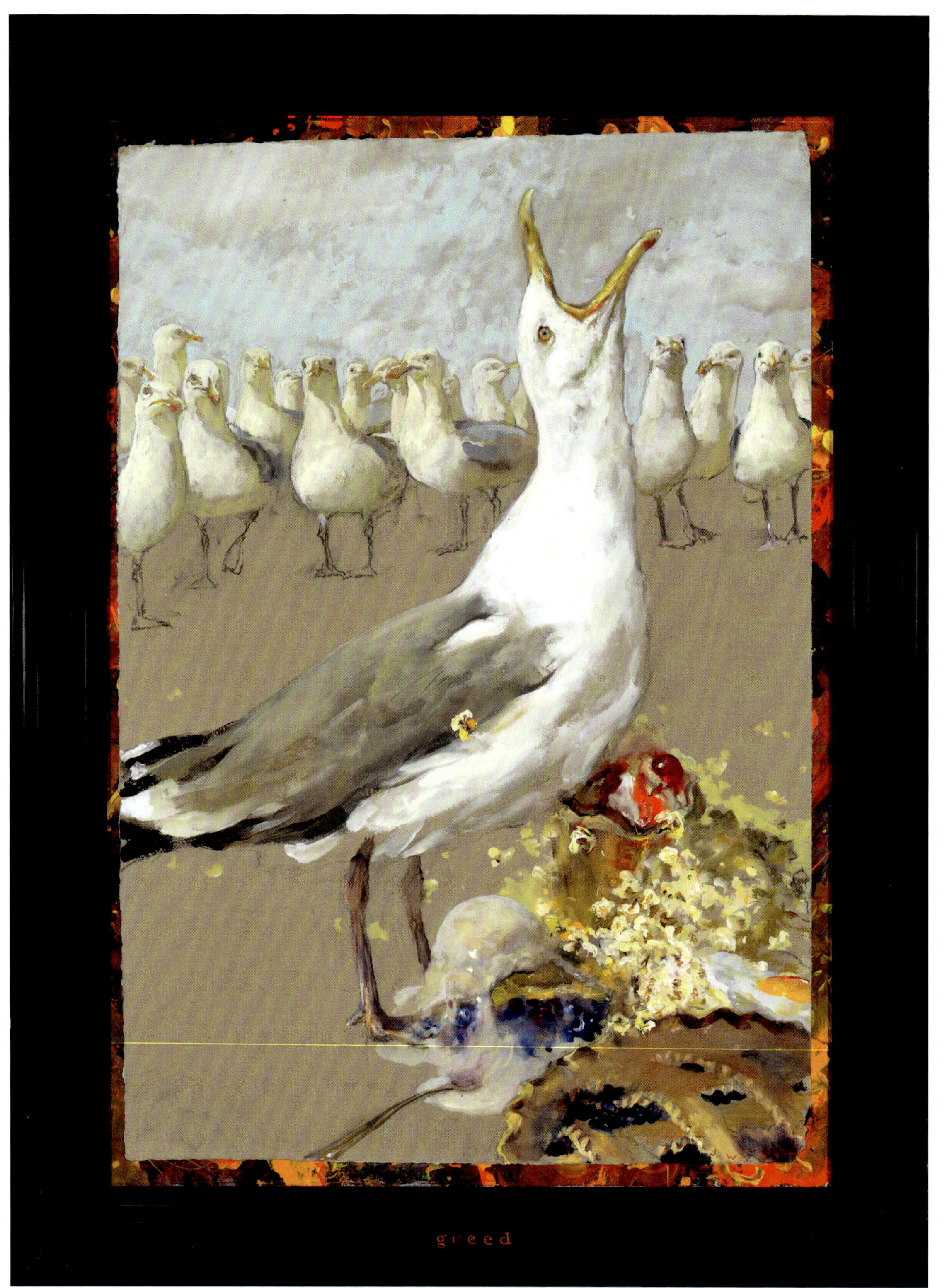

97. *Greed—The Seven Deadly Sins*, 2008. Watercolor and gouache on toned, hand-woven rag paper mounted on archival board, 87.6 x 61.6 cm (34½ x 24¼ in.)

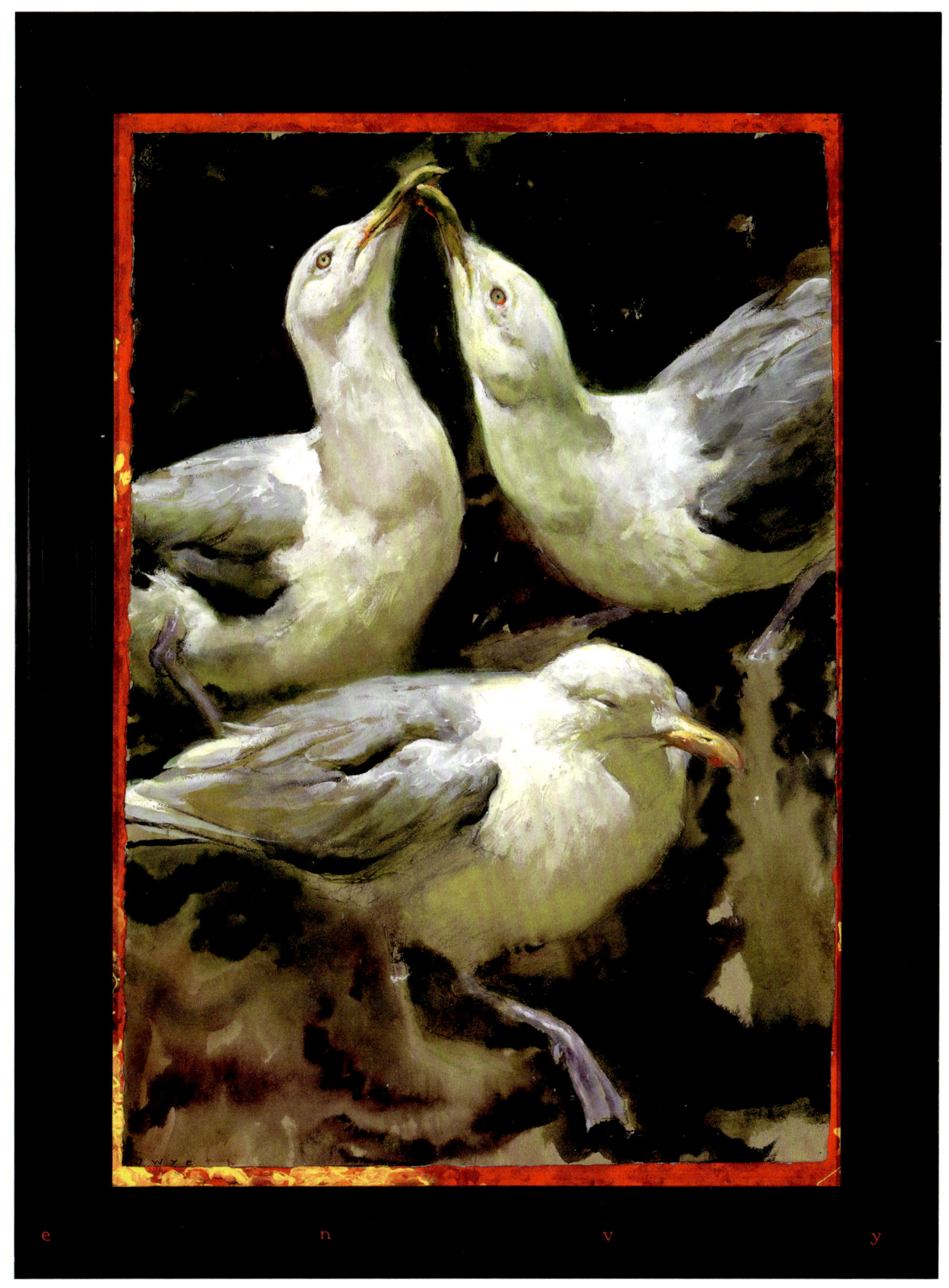

98. *Envy—The Seven Deadly Sins*, 2005. Watercolor and gouache on toned, hand-woven rag paper mounted on archival board, 87.6 x 61.6 cm (34½ x 24¼ in.)

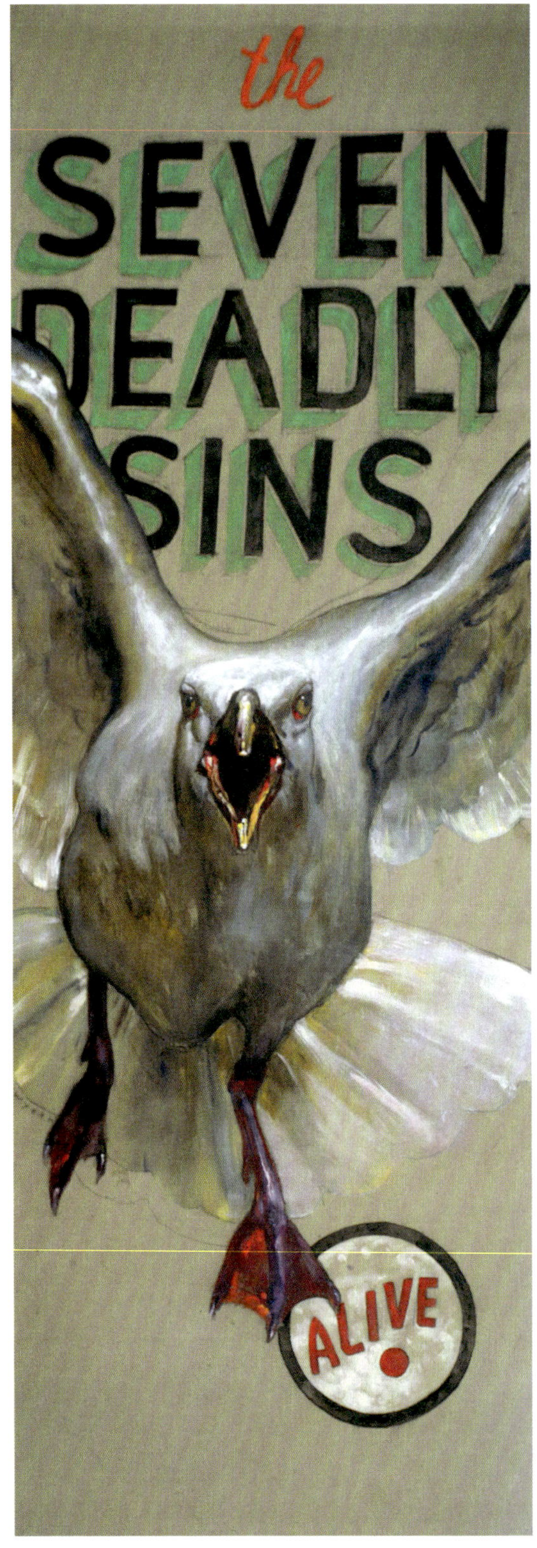

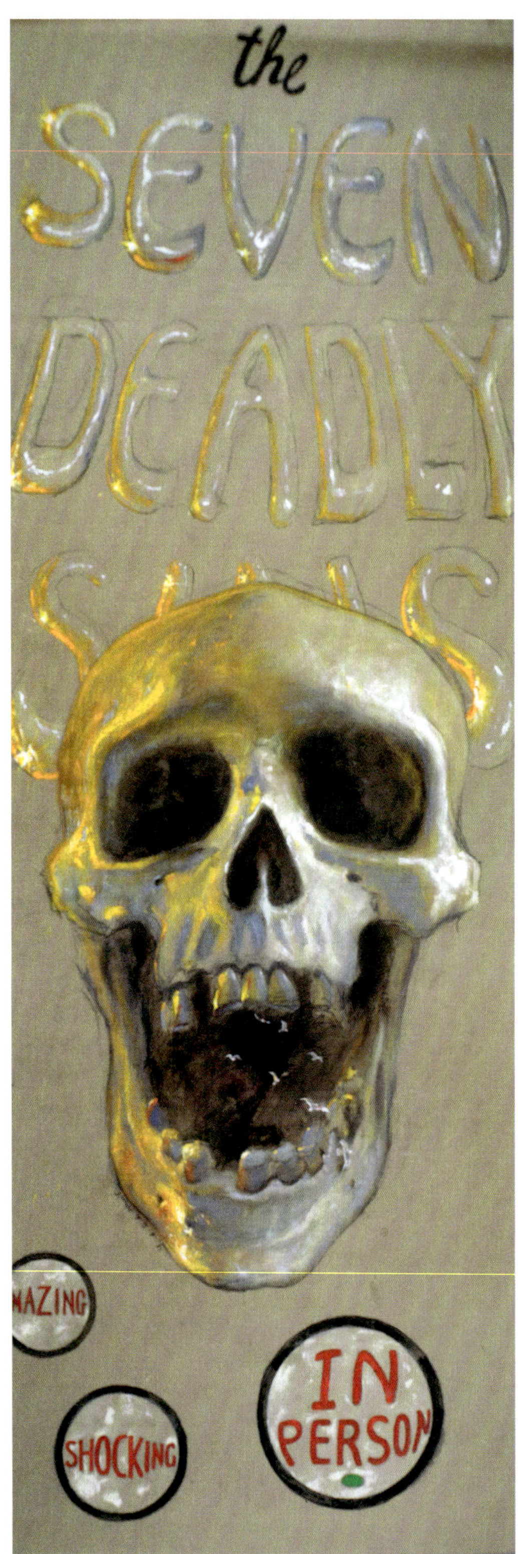

99. *Carney Banner, Gull*, 2009.
Acrylic, gouache, and India ink on linen fabric, 518.2 x 182.9 cm (204 x 72 in.)

100. *Carney Banner, Skull*, 2009.
Acrylic, gouache, and India ink on linen fabric, 518.2 x 182.9 cm (204 x 72 in.)

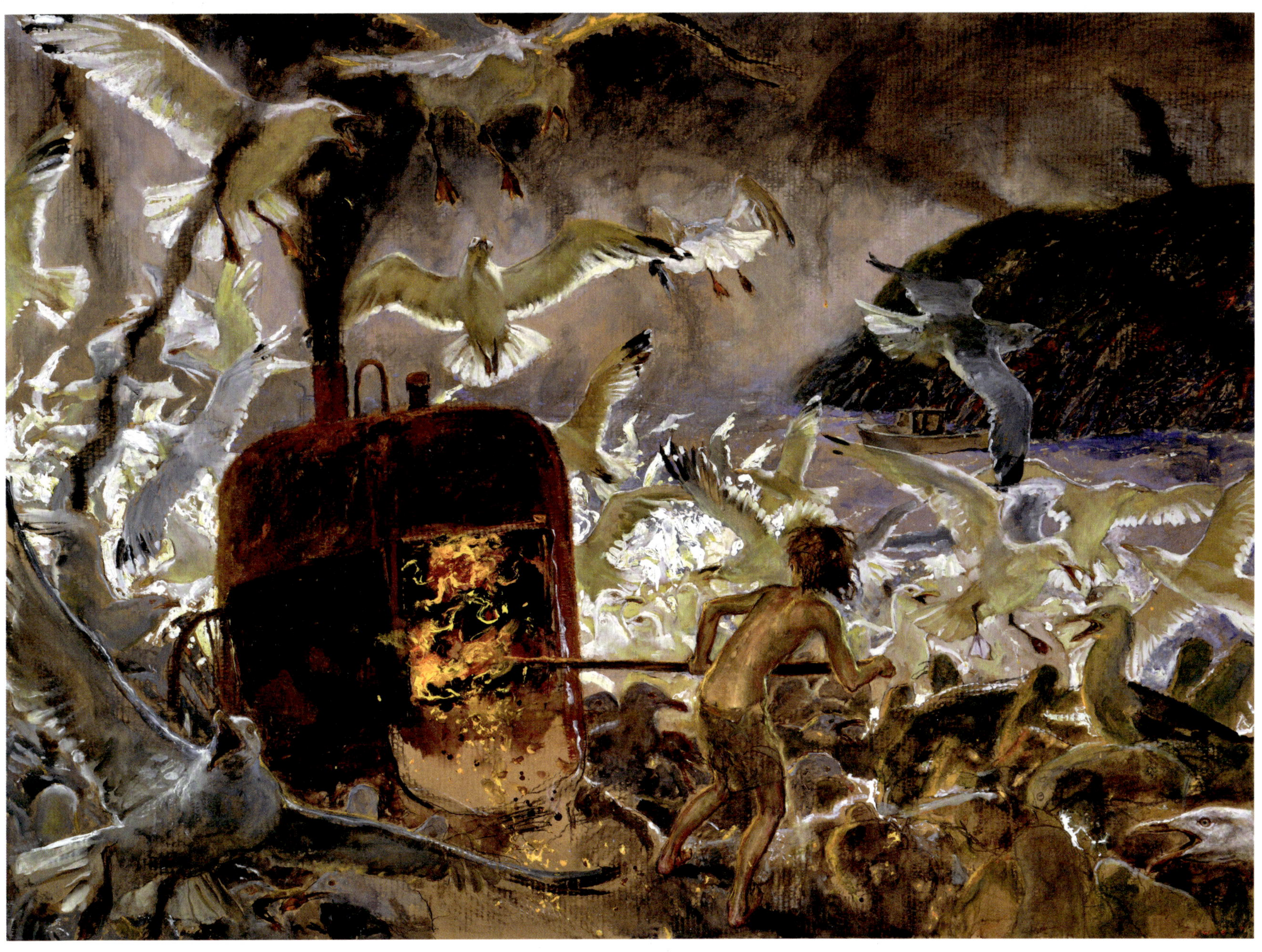

101. *Inferno, Monhegan*, 2006. Watercolor, gouache, and enamel on archival cardboard, 152.4 x 203.2 cm (60 x 80 in.)

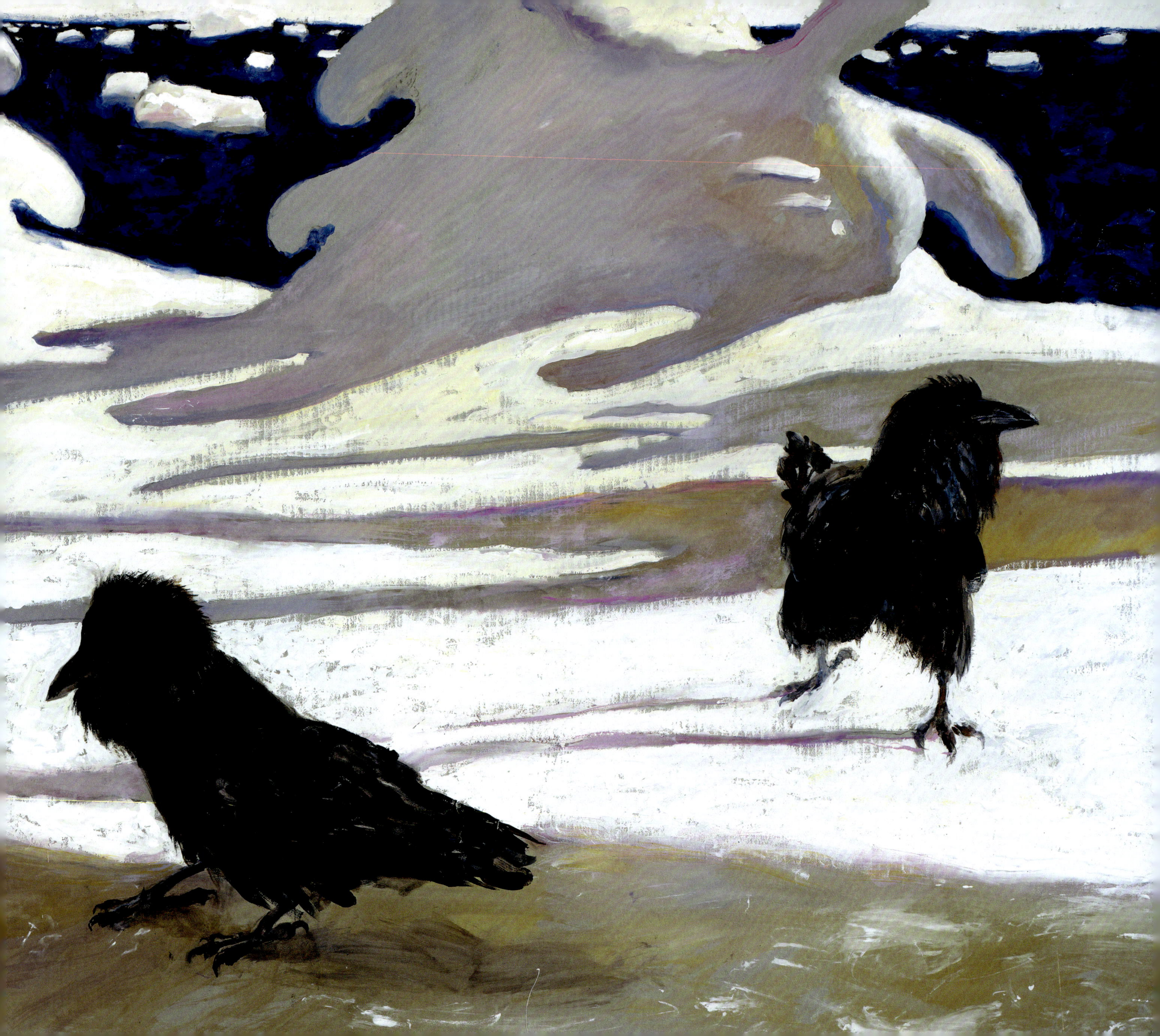

Recent Work

Since his father's death in January 2009, Wyeth's work has taken on new perspectives that suggest he is in the role of filming his own life, as the important figures of his formation become the stars of the moment. A series of images associated with the Headlands of Monhegan emerged recently during a recurring dream sequence in which Wyeth pictured his various mentors looking out over the ocean. In visualizing the dreams in his mind's eye, and subsequently painting the series of images on canvas and cardboard with his distinctive mixture of combined media, Wyeth himself is the director of his own documentary.

The first scene, *Sea Watchers*, is populated by four figures: Warhol farthest from the sea, Winslow Homer standing confidently in the middle ground, and Newell Convers and Andrew Wyeth standing together as they gaze at the sea in a pose approximating a 1930 photograph of them standing on the cliffs wearing foul-weather gear.[1] In *The Sea, Watched*, Homer has vanished. Once again Warhol observes from the far left, depicted from behind in profile, as he appeared in studies that were part of the initial Wyeth-Warhol portrait exchange, staring out at the two Wyeths, father and son, standing nearer the shoreline, as before. Andrew, closer to the sea, points out at the water, and N.C. stands behind him, crossing his arms in front of his burly frame. In this instance, Wyeth's sea is roiling with emotion, richly swirling pigment, spray, and color, more freely applied than in his earlier seascapes. The artist places the Headlands right up against the upper edge of the horizontally shaped canvas, effectively cutting off any chance of seeing the sky. The composition forces us to examine the intense juxtaposition of land and sea and how the stationary, material forms of the rocky coast clash with the infinite droplets of water in constant motion as they mass together in the ever-changing sea. Wyeth focuses on elemental collisions of contrasts: that which is real—the rocks and the waves—and that which is imagined as real in his mind's eye.

The third composition, *A Recurring Dream*, removes Warhol, and now we are down to those two mentors who represent the past generations of the artist's family. The brilliant blue shade of Monhegan evening surrounds them, and stars now speckle the night sky. Andrew does not point, but stands like a vertical post, pushed back farther from the sea than in the second version, while his stout father, N.C., still with his arms crossed over his chest, stands stolidly beside his son. Jamie Wyeth fits these two figures within a visual crescendo of lavender-tinged water that stretches back into the inlet before opening up to the wider ocean, much like the sweeping beam from a lighthouse. The composition recalls *Moon Landing*, Wyeth's earlier response from Monhegan in coming to terms with the infinity of the universe during the historic flight of 1969 (see cat. 24). From his now-distant vantage point, the artist's familial patriarchs and most important aesthetic mentors are transformed into simple shapes that resemble more slender versions of the stout bollards so securely fastened to Monhegan's shoreline, where they could offer safety to ships needing to be tethered. Now, in relation to the whole, the two figures are far less significant; indeed, they are relegated to the position of viewing the seascape

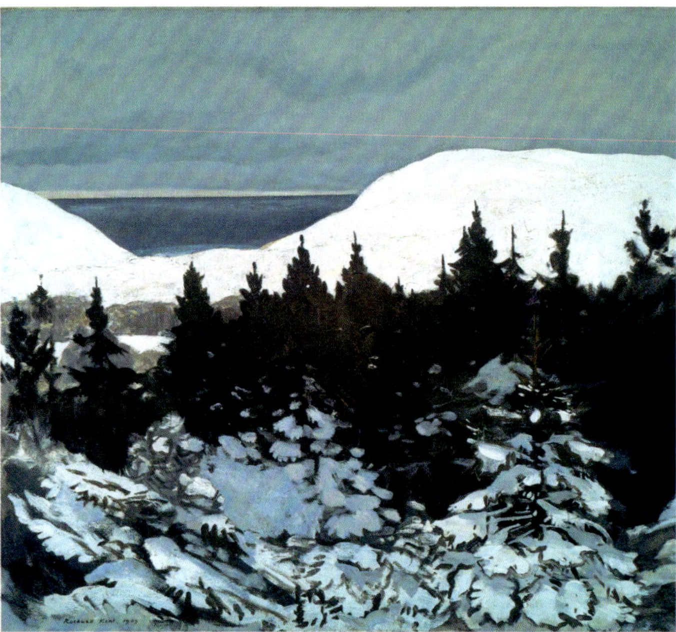

Fig 21. Rockwell Kent (1882–1971)
Maine Coast, Winter, 1909
Oil on canvas
96.2 x 113.4 cm (37⅞ x 44⅝ in.)

that Jamie Wyeth freely stretches out before them to represent the surroundings that were a touchstone for all three artists. *A Recurring Dream* claims the view from the Monhegan Headlands as Jamie Wyeth's own, one that takes its leave from his grandfather and father, who are left behind to watch him from the safe vantage of the shore.

Just as the cast of artistic mentors exits the dramatic stage of the Monhegan Headlands, Wyeth envisions Rockwell Kent, yet another highly significant mentor in the spiritual sense more than in a technical or formal sense, in a portrait that belongs to the current, ongoing *Series of Untoward Occurrences on Monhegan Island*. Although Wyeth avoided portraying any of his other mentors at work, in this enigmatic image Kent appears painting right before our very eyes (cat. 105). Wyeth chooses a vertical canvas, distinctly different from the horizontal compositions of his dream sequence, with proportions that closely approximate the shape of his own first acquisition of a work by Rockwell Kent, *Rocks, Monhegan* (1906). In the earlier scene of *Kent House*, Wyeth projects Kent's Monhegan legacy high above the cliff, out of reach (see cat. 72). In this composition Wyeth dares to paint the same landscapes of Monhegan that he so admired from Kent's first winters spent on the island, between 1905 and 1909. Just to the left of Kent are bold, dark pine trees resembling jagged teeth that bite into the sheer drop of snow-capped cliffs, a reprise of the landscape in Kent's earlier series such as *Maine Coast, Winter* (fig. 21) and Wyeth's own winter landscape odes to black and white, in which ravens strut against the surreal snow formations depicted in *Ice Storm—Maine (Study)*. Kent wears a red-and-black plaid Mackinaw and a loose brown tie that may be a nod to popular notions of an artist's costume, or even a reference to Kent's socialist sympathies. Wyeth highlights Kent's shiny, bald dome and his ruddy cheeks, and he paints him from his imagination with his intensely blue eyes (even though they were brown) that fix on us as Helen Taussig and Andy Warhol did in Wyeth's earlier versions of his powerful head-on portraits (see cats. 10 and 33).

The most intriguing details of this scene are found right up front in the position of Kent's brushes and palette, and in the far distance at the right, where we see a silhouette of a figure in free fall. The lower corner of the palette and Kent's paintbrush butt up against and visually project beyond the canvas into our space, effectively offering up several juicy squeezes of the oil that so attracted Wyeth as a child in his aunt Carolyn's studio. Kent, the painter, engages us with his expression and lures us into his work and his world with the tools of his trade. In this installment of the *Series of Untoward Occurrences on Monhegan Island*, Kent seems to be posing the fundamental question of his art directly to us. Pressing Kent up against the foreground of the composition, Wyeth seems to create his own morality painting, a modern and very personal interpretation that combines elements of Warhol's Suicide paintings of 1963 and Pieter Brueghel's *Landscape with the Fall of Icarus* (about 1558, Royal Museums of Fine Arts, Belgium). In Brueghel's scene, a farmer goes about his work tilling the soil, while far in the distance the ancient legend of Icarus unfolds. Icarus ends up plunging headlong into the sea, which Brueghel relegates to a small detail of two legs about to slip under the surface of the water. In Warhol's stark black-and-white paintings of suicide, a male figure appears suspended between life and death, light and darkness, good and evil.[2] Kent, the great lover of the Monhegan landscape and notorious lover on Monhegan, left behind him a complex web of personal relationships fraught with sorrow.[3] Here he is associated with a falling figure that alludes to the mysterious death of Kent's model and mistress, Sally Moran, who fell into the sea off the Headlands in 1953 while Kent himself was off island.[4] Surrounded by Monhegan, a place of great vistas, topographic extremes, and telescoped perspectives, Wyeth's Kent brings his art and his life into intense focus, confronting us with the question of whether the two can ever be reconciled.

For Wyeth, Kent ultimately becomes the last in a long line of mentors who could be described according to Malcolm Gladwell's recent interpretation of outliers.[5] From Newell Convers and Andrew Wyeth to Andy Warhol, Winslow Homer, and Rockwell Kent, all shared a distinct sense of what it would take to distinguish their own manner of artistic expression from those of their contemporaries, whether in the form of book illustration, tempera, Pop Art, genre painting, or landscapes. The many mentors and muses Jamie Wyeth engaged with for extended periods of time—Lincoln Kirstein, the Kennedy brothers, Arnold Schwarzenegger, Rudolf Nureyev, and Phyllis Mills Wyeth—could also be seen as outliers who rose beyond the realm of their peers through the intense practice by which they honed their respective talents. And, as Gladwell himself eloquently describes his own experience of being an outlier in terms of his upbringing as a multiracial child, Orca Bates and his brother, Cat, born on Monhegan, would also fall within the category.[6]

Wyeth's recent series of recurring dream imagery and the imaginary portrait of Rockwell Kent shown with a woman falling from the cliffs, all firmly situated on Monhegan, effectively bind together the personal narrative of portraying the outlier and the physical place, an island that bears witness to extremes of physical beauty, dizzying cliffs, and distant, knife-edged horizons, that itself is an outlier, situated some ten miles from the mainland. For Wyeth these are the relationships and experiences that populate his rich, imaginative world and that ultimately circumscribe his own, self-imposed boundaries as an outlier himself, who is most at home on Monhegan, or on his closer-to-home outlier, Southern Island.

Thoreau, encountering the forces of nature in Maine, was provoked to ask: "What is it to be admitted to a museum, to see a myriad of particular things, compared with being shown some star's surface, some hard matter at home! . . . Think of our life in nature, —daily to be shown matter, to come in contact with it,—rocks, trees, wind on our cheeks! the solid earth! The actual world! The common sense! Contact! Contact! Who are we? Where are we?"[7] That sense of contact, of making sense of the material world as a visual artist depicting nature, is at the core of Wyeth's work. We discover this interest from his very earliest drawings, such as the one in which he envisioned a fishing boat poised at the waterline beneath his father's portrait of him in 1949 (see cat. 7) to his series based on the ghosts of his dreams, and also in his recent series of

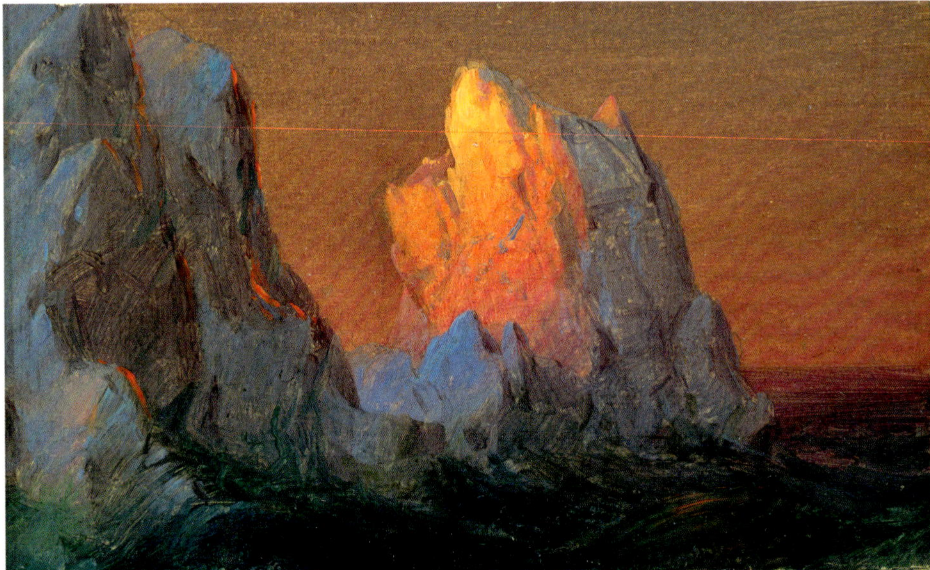

Fig. 22. Frederic Edwin Church (1826–1900)
Icebergs, 1863
Oil on canvas
8.25 x 14.29 cm (3¼ x 5⅝ in.)

compositions, created of mixed media on paperboard, inspired by an experience, traveling across the ice-clogged waters of Tenants Harbor to his studio on Southern Island in his inflatable launch, when he was thrown headlong into the frigid waters.[8]

In *Ice Floe* and *Berg*, Wyeth bears down on us with an extreme jolt to the senses between the looming berg in the foreground and the diminutive buildings of the lighthouse and bell tower on Southern Island that seem so far away as to be all but unattainable. As the sun appears to be setting, chunks of ice floating in the harbor during the winter months appear deceptively large and threatening, as surely they would be when seen face-to-face. The waterline looms above our perspective as though we are rapidly sinking or the waves are undulating above us; the skewed bergs of ice evoke the feeling of being off-kilter and effectively bobbing up and down with the tide. Although land is in sight, its tiny scale indicates that it is off in the distance, beyond a field of ice remade with licks of pigment lavished on the surface like whipped cream on a frozen dessert.

In *Berg* and related compositions still emerging from the studio as part of his current work, Jamie Wyeth attains a new level of artistic expression that grows organically from his work over many decades, extending as far back as his earliest drawings, such as *Boys Sledding*, in which he imagines the action taking place close to and far from the viewer simultaneously (see cat. 4). The artist has described his paintings as miniature worlds, and in *Berg* we find that he has created the world of Southern Island in miniature, tightly compressed right under the uppermost edge of the composition. Many artists work out their compositions on smaller-scale canvases that are easily transported to and from the locations where they are painting. Frederic Church's memorable experiences traveling by boat inside the Arctic Circle later inspired a series of diminutive fantasy paintings, including *Icebergs* (1863), only three by five inches in size, that the artist painted from memory (fig. 22). Thomas Hart Benton was also known to construct small-scale three-dimensional maquettes that enabled him to work out perspective for his genre scenes.[9]

On Southern Island, Wyeth has reconstructed a half-life-scale building of Daniel Webster's home and has recently assembled two one-sixth-life-scale rooms as a way of remembering his earlier years in New York City with Warhol, Kirstein, and Nureyev (see cats. 13 and 29). His process of envisioning the miniature worlds of his past in these tableaux is not merely a case of enlarging a smaller sketch or building a maquette to work out perspectival details. Rather, it is more a hybrid, closer to Church's fantasy painting *Icebergs*, in that Wyeth freely combines his experiences of the past in works that inspire his present. That these two recent assemblages, or tableaux vivant, as the artist prefers to call them, are part of his world on Southern Island fits right into the idea of the *Gesamtkunstwerk*, or total work of art, that he has created there in and around the original bell tower and lighthouse of Southern Island. His is a carefully constructed world, extending from full scale down to one-sixth scale, that continues to inspire his imagination and in turn the creation of his paintings.

In describing the particular kind of ice that he comes to know at Walden Pond, Thoreau himself adopts the view of the artist in envisioning the perspective of the near, close to the canvas, and the far, that of the viewer's perspective at a distance. He launches from the experience of the real world to explore the philosophical realm of the abstract, observing, "Like the water, the Walden ice, seen near at hand, has a green tint, but at a distance is beautifully blue, and you can easily tell it from the white ice of the river, or the merely greenish ice of some ponds, a quarter of a mile off." He further offers that ice "is an interesting subject for contemplation," and goes on to pose the rhetorical question he proceeds to answer, "Why is it that a bucket of water soon becomes putrid, but frozen remains sweet forever? It is commonly said that this is the difference between the affections and the intellect."[10] For Thoreau these dichotomies expressed by ice allow him to approach what he believes to be truth in nature and for eternity. For Jamie Wyeth, these dichotomies between making and matching, between the worlds he inhabits and the art world all around him, worlds real and imagined, small and large, visible and invisible, past and present, are what energize and electrify his best works. And, in the purest form of his artistic expression, time and again over the course of his career, he reveals that what meets the eye is far more than we may ever expect.

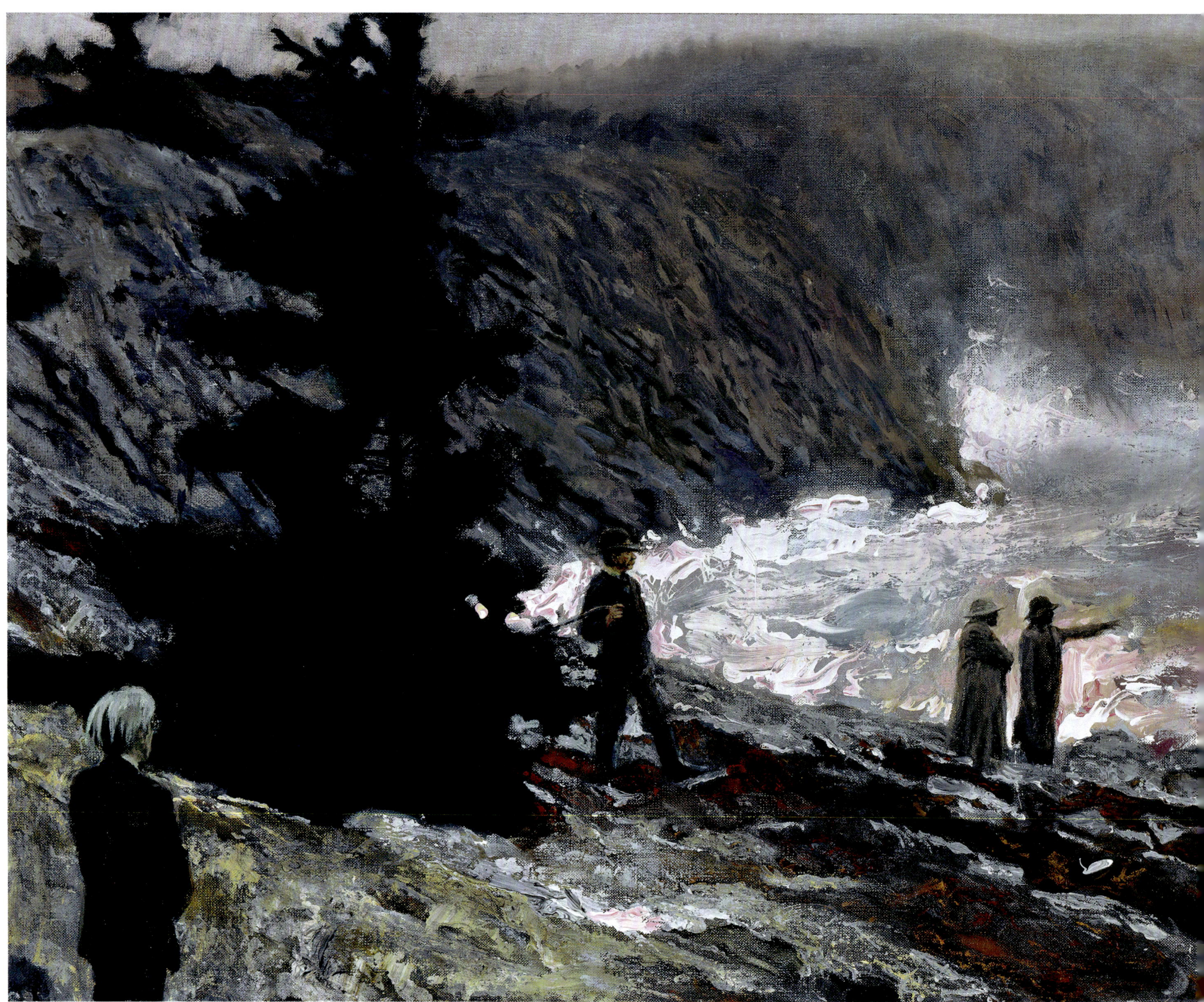

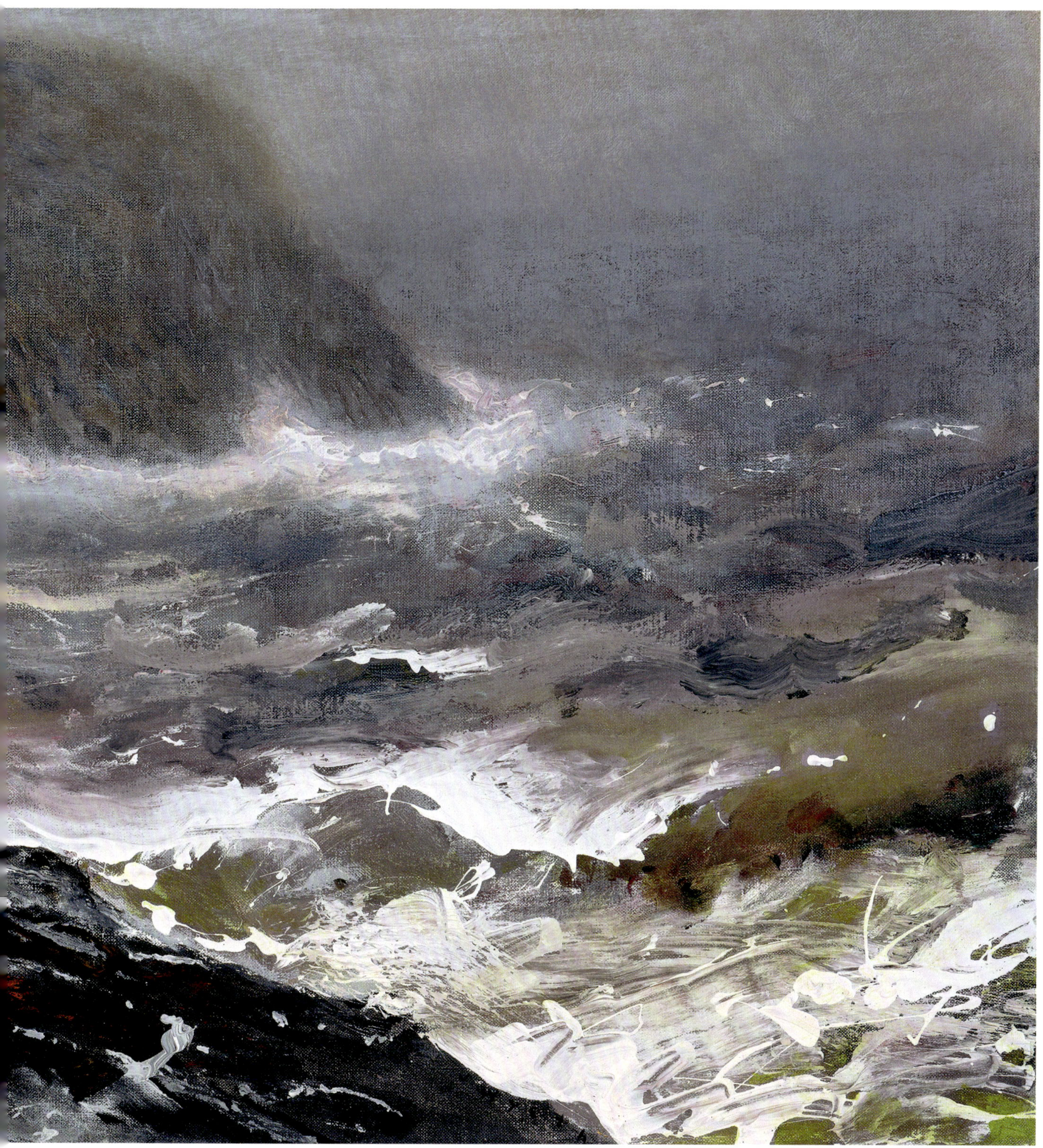

102. *Sea Watchers*, 2009. Oil on canvas, 61 x 134.6 cm (24 x 53 in.)

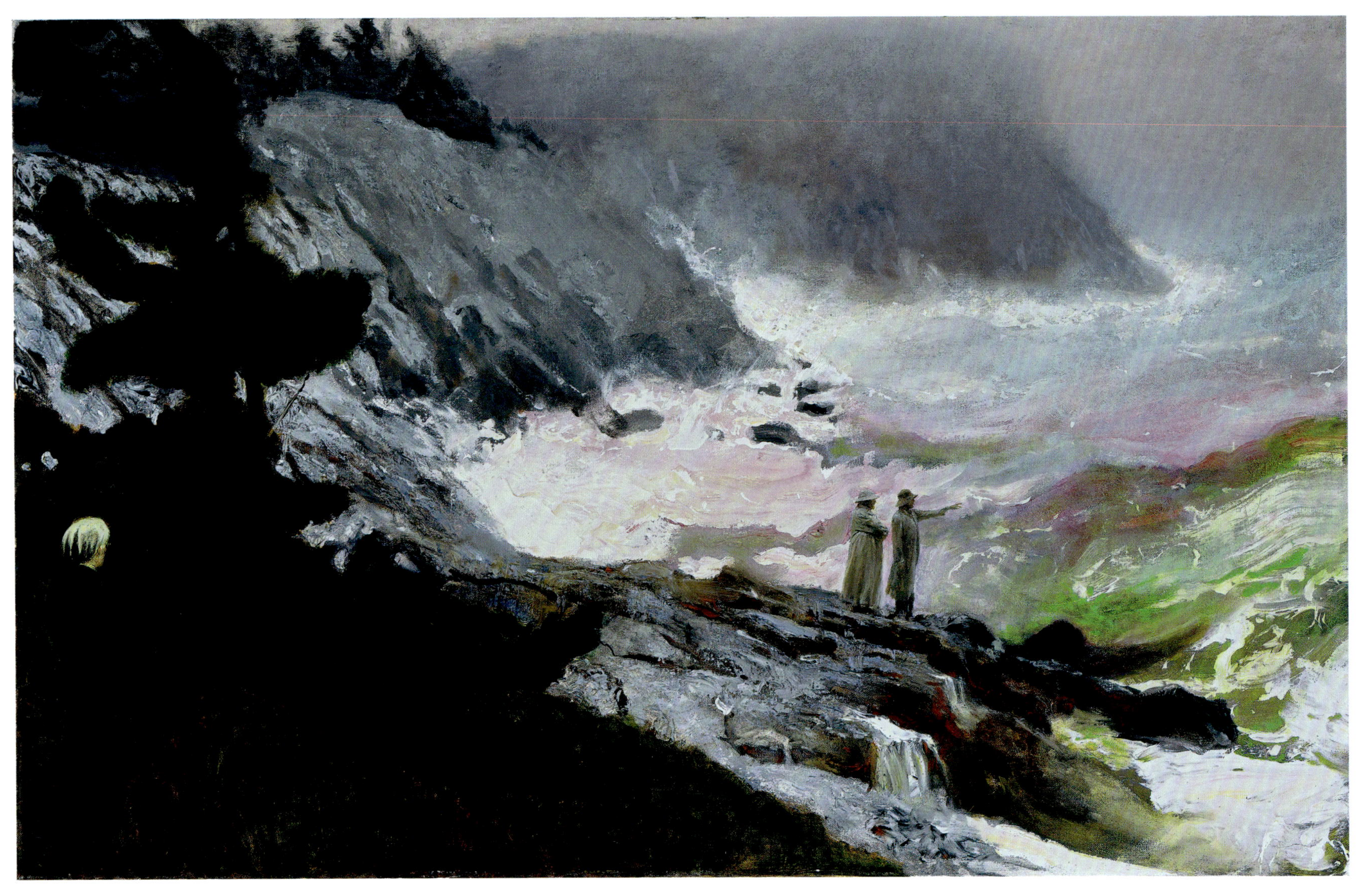

103. *The Sea, Watched*, 2009. Oil on canvas, 76.2 x 121.9 cm (30 x 48 in.)

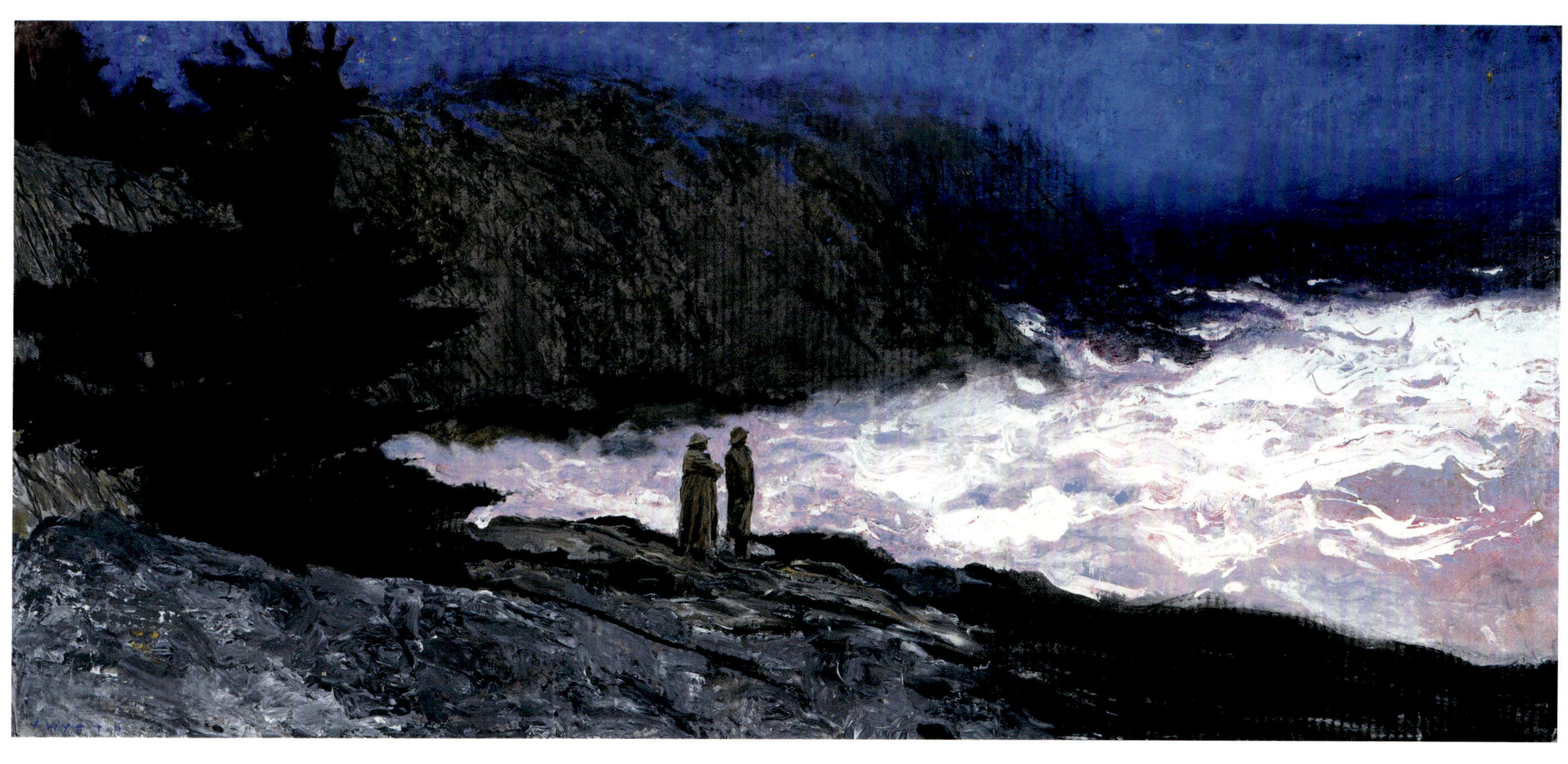

104. *A Recurring Dream*, 2011. Acrylic, oil, and watercolor on archival cardboard, 59.7 x 132.1 cm (23½ x 52 in.)

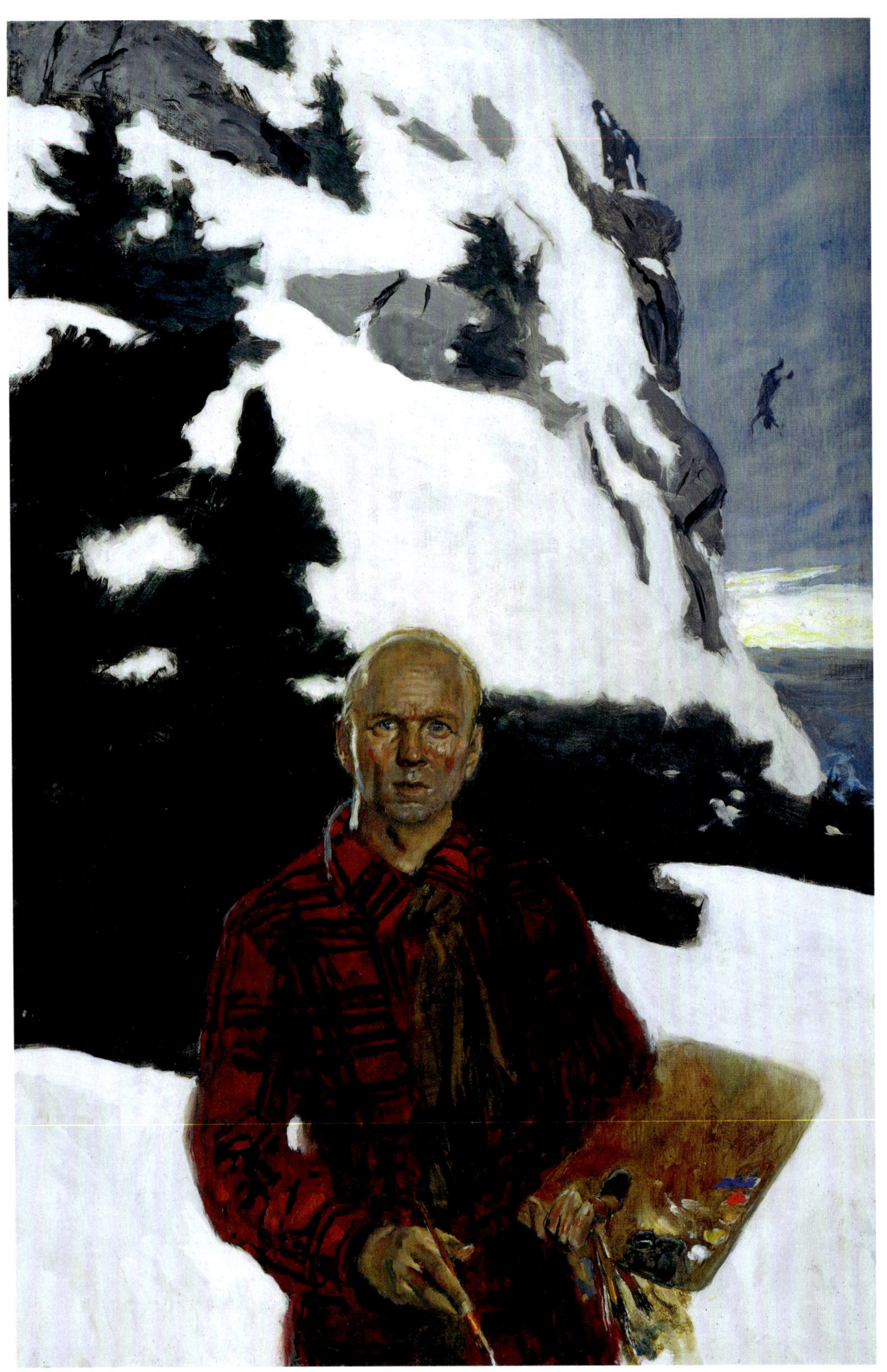

105. *Rockwell Kent—Second in a Series of Untoward Occurrences on Monhegan Island*, 2013. Enamel, gesso, and oil on composite board, 86.4 x 66 cm (34 x 26 in.)

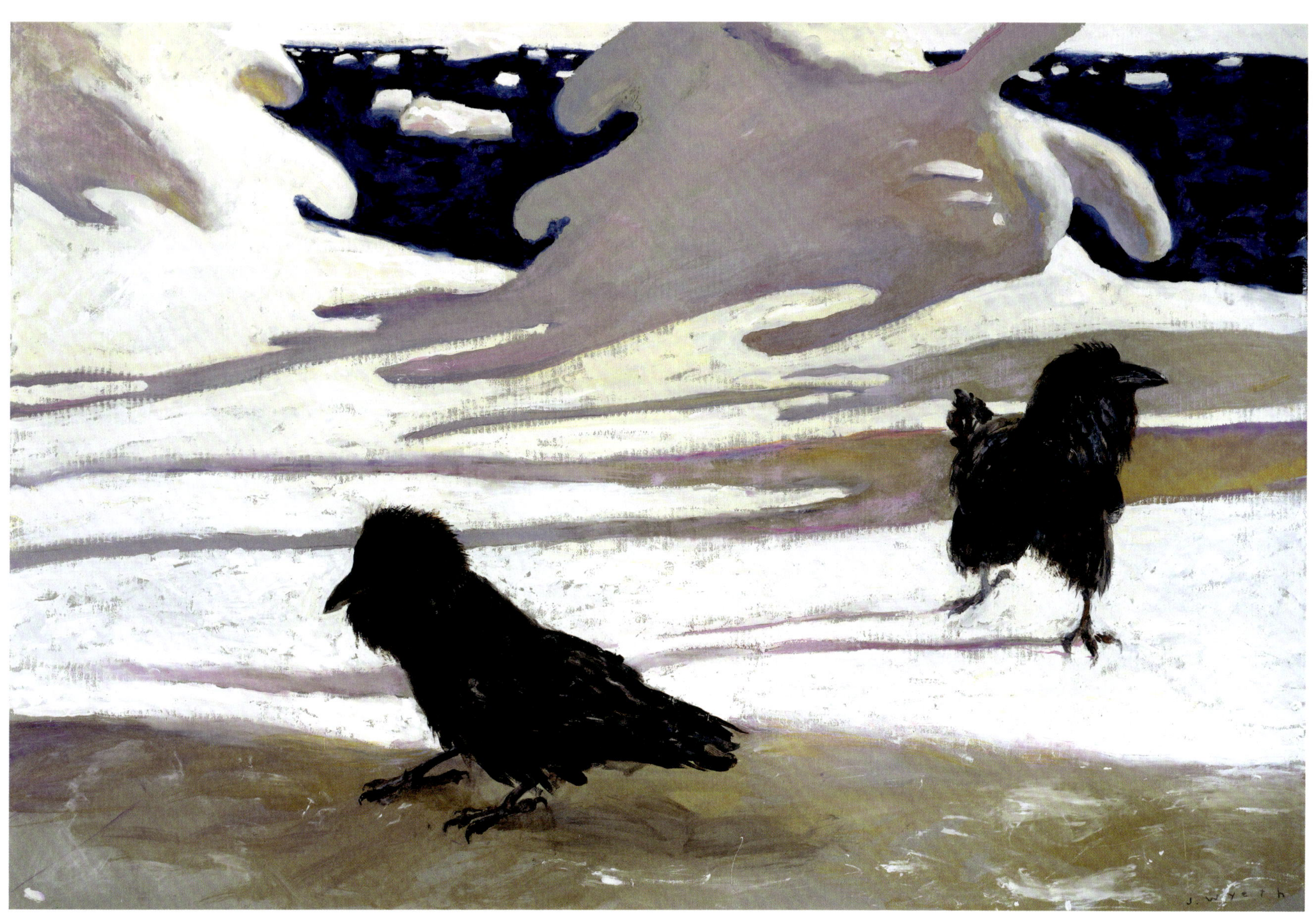

106. *Ice Storm—Maine (Study)*, 1998. Watercolor and gouache on archival cardboard, 101.6 x 152.4 cm (40 x 60 in.)

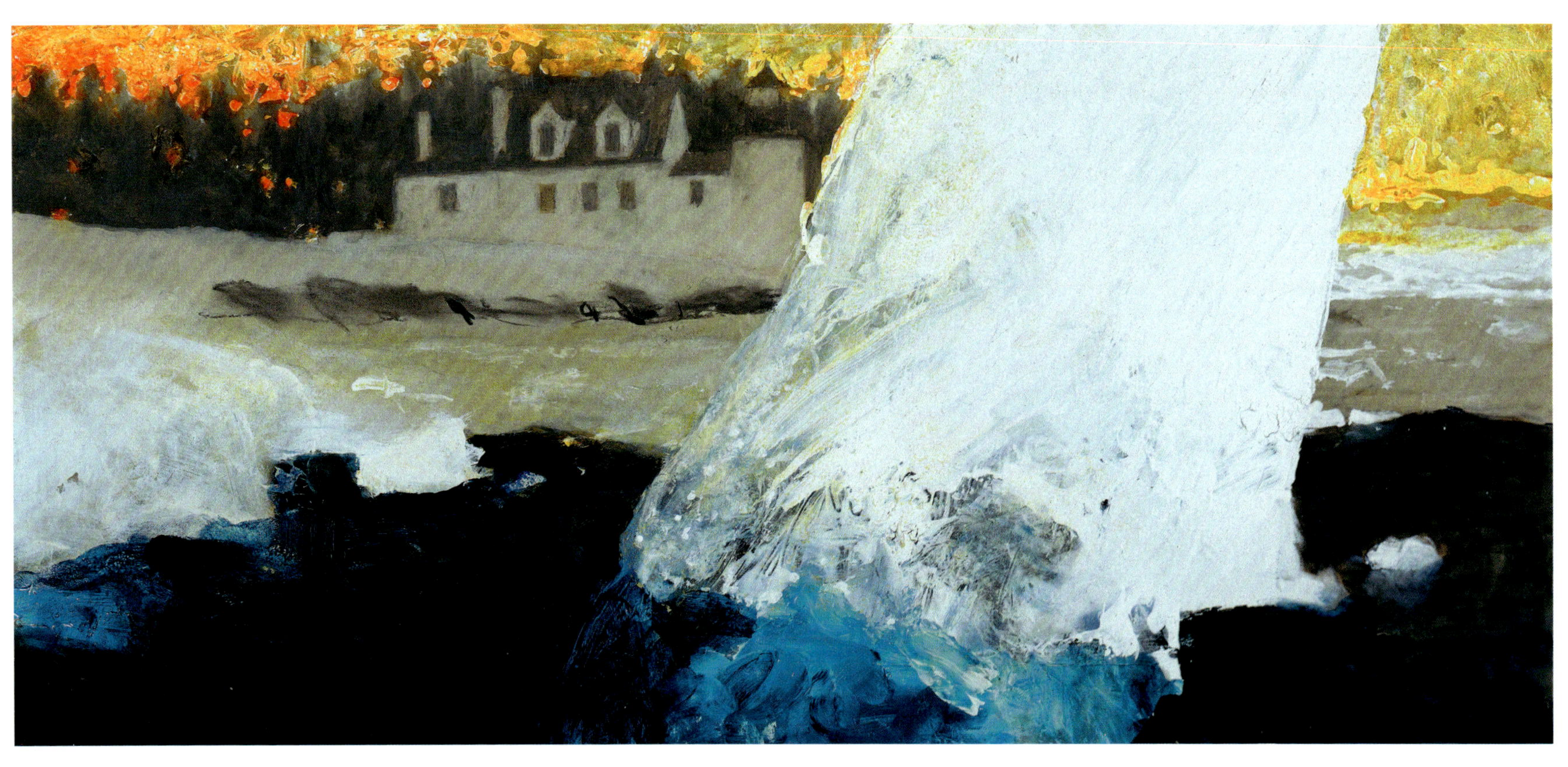

107. *Ice Floe*, 2012. Watercolor, gouache, and varnish on toned rag board, 41.9 x 91.4 cm (16½ x 36 in.)

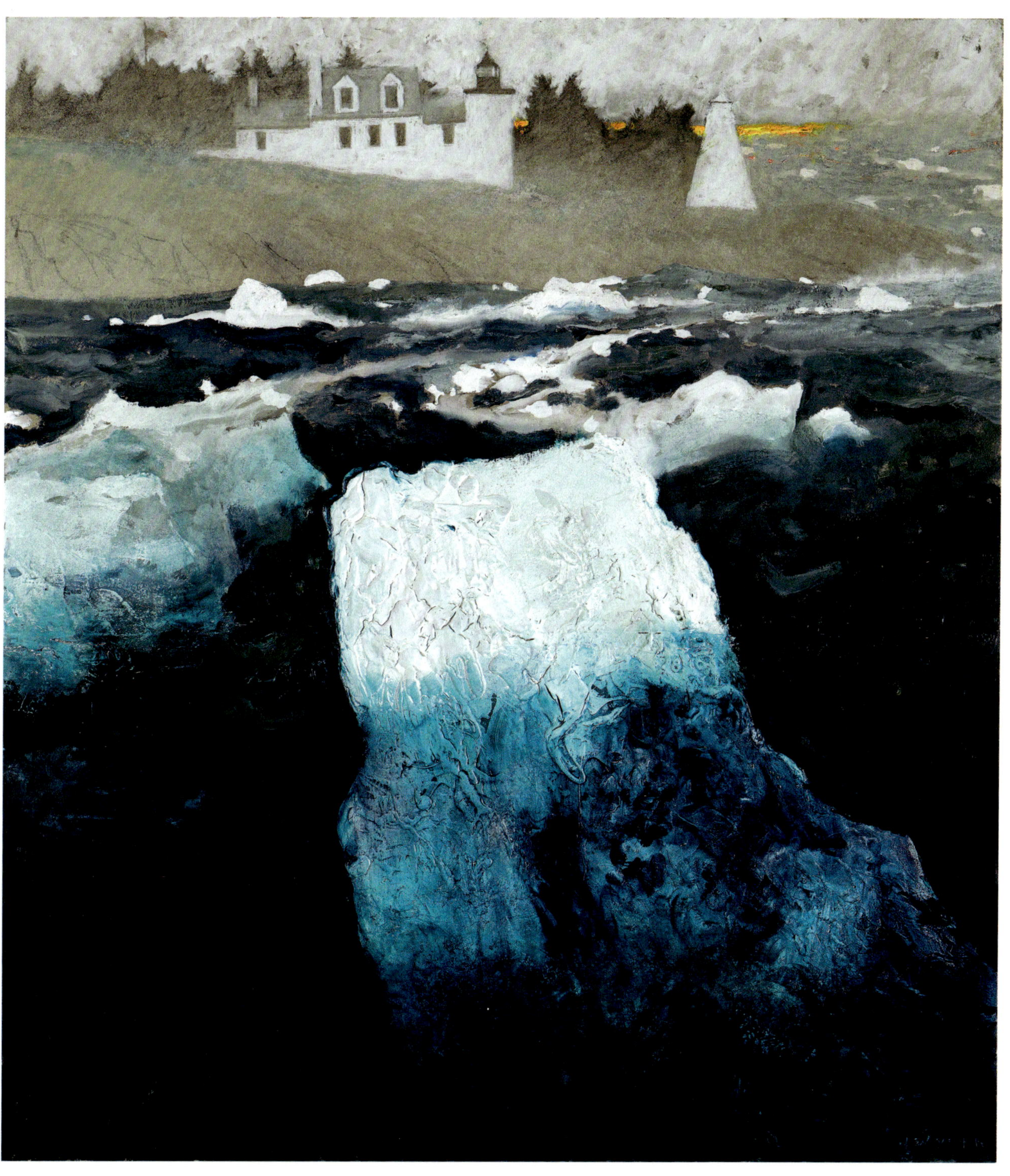

108. *Berg*, 2012. Watercolor, gesso, and enamel on joined rag boards, 102.2 x 91.4 cm (40¼ x 36 in.)

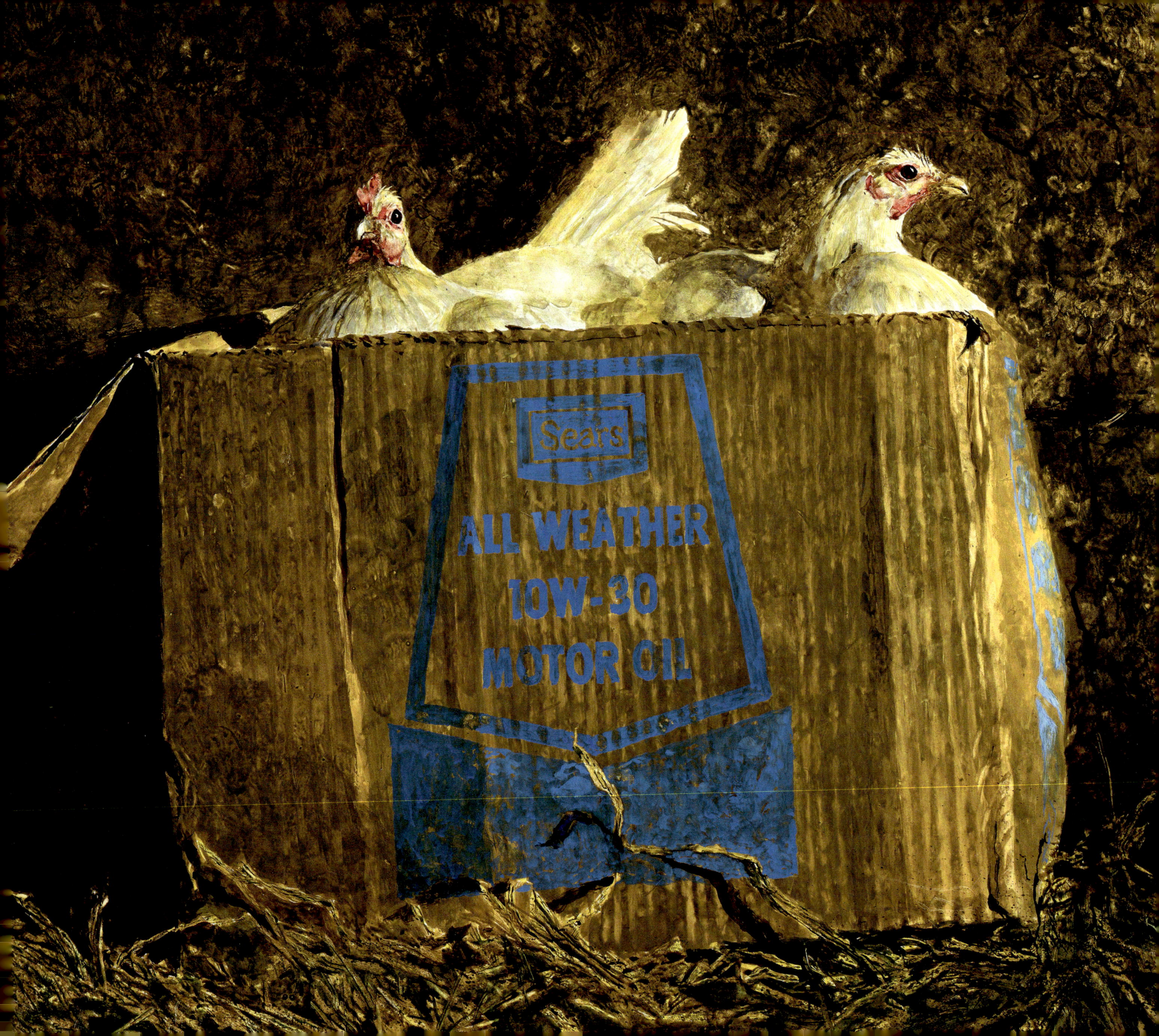
Sears
ALL WEATHER
10W-30
MOTOR OIL

Chronology

James Browning Wyeth born on July 6, 1946, in Chadds Ford, Pennsylvania, to Andrew Wyeth (1917–2009) and Betsy James Wyeth (born 1922). He has one brother, Nicholas (born 1943).

1957
Leaves school after sixth grade to concentrate on painting and studies drawing with his aunt Carolyn.

1963
First museum acquisition, *The Capstan* (1963), by the Farnsworth Art Museum, Rockland, Maine.

1965
Studies anatomy with Dr. Emanuel B. Kaplan at a hospital morgue in New York City.

Paints portrait of Lincoln Kirstein.

1966–1971
Serves in the Delaware Air National Guard.

1966
First solo exhibition, at Knoedler Gallery in New York, consisting of forty-two paintings.

1968
Purchases Kent House, built by Rockwell Kent in 1908, on Monhegan Island, Maine.

December 11, marries Phyllis Mills, daughter of James and Alice du Pont Mills.

1969
Participates in Eyewitness to Space, a program of the National Aeronautics and Space Administration. Other participants include Robert Rauschenberg, Peter Hurd, Norman Rockwell, and Andy Warhol.

First solo museum exhibition, *Oils, Watercolors and Drawings by Jamie Wyeth*, Farnsworth Art Museum, Rockland, Maine.

1972
Appointed council member of the National Endowment for the Arts.

1974
Harper's Magazine publishes drawings made during the Watergate hearings.

1975
Awarded honorary degree by Elizabethtown College, Elizabethtown, Pennsylvania.

1975–76
First full retrospective, *Jamie Wyeth*, Joslyn Art Museum, Omaha, Nebraska.

1976
Paints at the Factory, Andy Warhol's studio in New York. Wyeth and Warhol portraits of each other exhibited at the Coe Kerr Gallery, New York; Everson Museum of Art, Syracuse; Cheekwood Botanical Gardens and Museum of Art, Nashville; Brandywine River Museum, Chadds Ford, Pennsylvania; and Hôtel de Paris, Monaco.

Jamie Wyeth's portrait of president-elect Jimmy Carter appears on the cover of *Time* when he is named the magazine's Man of the Year.

1977
Completes more than thirty studies and an oil of Rudolf Nureyev.

1979
Illustrates *The Stray*, by Betsy James Wyeth.

1980
First major retrospective, *Jamie Wyeth*, Pennsylvania Academy of the Fine Arts, Philadelphia; Greenville County Museum of Art, Greenville, South Carolina; and Amon Carter Museum of Art, Fort Worth.

1981
Included in group exhibition *Contemporary American Realism since 1960*, Pennsylvania Academy of the Fine Arts, Philadelphia.

Christmas Eve at the White House reproduced as a Christmas card for President and Mrs. Reagan.

1983
Receives honorary degree from Dickinson School of Law, Dickinson College, Carlisle, Pennsylvania.

Jamie Wyeth in Alaska, Anchorage Fine Arts Museum, Anchorage; University of Alaska Museum, Fairbanks; and Alaska State Museum, Juneau.

1984
Christmas Morning at the White House reproduced as a Christmas card for President and Mrs. Reagan.

Jamie Wyeth: An American View, Portland Museum of Art, Portland, Maine; Columbia Museum, South Carolina; and Oklahoma Art Center, Oklahoma City.

1986
An American Vision: Three Generations of Wyeth Art, organized by the Brandywine River Museum, shown in Washington, D.C., Dallas, Chicago, Italy, England, Japan, and Russia.

1987
Receives honorary degree from Pine Manor College, Chestnut Hill, Massachusetts.

1988
Receives honorary degree from the University of Vermont.

1993
Receives honorary degree from Westbrook College, Portland, Maine.

1997
Illustrates *Cabbages and Kings*, by Elizabeth Seabrook.

N. C. Wyeth and His Grandson: A Legacy, Terra Museum of American Art, Chicago, and Brandywine River Museum, Chadds Ford, Pennsylvania.

1998–99
Wondrous Strange: The Wyeth Tradition, Farnsworth Art Museum, Rockland, Maine, and Delaware Art Museum, Wilmington.

2000–2002
One Nation: Patriots and Pirates, Portraits by N. C. Wyeth and James Wyeth, Farnsworth Art Museum, Rockland, Maine; the Russell Rotunda, Capitol Building, Washington, D.C.;

New Britain Museum of American Art, New Britain, Connecticut; Brandywine River Museum, Chadds Ford, Pennsylvania; and Ringling Museum of Art, Sarasota, Florida.

2001
Receives honorary degree from the University of Maine, Orono.

2002
Receives honorary degree from the University of Delaware.

2002–3
Capturing Nureyev: James Wyeth Paints the Dancer, John F. Kennedy Center for the Performing Arts, Washington, D.C.; New York Public Library for the Performing Arts at Lincoln Center, New York; Farnsworth Art Museum and Wyeth Center, Rockland, Maine; Brandywine River Museum, Chadds Ford, Pennsylvania.

2006
Capturing Nureyev: James Wyeth Paints the Dancer, Kemper Museum of Contemporary Art, Kansas City, Missouri.

2006–7
Factory Work: Warhol, Wyeth, Basquiat, Brandywine River Museum, Chadds Ford, Pennsylvania; McNay Museum of Art, San Antonio, Texas; and Wyeth Center at the Farnsworth Art Museum, Rockland, Maine.

2007
Dog Days of Summer: Works of Jamie Wyeth, Brandywine River Museum, Chadds Ford, Pennsylvania.

2008–11
Included in *NASA Art: 50 Years of Exploration*, organized by the Smithsonian Institution Traveling Exhibition Service and shown at the Art Students League of Bonita Springs, Florida; Huntsville Museum of Art, Alabama; Irving Arts Center, Texas; Colorado Springs Fine Arts Center, Colorado; Lauren Rogers Museum of Art, Laurel, Mississippi; and Clay Center for the Arts and Sciences of West Virginia, Charleston.

2009–10
Jamie Wyeth: Seven Deadly Sins, Wyeth Center at the Farnsworth Art Museum, Rockland, Maine; Brandywine River Museum, Chadds Ford, Pennsylvania; and Salt Lake City Art Center, Utah.

2011
Farm Work, Brandywine River Museum, Chadds Ford, Pennsylvania.

2012–13
Jamie Wyeth, Rockwell Kent, and Monhegan, Farnsworth Art Museum, Rockland, Maine; Greenville County Museum of Art, Greenville, South Carolina; and Brandywine River Museum, Chadds Ford, Pennsylvania.

Notes

Preface

1. For examples of thematic exhibitions, see in the Bibliography: *Jamie Wyeth: Islands* (1993), *Capturing Nureyev* (2002), *Dog Days* (2007), *Seven Deadly Sins* (2009), *Farm Work* (2011), and *Rockwell Kent, Jamie Wyeth, and Monhegan* (2012).

2. *Jamie Wyeth*, exh. cat. (Boston: Houghton Mifflin, 1980).

3. For major exhibitions devoted to multiple generations of Wyeths, see in the Bibliography: *An American Vision: Three Generations of Wyeth Art* (1987), *Wondrous Strange: The Wyeth Tradition* (1998), *One Nation: Patriots and Pirates Portrayed by N. C. Wyeth and Jamie Wyeth* (2000), and *Wyeth Vertigo* (2013).

4. Robert Rosenblum, Joyce Hill Stoner, and Margaret Rose Vendryes, *Factory Work: Warhol, Wyeth, Basquiat*, exh. cat. (Hanover, N.H.: Brandywine River Museum in association with University Press of New England, 2006). See also *Farm Work* (2011).

5. See Christopher Crosman, "Betsy's World," in Anne Classen Knutson, *Andrew Wyeth: Memory & Magic*, exh. cat. (New York: High Museum of Art and Philadelphia Museum of Art in association with Rizzoli, 2006), pp. 107–22. See also Richard Meryman, *Andrew Wyeth: A Secret Life* (New York: HarperCollins, 1996), pp. 263–64.

6. The representation of the tension between these worlds is perhaps most clearly expressed by Andrew Wyeth in *Otherworld* (2002, private collection); see Joyce Hill Stoner, "Wyeth Vertigo: On Land and Sea, in the Air, and at the Dinner Table," in Thomas Denenberg et al., *Vertigo*, exh. cat. (Hanover, N.H: Shelburne Museum in association with University Press of New England, 2013).

7. Marsden Hartley, "On the Subject of Nativeness—A Tribute to Maine," in *On Art*, ed. Gail R. Scott (New York: Horizon Press, 1982), pp. 112–15. Living in Berlin just before the First World War, Hartley was moved to explore his American heritage in Native American signs and symbols, producing a series of paintings on the theme of "Amerika" inspired by visits to Berlin's Ethnographical Museum. See Barbara Haskell, *Marsden Hartley*, exh. cat. (New York: Whitney Museum of Art in association with New York University Press, 1980), p. 42; Wanda M. Corn, "Marsden Hartley's Native Amerika," in Elizabeth Mankin Kornhauser, *Marsden Hartley*, exh. cat. (New Haven: Wadsworth Atheneum Museum of Art in association with Yale University Press, 2003), pp. 69–94.

8. Rockwell Kent, *It's Me, O Lord: The Autobiography of Rockwell Kent* (New York: Dodd, Mead, 1955), p. 138. This statement is quoted by Jamie Wyeth in his foreword to *Rockwell Kent: An Anthology of His Works*, ed. Fridolf Johnson (New York: Knopf, 1982), p. 11.

Jamie Wyeth and Recent American Realism

1. Michael Kimmelman, "Andrew Wyeth, Painter, Dies at 91," *New York Times*, January 16, 2009.

2. Lincoln Kirstein, "James Wyeth," in *An American Vision: Three Generations of Wyeth Art*, exh. cat. (Boston: Little, Brown, 1987), p. 157.

3. Ibid., 156.

4. Bruce Glaser, "Questions to Stella and Judd," *Art News* 65 (September 1966): 55–61.

5. Udo Kultermann, *New Realism* (Greenwich, Conn.: New York Graphic Society, 1972), p. 9.

6. Ibid., p. 8.

7. See, for example, Frank Goodyear, *Contemporary Realism since 1960*, exh. cat. (Boston: New York Graphic Society, 1981).

8. Ihab Hassan, "From Postmodernism to Postmodernity: The Local/Global Context," *www.ihabhassan.com/postmodernism_to_postmodernity.htm* (accessed October 6, 2013). See also Charles Jencks, *Post-Modernism: The New Classicism in Art and Architecture* (London: Academy Editions, 1987).

9. Ralph Waldo Emerson, "Nature," in *The Complete Works of Ralph Waldo Emerson* (Boston: Houghton Mifflin, 1903), 1:26.

10. William Ritter, *Giovanni Segantini* (Vienna: Verlag der Gesellschaft für Vervielfältigende Kunst, 1897).

11. *Andrew Wyeth: A Spoken Self-Portrait*, ed. Richard Meryman (Washington, D.C.: National Gallery of Art, 2013).

12. Ralph Waldo Emerson, "Art," in *The Complete Works of Ralph Waldo Emerson* (Boston: Houghton Mifflin, 1898), p. 131.

Early Life and Work

1. Quoted in William K. Stevens, "Sketching the Wyeth Dynasty," *New York Times*, November 23, 1986.

2. See David Michaelis, *N. C. Wyeth: A Biography* (New York: Knopf, 1998); Christine B. Podmaniczky, *N. C. Wyeth: Catalogue Raisonné of Paintings*, 2 vols. (London: Scala, 2008); Betsy James Wyeth, ed., *The Wyeths: The Letters of N. C. Wyeth, 1901–1945* (Boston: Gambit, 1971).

3. Michaelis, *N. C. Wyeth*, p. 171; Podmaniczky, *N. C. Wyeth*, vol. 1, p. 38. N.C. briefly moved to Needham in 1921, returning to Chadds Ford two years later. Ibid., p. 18.

4. Michaelis, *N. C. Wyeth*, pp. 6, 16–18, 281; Podmaniczky, *N. C. Wyeth*, vol. 1, p. 17.

5. See James Gardner, "The Last Dynasty," *The Magazine Antiques* 183, no. 3 (May–June 2013): 127–32.

6. As Andrew Wyeth reflected on his own training by his father, N. C. Wyeth, he recalled: “He taught me anatomy, brought in nude models, made me draw from casts, did everything in his power to help me see. I tried to encourage [Jamie] and still to let him go his own way. He must find out for himself if it is what he wants to do. All I can teach him is self-reliance and respect for his craft.” *Realism Now: Traditions and Departures: Mentors and Protégés* (Boston: Vose Gallery, 2003), p. 36.

7. For accounts of Andrew Wyeth’s life and work, see Thomas Hoving and Andrew Wyeth, *Two Worlds of Andrew Wyeth: A Conversation with Andrew Wyeth* (Boston: Houghton Mifflin, 1978); Wanda M. Corn, *The Art of Andrew Wyeth*, exh. cat. (Greenwich, Conn.: New York Graphic Society, 1973); Richard Meryman, *Andrew Wyeth: A Secret Life* (New York: HarperCollins, 1996); and Anne Classen Knutson et al., *Andrew Wyeth: Memory & Magic* (Atlanta: High Museum of Art, in association with Rizzoli, 2005).

8. Richard Meryman, “Andrew Wyeth: An Interview,” in Corn, *The Art of Andrew Wyeth*, p. 58.

9. See Brian O’Doherty, *American Masters: The Voice and the Myth* (New York: Random House, 1973), pp. 229–53; Meryman, *Andrew Wyeth*, p. 22.

10. For further insight into the broader topic of children’s drawings, see Jonathan Fineberg, ed., *When We Were Young: New Perspectives on the Art of the Child*, exh. cat. (Washington, D.C.: Phillips Collection; Berkeley: University of California Press, 2006), esp. pp. 1–17. See also Elliot Bostwick Davis, “Hopper’s Foundation,” in Carol Troyen et al., *Edward Hopper*, exh. cat. (Boston: Museum of Fine Arts, 2007), p. 31.

11. Phyllis Mills Wyeth, interview by the author, Tenants Harbor, July 14, 2011.

12. I am grateful to Mary Beth Dolan and Helene Sutton for tracking down this drawing at the Wyeths’ home.

13. For the persistence of the story of Giotto in American art, see John Gadsby Chapman, *The American Drawing Book: A Manual for the Amateur, and Basis of Study for the Professional Artist* (New York: J. S. Redfield, 1847), p. 22. The original story is described in Giorgio Vasari, *Lives of the Artists* (1550).

14. Gian Carlo Menotti, “The Hero,” *New York Post*, November 6, 1974, p. 42.

15. Wyeth, *The Wyeths: The Letters of N. C. Wyeth*, pp. 657–58, 667.

16. The Jamie Wyeth Archives and Database at the Farnsworth Art Museum includes various drawing examinations that were signed and dated by Jamie Wyeth to document his progress. His initial curriculum derived from the University of Chicago’s American School. I am grateful to Mary Beth Dolan for this information.

17. Carolyn Wyeth is a fascinating figure in Jamie Wyeth’s life and an artist who would benefit from greater study. The most comprehensive catalogue of her work was published by the Brandywine River Museum of Art. See Richard Meryman, *Carolyn Wyeth, Artist: An Interview with Carolyn Wyeth*, exh. cat. (Chadds Ford: Brandywine Conservancy, 1979).

18. David R. Boldt, “True Art,” *Today Magazine, Philadelphia Inquirer*, September 21, 1980, p. 43.

19. Menotti, “The Hero,” p. 42.

20. He added, “My father works in tempera, which I did try. All the properties he likes I dislike and vice versa. I think these choices are purely personal.” *Realism Now*, p. 37.

21. Joyce Hill Stoner, “Wyeth Vertigo: On Land and Sea, in the Air, and at the Dinner Table,” in Stoner et al., *Wyeth Vertigo* (Shelburne, Vt.: Shelburne Museum, 2013), p. 44, refers to a painting that Jamie Wyeth made following the death of his aunt Carolyn in 1994, but it has not been located.

22. Meryman, *Andrew Wyeth: A Secret Life*, pp. 272–73.

23. For a description of the “properties,” as Howard Pyle called them, that N. C. Wyeth assembled in his studio, see Podmaniczky, *N. C. Wyeth*, vol. 1, pp. 31–33. Christopher Crosman in collaboration with Jamie Wyeth mounted an exhibition at the Farnsworth Art Museum, *Paintings, Props, and Costumes: Objects of Inspiration* (1999–2000), that explored the role of props in Jamie Wyeth’s painting.

24. Marilyn Lois Polak, “Prince on the Brandywine,” *Baltimore Sun*, March 21, 1976: “Some of Jamie Wyeth’s early subjects were slightly exploitive. Shorty was a taciturn derelict he found walking on the railroad tracks. ‘I must say he was marvelous,’ he grins. ‘When I asked him to pose, he didn’t know what I meant, so I finally said, well just sit there.’”

25. Jamie Wyeth, interview by the author, Tenants Harbor, Maine, August 15, 2012.

26. See Lincoln Kirstein, foreword to *James Wyeth: Paintings*, exh. cat. (New York: Knoedler, 1966): “Jamie considers himself the spiritual great-grandson of John Singleton Copley, before he left Boston for London and the Royal Academy” (n.p.).

27. John W. McCoubrey, *American Art, 1700–1960: Sources and Documents* (Englewood Cliffs, N.J.: Prentice-Hall, 1965), pp. 15–16.

Formation

1. *Portrait of Shorty* was first exhibited at the Wilcox Gallery, Swarthmore College, Swarthmore, Pennsylvania in 1964.

2. Marilyn Lois Polak, “Prince on the Brandywine,” *Baltimore Sun*, March 21, 1976.

3. See Baldwin, *To Heal the Heart of a Child*, pp. 96–106; Patricia Meisol, “The Changing Face of a Strong Woman,” *New York Times*, August 14, 2013.

4. Arthur White Franklin, “Not Men, but a Method,” *The British Medical Journal* 2, no. 5411 (September 19, 1964): 749.

5. Dr. Charlotte Ferencz, quoted in Baldwin, *To Heal the Heart of a Child*, p. 102.

6. Ibid.

7. Ibid., p. 101.

8. This account of the painting *Draft Age* is found in David R. Boldt, “True Art,” *Today Magazine, Philadelphia Inquirer*, September 21, 1980, p. 47. When Lynch was awake (if indeed he was behind the dark glasses), the artist held his attention by playing four or five Beatles albums in a row. Only after all of the albums had been played would the hard-driving Wyeth grant Lynch a fifteen-minute break.

9. Ibid.

10. Ibid. Lincoln Kirstein proposes an alternative interpretation from the perspective of an army veteran and member of the distinguished corps of “Monuments Men,” noting that the iron teeth of Lynch’s jacket zipper suggest “a future soldier’s battle dress,” and that “plastic sunglasses mock the armored visors of chivalry in desuetude.” Lincoln Kirstein, “James Wyeth,”

in James H. Duff et al., *An American Vision: Three Generations of Wyeth Art: N. C. Wyeth, Andrew Wyeth, James Wyeth* (Boston: Little, Brown, 1987), p. 157.

11. Jerry L. Thompson, "Lincoln Kirstein at Eighty," *Yale Review* 95, no. 3 (2007): 16.

12. Kirstein also managed to found a literary magazine, *Hound & Horn*, financed by his father and sealed with a logo designed by Rockwell Kent. The publication featured many of the foremost writers, artists, and photographers of the day.

13. John Russell, "Lincoln Kirstein: A Life in Art," *New York Times*, June 20, 1982.

14. See Martin Duberman's biography, *The Worlds of Lincoln Kirstein* (New York: Knopf, 2007), pp. 355–56.

15. Andrew, who was effectively replaced by Jamie as the object of Kirstein's interest, noted, "Lincoln was the one person who took Jamie seriously." Betsy felt that Kirstein "could give Jamie a different kind of education than we could." Ibid., p. 566.

16. Ibid.

17. Andrew Wyeth had recommended Jamie for the Helen Taussig portrait commission that came to him via his Chadds Ford neighbor Dr. Margaret Handy. In addition to turning down the Kirstein portrait in favor of Jamie, Andrew Wyeth later recommended him for the Eyewitness to Space program.

18. Duberman, *The Worlds of Lincoln Kirstein*, p. 567.

19. Copley, the master of sartorial detail, painted Adams in a ruddy suit of coarse wool that would have been easily identified at the time as a distinctly homespun cloth made in the New England colonies, and therefore not subject to the oppressive British import taxes that he and his fellow Patriots vociferously opposed.

20. Claudia Roth Pierpont, "The Prince of the City," *New Yorker*, April 16, 2007, p. 143.

21. A student at the School of American Ballet noted that Kirstein was often seen the way that Jamie Wyeth painted him, observing that his attire and "his habitual stance with arms behind his back were probably subconscious efforts to deemphasize his massive frame." Wendy Wick Reeves, *Modern American Portrait Drawings from the National Portrait Gallery*, exh. cat. (Washington, D.C.: Smithsonian Institution, 2002), p. 206. See also Colta Ives, "Jamie Wyeth," in Nancy Reynolds, ed., *Remembering Lincoln* (New York: Ballet Society, 2007), p. 221.

22. Jamie Wyeth, "Collector of Memories and Lessons," in *The Person Who Changed My Life: Prominent People Recall Their Mentors*, ed. Matilda Raffa Cuomo (1999; repr., Emmaus, Pa.: Rodale Books, 2012), p. 189.

23. See Barbara Cohen-Stratyner et al., *Capturing Nureyev: Jamie Wyeth Paints the Dancer*, exh. cat. (Rockland, Maine: Farnsworth Art Museum in association with University Press of New England, 2002).

24. Jamie Wyeth, "Collector of Memories and Lessons," p. 189.

25. Ives, "Jamie Wyeth," p. 202. Wyeth notes that Kirstein purchased two portraits of Nureyev from his first show and later invited him to his house, along with the dancer: "I just sat there in silence, while Lincoln and Nureyev went on and on. I mean, talk about two giants in their fields. Nureyev was very bright in terms of the history of dance."

26. In *Interview Magazine* (February 1974), Wyeth recalled an encounter with a taxi driver upon leaving the morgue following the Thanksgiving holiday. Recognizing the smell of the formaldehyde, the cabbie greeted him as "Doc" and offered him a turkey sandwich. "I couldn't resist it and said, 'I'd love to but I've just been cutting up bodies all day.' This guy turned his rear view mirror to look at me. I suddenly became Baron Frankenstein."

27. For an image of Jamie Wyeth's portrait of Lincoln Kirstein installed in Kirstein's New York City apartment, see Lincoln Kirstein, *Quarry: A Collection in Lieu of Memories, with Photographs by Jerry Thompson* (Pasadena: Twelvetrees Press, 1986), p. 28. See also Michael K. Komanecky, *Jamie Wyeth: Seven Deadly Sins*, exh. cat. (Rockland, Maine: Farnsworth Art Museum, 2009), p. 12.

28. He also contributed a trenchant commentary to Duff et al., *An American Vision*, pp. 156–162.

29. Jamie Wyeth, "The Collector of Memories and Lessons," p. 188.

30. Duberman, *The Worlds of Lincoln Kirstein*, p. 567.

31. Quoted by Sally Quinn, *Washington Post*, November 28, 1974. "I don't want to do an official portrait thing . . . and also . . . it scared the hell out of me. I'd never laid eyes on him." *Look* magazine published an account of Jamie Wyeth's intent observation of the late president's brother Edward to catch "the calculating gaze that masks the political mind forever diverted to some scene still unplayed." "Another Wyeth: The Portrait Artist Is a Young Man," *Look*, April 2, 1968, p. 58.

32. Sandra Carpenter and Greg Schaber, "Jamie Wyeth: His Art and Insights," *Artist's Magazine* 14, no. 8 (August 1997): 38.

33. Kitty Kelley, *Capturing Camelot: Stanley Tretick's Iconic Images of the Kennedys* (New York: Thomas Dunne Books, 2012), p. 202.

34. See Wanda Corn, *The Art of Andrew Wyeth* (Greenwich, Conn.: New York Graphic Society, 1973), p. 96.

35. For notes on *C-97 Landing in Vietnam*, see Individual Profile, Biography, Jamie Wyeth, comments 2004, Jamie Wyeth Archives and Database, Farnsworth Art Museum.

36. Walter Friedlaender, *Mannerism and Anti-Mannerism in Italian Painting, Two Essays* (1957; repr., New York: Columbia University Press, 1990), p. 54.

37. Michael Komanecky and Jamie Wyeth, "A Dialogue," held at the Strand Theatre, Rockland, Maine, August 14, 2012. Transcript available at the Farnsworth Art Museum, Department of Education, Rockland, Maine.

38. Meryman, *Andrew Wyeth: A Secret Life*, p. 281.

39. Jamie Wyeth notes that in 1968, when he produced a series of drawings of his cousin Robin McCoy in the nude, one of the sheets went missing and later turned up in his father's studio. In the wake of the family brouhaha over the drawings, Andrew Wyeth surreptitiously began his own series of nudes at the Kuerners', later revealed in the body of work inspired by Helga Testorf. For the Helga series of drawings and paintings, see John Wilmerding, *Andrew Wyeth: The Helga Pictures*, exh. cat. (New York: Abrams, 1987). See also David Michaelis, *N. C. Wyeth: A Biography* (New York: Knopf, 1998), p. 390: "Father and son had been collaborating on book illustrations since Andy was sixteen. In the mid-1930s, be-

fore his emergence as a watercolor painter, Andy had illustrated several books with which N. C. had helped. Andy, in turn, had assisted his father with the pen-and-ink work in N. C. Wyeth's *Men of Concord*, a selection from Thoreau's journals. Andy had produced twenty-four pen-and-ink drawings, and Houghton Mifflin and the public had never been the wiser." On Andrew's early promise as an artist and his father's subsequent disappointment, see Wyeth, *The Wyeths: The Letters of N. C. Wyeth*, pp. 819–20.

40. Peter Hurd, "Countdown at Canaveral," *Art in America* 5 (1963): 61, 64.

41. Jamie Wyeth's illustrations for the Eyewitness to Space program can be found in the catalogue by Hereward Lester Cooke and James D. Dean, *Eyewitness to Space: Paintings and Drawings Related to the Apollo Mission to the Moon* (New York: Abrams, 1972), pp. 15, 32, 39, 69, 74, 75, 90, 179, 197.

42. Recounted in Lincoln Kirstein, "James Wyeth," in Duff et al., *An American Vision*, pp. 158–159.

43. Phyllis Mills Wyeth, interview by the author, Tenants Harbor, Maine, July 14, 2011.

44. Jamie Wyeth, *Ehrlichman Pleading before Jury, Policeman Guarding Room 6*, 1974, pencil on paper, 27.9 x 35.6 cm (11 x 14 in.) and *Ehrlichman and Jury*, 1964, pencil on paper, 27.9 x 35.6 cm (11 x 14 in.).

45. Jamie Wyeth, interview by the author, Tenants Harbor, August 15, 2012. Lincoln Kirstein also notes the resemblance to Daumier in *An American Vision*, p. 158.

New York and the Factory

1. Bob Colacello, *Holy Terror: Andy Warhol Close Up* (New York: HarperCollins, 1990), pp. 29, 30.

2. Ibid., p. 92.

3. John Buckland, "The Brandywine Tradition Meets the Big Apple: The Twain Meet," *Delaware Today*, August 1976, p. 18.

4. Robert Rosenblum et al., *Factory Work: Warhol, Wyeth, Basquiat* (Rockland, Maine: Farnsworth Art Museum, 2006), p. 22.

5. See Robert Rosenblum, "Warhol's Identity Thefts," ibid., pp. 10–22.

6. Victor Bockris, *The Life and Death of Andy Warhol* (New York: Bantam Books, 1989), p. 309: "Andy let his victims feel the lash with the slightest lessening of approval. Bianca Jagger's fall from grace would eventually cause her to think of her once 'magical, beautiful' friend as a 'vampire.' It was an apt choice of words, for once Andy's suction stopped, his victims felt drained."

7. Rosenblum et al., *Factory Work*, p. 33.

8. A 1978 *Oxidation Painting* from this series is in the collection of the Museum of Fine Arts, Boston (1993.685).

9. Pat Hackett, ed., *The Andy Warhol Diaries* (New York: Warner, 1989), p. 55. Warhol directed Cutrone, "Try to hold it until he gets to the office, because he takes lots of vitamin B so the canvas turns a really pretty color when it's his piss." See also Christine Daulton, "Technical Notes: Chemistry and Art: Andy Warhol's Oxidation Paintings," in Robert Rosenblum et al., *Factory Work*, pp. 24–27.

10. Lincoln Kirstein, foreword to *James Wyeth Paintings* (New York: M. Knoedler, 1966), n.p.

11. Roberta Brandes Gratz, *New York Post*, June 1, 1976, n.p.

12. See Joyce Hill Stoner, "Andy Warhol and Jamie Wyeth," in Rosenblum et al., *Factory Work*, p. 70.

13. Hilton Kramer, "Art: Warhol Meets Wyeth," *New York Times*, June 4, 1976, p. 66.

14. Robert Rosenblum, "Warhol's Identity Thefts," p. 13.

15. Stoner, "Andy Warhol and Jamie Wyeth," p. 63.

16. Andy Warhol, *The Philosophy of Andy Warhol: From A to B and Back Again* (New York: Harcourt Brace Jovanovich, 1975), pp. 51, 62.

17. Colacello, *Holy Terror*, p. 16. In third grade, Warhol contracted a rare disease, "St. Vitus's dance—a virus of the nerves, thought to be a complication from scarlet fever, that would change his looks, and his life, forever. Its obvious symptoms were shaky limbs and blotchy skin." Ibid.

18. Gerrit Henry, *Art News*, September 1976, p. 121. See also Meryman, *Andrew Wyeth: A Secret Life*, p. 277.

19. Buckland, "The Brandywine Tradition Meets the Big Apple," p. 17.

20. The full-length study is *Andy Warhol—with Archie in Profile (Study #8)* (1976, private collection). For Warhol's interest in portraying feet of famous people, see *Andy Warhol: Still Lifes and Feet, 1956–1961*, exh. cat. (New York: Paul Kasmin Gallery, 2010). *Andy's Feet* was given to Wyeth after Warhol's death.

21. "Arnold Schwarzenegger: This Hunk Is Not a Fruit," *Village Voice*, June 24, 1977, p. 56.

22. Richard Hamilton to Alison and Peter Smithson, January 16, 1957; *www.kunsthalle-tuebingen.de*, accessed May 16, 2013.

23. Colacello, *Holy Terror*, p. 107.

24. Barbara Cohen-Stratyner and Lauren Raye Smith, *Capturing Nureyev: Jamie Wyeth Paints the Dancer* (Rockland, Maine: Farnsworth Art Museum in association with University Press of New England), p. 42.

25. Michael Komanecky and Jamie Wyeth, "A Dialogue," held at the Strand Theatre, Rockland, Maine, August 14, 2012; transcript available at the Farnsworth Art Museum, Department of Education, Rockland, Maine.

26. Clive Barnes, "Nureyev: An Introduction," in *Capturing Nureyev*, pp. 11–13.

27. Lauren Raye Smith, "Nureyev Revisted: James Wyeth's Portraits," in Cohen-Stratyner and Smith, *Capturing Nureyev*, p. 45. Phil Patton, "Painting's Favorite Son," *United Mainliner*, October 1980, p. 112.

28. See Barbara Cohen-Stratyner, "Presenting Nureyev: Visual Cues in Promotional Dance Photography," in Cohen-Stratyner and Smith, *Capturing Nureyev*, pp. 27–40.

29. Susan Watters, "What's Nude?" *Women's Wear Daily*, February 14, 2002, p. 13. See also Ronnie Cutrone, "An Artist's Take on the Work of Warhol," in Joseph O'Connor and Benjamin Liu, *Unseen Warhol* (New York: Rizzoli, 1996), esp. pp. 68–69.

30. Jamie Wyeth, conversation with the author, June 28, 2013.

Brandywine

1. Marshall Ledger, "Jamie's World," *Philadelphia* magazine, September 1980, p. 138.

2. Jamie Wyeth, interview by the author, July 17, 2012, Southern Island, Maine.

3. Richard Meryman, *Andrew Wyeth: A Secret Life* (New York: HarperCollins, 1996), p. 100.

4. Jamie Wyeth, *Farm Work*, exh. cat. (Chadds Ford, Pa.: Brandywine River Museum, 2011), p. 22.

5. Ibid., p. 33.

6. Wyeth described the painting as "one of the most breathtaking pictures I've ever seen. [It] just blows me away. I can't even believe human hands did the painting." Jamie Wyeth, interview by Christopher Crosman, in Crosman, *Jamie Wyeth: Islands*, exh. cat. (Rockland, Maine: Farnsworth Library and Art Museum, 1993), p. 5.

7. David R. Boldt, "True Art," *Today Magazine, Philadelphia Inquirer*, September 21, 1980, p. 51; Phyllis Mills Wyeth, conversation with the author, July 14, 2011, Tenants Harbor, Maine.

8. When the work appeared in Jamie Wyeth's 1980 retrospective, David Boldt, writing for the magazine of the *Philadelphia Inquirer*, observed that it had a "surreal, dreamlike quality that seems to have something to do with the intensity of the color of the leaves. More, perhaps than any of Jamie Wyeth's other paintings, it reminds a viewer of Carolyn Wyeth's hauntingly expressive paintings." In the same article, Frank Goodyear is quoted as saying, "I've never understood that picture. I think there's some secret in it that has to do with their relationship." Boldt, "True Art," p. 43.

9. See especially Randall C. Griffin, "Andrew Wyeth's *Christina's World*: Normalizing the Abnormal Body," *American Art* 24, no. 2 (2010): 30–49; Laura Hoptman, *Wyeth: Christina's World* (New York: Museum of Modern Art, 2012); and Betsy James Wyeth, *Christina's World: Paintings and Pre-Studies of Andrew Wyeth* (Boston: Houghton Mifflin, 1982).

10. Phyllis Mills Wyeth, conversation with the author, July 14, 2011, Tenants Harbor, Maine.

11. N. C. Wyeth, with Howard Pyle's blessing and funding provided by the *Saturday Evening Post* and *Scribner's*, traveled west in 1904, becoming a wrangler as a means of gaining first-hand experience that would help him portray life on the Great Plains. Douglas Allen and Douglas Allen Jr., *N. C. Wyeth: The Collected Paintings, Illustrations, and Murals* (New York: Crown, 1972), p. 31. For Homer, see Kathleen A. Foster, *Shipwreck! Winslow Homer and* The Life Line, exh. cat. (Philadelphia: Philadelphia Museum of Art, 2012), p. 80.

12. Phyllis Mills Wyeth also notes that she was distracted by the way the horses had been hitched to the coach. Conversation with the author, June 15, 2013, Wilmington.

13. When Muybridge circulated his first motion photographs of Leland Stanford's racehorses in 1878, Rogers and Eakins immediately tested the results by "reanimating" them in a zoetrope. For his painting, "Eakins measured the coach for a perspective drawing, made pencil and color oil sketches, and, very likely with Rogers's help, photographed the four-in-hand and its passengers." Additionally, Eakins modeled the horses in wax, which he could then manipulate and rearrange to fit the chosen perspective. On Fairman Rogers, see W. Douglass Paschall, "The Camera Artist," in Darrel Sewell, org., *Thomas Eakins*, exh. cat. (Philadelphia: Philadelphia Museum of Art in association with Yale University Press, 2001), p. 243. Jamie Wyeth also studied some of his natural subjects closely. Seeking to attract a pair of ravens, Wyeth consulted with the biologist and bird expert Bernd Heinrich, who advised him to acquire a dead cow carcass. This was accomplished with the help of local dairy farmers and other community members, who transported it to Southern Island. See Bernd Heinrich, "Adapting to Ravens," in *Gulls, Ravens, and a Vulture: The Ornithological Paintings of James Wyeth*, exh. cat. (Rockland, Me.: Farnsworth Art Museum and Wyeth Center, 2005), pp. 52–71.

14. Phyllis Wyeth has continued to have success breeding and racing thoroughbreds, including the 2012 Belmont Stakes champion, Union Rags.

15. Notes to *Twins*, 1990, Individual Profile, Biography, Jamie Wyeth, March 2004, documented in the Jamie Wyeth Archives and Database at the Farnsworth Art Museum.

16. Joyce Hill Stoner, "Jamie Wyeth: Proteus in Paint" (1998), *www.tfaoi.com/newsmu/nmus82f.htm* (accessed June 12, 2013).

17. Wyeth, *Farm Work*, pp. 85 and 91.

18. See Joyce Hill Stoner, "The Patriarch of Pop and the Prince of Realism: Andy Warhol and Jamie Wyeth in the 1970s," in Robert Rosenblum et al., *Factory Work: Warhol, Wyeth, Basquiat* (Rockland, Maine: Farnsworth Art Museum, 2006), p. 40.

19. On this distinction, see Ernst H. Gombrich, *Art and Illusion: A Study in the Psychology of Pictorial Representation*, 4th ed. (Princeton: Princeton University Press, 1972), esp. pp. 291–329. See also Barbara Novak, *American Painting of the Nineteenth Century: Realism, Idealism, and the American Experience*, 2nd ed. (New York: Harper & Row, 1979), esp. pp. 15–26.

20. Kent's *Late Afternoon, Monhegan Island* (1906–1907), a painting Wyeth now owns, is one example. See Michael K. Komanecky, *Jamie Wyeth, Rockwell Kent, and Monhegan*, exh. cat. (Rockland, Maine: Farnsworth Art Museum, 2012), p. 45.

21. Boldt, "True Art," p. 41.

22. See Andy Warhol, *The Philosophy of Andy Warhol* (New York: Harcourt Brace Jovanovich, 1975), p. 79

23. For an overview of Warhol's collections, see John W. Smith, ed., *Possession Obsession*, exh. cat. (Pittsburgh: Andy Warhol Museum, 2002), and Daniel Robbins, *Raid the Icebox 1 with Andy Warhol*, exh. cat. (Providence: Rhode Island School of Design, 1969). See also Sotheby's auction catalogue *The Andy Warhol Collection*, April 12–May 3, 1988.

24. Boldt, "True Art," p. 41; see also Wyeth, *Farm Work*, p. 61.

Maine

1. Jamie Wyeth, interview by Christopher Crosman, in Crosman, *Jamie Wyeth: Islands*, exh. cat. (Rockland, Maine: Farnsworth Library and Art Museum, 1993), p. 11.

2. See Michael Komanecky, foreword to *Jamie Wyeth, Rockwell Kent, and Monhegan* (Rockland, Maine: Farnsworth Library and Art Museum).

3. Rockwell Kent, *It's Me, O Lord: The Autobiography of Rockwell Kent* (New York: Dodd, Mead, 1955), p. 137.

4. Ibid., p. 50.

5. Ibid.

6. Ibid., pp. 151–154.

7. Ibid., pp. 154–155.

8. Ibid., p. 177.

9. Notes to *Southern Light*, 1994, Individual Profile, Biography, Jamie Wyeth, 2011, documented in the Jamie Wyeth Archives and Database at the Farnsworth Art Museum.

10. The drawing, on a scrap of orange memo paper, appeared in the exhibition *Farm Work by Jamie Wyeth*; see *Farm Work*, exh. cat. (Chadds Ford, Pa.: Brandywine River Museum, 2011), p. 58.

11. At this time Warhol was embarking on a series of shadow paintings. See Ronnie Cutrone, "An Artist's Take on the Work of Warhol," in Joseph O'Connor and Benjamin Liu, *Unseen Warhol* (New York: Rizzoli, 1996), esp. p. 63.

12. Henry David Thoreau, *Walden* (1854; repr., New Haven: Yale University Press, 2006), p. 38.

13. See Jamie Wyeth, "Monhegan, My Lover," in Carl Little, *The Art of Monhegan Island* (Camden, Maine: Down East Books, 2004), esp. pp. 6–7.

14. Joyce Hill Stoner et al., *Wyeth Vertigo*, exh. cat. (Shelburne, Vt.: Shelburne Museum). p. 41.

15. Joyce Hill Stoner, "Jamie Wyeth: Proteus in Paint," *www.tfaoi.com/newsmu/nmus82f.htm* (accessed June 12, 2013).

16. Steve Ausplund, conversation with the author, Tenants Harbor, Maine, July 16, 2013.

17. Michael Komanecky, *Jamie Wyeth: Seven Deadly Sins*, exh. cat. (Rockland, Maine: Farnsworth Art Museum, 2009), p. 11. The film *Seven* has many disturbing sequences that, like Hitchcock's, achieve their effect of horror by leaving a great deal to the imagination of the viewer.

18. Wyeth's childhood drawings in the Jamie Wyeth Archives and Database at the Farnsworth Art Museum include many scenes of movie actors such as Douglas Fairbanks Jr. and Danny Kaye.

19. Nancy Reynolds, ed., *Remembering Lincoln* (New York: Ballet Society, 2007), pp. 201–2; Duberman, *The Worlds of Lincoln Kirstein*, p. 138.

20. "Jamie Wyeth: Works from Kingdom Hospital," *www.adelsongalleries.com/exhibitions/2004-03-04_jamie-wyeth/press-release/* (accessed June 1, 2013).

21. D'Arcy Marsh and Jamie Wyeth, *Inferno* (2009).

22. See *The Rookery* (1977, oil, PepsiCo., Inc., World Headquarters, Purchase, N.Y.), and *The Rookery—Study* (1977, mixed media, private collection), in *Jamie Wyeth*, exh. cat. (Boston: Houghton Mifflin, 1980), pp. 132–33.

23. The tiny shells placed cheek by jowl also evoke the tightly coiled nautilus curls found on frames attributed to Tiffany Glass and Decorating Co. See Alice Cooney Frelinghuysen et al., *Splendid Legacy: The Havermeyer Collection*, exh. cat. (New York: Metropolitan Museum of Art, 1993), plate 173, p. 186.

24. Jamie Wyeth and Barbara Alfond, conversation with the author, Tenants Harbor, Maine, July 2011.

25. *Portrait of Vulture*, 1997, private collection; reproduced in Stoner et al., *Wyeth Vertigo*, p. 54.

26. Komanecky, *Jamie Wyeth: The Seven Deadly Sins*, p. 14.

Recent Work

1. David Michaelis, *N. C. Wyeth: A Biography* (New York: Knopf, 1998), p. 334.

2. See Ronnie Cutrone, "An Artist's Take on the Work of Warhol," in Joseph O'Connor and Benjamin Liu, *Unseen Warhol* (New York: Rizzoli, 1996), p. 61.

3. The artist describes his struggle between vice and his "better self" in Rockwell Kent, *It's Me, O Lord: The Autobiography of Rockwell Kent* (New York: Dodd, Mead, 1955), pp. 154–55. See also Kent's drawing *Sorrow, Monhegan* (1907), reproduced in Amanda C. Burdan, *Jamie Wyeth, Rockwell Kent, and Monhegan at the Brandywine River Museum*, exh. cat. (Chadds Ford, Pa.: Brandywine River Museum, 2013).

4. See "Searchers Fail to Find Socialite," *Post-Standard*, July 12, 1953, p. 31, and "Police See Foul Play in Death of Rich Socialite," *Daily Messenger*, October 5, 1953, p. 1.

5. Malcolm Gladwell, *Outliers: The Story of Success* (New York: Little, Brown, 2008), esp. pp. 35–36.

6. Ibid., pp. 270–85.

7. Henry David Thoreau, *The Maine Woods* (1864; repr., New York: Perennial Library, 1987), p. 95.

8. As a child he had nearly drowned in a pond near his family's home in Maine, purportedly while his father was painting him. Richard Meryman, *Andrew Wyeth: A Secret Life* (New York: HarperCollins, 1996), p. 264.

9. See, for example, *Maquette for the Painting "Cotton Weighing,"* about 1939, Milwaukee Art Museum.

10. Thoreau, *Walden* (1854; repr., New Haven: Yale University Press, 2006), p. 321.

Bibliography

Exhibition Catalogues

1960. *Famous Families in American Art*. Foreword by Jerry Bywaters, introduction by Barney Delatano. Dallas: Dallas Museum of American Art.

1966. *James Wyeth: Paintings*. Foreword by Lincoln Kirstein. New York: Knoedler.

1969. *Oils, Watercolors, Drawings by James Wyeth*. Foreword by Priscilla Adams. Rockland, Maine: Farnsworth Art Museum.

1971. *The Brandywine Heritage: Howard Pyle, N. C. Wyeth, Andrew Wyeth, James Wyeth*. Introduction by Richard McLanathan. Chadds Ford, Pa.: Brandywine River Museum.

1974. *James Wyeth: Recent Paintings*. Theodore E. Stebbins Jr. New York: Coe Kerr Gallery.

1976. *Andy Warhol and Jamie Wyeth: Portraits of Each Other*. Warren Adelson. New York: Coe Kerr Gallery.

1976. *James Wyeth*. Theodore E. Stebbins Jr. Omaha, Neb.: Joslyn Art Museum.

1977. *Jamie Wyeth: Recent Paintings*. Warren Adelson. New York: Coe Kerr Gallery.

1980. *Jamie Wyeth*. Boston: Houghton Mifflin.

1983. *Jamie Wyeth: Exhibition of Original Paintings and Etchings*. Anchorage: Artique Ltd. Fine Art Gallery.

1983. *Jamie Wyeth in Alaska*. Warren Adelson. Anchorage: Anchorage Fine Arts Museum.

1984. *Jamie Wyeth: An American View*. John Holverson. Portland, Maine: Portland Museum of Art.

1984. *Jamie Wyeth: Recent Works*. R. Frederick Woolworth. New York: Coe Kerr Gallery.

1985. *Jamie Wyeth: Special Works*. Peter Fairbanks. San Francisco: Montgomery Gallery.

1986. *Jamie Wyeth: New Works*. Ronald R. Hall and Susan R. Petty. Dallas: Hall Galleries.

1987. *An American Vision: Three Generations of Wyeth Art*. Essays by James H. Duff, Andrew Wyeth, Thomas Hoving, and Lincoln Kirstein. Boston: Little, Brown.

1987. *A Proud Heritage: Two Centuries of American Art*. Terry A. Neff et al. Chicago: Terra Museum of American Art.

1988. *Jamie Wyeth: Recent Works*. Warren Adelson. New York: Coe Kerr Gallery.

1991. *Jamie Wyeth on Monhegan*. Peter Ralston and Richard McClanathan. Rockland, Maine: Island Institute.

1993. *Jamie Wyeth: Islands*. Christopher Crosman. Rockland, Maine: Farnsworth Library and Art Museum.

1997. *N. C. Wyeth and His Grandson: A Legacy*. Stephen May. Chicago: Terra Museum of American Art. Rockland, Maine: MBNA, 1998.

1998. *A Closer Look: Howard Pyle, N. C. Wyeth, Andrew Wyeth, and Jamie Wyeth*. Joyce Hill Stoner. Wilmington: Delaware Art Museum.

1998. *Wondrous Strange: The Wyeth Tradition: Howard Pyle, N. C. Wyeth, Andrew Wyeth, James Wyeth*. Essays by Stephen T. Bruni, Betsy James Wyeth, Theodore F. Wolff, and Christopher Crosman. Boston: Little, Brown.

1999. *A Century of Wyeths*. Essays by Christopher Crosman, Charles M. Cawley, and Lauren Raye Smith. Rockland, Maine: Farnsworth Art Museum.

1999. *Dead Cat Museum, Monhegan Island and Other Recent Paintings by James Wyeth*. New York: James Graham and Sons Gallery.

2000. *Monhegan*. Jamie Wyeth and Lauren Raye Smith. Rockland, Maine: Farnsworth Art Museum.

2000. *One Nation: Patriots and Pirates Portrayed by N. C. Wyeth and James Wyeth*. Introduction by Lauren Raye Smith, essays by Tom Brokaw and David Michaelis. Boston: Bulfinch.

2002. *Capturing Nureyev: Jamie Wyeth Paints the Dancer*. Introduction by Clive Barnes, essays by Barbara Cohen-Stratyner and Lauren Raye Smith with contributions by Phyllis Wyeth and Lynn Seymour. Rockland, Maine: Farnsworth Art Museum in association with University Press of New England.

2004. *Jamie Wyeth: Works from Kingdom Hospital*. Foreword by Warren Adelson. New York: Adelson Galleries.

2005. *Gulls, Ravens and a Vulture: The Ornithological Paintings of James Wyeth*. Introduction by Chris Crosman, essays by Bernd Heinrich, Richard Podolsky, and Victoria Woodhull. Rockland, Maine: Farnsworth Art Museum.

2006. *A Collector's Passion: Three Generations of Wyeth Art—1938 to 2004*. Essay by Joyce Hill Stoner. West Long Branch, N.J.: Monmouth University.

2006. *Cryptozoology: Out of Time Place Scale*. Mark Bessire, Walmor Correa, Sean Foley, Loring M. Danforth, Loren Coleman, Charles Fort, David Filipi, Raechell Smith, and Nato Thompson. Lewiston, Maine: Bates College of Art; Zurich: JRP Ringier; Kansas City, Mo.: Kansas City Art Institute.

2006. *Factory Work: Warhol, Wyeth, Basquiat*. Essays by Robert Rosenblum, Christine Daulton, Joyce Hill Stoner, and Margaret Rose Vendryes. Rockland, Maine: Farnsworth Art Museum and Wyeth Center.

2007. *Dog Days of Summer*. Preface by James H. Duff, commentary by the artist. Chadds Ford, Pa.: Brandywine River Museum.

2008. *Seven Deadly Sins and Recent Works*. Warren Adelson. New York: Adelson Galleries.

2009. *Jamie Wyeth: Seven Deadly Sins*. Foreword and essay by Michael K. Komanecky. Rockland, Maine: Farnsworth Art Museum.

2009. *The Thaw Collection of Master Drawings*. Rhoda Eitel-Porter and Colin J. Bailey. New York: Morgan Library and Museum.

2009. *Wyeth: Three Generations of Artistry*. Edited by Michelle Bolton King. Kansas City, Mo.: Kemper Museum of Contemporary Art.

2010. *Jamie Wyeth Paintings*. Foreword by Meredith Long. Houston: Meredith Long and Co.

2011. *Farm Work*. Foreword by James H. Duff, commentary by the artist. Chadds Ford, Pa.: Brandywine River Museum.

2011. *The Wyeths: Three Generations of American Art*. Henry Adams and Joyce Hill Stoner. Paris: Mona Bismarck American Center for Art and Culture.

2012. *Jamie Wyeth, Rockwell Kent, and Monhegan*. Foreword by Michael Komanecky. Rockland, Maine: Farnsworth Library and Art Museum.

2012. *The Wyeths across Texas*. Henry Adams. Tyler, Tex.: Tyler Museum of Art.

2013. *Jamie Wyeth, Rockwell Kent, and Monhegan at the Brandywine River Museum*. Amanda C. Burdan. Chadds Ford, Pa.: Brandywine River Museum.

2013. *Wyeth Vertigo*. Essays by Joyce Hill Stoner, Alexander Nemerov, Thomas Denenberg. Shelburne, Vt.: Shelburne Museum.

Related Books

1969. Henry C. Pitz. *The Brandywine Tradition*. Boston: Houghton Mifflin.

1971. Hereward Lester Cooke. *Eyewitness to Space: Paintings and Drawings Related to the Apollo Mission to the Moon*. New York: Abrams.

1979. Betsy James Wyeth. *The Stray*. Illustrated by Jamie Wyeth. New York: Farrar, Straus & Giroux.

1987. "Renowned Artist Unveils *Night Vision*." In *Reflections on the Wall: Vietnam Veterans Memorial* (New York: Stackpole).

1989. Andy Warhol. *The Andy Warhol Diaries*. Edited by Pat Hackett. New York: Warner Books.

1992. Joyce Baldwin. *To Heal the Heart of a Child: Helen Taussig, M.D.* New York: Walker.

1997. Elizabeth Seabrook. *Cabbages and Kings*. Illustrated by Jamie Wyeth. New York: Viking Children's Books.

1999. Nicholas Baume, ed. *About Face: Andy Warhol Portraits*. Exh. cat. Hartford: Wadsworth Atheneum; Pittsburgh: Andy Warhol Museum.

1999. Susan Lawson-Bell, James Dean, Robert Schulman, and Bertram Ulrich. *Artistry of Space: The NASA Art Program*. Exh. cat. Ann Arbor: Artrain.

2001. Carolyn Kinder Carr and Ellen G. Miles. *A Brush with History: Paintings from the National Portrait Gallery*. Exh. cat. Washington, D.C.: National Portrait Gallery, Smithsonian Institution.

2002. Wendy Wick Reaves, Bernard F. Reilly Jr., et al. *Eye Contact: Modern American Portrait Drawings from the National Portrait Gallery*. Exh. cat. Washington, D.C.: National Portrait Gallery, Smithsonian Institution.

2003. Kenneth E. Silver. *JFK and Art*. Exh. cat. Greenwich, Conn.: Bruce Museum of Arts and Science.

2004. Carl Little. *The Art of Monhegan Island*. Foreword by Jamie Wyeth. Camden, Maine: Down East Books.

2006. Carl Little. *Paintings of Maine: A New Collection*. Camden, Maine: Down East Books.

2010. Louis A. Zona. *Masterworks from the Butler Institute of American Art*. Youngstown, Ohio: Butler Institute of American Art.

2011. Barbara Walsh. *Sammy in the Sky*. Illustrated by Jamie Wyeth. Somerville, Mass.: Candlewick Press.

2012. Kitty Kelley. *Capturing Camelot: Stanley Tretick's Iconic Images of the Kennedys*. New York: Thomas Dunne Books.

2013. Susan Goldman Rubin. *Everybody Paints! The Lives and Art of the Wyeth Family*. San Francisco: Chronicle Books.

Magazine and Online Articles

December 1960."Heir Apparent." *Newsweek*.

March 1964. "Art: Wyeth the Youngest." *Time*.

April 1968. "Another Wyeth: The Portrait Artist as a Young Man." *Look*.

January–March 1972. "The Artist in His Environment." *Historic Preservation*.

February 1974. "Down on the Farm with Jamie Wyeth." Scott Heiser. *Interview Magazine*.

February 1975. "James Wyeth." Susan Meyer. *American Artist*.

November 1977. "Observation, Distillation, and Time: A Seaside Interview with Jamie Wyeth." *Impresario: Magazine of the Arts and Leisure*.

September 1980."Jamie's World." Marshall Ledger. *Philadelphia*.

February 1981. "Jamie Wyeth's Studio Retreat." M. Steven Dougherty. *American Artist*.

May 1981. "Artist's Dialog: A Conversation with Jamie Wyeth." *Architectural Digest*.

July 1984. "The Young Wyeths." Judith Thurman. *House and Garden*.

September 1989. "Jamie Wyeth Goes beyond the Picturesque." Colin Sargent. *Portland*.

January 1991. "Jamie Wyeth on Monhegan." Richard McLanathan. *Island Journal*.

July 1991. "The Wyeth Family—American Visions." Richard Meryman. *National Geographic*.

December 1993. "Jamie Wyeth—Review." Stephen May. *Art News*.

January 1995. "Southern Island Light." Chris Crosman. *Island Journal*.

September 1996. "A Portrait of Orca Bates." Cindy Anderson. *Yankee Magazine*.

August 1997. "Jamie Wyeth: His Art and Insights." Sandra Carpenter and Greg Schaber. *Artist's Magazine*.

December 1998. "An American Legacy: Howard Pyle and the Wyeths." Stephen May. *American Artist*.

October 1999. "Andy Warhol and Jamie Wyeth: Interactions." Joyce Hill Stoner. *American Art*.

April 2001. "Jamie Wyeth: Painter of Patriots, Presidents, Seagulls and the White House." Gordon Wetmore. *International Artist*.

June 2002. "James Browning Wyeth. 2002 Gold Medal Recipient." *Art of the Portrait*.

August 2002. "The Legendary Dancer though the Eyes of Jamie Wyeth." Paul Theroux. *Architectural Digest*.

April 2003. "When Nureyev Stood Still." Lewis Whittington. *Advocate*.

April 2004. "Altered States." *Art + Auction*.

March 2005. "Seeing People: Paintings from the National Academy Museum." David Dearinger. *American Art Review*.

August 2005. "Jamie Wyeth on Art and Islands." Marianne R. Stanton. *Nantucket Today*.

August 2005. "Three Generations of Wyeth Painters." Susan Lorenzo. *Nantucket Times*.

October 2005. "Today's Masters: The Spirits Keep Watch." Susan Gray. *Art and Antiques*.

November 2005. "About the Cover." *Journal of the Veterinary Medical Association*.

August 2006. "Painting Maine: Three Wyeths." Lori Douglas Clark. *Bangor Metro*.

September 2006. "Jamie Wyeth: Combining Water Soluble Paints." M. Stephen Dougherty. *American Artist*.

January 2007. "About the Cover." *Journal of the Veterinary Medical Association*.

April 2007. "The Prince of the City." Claudia Roth Pierpoint. *New Yorker*.

December 2007. "Season's Greetings." Dana Schmidt. *Artist's Magazine*.

April 2008. "Art Gallery, Chronicle." James Panero. *New Criterion*.

Summer 2009. "Isle of Wyeth." Annaliese Jakimides. *Bangor Metro*.

2010. "Jamie Wyeth: Proteus in Paint." Joyce Hill Stoner. Traditional Fine Arts Organization, *www.tfaoi.com/newsmu/nmus82f.htm* (accessed July 2, 2013).

October 2011. "The Artist's Refuge." James Schwartz. *Historic Preservation*.

October 2011. "Take a Peek at Jamie Wyeth's Watercolors." *Artist Daily*.

December 2011. "Les Wyeth, une retrospective." Laurent Benoist. *L'Art de l'aquarelle*.

September–October 2012. "The Wyeths across Texas." Henry Adams. *American Art Review*.

2013. "The Wyeths: A Family Legacy." Megan Holloway Fort. *Heritage: Magazine of the New York State Historical Association*, vol. 28.

Spring 2013. "Jamie Wyeth." Suzanne Gannon. *Heritage Magazine for the Intelligent Collector*.

April 2013. "The Walkover." Kane Webb. *Louisville Magazine*.

May 2013. "The 10 Most Creative Families." *Town and Country*.

May–June 2013. "The Last Dynasty." James Gardner. *The Magazine Antiques*.

May–June 2013. "Wyeth Vertigo." Joyce Hill Stoner. *American Art Review*.

Undated. "Andy Warhol's Piss Paintings." Gary Comenas. *www.warholstars.org/aw76p.html* (accessed December 5, 2012).

Newspaper Articles

1961. "James Wyeth, 14, wins honor at exhibit." *Wilmington Evening Journal*, March 16.

1961. "Another Wyeth makes a bow on the art horizon—James, 14." Betty Bourroughs. *Wilmington Morning News*, April 28.

1962. "Young Wyeth's painting is admired." *Wilmington Morning News*, May 1.

1962. "Wyeth show has first preview." *Buffalo Evening News*, November 2.

1963. "Shorty, Wyeth Jr. model, gone." *Wilmington Evening Journal*, November 22.

1964. "Another Wyeth day is dawning." *Wilmington Morning News*, March 16.

1964. "Jamie Wyeth plans summer at home." *Wilmington Evening Journal*, March 18.

1964. "No soup cans for Jamie Wyeth." Barbara Goldsmith. *New York Tribune*, November 17.

1966. "Art: Jamie Wyeth's works at Knoedler." Hilton Kramer. *New York Times*, November 30.

1966. "James Wyeth's work: To the editor." Maxwell Davidson. *New York Times*, December 1.

1966. "Jamie Wyeth shows his art in New York—and everybody is there." Ruth Seltzer. *Philadelphia Evening Bulletin*, December 1.

1966. "Friendship and hard cider—Wyeth seeks a 'certain thing.'" Charles Eisendrath. *Baltimore Evening Sun*, December 2.

1966. "Jamie Wyeth watercolors." Charlotte Lichblau. *Philadelphia Inquirer*, December 4.

1966. "Funk and fun at the Whitney: Pure heir." Grace Glueck. *New York Times*, December 11.

1967. "The young man likes to work." Don Weldon. *Philadelphia Inquirer*, April 23.

1971. "Brandywine Museum honors three Wyeths with display." *New York Times*, June 17.

1975. "The lady is a pig." Eugenia Sheppard. *New York Post*, November 14.

1976. "At gallery, the crowd was ogling itself." Judy Klemesrud. *New York Times*, June 6.

1978. "Rudi and Jamie: Art's incredible pas de deux." Nessa Forman. *Philadelphia Sunday Bulletin*, February 19.

1980. "Ars longa: Just take a Wyeth's word for it." Maryanne Conheim. *Philadelphia Inquirer*, September 18.

1981. "The artist is a lonely hunter." *Christian Science Monitor*, November 3.

1984. "Painting puts a drain on famed state artist." *Louisville Courier-Journal*, July 5.

1985. "Jamie Wyeth: A rare portrait of America's premier portraitist." Nan Robertson. *New Haven Register*, August 18.

1986. "Sketching the Wyeth dynasty." William K. Stevens. *New York Times*, November 23.

1988. "Jamie Wyeth is out of the shadow." Michael Killian. *Philadelphia Daily News*, December 31.

1993. "In Jamie Wyeth's eye, the coast is not clear." *Maine Sunday Telegram*, July 25.

1994. "A portrait of laundry." Maggie Lewis. *Christian Science Monitor*, June 27.

1997. "Jamie Wyeth: His art and insight." Greg Schaber. *Maine Sunday Telegram*, August 1.

1997. "Artistic bloodline." Deborah Wilk. *Chicago Tribune*, July 1.

1997. "Wyeth feels connected to his grandfather—even though they never met." *Chicago Sun Times*, July 13.

1998. "Paying tribute to Maine's no. 1 family." *New York Times*, July 19.

1998. "Worshiping Wyeths." Edger Allen Beem. *Maine Times*, September 1.

1999. "Images of heaven and hell at the old church." David Grima. *Camden Herald*, June 3.

2000. "Jamie Wyeth draws the viewer into his paintings." Nancy M. Kendall. *Christian Science Monitor*, February 7.

2000. "Political lines." *New York Times*, August 7.

2001. "Pirates and patriots by N. C. Wyeth and James Wyeth." Stephen May. *Antiques and the Arts Weekly*, January 12.

2001. "New White House portrait done by a Wyeth." Carl Hartman. *Citizen's Voice* (Wilkes-Barre, Pa.), January 14.

2001. "Wyeths share patriotic views." *Washington Times*, January 20.

2001. "Bombast and ambivalence." Tracy O'Shaughnessy. *Republican-American* (Waterbury, Conn.), March 4.

2001. "Jamie Wyeth celebrates rescue workers in New York." Anthony Ronzio. *k2Bh.com*, October 16.

2002. "Capturing Nureyev: Jamie Wyeth paints the dancer." Stephen May. *Antiques and the Arts Weekly*, February 2.

2002. "Still life of a dancer: Capturing Nureyev." Philip Kennicott. *Washington Post*, February 7.

2002. "America's true spirit on display." Joanna Shaw-Eagle. *Washington Times*, February 23.

2002. "A dancer made still: Portraits of Nureyev created by James Wyeth." Mel Gussow. *New York Times*, March 27.

2002. "One artist's anatomy of Nureyev." Susan Reiter. *Long Island Newsday*, April 11.

2002. "Great dancer, touchy subject." David Tyler. *Times Record* [Brunswick, Maine], June 27.

2003. "Wyeth's revealing portrait of the unseen." *Christian Science Monitor*, October 31.

2004. "A hospital that is a real horror show." Bill Carter. *New York Times*, February 29.

2005. "Wyeth's card is indisputably elegant picture." Harry Themal. *Delaware News Journal*, December 12.

2006. "Wyeth and Warhol: An odd couple of art world." Edward J. Sozanski. *Philadelphia Inquirer*, October 1.

2007. "Strange bedfellows." Frank Hammel. *San Antonio Current*, January 16.

2007. "Dog days with Jamie Wyeth at the Brandywine." Victoria Donohoe. *Philadelphia Inquirer*, June 15.

2008. "Show and tell." Bill Cunningham. *New York Times*, January 20.

2009. "They're fowl." Jessica Bloch. *Bangor Daily News*, July 7.

2009. "Artist Wyeth shows 'sins' are for the birds." Joann Lovaglio. *Associated Press*, October 6.

2010. "Seagulls of sin: Jamie Wyeth brings his brush and birds to Utah." Ben Fulton. *Salt Lake City Tribune*, January 21.

2011. "Jamie Wyeth dog painting sells for $218,000 in New York auction." *New York Post*, March 3.

2011. "NASA/art exhibition on display now at LRMA." Holly Green. *Laurel (Miss.) Leader-Call*, April 19.

2011. "Wyeth: Une famille d'artistes en Amérique. " Valerie Duponchelle. *Le Figaro*, November 9.

2012. "Life on the farm—Wyeth style." Betsy Price. *Sunday News Journal* (Delaware), June 26.

2012. "Jamie Wyeth's barnyard critters." Edward J. Sozanski. *Philadelphia Inquirer*, July 3.

2013. "Re-evaluating the Wyeth dynasty." *Wall Street Journal*, May 16.

2013. "Rugged beauty." Betsy Price. *Wilmington News Journal*, June 22.

2013. "Art: Two artists' response to a Maine island." Edward J. Sozanski. *Philadelphia Inquirer*, June 23.

2013. "The Wyeths: Seen at their extreme." Sebastian Smee. *Boston Globe*, June 29.

Television and Video

1975. James Wyeth interview by Warren Adelson at Joslyn Museum.

1982. "Exploring the Arts: A Visit with Jamie Wyeth." Interview by Eric Wallace. Alaska Public TV.

1984. "Robin Young Profiles: People Who Count." Interview by Robin Young. WBZ-TV, Boston.

1986. "The Wyeths: A Father and His Family." Smithsonian Institution and WETA-TV, Washington, D.C.

1987. "CBS Sunday Morning: An American Vision." Charles Kuralt. CBS, New York.

1987. "The Today Show: Jamie Wyeth at the Brandywine Museum." Interview by Jamie Gangel. NBC, New York.

1997. "CBS Sunday Morning: This Old House and the Portrait of an Artist as a Younger Man." Martha Teischner. CBS, New York.

1998. "Jamie Wyeth: Interview for Wondrous Strange Exhibition at the Farnsworth Art Museum." PBS.

1999. "Interview with Andrew and Jamie Wyeth." Kim Block. WGME-TV, Portland, Maine.

2001. "Interview with Jamie Wyeth for the September 11th Print Fundraising Program." WABI, Bangor, Maine.

2001. "One Nation: Patriots and Pirates." Crystal Productions.

2002. "Breakfast with the Arts." A&E television network, New York.

2002. "Capturing Nureyev: James Wyeth Paints the Dancer. Interview with Jamie Wyeth and Clive Barnes." Steve Labovsky. Farnsworth Art Museum, Rockland, Maine.

2002. "Interview with Jamie Wyeth for the Capturing Nureyev Exhibition." Jennifer Rooks. WCSH-TV, Portland, Maine.

2003. "CBS Sunday Morning with Charles Osgood: Rockwell Kent." Tim Sample. CBS, New York.

2003. "Crossroads with Jill Pasternak." WRTI Radio Network, Philadelphia.

2009. *Inferno: A Film by D'Arcy Marsh and Jamie Wyeth*. Otter Island Films, Rockland, Maine.

2013. "Andrew Wyeth." Eleanor Yule and Michael Palin. BBC2, London.

2013. "CBS Sunday Morning: Bird Houses." CBS, New York.

2014. "Michael Palin in Wyeth's World," BBC2, London.

Checklist

All works are by Jamie Wyeth unless stated otherwise.

1
Cowboys Fighting, 1952
Graphite on paper
9.5 x 9.5 cm (3¾ x 3¾ in.)
Phyllis and Jamie Wyeth Collection, CF11.074

2
Musketeers, 1951
Graphite on paper
27.9 x 21.6 cm (11 x 8½ in.)
Phyllis and Jamie Wyeth Collection, CF23.20

3
D'Artagnan, 1951
Graphite on paper
27.9 x 21.6 cm (11 x 8½ in.)
Phyllis and Jamie Wyeth Collection, CF23.21

4
Boys Sledding, 1951
Graphite on paper
27.9 x 21.6 cm (11 x 8½ in.)
Phyllis and Jamie Wyeth Collection, CF28.27

5
Ardent Lover, 1958
Graphite on paper
21.3 x 27.6 cm (8⅜ x 10⅞ in.)
Phyllis and Jamie Wyeth Collection, CF5-042R

6
Aunt Carolyn, 1958
Graphite and ink on paper
15.9 x 8.3 cm (6¼ x 3¼ in.)
Phyllis and Jamie Wyeth Collection

7
Andrew Wyeth and Jamie Wyeth
Jamie in Blue Sweater, 1949
Watercolor on paper; graphite on paper
40.6 x 50.8 cm (16 x 20 in.)
Phyllis and Jamie Wyeth Collection
© Andrew Wyeth
© Jamie Wyeth

8
The Children's Illustrator, 2005
Oil on canvas
71.1 x 66 cm (28 x 26 in.)
Collection of Mr. and Mrs. Frank E. Fowler

9
Portrait of Shorty, 1963
Oil on canvas
45.7 x 55.9 cm (18 x 22 in.)
Collection of Andrew and Betsy Wyeth

10
Portrait of Helen Taussig, 1963
Oil on canvas
40 x 55.2 cm (15¾ x 21¾ in.)
Courtesy of The Johns Hopkins University School of Medicine, Baltimore, Maryland

11
Draft Age, 1965
Oil on canvas
91.4 x 76.2 cm (36 x 30 in.)
Collection of Brandywine River Museum of Art
Purchase made possible by Mr. and Mrs. Randy L. Christofferson, Mr. and Mrs. George Strawbridge, Jr., Mary Alice Dorrance Malone Foundation, The Margaret Dorrance Strawbridge Foundation of Pennsylvania I, Inc., The William Stamps Farish Fund, Mr. and Mrs. James W. Stewart III, and MBNA America, 1999, 99.4

12
Portrait of Lincoln Kirstein, 1965
Oil on canvas
97.8 x 73.7 cm (38½ x 29 in.)
National Portrait Gallery, Smithsonian Institution
Bequest of Lincoln Kirstein, NPG.96.97

13
La Côte Basque, 2013
Combined media, assemblage
76.2 x 101.6 x 53.3 cm (30 x 40 x 21 in.)
Phyllis and Jamie Wyeth Collection

14
Skull, 1965
From *Morgue Drawing* sketchbook, page 8
Graphite on paper
27.9 x 35.6 cm (11 x 14 in.)
Phyllis and Jamie Wyeth Collection

15
Five Hands, 1965
From *Morgue Drawing* sketchbook, page 4
Graphite on paper
27.9 x 35.6 cm (11 x 14 in.)
Phyllis and Jamie Wyeth Collection

16
Senator Robert F. Kennedy and Senator Edward M. Kennedy, 1966
Graphite on paper
26.7 x 34.3 cm (10½ x 13½ in.)
Phyllis and Jamie Wyeth Collection

17
Senator Edward M. Kennedy's Eyes, 1966
Graphite on paper
27.9 x 33.7 cm (11 x 13¼ in.)
Phyllis and Jamie Wyeth Collection

18
Senator Edward M. Kennedy, 1966
Graphite on paper
35.6 x 27.9 cm (14 x 11 in.)
Phyllis and Jamie Wyeth Collection

19
Portrait of John F. Kennedy, 1967
Oil on canvas
40.6 x 73.7 cm (16 x 29 in.)
Phyllis and Jamie Wyeth Collection

20
Portrait of Andrew Wyeth, 1969
Oil on canvas
61 x 81.3 cm (24 x 32 in.)
Private collection

21
Self-Portrait, about 1969
Oil on canvas
61.6 x 51.1 cm (24¼ x 20⅛ in.)
National Academy Museum, New York, 1979.12
Photograph: Glenn Castellano

22
Gemini Launch Pad, 1969
Watercolor on watercolor paper
68.6 x 86.4 cm (27 x 34 in.)
Smithsonian National Air and Space Museum, Washington, D.C.

23
Apollo XI—To the Moon, July 16, 1969, 1969
Watercolor on Twinrocker handmade paper
71.1 x 52.1 cm (28 x 20½ in.)
Phyllis and Jamie Wyeth Collection

24
Moon Landing, 1969
Oil on canvas
73.7 x 109.2 cm (29 x 43 in.)
Courtesy of Adelson Galleries and Frank Fowler
Photograph: John Bigelow Taylor

25
Judge John Sirica, 1974
Graphite on paper
27.9 x 35.6 cm (11 x 14 in.)
Phyllis and Jamie Wyeth Collection

26
Albert Jenner, 1974
Graphite on paper
27.9 x 35.6 cm (11 x 14 in.)
Phyllis and Jamie Wyeth Collection

27
Special Prosecutor James Neal Tries to Impeach John Ehrlichman's Prior Testimony, 1974
Graphite on paper
27.9 x 35.6 cm (11 x 14 in.)
Phyllis and Jamie Wyeth Collection

28
Fred Hughes and Andy Warhol, 2005
Oil on canvas
121.9 x 76.2 cm (48 x 30 in.)
Private collection

29
Factory Dining Room, 2013
Oil and combined media, assemblage
109.2 x 78.7 x 55.9 cm (43 x 31 x 22 in.)
Phyllis and Jamie Wyeth Collection

30
A.W. Working on Piss Series, 2007
Acrylic, oil, and watercolor on cardboard
121.9 x 76.2 cm (48 x 30 in.)
Phyllis and Jamie Wyeth Collection

31
Andy's Feet, 1976
Charcoal, gouache, and watercolor on brown cardboard
66 x 48.3 cm (26 x 19 in.)
Phyllis and Jamie Wyeth Collection

32
Andy Warhol (1928–1987)
Jamie Wyeth, 1976
Oil on canvas
101.6 x 101.6 cm (40 x 40 in.)
Phyllis and Jamie Wyeth Collection
© 2014 The Andy Warhol Foundation for the Visual Arts, Inc./Artists Rights Society (ARS), New York

33
Portrait of Andy Warhol, 1976
Oil on gessoed panel
76.2 x 61 cm (30 x 24 in.)
Permanent Collection of Cheekwood Botanical Garden and Museum of Art

34
Andy Warhol—Facing His Right (Study #15), 1976
Graphite on paper
55.9 x 76.2 cm (22 x 30 in.)
Collection of Brandywine River Museum of Art
Gift of Amanda K. Berls, 1980, 80.3.33

35
Andy Warhol—Facing Left (Study #2), 1976
Graphite, India ink, and opaque white watercolor on board
40.6 x 33.7 cm (16 x 13¼ in.)
The Morgan Library and Museum, New York
Thaw Collection, 2010.141

36
Portrait of Arnold Schwarzenegger, 1977
Oil on canvas
83.8 x 83.8 cm (33 x 33 in.)
Collection of Arnold Schwarzenegger

37
Nureyev—Purple Scarf, 2001
Graphite, gouache, and watercolor on toned rag board
90.2 x 64.8 cm (35½ x 25½ in.)
Phyllis and Jamie Wyeth Collection

38
Nureyev—Don Quixote—Yellow Background, 2001
Graphite, gouache, and watercolor on cardboard
121.3 x 91.4 cm (47¾ x 36 in.)
Collection of Brandywine River Museum of Art
Purchase made possible by the Robert J. Kleberg, Jr. and Helen C. Kleberg Foundation; the Roemer Foundation; The Margaret Dorrance Strawbridge Foundation of Pennsylvania I, Inc.; and an anonymous donor, 2006.6.1

39
Profile with Black Wash Background, Head, Nureyev (Study #23), 1977
Graphite, gouache, and watercolor on toned rag board
52.7 x 54 cm (20¾ x 21¼ in.)
Collection of Philip and Tina DeNormandie

40
Profile, in Fur, Nureyev (Study #9), 1977
Graphite, gouache, and watercolor on toned rag board
50.8 x 40.6 cm (20 x 16 in.)
Collection of Andrew and Betsy Wyeth

41
Nureyev Sketchbook, Image N-31b, 1977
Pen and ink on paper
27.9 x 35.6 cm (11 x 14 in.)
Collection of Brandywine River Museum of Art
Purchase made possible by the Robert J. Kleberg, Jr. and Helen C. Kleberg Foundation; the Roemer Foundation; The Margaret Dorrance Strawbridge Foundation of Pennsylvania I, Inc.; and an anonymous donor, 2006, 2006.6.19.19a, b

42
Nude Three-Quarter Figure, Nureyev (Study #18), 1977 (finished in 1993)
Graphite, charcoal, watercolor, and gouache on toned rag paper
121.9 x 87.6 cm (48 x 34½ in.)
Collection of Brandywine River Museum of Art
Purchase made possible by the Robert J. Kleberg, Jr. and Helen C. Kleberg Foundation; the Roemer Foundation; The Margaret Dorrance Strawbridge Foundation of Pennsylvania I, Inc.; and an anonymous donor, 2006, 2006.6.13

43
Pumpkinhead—Self-Portrait, 1972
Oil on canvas
76.2 x 76.2 cm (30 x 30 in.)
Private collection

44
And Then Into the Deep Gorge, 1975
Oil on canvas
91.4 x 116.8 cm (36 x 46 in.)
Phyllis and Jamie Wyeth Collection

45
The Weathervane, 1959
Watercolor on Strathmore high-surface paper
56.5 x 35.6 cm (22¼ x 14 in.)
Collection of Andrew and Betsy Wyeth

46
Lime Bag, 1964
Oil on board
40.6 x 31.1 cm (16 x 12¼ in.)
Brandywine River Museum of Art
Gift of Mr. and Mrs. Andrew Wyeth, 70.3.9

47
Catching Snowflakes, 2004
Watercolor and gouache on toned rag board
101.6 x 71.1 cm (40 x 28 in.)
Phyllis and Jamie Wyeth Collection

48
Stealing Holly, 2004
Watercolor and gouache on toned rag board
14.6 x 18.1 cm (5¾ x 7⅛ in.)
Phyllis and Jamie Wyeth Collection

49
Connemara, 1987
Oil on canvas
94 x 185.4 cm (37 x 73 in.)
Phyllis and Jamie Wyeth Collection

50
Connemara Four, 1991
Oil on panel
121.9 x 243.8 cm (48 x 96 in.)
Phyllis and Jamie Wyeth Collection

51
Brandywine Spiders, 1973
Watercolor on Strathmore plate-finish paper
63.5 x 89.5 cm (25 x 35¼ in.)
Private collection

52
Patriot's Barn, 2001
Watercolor, gouache, and pastel on toned rag board
66.7 x 99 cm (26¼ x 39 in.)
Bank of America Collection, M61

53
Dragonflies, 1986
Watercolor on three-ply Strathmore paper
76.2 x 101.6 cm (30 x 40 in.)
Collection of Brock and Yvonne Vinton

54
Dragonfly, 1994
Essence of pearl, gouache, varnish, and watercolor on Strathmore paper
49.5 x 39.4 cm (19½ x 15½ in.)
Private collection

55
Twins, 1990
Watercolor on three-ply Strathmore paper
58.4 x 73.7 cm (23 x 29 in.)
Private collection

56
Birds' House, 1989
Varnish and watercolor on white Strathmore paper
76.8 x 54.6 cm (30¼ x 21½ in.)
Phyllis and Jamie Wyeth Collection

57
"They were seated around tables, roaring with laughter, drinking mugs of beer," 1979
Illustration for *The Stray*, by Betsy Wyeth
Pen and ink and watercolor on rag paper
16.5 x 25.4 cm (6½ x 10 in.)
Phyllis and Jamie Wyeth Collection

58
"Too late, he chirped, after he carefully studied the ground," 1996
Illustration for *Cabbages and Kings*, by Elizabeth Seabrook
Gouache and watercolor on toned rag board
31.8 x 24.1 cm (12½ x 9½ in.)
Phyllis and Jamie Wyeth Collection

59
P.W. and Ziggy, 1998
Watercolor and gouache on toned rag board
33 x 24.8 cm (13 x 9¾ in.)
Phyllis and Jamie Wyeth Collection

60
Christmas Morning 2006, 2006
Watercolor and gouache on toned rag board
13.7 x 21 cm (5⅜ x 8¼ in.)
Phyllis and Jamie Wyeth Collection

61
Barn Owls, Immature, 2006
Watercolor and gouache on Strathmore paper
89.9 x 64.8 cm (35⅜ x 25½ in.)
Private collection

62
Goat Tree, 2006
Watercolor and gesso on toned rag board
90.1 x 69.9 cm (35½ x 27½ in.)
Phyllis and Jamie Wyeth Collection

63
10 W 30, 1981
Watercolor and varnish on white Strathmore rag paper
58.4 x 78.7 cm (23 x 31 in.)
Collection of Andrew and Betsy Wyeth

64
Cornflakes, 1985
Watercolor and varnish on white Strathmore rag paper
71.1 x 55.9 cm (28 x 22 in.)
Crystal Bridges Museum of American Art, Bentonville, Arkansas
Photograph: Dwight Primiano

65
Kleberg, 1984
Oil on canvas
77.5 x 108 cm (30½ x 42½ in.)
Terra Foundation for American Art
Daniel J. Terra Collection, 1992.184

66
Bale, 1972
Oil on canvas
72.4 x 88.9 cm (28½ x 35 in.)
Phyllis and Jamie Wyeth Collection

67
Orca, 1990
Oil on panel
101.6 x 76.2 cm (40 x 30 in.)
Collection of Helen C. Alexander

68
Orca Bates, 1990
Oil on panel
101.6 x 101.6 cm (40 x 40 in.)
Crystal Bridges Museum of American Art, Bentonville, Arkansas
Photograph: Dwight Primiano

69
Whale, 1978
Oil on canvas
91.4 x 116.8 cm (36 x 46 in.)
Collection of Louise Philibosian Danelian

70
Southern Light, 1994
Enamel and oil on board
91.4 x 122 cm (36 x 48 in.)
Phyllis and Jamie Wyeth Collection

71
Twin Houses, 1969
Watercolor on watercolor paper
48.3 x 76.2 cm (19 x 30 in.)
Collection of UMB Financial Corporation

72
Kent House, 1972
Oil on canvas
76.2 x 101.6 cm (30 x 40 in.)
Collection of Brandywine River Museum of Art
Gift of Mr. and Mrs. Andrew Wyeth, 1985

73
Head Tide—Maine, 1991
Watercolor on rag paper
58.4 x 73.7 cm (23 x 29 in.)
Collection of Mr. and Mrs. Robert Rans

74
Bell Tower, 1963
Watercolor on paper
58.4 x 47 cm (23 x 18½ in.)
Collection of Andrew and Betsy Wyeth

75
Lighthouse Iris, 1993
Gouache and watercolor on toned rag board
71.1 x 53.3 cm (28 x 21 in.)
Collection of Richard and Marsha Rothman

76
A Murder of Crows, 2003
Oil on canvas
91.4 x 76.2 cm (36 x 30 in.)
Phyllis and Jamie Wyeth Collection

77
Pumpkin Shadow, 1977
Watercolor on paper
76.2 x 54.6 cm (30 x 21½ in.)
Private collection

78
Mischief Night, 1986
Watercolor and varnish on Strathmore rag paper
57.2 x 78.7 cm (22½ x 31 in.)
Delaware Art Museum
Photograph: Rick Echelmeyer
Delaware Art Museum
F. V. du Pont Acquisition Fund, 1991

79
The Headlands of Monhegan Island, Maine, 2007
Oil on canvas
101.6 x 152.4 cm (40 x 60 in.)
Phyllis and Jamie Wyeth Collection

80
The Islander, 1975
Oil on canvas
86.4 x 112.7 cm (34 x 44⅜ in.)
Collection of Andrew and Betsy Wyeth

81
Portrait of Lady, 1968
Oil on canvas
91.4 x 161.3 cm (36 x 63½ in.)
Alexander M. Laughlin Family Trust

82
Wreck of the Polias, 2002
Oil on board
70.5 x 78.7 cm (27¾ x 31 in.)
Collection of Mr. and Mrs. Frank E. Fowler

83
Thanks for Saving My Life, 2008
Watercolor and gouache on toned rag board
17.5 x 20.6 cm (6⅞ x 8⅛ in.)
Collection of Steve Ausplund and Viki Reed

84
Homer, 2003
Watercolor and gouache on toned rag board
13.7 x 16.2 cm (5⅜ x 6⅜ in.)
Collection of Mary Beth Dolan

85
Raven, 1980
Oil on canvas
152.4 x 182.9 cm (60 x 72 in.)
Brandywine River Museum of Art
Museum purchase, 1992, 92.6

86
Meteor Shower, 1993
Oil and essence of pearl on panel
83.8 x 121.9 cm (33 x 48 in.)
Collection of Andrew and Betsy Wyeth

87
"I stared up at the sky and shouted, 'I love you Sammy. You are still the best,'" 2011
Illustration for *Sammy in the Sky*, by Barbara Walsh
Watercolor, graphite, and gouache on toned rag board
30.5 x 25.4 cm (12 x 10 in.)
Phyllis and Jamie Wyeth Collection

88
Sea Star, 1985
Oil on gessoed panel; frame of assembled found objects
78.7 x 116.8 cm (31 x 46 in.)
Frame: 94.3 x 132.4 cm (37⅛ x 52⅛ in.)
Terra Foundation for American Art
Daniel J. Terra Collection, 1992.165

89
Butterscotch, Gull, and Hot Fudge Sundae, 2004
Watercolor and gouache on toned rag paper
74.9 x 57.2 cm (29½ x 22½ in.)
Collection of Barbara and Theodore Alfond

90
Run, 1999
Watercolor, gouache, and bone on toned rag paper
55.9 x 76.2 cm (22 x 30 in.)
Phyllis and Jamie Wyeth Collection

91
The Monhegan Island Schoolhouse, 2007
Gouache and watercolor on toned rag board
81.3 x 101.6 cm (32 x 40 in.)
Phyllis and Jamie Wyeth Collection

92
Anger—The Seven Deadly Sins, 2005
Watercolor and gouache on toned, hand-woven rag paper mounted on archival board
87.6 x 61.6 cm (34½ x 24¼ in.)
Private collection

93
Lust—The Seven Deadly Sins, 2007
Watercolor and gouache on toned, hand-woven rag paper mounted on archival board
87.6 x 61.6 cm (34½ x 24¼ in.)
Private collection

94
Gluttony—The Seven Deadly Sins, 2005
Watercolor and gouache on toned, hand-woven rag paper mounted on archival board
87.6 x 61.6 cm (34½ x 24¼ in.)
Private collection

95
Pride—The Seven Deadly Sins, 2008
Watercolor and gouache on toned, hand-woven rag paper mounted on archival board
87.6 x 61.6 cm (34½ x 24¼ in.)
Private collection

96
Sloth—The Seven Deadly Sins, 2007
Watercolor and gouache on toned, hand-woven rag paper mounted on archival board
87.6 x 61.6 cm (34½ x 24¼ in.)
Private collection

97
Greed—The Seven Deadly Sins, 2008
Watercolor and gouache on toned, hand-woven rag paper mounted on archival board
87.6 x 61.6 cm (34½ x 24¼ in.)
Private collection

98
Envy—The Seven Deadly Sins, 2005
Watercolor and gouache on toned, hand-woven rag paper mounted on archival board
87.6 x 61.6 cm (34½ x 24¼ in.)
Private collection

99
Carney Banner, Gull, 2009
Acrylic, gouache, and India ink on linen fabric
518.2 x 182.9 cm (204 x 72 in.)
Phyllis and Jamie Wyeth Collection

100
Carney Banner, Skull, 2009
Acrylic, gouache, and India ink on linen fabric
518.2 x 182.9 cm (204 x 72 in.)
Phyllis and Jamie Wyeth Collection

101
Inferno, Monhegan, 2006
Watercolor, gouache, and enamel on archival cardboard
152.4 x 203.2 cm (60 x 80 in.)
Private collection

102
Sea Watchers, 2009
Oil on canvas
61 x 134.6 cm (24 x 53 in.)
Private collection, Houston, Texas

103
The Sea, Watched, 2009
Oil on canvas
76.2 x 121.9 cm (30 x 48 in.)
Private collection

104
A Recurring Dream, 2011
Acrylic, oil, and watercolor on archival cardboard
59.7 x 132.1 cm (23½ x 52 in.)
Phyllis and Jamie Wyeth Collection

105
Rockwell Kent—Second in a Series of Untoward Occurrences on Monhegan Island, 2013
Enamel, gesso, and oil on composite board
86.4 x 66 cm (34 x 26 in.)
Phyllis and Jamie Wyeth Collection

106
Ice Storm—Maine (Study), 1998
Watercolor and gouache on archival cardboard
101.6 x 152.4 cm (40 x 60 in.)
Phyllis and Jamie Wyeth Collection

107
Ice Floe, 2012
Watercolor, gouache, and varnish on toned rag board
41.9 x 91.4 cm (16½ x 36 in.)
Phyllis and Jamie Wyeth Collection

108
Berg, 2012
Watercolor, gesso, and enamel on joined rag boards
102.2 x 91.4 cm (40¼ x 36 in.)
Phyllis and Jamie Wyeth Collection

Figure Illustrations

Exhibited but not illustrated

Barney and Miss Beazley Conferring, India Off (Study #2), 2005
Pen and ink on paper
102.2 x 91.4 cm (40 1/4 x 36 in.)
Phyllis and Jamie Wyeth Collection

Cabbages and Kings, by Elizabeth Seabrook, 1997
Printed book
22.2 x 30.2 cm (8 3/4 x 11 7/8 in.)
Phyllis and Jamie Wyeth Collection

"John F. Kennedy" Irish postal stamp, 1988
2.9 x 4 cm (1 1/8 x 1 9/16 in.)
Courtesy of Elliot Bostwick Davis

"Partridge in a Pear Tree" U.S. Postal Service stamp, 1971
4 x 2.5 cm (1 9/16 x 1 in.)
Courtesy of Elliot Bostwick Davis

Sammy in the Sky, by Barbara Walsh, 2011
Printed book
29.5 x 27 cm (11 5/8 x 10 5/8 in.)
Phyllis and Jamie Wyeth Collection

The Stray, by Betsy Wyeth, 1979
Printed book
24.5 x 19.7 cm (9 5/8 x 7 3/4 in.)
Phyllis and Jamie Wyeth Collection

Works not otherwise attributed are by Jamie Wyeth.

1
Peter Ralston (born in 1950)
Of a Feather, 2008
Archival pigment print
43.2 x 55.9 cm (17 x 22 in.)
Museum of Fine Arts, Boston
Museum purchase with funds donated anonymously, 2013.598

2
Andrew Wyeth (1917–2009)
Oil Lamp, 1945
Tempera on panel
86.4 x 106.7 cm (34 x 42 in.)
Private collection
© Andrew Wyeth

3
Robert Rauschenberg (1925–2008)
Retroactive I, 1963
Oil and silkscreen ink on canvas
213.4 x 152.4 cm (84 x 60 in.)
Wadsworth Atheneum Museum of Art
Gift of Susan Morse Hilles, 1964.30
© Robert Rauschenberg Foundation/Licensed by VAGA, New York, NY
Photograph: Wadsworth Atheneum Art Museum/Art Resource, NY

4
Adam and Eve and the C-97, 1969
Oil on parachute nylon
2.29 x 7.03 m (7 ft. 6 in. x 23 ft. 3/4 in.)
Courtesy of the Delaware Military Heritage and Education Foundation

5
James Rosenquist (born in 1933)
F-111, 1964–65
Oil on canvas with aluminum, 23 sections
3.05 x 26.21 m (10 x 86 ft.)
Museum of Modern Art
Gift of Mr. and Mrs. Alex L. Hillman and Lillie P. Bliss Bequest (both by exchange), 473.1996a–w
Art © James Rosenquist/Licensed by VAGA, New York, NY
Digital image © The Museum of Modern Art/Licensed by SCALA/Art Resource, NY

6
Stanley Tretick (1921–1999)
Andy Warhol and Jamie Wyeth, 1976
Photograph
© Estate of Stanley Tretick, LLC

7
Portrait of Pig, 1970
Oil on canvas
130.8 x 211.5 cm (51 1/2 x 83 1/4 in.)
Collection of Brandywine River Museum of Art
Gift of Betsy James Wyeth, 1984

8
Damien Hirst (born in 1965)
This Little Piggy Went to Market, This Little Piggy Stayed at Home, 1996
Glass, pig, painted steel, acrylic, stainless steel, plastic, formaldehyde solution, and painted steel with motorized base. Two parts, each 120 x 210 x 60 cm (47 1/4 x 82 5/8 x 23 5/8 in.)
© Damien Hirst and Science Ltd. All rights reserved/DACS, London/ARS, NY 2014
Photograph: Stephen White, courtesy White Cube

9
John Singleton Copley (1738–1815)
A Boy with a Flying Squirrel (Henry Pelham), 1765
Oil on canvas
77.2 x 63.8 cm (30 3/8 x 25 1/8 in.)
Museum of Fine Arts, Boston
Gift of the artist's great-granddaughter, 1978.297

10
Thomas Eakins (1844–1916)
The Writing Master, 1882
Oil on canvas
76.2 x 87 cm (30 x 34 1/4 in.)
The Metropolitan Museum of Art
John Stewart Kennedy Fund, 1917, 17.173
Image © The Metropolitan Museum of Art. Image source: Art Resource, NY

11
Support, 1969
Watercolor on paper
53.3 x 61 cm (21 x 24 in.)
Courtesy of NASA and the NASA Art Program
Photograph: National Air and Space Museum, Smithsonian Institution

12
Stanley Tretick (1921–1999)
Jamie Wyeth Measuring Andy Warhol with Calipers, about 1976
Photograph
© Estate of Stanley Tretick, LLC

13
Stanley Tretick (1921–1999)
Jamie Wyeth Placing Calipers on the Portrait of Andy Warhol, about 1976
Photograph

14
Portrait of Rudolf Nureyev, 1977
Oil on canvas
114.9 x 102.9 cm (45¼ x 40½ in.)
Private collection

15
N. C. Wyeth (1882–1945)
Treasure Island, 1911
Oil on canvas
Endpaper illustration for Robert Louis Stevenson, *Treasure Island* (New York: Charles Scribner's Sons, 1911)
83.2 x 119.7 cm (32¾ x 47⅛ in.)
Collection of Brandywine River Museum of Art
Purchased in memory of Hope Montgomery Scott, 1997

16
Phyllis Mills, 1967
Oil on canvas
50.8 x 61 cm (20 x 24 in.)
Private collection

17
Mary Stevenson Cassatt (1844–1926)
A Woman and a Girl Driving, 1881
Oil on canvas
89.7 x 130.5 cm (35 5/16 x 51⅜ in.)
Philadelphia Museum of Art
Purchased with the W. P. Wilstach Fund, 1921, W1921-1-1

18
Henrietta Alexander (born in 1958)
Jamie and His Pig, Frank Fowler, 1981
Color photograph
20.3 x 25.4 cm (8 x 10 in.)

19
Winslow Homer (1836–1910)
The Lookout—All's Well, 1896
Oil on canvas
101.3 x 76.5 cm (39⅞ x 30⅛ in.)
Museum of Fine Arts, Boston
Warren Collection—William Wilkins Warren Fund, 99.23

20
Andrew Wyeth (1917–2009)
Soaring, 1942–50
Tempera on Masonite
121.9 x 221 cm (48 x 87 in.)
Shelburne Museum

Photograph: J. David Bohl

21
Rockwell Kent (1882–1971)
Maine Coast, Winter, 1909
Oil on canvas
96.2 x 113.4 cm (37⅞ x 44⅝ in.)
Museum of Fine Arts, Boston
Bequest of John T. Spaulding, 48.567
Courtesy of Plattsburgh State Art Museum, State University of New York, USA, Rockwell Kent Collection, Bequest of Sally Kent Gorton.

22
Frederic Edwin Church (1826–1900)
Icebergs, 1863
Oil on canvas
8.25 x 14.29 cm (3¼ x 5⅝ in.)
Museum of Fine Arts, Boston
Emily L. Ainsley Fund, 1984.583

Details

pp. 2–3, cat. 103; p. 4, cat. 72; p. 6, cat. 52; p. 8, cat. 70; p. 12, cat. 9; p. 26, cat. 8; p. 38, cat. 20; p. 66, cat. 39; p. 90, cat. 53; p. 124, cat. 81; p. 168, cat. 106; p. 182, cat. 63

Acknowledgments

The exceptional staff members of the Museum of Fine Arts, Boston, contributed their considerable expertise and energy to ensure the success of *Jamie Wyeth*, and I extend my gratitude to each and every one. I am especially grateful to Malcolm Rogers, Ann and Graham Gund Director, for his enthusiasm throughout this project while the MFA was undergoing its historic transformation with the opening of the Art of the Americas Wing in November 2010 and the opening of the Linde Family Wing for Contemporary Art in September 2011. Together, we express our profound thanks to our funders, without whose support and encouragement we could not have brought the exhibition and its accompanying catalogue to fruition.

The exhibition has been enhanced significantly by loans from members of the Wyeth family, including Mrs. Andrew Wyeth, the artist's first and most dedicated collector, beginning with his childhood drawings, as well as Jamie and Phyllis Wyeth, who have been extraordinarily generous in sharing their collections with the public. I express my heartfelt thanks to the Wyeths for extending their exceptionally warm hospitality, knowledge, good humor, and friendship to me throughout this project. Mary Beth Dolan, curator of the Jamie Wyeth Collection, has been steadfast in her dedication to the success of this exhibition and publication, and I cannot thank her enough for her insights, expertise, patient assistance, and kindness in dealing with countless crucial details. Helene Sutton, assistant to Jamie and Phyllis Wyeth, offered gracious support and good cheer in performing many tasks, including tracking down works of art, completing paperwork of all kinds, and facilitating electronic communications, and I am very grateful to her. I would also like to extend my thanks to all of the members of the Wyeths' broader circle of friends who have kindly welcomed me in Delaware and Maine: George A. Weymouth, Anne and Gregg Fields, Muffy and Louis Cabot, Cindy Lang, Paige Nolan, Victoria Woodhull, Peggy Leighton, Nancy Carlson, Marsha Skoglund, Steve Bailey, Brendan Chase, and Willi Dolan. Any project involving Jamie Wyeth's work is also indebted to his champions Warren and Jan Adelson, who have generously shared their interest and expertise, along with their personal collection, as well as to Mr. and Mrs. Frank E. Fowler, who graciously welcomed me to their plantation in South Carolina. The artist wishes to thank the following individuals for their contributions: Lowell Sibole, Susan Singer, David Paffhausen, and Steve Morrison.

At the MFA, I thank especially Katie Getchell, Chris Newth, and Patrick McMahon, all dedicated advocates of the project, for their practical advice; Maria Muller and Andrew Russell for their support; and Edward Saywell, Chair, Linde Family Wing for Contemporary Art and Arthur K. Solomon Curator of Modern Art; Jen Mergel, Robert L. Beal, Enid L. Beal and Bruce A. Beal Senior Curator of Contemporary Art; and Jasmine Hagans, for their enthusiasm and encouragement. I am grateful to Tomomi Itakura, Keith Crippen, Dustin Williams, Nick Pioggia, and all of their colleagues in the Exhibitions and Design Department, in particular Gillian Fruh, Anna Bursaux, and Martha Clawson, who have worked tirelessly to coordinate the exhibition at the MFA and during its tour. The installation has also benefited tremendously from the work of Jill Kennedy-Kernohan; Rhona MacBeth, Eijk and Rose-Marie van Otterloo Conservator of Paintings; Irene Konefal; Charlotte Ameringer; Katrina Newbury, Saundra B. Lane Associate Conservator; Andrew Haines; and Gail B. English in Conservation and Collections Management; the interpretive talents of Barbara T. Martin, Barbara and Theodore Alfond

Curator of Education, and Adam Tessier in Education; and the expertise of Janet O'Donoghue, Michael Roper, Jeff Bradford, and George Scharoun in Creative and Interactive Media.

For creating this beautiful volume, I am indebted to our colleagues in MFA Publications: Emiko K. Usui, Jennifer Snodgrass, Anna Barnet, Terry McAweeney, Cynthia R. Randall, and Ann Twombly. I also thank MFA colleagues past and present: Clifford S. Ackley, Ruth and Carl J. Shapiro Curator of Prints and Drawings; Mary Frances Allen; Laurie Boganski; Tom Catalini; Scott Cina; Chris Daunais; Zachary Dollar; Catherine East; Ann Ghormley; Deanna Griffin; Anne E. Havinga, Estrellita and Yousuf Karsh Senior Curator of Photographs; Karen E. Haas, Lane Curator of Photographs; Karen Frascona; David Geldart; Lawrence Gibbons; Dawn Griffin; Amelia Kantrovitz; Mark Kerwin and his team; Christine Kondoleon, George D. and Margo Behrakis Senior Curator of Greek and Roman Art, and Frederic E. Whittmann; Debra Lakind; Ralph LaVoie and the facilities crew; Kenneth Leibe; Peter Matthews; Julia McCarthy; Maureen Melton, Susan Morse Hilles Director of Libraries and Archives; Al Miner; Bob Morneau; Myriam Negrón; Jane O'Reilly; Quinn Papazian; Molly Papows; Kim Pashko; Christine Pollock; Kay Satomi; George Shackelford; Matthew Siegal; Siobhan Wheeler; Bob Wilson; and John Woolf. For giving me newfound freedom to write in offsite locations, I thank Paula Matthews and the Pauline Thayer Starr Trust, and I am forever appreciative for the Museum's William Morris Hunt Library staff and volunteers, who provided me with a peaceful haven, along with plenty of water and chocolate to sustain my efforts: Deborah Barlow Smedstad, Lee-Ann Famolare, Paul McAlpine, and Hee Jung Lee. At the W. Van Alan Clark Jr. Library, School of the Museum of Fine Arts, I thank Lauren Kimball-Brown and Darin Murphy for all of their help.

To my extraordinarily dedicated colleagues, both past and present, in the Art of the Americas department, I offer my gratitude for their patience and support while this exhibition and the accompanying catalogue occupied my attention: Erica Hirshler, Croll Senior Curator of American Paintings; Nonie Gadsden, Katharine Lane Weems Senior Curator of American Decorative Arts and Sculpture; Karen E. Quinn, Kristin and Roger Servison Curator of Paintings; Dennis Carr, Carolyn and Peter Lynch Curator of American Decorative Arts and Sculpture; Kelly L'Ecuyer, former Ellyn McColgan Curator of Decorative Arts and Sculpture; Caroline Cole, current Ellyn McColgan Curator of Decorative Arts and Sculpture; Molly Richmond; Katie DeMarsh; Toni Pullman; Jamieson Bunn; Meredith Crawford; Victoria Ross; and Gerry Ward. Research for the catalogue and a whole host of initiatives supporting the exhibition were handled with exceptional skill and aplomb by Taylor L. Poulin, Horowitz Curatorial Research Associate, and by Janet Comey; I am indebted to both of them for their many contributions. To the Art of the Americas volunteers and interns who have contributed hundreds of hours of their time to this project, I am forever grateful: Eliza H. Kontulis; Katie Dammers; Lisa Hartung, Lunder Summer Intern; Lauren Spengler; Melissa Tully; and Michelle Walsh.

The extraordinary range of works presented in this retrospective reflects the unstinting generosity of many private collectors who extended themselves and their art for the benefit of the public. I offer heartfelt appreciation and thanks to those donors who wish to remain anonymous and to Helen C. Alexander; Barbara and Theodore Alfond; Steve Ausplund and Viki Reed; Louise Philibosian Danelian; Tina and Philip DeNormandie; Mary Beth Dolan; Mr. and Mrs. Frank E. Fowler; The Alexander M. Laughlin Family Trust and Mr. David W. Laughlin; Mrs. Amy Morey; Mr. and Mrs. Robert Rans; Richard and

Martha Rothman; the Honorable Mr. Arnold Schwarzenegger and Ms. Rebecca Lombino; the UMB Financial Corporation and Ms. Carol Sturm; and Brock and Yvonne Vinton.

Colleagues at many institutions have given their generous support by way of providing access to works, imparting information, offering expertise, and supporting loans to the exhibition. I am indebted to Lillian Lambrecht and Alicia Verity at Bank of America; James Duff, Virginia Logan, Thomas Padon, Audrey Lewis, Amanda Burdan, and Jean Gilmore at the Brandywine River Museum of Art and Conservancy; Jane MacLeod and Jochen Wierich at Cheekwood Botanical Garden and Museum of Art; Alice Walton, Rod Bigelow, Don Bacigalupi, and Kate Sbarra at the Crystal Bridges Museum of American Art; Kevin Murphy and Tracy Cude, formerly at the Crystal Bridges Museum of American Art; Katherine C. Luber, The Kelso Director, and William Rudolph, San Antonio Museum of Art; Mike Miller and Heather Campbell Coyle at the Delaware Art Museum; Christopher Brownawell, Michael Komanecky, and Roger Dell at the Farnsworth Art Museum; Jeanne Janney; Cameron M. Shay at Graham Gallery; Nancy McCall and Andrew Harrison at the Alan Chesney Medical Archives, Johns Hopkins Medical School; D'Arcy Marsh of D'Arcy Marsh Films; William Griswold and Isabelle Dervaux at the Morgan Library and Museum; Carmine Branagan and Malcolm Price at the National Academy of Design; Kathleen A. Foster at the Philadelphia Museum of Art; Thomas Denenberg at the Shelburne Museum; Kim Sajet, Wendy Wick Reeves, and Brandon Fortune at the Smithsonian National Portrait Gallery; Thomas Crouch at the Smithsonian National Air and Space Museum; Wanda Corn at Stanford University; Elizabeth Glassman and Peter John Brownlee at the Terra Founda-tion for American Art; and Joyce Hill Stoner at the University of Delaware and Winterthur Museum, Garden, and Library. Christopher Crosman offered many insightful comments, observations, and suggestions in reading an early draft of the catalogue essay, and to him I extend my heartfelt thanks. David Houston, formerly curator at the Crystal Bridges Museum of American Art, and now the Director of the Bo Bartlett Center, has been a steadfast and generous collaborator, and I cannot thank him enough for his contribution to the catalogue, as well as for his warmth and collegiality.

For their great patience while I have been at work on the exhibition, as well as their love and support throughout, I thank John, William, and James Paolella, who traveled to midcoast Maine and explored the cliffs and trails of Monhegan with me. It has been an honor and a joy to work with so many dear colleagues and friends who have freely shared their time and expertise with me in presenting the imaginative works by Jamie Wyeth to audiences here at the Museum of Fine Arts, Boston, the Brandywine River Museum of Art, the San Antonio Museum of Art, and Crystal Bridges Museum of American Art. Thank you all so much for your many gifts.

Elliot Bostwick Davis
John Moors Cabot Chair
Art of the Americas
Museum of Fine Arts, Boston

Index

All works are by Jamie Wyeth unless otherwise indicated. Page numbers in *italics* refer to illustrations.

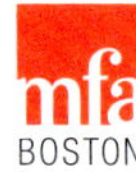

MFA Publications
Museum of Fine Arts, Boston
465 Huntington Avenue
Boston, Massachusetts 02115
www.mfa.org/publications

This book was published in conjunction with the exhibition *Jamie Wyeth*, organized by the Museum of Fine Arts, Boston.

Museum of Fine Arts, Boston:
July 16–December 28, 2014

Brandywine River Museum of Art,
Chadds Ford, Pennsylvania:
January 17–April 5, 2015

San Antonio Museum of Art,
San Antonio, Texas:
April 25–July 5, 2015

Crystal Bridges Museum of American Art, Bentonville, Arkansas:
July 23–October 5, 2015

Generous support for this publication was provided by the Ann and William Elfers Publications Fund at the Museum of Fine Arts, Boston.

Jamie Wyeth at the Museum of Fine Arts, Boston, is sponsored by Bank of America.

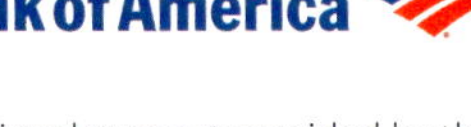

Additional support provided by the Mr. and Mrs. Raymond J. Horowitz Foundation for the Arts, as well as Mr. and Mrs. Jeffrey E. Marshall and the Shelly and Michael Kassen Fund.

ISBN 978-0-87846-814-0
Library of Congress Control Number:
2013957257

The Museum of Fine Arts, Boston, is a nonprofit institution devoted to the promotion and appreciation of the creative arts. The Museum endeavors to respect the copyrights of all authors and creators in a manner consistent with its nonprofit educational mission. If you feel any material has been included in this publication improperly, please contact the Department of Rights and Licensing at 617 267 9300, or by mail at the above address.

While the objects in this publication necessarily represent only a small portion of the MFA's holdings, the Museum is proud to be a leader within the American museum community in sharing the objects in its collection via its website. Currently, information about more than 330,000 objects is available to the public worldwide. To learn more about the MFA's collections, including provenance, publication, and exhibition history, kindly visit *www.mfa.org/collections*.

For a complete listing of MFA publications, please contact the publisher at the above address, or call 617 369 3438.

Edited by Ann Twombly and
Jennifer Snodgrass
Proofread by Kathryn Blatt

Designed by Cynthia Rockwell Randall
Production by Terry McAweeney
Production assistance by Anna Barnet
Printed on 135 gsm GardaPat Kiara and bound at Graphicom, Verona, Italy

Distributed in the United States of America and Canada by
ARTBOOK | D.A.P.
155 Sixth Avenue
New York, New York 10013
www.artbook.com

Distributed outside the United States of America and Canada by
Thames & Hudson, Ltd.
181A High Holborn
London WC1V 7QX
www.thamesandhudson.com

SECOND PRINTING
Printed and bound in Italy
This book was printed on acid-free paper.